Chronicles of a Two-Front War

Civil Rights and Vietnam in the African American Press

Chronicles of a Two-Front War

Civil Rights and Vietnam in the African American Press

Lawrence Allen Eldridge

University of Missouri Press   Columbia and London

Copyright © 2011 by
The Curators of the University of Missouri
University of Missouri Press, Columbia, Missouri 65201
Printed and bound in the United States of America
All rights reserved
5 4 3 2 1   15 14 13 12 11

Cataloging-in-Publication data available from the Library of Congress.
ISBN 978-0-8262-1939-8

∞™ This paper meets the requirements of the
American National Standard for Permanence of Paper
for Printed Library Materials, Z39.48, 1984.

Design and composition: Jennifer Cropp
Printing and binding: Thomson-Shore, Inc.
Typefaces: Minion, Haettenschweiler, Arial, and Impact

For Lynn, my wife and my emotional and intellectual companion, whose steadfast support enriched every step in the preparation of this book

Contents

Acknowledgments

A number of individuals and institutions have contributed in a variety of ways to aid me in the research and writing of this book and to improve the final quality of the finished product. The project owed its beginnings in large measure to the indulgence of one of my history professors, Dr. Perry Duis, at the University of Illinois—Chicago. He let me talk him into accepting my proposal for a paper on how the *Chicago Daily Defender* covered the Vietnam War for its primary audience, the city's African American community. My argument supporting the topic for his seminar on urban history was something of a stretch, but Professor Duis approved the proposal and thus began my journey into the subject of this book. By the end of the term I was hooked and knew I had found a subject I wanted to pursue much more thoroughly.

Other professors who provided early guidance and encouragement include my doctoral adviser, Robert L. Messer; Richard Fried; James Sack; and Richard R. John. Ronald L. Numbers, Hilldale Professor of the History of Science and Medicine at the University of Wisconsin, provided invaluable suggestions early in the gestation of the book.

The archivists at the Lyndon B. Johnson and Richard Nixon presidential libraries were very helpful in steering me through the thicket of sources to locate key documents pertaining to the African American press during the Vietnam War. During my visit to the LBJ library, the archivist Allen Fisher was particularly helpful. Later, Denise Gamino, a researcher, dug through the archives at the library to find additional materials. At the Nixon library the head archivist, Greg Cumming, and his associate Pam Eisenberg were indispensable.

The librarians at the UIC Microfilm Library efficiently and patiently supported months of research in the library's collection of African American newspapers and magazines, as well as microfilm tape acquired on loan from collections around the country. The reference librarians at the Oak Brook and Elmhurst public libraries near my residence also sought out additional microfilm collections and generously made space available to me to continue the research.

The staff of the Auburn Avenue Research Library on African American Culture and History in Atlanta provided help with primary source materials during several visits.

Columbia University generously supplied material from its Black Journalists Oral History Project.

Michigan State University Library in East Lansing provided access to its Women in Journalism collection, part of the Washington Press Club Foundation Oral History Project, which contains important oral histories of several African American journalists.

The reference staff of the Vivian G. Harsh Research Collection of Afro-American History and Literature, in the Carter G. Woodson Regional Library, a branch of the Chicago Public Library, was helpful in ferreting out important documents from the Abbott-Sengstacke Family Papers that illuminate the work of John Sengstacke, publisher of the *Chicago Daily Defender*, head of the Sengstacke group of black newspapers, and dean of black newspaper publishers during the Vietnam War era.

Audie Myers, a private researcher, helped immensely with collection of material from the Ethel Payne Papers at the Library of Congress and additional Ethel Payne papers held by the Civil Rights Documentation Project, Moorland-Spingarn Research Center, Howard University, Washington, D.C.

David Williams, an archive researcher, helped locate materials in the Wisconsin Historical Society's extraordinary collection of African American newspapers in Madison.

All the interview subjects who gave their time and recollections so generously deserve special thanks. Among them I must single out Eleanor Ohman, retired *San Francisco Sun-Reporter* cartoonist and aide to the *Sun-Reporter* publisher, Carleton B. Goodlett; she provided extremely useful information in conversations and supplied copies of several of her own original cartoon drawings, for which I am especially grateful. She also introduced me to one of the founders of her newspaper, Thomas Fleming, with whom I spent an unforgettable afternoon, picking through his vivid memories of his paper's history and enjoying the pleasure of his company.

I must acknowledge also the help and encouragement of two friends in academia, Ben McArthur, academic dean, and Eric Anderson, president of Southwestern Adventist University, who steered me to the University of

Missouri Press. Another long-time friend, Jerry Keith, provided invaluable technical assistance along the way.

I am indebted to Clair Willcox, editor-in-chief of the University of Missouri Press; Sara Davis, managing editor; and other dedicated professionals and specialists at the press. I owe special thanks to my editor, Polly Kummel, who skillfully refined my manuscript to make it a better book.

Chronicles of a Two-Front War

Civil Rights and Vietnam in the African American Press

Introduction

Negro newspapers . . . became the medium through which the yearnings of the race were expressed, the platform from which the Negro leaders could speak, the coordinator of mass action which Negroes felt compelled to take, and the instrument by which many Negroes were educated with respect to public affairs.—John Hope Franklin, *From Slavery to Freedom*

On the morning of August 2, 1964, Captain John J. Herrick, skipper of the American destroyer *Maddox*, steered his warship to within ten miles of North Vietnam's Red River delta on the western edge of the Gulf of Tonkin. The sea was calm and the day was clear, but Herrick was edgy. Before dawn his ship had encountered a flotilla of Vietnamese junks. Unsure of the enemy's intentions, he sounded general quarters and radioed the Seventh Fleet. Although his crew picked up some radio crackle indicating the enemy might be gearing up for military operations, the night passed quietly.

Then, shortly before noon, Herrick spotted three enemy patrol boats moving out of the estuary and behind an island that had been raided by South Vietnamese commandos two days earlier. As the *Maddox* headed out to sea, its crew intercepted an order telling the patrol boats to attack after they finished refueling. The North Vietnamese boats soon reappeared and headed for the destroyer. What followed was a lopsided skirmish that was over in twenty minutes.

Herrick ordered his crew to open fire when the enemy craft were within ten thousand yards. The patrol boats kept coming, two closing to within five thousand yards of the *Maddox* and haphazardly launching several torpedoes

1

at the destroyer. None of the torpedoes struck its target. The third enemy boat came even closer, its guns blazing, seeking a good firing position for its torpedoes. But before it could do any damage, four American jets roared in from the carrier *Ticonderoga* and began strafing two torpedo boats while *Maddox* gunners struck the third. One attacking boat was badly damaged. The other two turned and fled. Four North Vietnamese sailors were killed and six wounded. The *Maddox* took a single bullet and suffered no casualties. By any tactical measure it was a clear-cut American victory.

Two days later the *Maddox*, now joined by another U.S. destroyer, the *Turner Joy*, was back in North Vietnamese waters to probe the enemy's new naval aggressiveness. Both ships were under Herrick's command for the operation. One of Herrick's superiors radioed that the communists had, as he put it, "cut down the gauntlet" and were to be "treated as belligerents from first detection." Plainly, the brass was eager for a fight. What it got was almost certainly something less. During the night of August 4 the weather was volatile, and sonar and radar images were imperfect. The radar operators on the destroyers thought they detected patrol boats and torpedoes in the water. Swerving sharply to avoid torpedoes and firing into the blackness at an invisible enemy, the destroyers seemed to be dueling with phantoms. Herrick sent off a message to his superiors saying he was under attack.

Ten minutes after his first cable reached the Pentagon, he sent a second one saying, "Am under continuous torpedo attack." A few minutes later Herrick sent a third message reporting another torpedo had churned past his ship and two more had been seen in the water. He said his ships were firing at the unseen attackers and might have destroyed one. The stream of cables continued, with more arriving every few minutes. For two hours the messages flowed from the waters off North Vietnam up the chain of command to the Pentagon.

After an hour or so since the last of his cables Herrick sent another message expressing doubts about the engagement after a review of the action. No one had actually sighted enemy boats or torpedoes, he wrote. The radar blips could have been "freak weather effects" (so common in subsequent naval experience in the area that they came to be called the "Tonkin Spook"). The indications of torpedoes could have resulted from an overeager sonar operator. Captain Herrick duly reported his misgivings to his commanders and suggested a full evaluation before any further action.[1]

As the two U.S. warships were steaming into history in the Gulf of Tonkin, half a world away searchers were digging into a dirt levee near Philadelphia, Mississippi, looking for the bodies of three young civil rights workers who had disappeared weeks earlier. Michael Schwerner, a young white social worker on Manhattan's Lower East Side, had come to Mississippi to organize local blacks on behalf of the Congress of Racial Equality. At twenty-four he was the oldest of the three missing men. Andrew Goodman, also white, was an anthropology major at a New York college and a summer volunteer. James Chaney, a nineteen-year-old African American and native Mississippian, had accompanied them despite his family's misgivings about his civil rights activities. The three had vanished on June 21 after setting out for Philadelphia to reassure local blacks whose church had been set on fire.[2]

On August 4, the date of the controversial incident in the Gulf of Tonkin, a U.S. Navy Seabee pushed his shovel into the dank, crusting soil of the earthen dam in Mississippi and broke into a shallow grave containing the bodies of three men. They were identified as the missing volunteers. Autopsies revealed that Schwerner and Goodman had each been killed with a single bullet to the head. The killers had reserved their special fury for Chaney, brutally beating the young black man, then shooting him three times. The pathologist reported he had "never seen bones so severely shattered" in twenty-five years of practice.[3]

Events on August 4, 1964, in the waters off North Vietnam and on the earthen levee in Mississippi were on opposite sides of the globe, but they were connected. The connection was intimated in bitter words at the memorial service held in Philadelphia, Mississippi, for the slain men. Bob Moses, a young civil rights leader, waved a copy of a newspaper from Jackson that bore the headline "LBJ Says Shoot to Kill in Gulf of Tonkin."

Moses said: "The President wants to send soldiers to kill people on the other side of the world, people we know nothing about, while here in Mississippi he refuses to send anyone to protect black people against murderous violence."[4] Moses was pointing out an awful incongruity: the violent response of the U.S. government abroad and its decades-long failure to act against murderers of African Americans in the South who were seeking only to claim rights guaranteed in the Constitution. Moses also was underscoring what he perceived to be the tragic moral failure of a policy that professed to fight for freedom in Vietnam without protecting Americans who were in Mississippi fighting for the freedom of its black citizens or protecting the black citizens themselves.

Moses was one of the first to criticize U.S. military intervention in Vietnam on moral grounds. By constructing an argument based on comparing the government's treatment of blacks in Mississippi and its prosecution of the war in Vietnam, he unwittingly anticipated the tone, if not the precise contour, of a moral calculus that would shape the response to the war by a number of African American leaders in the civil rights movement, most notably, Martin Luther King Jr.

When Moses expressed his angry vision during that sweltering memorial service, he was also one of the first to view the war in Vietnam through the prism of black experience. Later Moses called Vietnam a "mirror of America."[5] The linkage of the war in Vietnam and the suffering of black Americans ultimately would become a commonplace in the lexicon of the black press and the rhetoric of civil rights protest. Moses helped blaze that ideological trail.

In the mid-1960s the administration's policy in Vietnam was supported in some of the black press and by several of the more moderate African American leaders, but a widening circle of younger voices in the civil rights movement began to express doubts, from misgivings about the war to outright opposition to America's role in Vietnam. As the war dragged on, much of the black press, and increasing numbers of prominent African American leaders, expressed growing disenchantment with American policy as the impact of the war on the domestic black agenda and on blacks generally became more apparent.

The war was threatening to eclipse the national effort to establish social and economic justice for black Americans. As the war escalated, the civil rights movement and Johnson's Great Society seemed to be losing the attention of the president. At the same time support in Congress for expensive reforms was weakening and the interest of the American people was flagging. The dwindling national support for vigorously pushing the black agenda and the shift of attention to prosecuting the war created anxiety in the black community. Black observers began to link escalation of the war and the declining fortunes of important social programs. This linkage was apparent in the way the black press interpreted the Vietnam War.

The war soon loomed even larger in the collective black experience because African Americans seemed to be fighting and dying in Vietnam in disproportionate numbers, even as their full participation in American life continued to be an elusive, unrealized dream. The painful irony was that the sacrifices of blacks on the battlefield, made ostensibly to secure the freedom of the South Vietnamese, failed to free African Americans from the shackles of discrimination at home. This inequity was an important element influencing how the black press viewed the war in Vietnam and places its interpretation of the conflict within the long tradition of the black press's fight for the rights of African Americans.

The black press was one of the two oldest, most enduring, and influential institutions in the African American community. Only the black church was older, beginning as a formal institution in Philadelphia, Pennsylvania, with the establishment of the African Methodist Episcopal Church in 1787. The black press was born forty years later when *Freedom's Journal* was published in New York City. Both institutions embraced the mission of protesting the mistreatment of blacks and the failure of American society to affirm their full rights of citizenship. Both the black press and the black church became powerful abolitionist voices.[6]

Freedom's Journal came into being after Mordecai M. Nash, editor of the *New York Enquirer*, voiced strong support for the Colonization Society, which advocated sending free blacks to Africa. Nash supported retention of "the institution of slavery" but favored the deportation of free blacks, because their freedom threatened the perpetuation of slavery. In response to Nash's editorial onslaught against the black citizens of New York, the founders of *Freedom's Journal* declared in their prospectus for the fledgling paper:

> We shall ever regard the constitution of the United States as our polar star. Pledged to no party, we shall endeavor to urge our brethren to use their right to the elective franchise as free citizens. . . . Daily slandered, we think that there ought to be some channel of communion between us and the public, through which a single voice may be heard, in defense of five hundred thousand free people of colour. For often has injustice been heaped upon us, when our only defense was an appeal to the Almighty: but we believe that the time has now arrived, when the calumnies of our enemies should be refuted by forcible arguments.[7]

One hundred and forty years after the birth of *Freedom's Journal*, Frank L. Stanley, president of the National Newspaper Publishers Association, the professional organization of the black press, wrote: "It is a historical fact that no racial group or people anywhere in the world since the invention of the printing press, have attained freedom or appreciably improved their status without the aid of their own militant press. . . . Never in the history of America, nor of the profession of journalism, has there been a greater need to keep the issue of social equality clear, and never has the opportunity for our press to become a truly great asset in the struggle for human dignity been so manifest."[8]

Throughout its long history since, the African American press has pursued its urgent mission of supporting black demands for equal justice, even when aggressive advocacy of black rights was unpopular or misunderstood by the dominant white culture. Sometimes this led to suppression or harassment by authorities, as happened all too often in the South, or during times of national crisis, such as World War I and, to a lesser extent, World War II. The government often viewed black demands for full equality during wartime as somehow unpatriotic and dangerous to national cohesion in the face of foreign enemies.[9]

The black press persisted in its pursuit of equal treatment and full citizenship rights for African Americans, providing news about—and editorial support of—civil rights activists to their readers as the modern civil rights movement was born and flourished shortly after midcentury. In the sixties the black press stood at the juncture of issues of black aspirations and the Vietnam War. Black newspapers and magazines actively reported and interpreted both the struggle for equal rights and the Vietnam War and did so from the unique perspective of a minority of the U.S. population that arguably was the group with the most riding on the outcome. The stake of African Americans in the civil rights movement and the goals of the Great Society made the liberal domestic social agenda the dominant story in the black press and inevitably influenced the way the black press and its readers interpreted the Vietnam War.

In this book I examine the coverage given the Vietnam War by the black press, from the Gulf of Tonkin incident in early August 1964 through the removal of U.S. ground forces in March 1973, with some retrospective observations made in the black press after the fall of Saigon in the spring of 1975. The primary sources for my research are a variety of African American news publications, including seventeen black newspapers and two newsmagazines. While I use other black publications to enrich the narrative and analysis, these nineteen print news sources form the core of the study. They are leading publications that represent diverse publishing companies and geographic regions. Within the universe of African American daily and weekly news organs, they are all part of mainstream black journalism and do not include such important, but sectarian and ideologically specialized, publications as *Muhammad Speaks* and the *Black Panther*.

Additional primary source materials included oral histories, private papers, and writings of participants in the relevant history, as well as interviews with, and books written by, actors in the narrative. The presidential libraries of Lyndon B. Johnson and Richard M. Nixon, and the published *Public Papers of the Presidents* also provided invaluable source material in documenting the governmental context in which the political and social aspirations of African Americans collided with the Vietnam War. Materials from the Gerald R. Ford Presidential Library shed light on the closing hours of the American presence in Saigon as the city was falling to the Vietnamese. Documents in the Harry S. Truman Presidential Library illuminate the early steps toward desegregation of the U.S. military in 1948, when Truman's Executive Order 9981 mandated the reform.

The coverage of the war in the black press provides a unique vantage point from which to observe the national scene at home as the war in Vietnam came to preoccupy the Johnson administration and exert pressure on the federal government's ability to meet its commitments to the social agenda of African

Americans. During the Johnson administration the pillars of the black press found themselves increasingly torn between a desire to support a president who had displayed a theretofore unprecedented level of presidential commitment to black goals and African American concerns about the diversion of scarce national resources to support a far-off war. The resulting ambivalence in black attitudes was scarcely eased by the internal conflict that would soon begin to tear at the civil rights movement.

The African American establishment found itself increasingly at odds with younger, more militant, leaders who began to assert themselves and articulate a more radical vision of black empowerment. These disruptive, often turbulent, tensions frequently spilled onto the pages of the black press as it reported on and debated the issues raised by the Vietnam conflict and its impact on the aspirations of black Americans. The intersecting arcs of the civil rights movement and the Vietnam struggle produced a perspective on the war that was both distinctly African American and deeply human.

1

Bringing the News Home

There is an important need for documenting the Negro soldier . . . in the light of the civil rights struggle back home.—Ethel Payne to U.S. official in Vietnam, December 28, 1966

Vietnam swarmed with reporters. Newspaper correspondents began filing stories from the combat zone early in the war. A few, like David Halberstam of the *New York Times*, became journalistic superstars who wrote compelling pieces that began to define the Vietnam story for millions of readers and to deepen hostility toward the media within the Johnson administration. After the Tet Offensive became big news in early 1968, the number of journalists in the country swelled to more than six hundred from all over the world. Although no military censors systematically restricted the flow of information from the war zone to news outlets, as was the case in World War II, U.S. officials in Vietnam sought to manage and control the news that was reported. Public information officers representing the U.S. command in Saigon tried ceaselessly to shape the story of the war. Their daily briefings were so disconnected from reality that they came to be known among reporters as the "Five O'Clock Follies."[1]

Among the horde of U.S. correspondents in Vietnam, few were African Americans. Despite more hiring of African Americans during the sixties, by 1970 only 5 percent of all reporters and photographers in the mainstream U.S.

media were black. None of the black publications could afford to keep permanent news staffs in South Vietnam.[2] To fill the gap various African American
news publications sent reporters on temporary assignment to Vietnam to observe the war and file stories chronicling their impressions.

Ethel Payne, a prominent journalist at the *Chicago Defender*, arrived in
Saigon on her first temporary assignment in Vietnam on Christmas Day 1966.
Three days later she wrote a memo to Barry Zorthian, chief information officer at the U.S. embassy, to say what she intended to do in Vietnam and to elicit
official cooperation. Her statement was an apt description of what other black
journalists on assignment from African American news publications went to
the war theater to do. She told Zorthian that her first purpose was "to try and
give an adequate picture of why we are involved in Vietnam," particularly to
inform "Negro communities." Payne's second stated goal was "to tell the full
role of Negro soldiers in this conflict," focusing especially on "the extent of integration in the services."

She noted that other African American journalists who had visited Vietnam
to report on the war were "in agreement" that they needed "more material
and cooperation" from U.S. officers in the war zone, particularly in ferreting out information about individual blacks in the battle zone that would re-
veal their "assignments, acts of heroism[,]" and "overall performance." She
lamented the absence of clear official documentation of the war-zone performance of black service people that had been reported by "other Negro
correspondents." The requests of these war correspondents for detailed information about African Americans' service had often been fruitless, Payne
reported, because military officials claimed racial statistics were not available
from personnel records.[3]

Payne later acknowledged that, although black service personnel hinted
at their "nagging doubts about the legitimacy and morality of the war," she
failed to focus on that aspect of the story. She even confessed that "maybe
I was a little brainwashed myself" because she did not concentrate on elements of the Vietnam story that might have reflected badly on the official
Washington line. "I've always regretted to this day that I didn't do what I felt
was an adequate job in reporting on the immorality of the war," she told an
interviewer in 1987.[4] Her statement was a remarkably honest expression of
what she regarded as a personal failure. It also sheds light on the pressures
that at least one journalist felt, to emphasize the positive elements in the story
of African American members of the U.S. military in Vietnam. Some of this
restraint may have reflected her innate caution or may have been influenced
by the editorial moderation that was typical of some black newspapers, including Payne's own *Chicago Defender*, when complete candor might have

meant criticizing Lyndon Johnson's Vietnam policy even as he championed civil rights programs beneficial to African Americans.

Another African American journalist who traveled to Vietnam on temporary assignment for a black paper was Mike Davis of the *Baltimore Afro-American*. During his four-month hitch in the second half of 1967, Davis produced a staggering volume of material, often filling several pages in a given issue of his paper. The *Afro-American* further enriched its war coverage by securing the services of Conrad Clark, an experienced black newspaperman who was in Vietnam as a GI in the Fourth Infantry Division and serving out the balance of his military commitment. The beauty of the arrangement for the paper was that it got a steady stream of stories from Clark while the U.S. Army picked up the tab.[5]

Payne's colleague at the *Defender*, Donald Mosby, also went to Vietnam on special assignment. He was sent to write a series on black soldiers in the war zone, after the newspaper received complaints from African American soldiers and some parents about the racist treatment of black GI's. Mosby's first report from Vietnam was published on May 6, 1968, barely a month after the assassination of Martin Luther King Jr. It was a time of tumult in the United States and of rising racial tensions among the troops in Vietnam. Mosby's lead article was followed by a series of pieces that provided a frequently raw, acerbic perspective on the experiences of blacks in the military during the war.[6]

Sometimes a chain of newspapers would send a correspondent to Vietnam to file stories that would be picked up by more than one paper in the group. Payne's articles which appeared frequently in the *Chicago Defender* also were picked up by other newspapers in the Sengstacke group. For example, after the *New Courier* joined the Sengstacke chain in 1966, it introduced Payne to its readers as a "*Courier* reporter."[7]

The two preeminent African American newsmagazines also used firsthand accounts from Vietnam to enrich their coverage of the war. *Jet* magazine sent its Washington bureau chief, Simeon Booker, to Vietnam in July 1965, making him one of the first African American journalists from a black news organization to be sent to Vietnam during the early stages of the buildup of U.S. forces there. Booker went to South Vietnam for two weeks to provide "a firsthand glimpse of activities in the war-torn country." The cover of the August 19, 1965, issue of *Jet* promoted his series of pieces this way: "Special Report: Negro Heroes in the Vietnam War." The main piece emphasized the dangers, including to Booker himself, who came under sniper fire, and discussed casualties among black troops.

Even this early in the war, Booker's reporting conveyed a sense of the racial ambiguities of the war; both allies and foes in the exotic land were dark skinned and strangely alien. As riots erupted back home, even this early in the conflict, the Vietcong tried to exploit the racial tension in the United States and turn black and white GIs against each other with clumsy propaganda. According to *Jet*, the efforts went nowhere. Later Booker returned to Vietnam, this time with a photographer in tow, to hook up with several frontline combat units and provide more on-the-spot reporting.[8]

Ebony magazine also published firsthand accounts from journalists in Vietnam. The culmination of the magazine's coverage of the Vietnam story occurred when it devoted its entire August 1968 issue to the story of black members of the U.S. military. Most of the articles dealt, directly or indirectly, with aspects of the African American experience in the Vietnam War, with much of the coverage based on reporting by black journalists who had visited the war zone.[9]

Based on her experience in Vietnam on temporary assignment, Payne recommended to John Sengstacke, her boss, that a reporter from the black press be stationed in the battle zone. In her memo of March 30, 1967, she told Sengstacke she was "more convinced than ever," after visiting Vietnam, that "there should be a correspondent stationed over there on at least a quasi-permanent basis to concentrate on the Negro in the war." She suggested that the National Newspaper Publishers Association (NNPA), which Sengstacke had founded, "send a pool correspondent over to defray the cost" of providing individual black newspapers with access to frontline war reporting.[10] Nothing came of the initiative.

As the last U.S. ground troops were leaving Vietnam in 1973, Sengstacke formally named Payne a war correspondent, the first African American woman to be given that designation. It was a belated gesture but a title she had earned during months of combat reporting in South Vietnam, even as she served as her newspaper's one-person Washington bureau.

All American journalists who visited South Vietnam to report on the war were given ground rules that had been laid down by the military. Among Payne's personal papers is a copy of a memo from the military press liaison brass addressed to "Media Representatives" that discusses the rules under which journalists and the service people with whom they interacted would operate in the gathering and dissemination of information. "The basic policy" of the U.S. information office in Vietnam, the memo announced, was "to provide media representatives maximum information consistent with requirements for security." The document went on to elaborate the customary rules distinguishing official and unofficial sources and how the media were to handle the attribution of information that was on the record, given on background only, or that was off the record entirely.[11]

Like every reporter in Vietnam, journalists representing black publications expressed frustration at the frequent difficulty of extracting reliable information from tight-lipped military press officers, particularly at staged briefings. Black reporters groused about the logistical difficulties of getting around the combat zone. But they also found combat personnel in the field very open and informative and were able to put together well-documented pieces for their publications.

The black newspapers also maintained a lively stable of commentators and editorial writers who grappled with issues raised by the war and their impact on the interests of the African American community. Several good columnists were appearing regularly in black newspapers. Some were figures known primarily in a particular newspaper's region or city. Others were prominent figures—mostly African Americans—whose columns were syndicated broadly to black newspapers. The widely circulated columnists were as professionally disparate as the civil rights leaders Roy Wilkins and Whitney Young and the former baseball player Jackie Robinson.

Cartoons were also used frequently to comment on the war in Vietnam, providing an often wry, usually provocative and thoughtful, perspective on the conflict. Political cartoons in mainstream U.S. publications sharpened their political bite during the Vietnam conflict. According to Joshua Brown, "Only when the Vietnam War reached its height in the late 1960s did many political cartoonists emerge from their torpor to take the unprecedented step of criticizing U.S. government foreign policy during wartime." This irreverence, at times rising to the pitch of polemics, had been common among cartoonists in the black press well before the Vietnam War, including during wartime.[12]

Pointedly critical cartoons directed at the nation's leaders had been a part of the black cartoonist's arsenal during foreign wars since World War I, when President Woodrow Wilson occasionally found himself ridiculed in them. For example, on July 19, 1917, the *New York Age* published a cartoon showing a group of blacks picketing the president with signs demanding an end to discrimination in the military and in civilian employment and challenging him to fulfill a promise made at the beginning of the war: "Absolute fair dealing" for black Americans. On March 23, 1918, the *Chicago Defender* ran a cartoon that showed a black nurse approaching the president about recruiting women to serve as Red Cross nurses. When the black woman says, "My brothers at the front desire my services," the president dismissively replies, "We can use your money—but not your services."[13]

Half a century later, during the Vietnam War, the black press was even bolder about aiming its messages at power and claiming full rights of citizenship for all African Americans. This blunt message of entitlement was amplified by the war and grounded in the sacrifices black soldiers were making on the battlefields of Vietnam. The cartoonists in the black press were warriors with pens in the fight of African Americans for justice. The result was a remarkable body of work in the literature of black protest.

A few cartoonists stood out from their peers by developing particularly memorable characters and a signature style that inspired a new generation of African American cartoonists. Sam Milai, a veteran *Courier* cartoonist, won first prize in the Russwurm Awards of the NNPA in 1966 for a 1965 Memorial Day cartoon celebrating the black GI in Vietnam. Milai frequently drew cartoons commenting on aspects of the Vietnam War and its impact on the lives of black Americans.[14]

The most celebrated of the black cartoonists was Ollie Wendell Harrington. According to the PBS Web site, he was "called the 'greatest' African-American cartoonist." He attended the Yale School of Fine Arts and the National Academy of Design and worked for a number of black newspapers, including the *New York Amsterdam News*, the *Pittsburgh Courier*, and the *Chicago Defender*. His most famous character was "Bootsie," who debuted in the *Amsterdam News* on December 28, 1935, and earned Harrington national recognition. During World War II, Harrington went to Europe as a war correspondent for the *Pittsburgh Courier*. It was, he said, "a wonderful solution," because the alternative was to join the U.S. military, which would have meant "fighting in a racially segregated army." He moved to Europe for good after the war, finally settling in communist East Berlin in 1961. During the sixties Harrington once again sent Bootsie off to war to comment on Vietnam. Harrington died in Berlin in November 1995, having lived to see the Berlin Wall come down.[15]

One of the most extensive portfolios of war cartoons in the black press appeared in the *Defender*, an iconic African American newspaper with a storied reputation as an influential force among black Americans. But even a small paper could nurture the talent of a skilled cartoonist whose work was imaginative yet who toiled in relative obscurity. Eleanor Ohman, cartoonist for the *Sun-Reporter*, was just such a talent. Her work appeared in the pages of the San Francisco Bay Area newspaper, which had a circulation of eight to nine thousand during the Vietnam era. Ohman joined the paper, which had been founded in 1944, when her boss, Dr. Carlton B. Goodlett, a physician, became publisher several years later to keep the fledgling publication afloat. She had been his secretary and administrative assistant in his medical office, but also brought to the paper a knack for drawing and the cartoonist's ability to reduce public issues to captivating visual metaphors within a few square inches of newspaper space. Her editor and the paper's founder, Thomas C. Fleming, stated emphatically that Ohman's cartoons were the best to be found in the black press.[16]

The publications also had the usual sections devoted to letters to the editor, which provided some of the sharpest opinions on the war, as well as other public opinion features; among the latter was the "Inquiring Photographer" in the *Defender*. Occasionally, letters to the editor took the form of poetry or contained a poem. Sometimes poems would be published in a special section, such as the "Poets' Nook" in the *Afro-American*. These sections were not permanent features but appeared occasionally, adding to the whimsy of the material. There was no confusing these poems with great literature, but they added a kind of sweetness to the dialog between the papers and their readers.[17]

Since the black press served a relatively small readership, sometimes a small-town intimacy crept into the reporting. When the *Afro-American*'s Mike Davis was sent to Vietnam for a four-month assignment, an editorial described his mission as being "to seek out husbands, sons, sweethearts and other relatives of AFRO readers and report on their impressions, activities and outlook on the controversial war on the other side of the world." The editorial then said: "In doing so, he will be perpetuating an AFRO tradition of bringing our readers a bit closer to their loved ones who have answered the call of duty." Once Mike Davis reached Vietnam, another editorial described how overwhelmed he had been by the reception from loyal readers who were serving in the combat zone. Then the editorial promised that "AFRO readers up and down the eastern seaboard can expect to look in the paper any day and see the pictures and stories about their hometown GIs serving in Vietnam."[18]

It was next to impossible for the black press, whether individual newspapers or a cooperative pool to serve multiple publications, to maintain a permanent presence in Vietnam. For one thing, it was just too costly. There was also something of a talent drain that was making it more difficult to develop and retain talent of the caliber of Ethel Payne, Donald Mosby, and Mike Davis. The top newspapers in the mainstream media were developing an appetite for African American talent to meet the challenge of adequately covering stories about black America. This exerted pressure on ambitious black reporters and other journalists to leave the black press to seize the opportunities these new positions offered. The black press could not compete either in salaries or in providing the kind of professional resources—travel budgets, technical support, and staff—necessary to help correspondents in the field do their work. These deficiencies sometimes led to frustration among black journalists, which could loosen their professional attachments to black newspapers and magazines, even when old loyalties and ideals made separation difficult.[19]

It was not uncommon for African American journalists working for black publications to supplement their income by picking up assignments from other media outlets or from nonjournalistic endeavors. Sometimes black journalists found the stimulation and glamour of mainstream media much more attractive professionally than laboring exclusively in the black press. A good example was Ethel Payne, whose work, particularly during her stint as White House correspondent, was read by mainstream journalists; this expanded her professional horizons and ultimately led to her leaving the Sengstacke newspaper group.

Payne was invited to host a CBS radio program called *Spectrum* in 1972, with the understanding that she would remain with the *Defender* as head of its Washington bureau. John Sengstacke watched Payne's burgeoning media presence with considerable uneasiness. She speculated that "there was a little jealousy and envy on the part of him and the Chicago paper." In an attempt to reinforce Payne's ties to the *Chicago Defender,* for which she had worked for twenty years, Sengstacke asked her to become associate editor with day-to-day responsibility for managing the news operation. The offer came just months after she began her six-year run with *Spectrum*. She took the editorial management position reluctantly but continued to do her pieces for *Spectrum*, including occasional television appearances.

Payne's motivation seemed to have been both the additional money she could earn and professional fulfillment. She remained on the *Defender* payroll but said the additional income from her CBS broadcast "helped immensely." She also reveled in the enjoyment and exposure she received from her broadcasts. Payne's dual career did not sit well with Sengstacke. Eventually, he reduced Payne's newspaper salary "to a minimum," then finally sent her a terse memo dated January 11, 1978, firing her. Despite the messy end to their professional relationship, Payne still remembered Sengstacke with affection and considerable admiration more than eight years after he terminated her. "He's a very complex man personally," she said. "He's a brooder. But he had more vision than any of the other black publishers that I knew, and so I remember that with fondness to this day. Whenever I see him, we have a very cordial relationship."[20]

During the Vietnam War, because of their small size and limited resources, black papers frequently relied on news services for stories and some features. Two of these were organizations developed by African Americans specifically to serve the black press. Claude Barnett founded the Associated Negro Press (ANP) in 1919. The ANP grew and prospered along with the black press it served. The service churned out its news reports on time, providing quality at reasonable cost to its subscribers. It successfully withstood all competitors within the African American community until World War II, when its dominant position was finally challenged by an association of its primary customers: major black newspapers. Under Sengstacke's leadership the NNPA decided to pool its newsgathering resources and do for its own constituent newspapers what the ANP had been doing for years—gather and disseminate news stories for common use. In 1955 the NNPA dropped the word *Negro* from its name, becoming the National Newspaper Publishing Association.[21]

By the time of the Vietnam War the NNPA had become a relatively minor factor in disseminating general national and international news to the black press. The ANP was even weaker, with only one secure niche; it circulated several columns by African American writers to black newspapers, including "Jackie Robinson Says," by Jackie Robinson; "Big Mouth," a humorous feature by Alfred Duckett (who also was the ghostwriter for Jackie Robinson's column and had purchased the ANP from its founder, Barnett), and "Thinking It Over," by Ernest Boynton.[22]

The black press used UPI for much of its straight news stories and photographs, as well as many signed feature articles. Occasionally, an African American news service was cited as the source for news items about the Vietnam War, but this occurred infrequently. UPI had vast resources, giving it the newsgathering capabilities necessary to offer a wide variety of news items, feature articles, and photographs. As the war escalated, UPI went from one permanent reporter to a fourteen-person staff at its bureau in South Vietnam in 1965. It established its own communications link from Saigon to regional offices in Manila and Tokyo and to its office in New York by leasing daily telex time, thereby giving it the ability to move material quickly and relatively inexpensively.[23]

UPI was not without its critics. As the war went on, some other news outfits in Vietnam began carping about the quality of UPI dispatches, arguing that the wire service tended to produce hasty copy before the dust of battle had settled, allowing little time for perspective, or even for clearing up erroneous information. Another criticism was that UPI tended to embroider the facts with color to liven up its stories, a process that continued in the New York office, which inevitably produced mistakes. Still, UPI had an enviable reputation for producing readable, well-organized copy. And its material constituted the core of hard news items about the Vietnam War in the black press. Black news services simply could not compete with the scope and quality of UPI material.[24]

The process black papers used to acquire and publish material from sources other than their own writers may have been necessary, but it may sometimes have been unethical. Payne told an interviewer that it was common for staffers on black newspapers to rework items for their own papers that had appeared in major newspapers and that the black papers would present the stories as original pieces. Payne did not identify particular newspapers but said that it "was a common practice, and everybody knew it," adding that she thought it was done "throughout the whole black press." She said she insisted on writing her own material and found the plagiarism she described "very distasteful." Payne attributed the custom to the slender budgets for legwork, investigation, and time required for independent reporting.[25] She made these comments while describing events in her career during the 1950s, so it is not clear from her comments alone whether this practice persisted into the Vietnam era.

Roland Wolseley, in his history of the black press published in 1971, confirmed the existence of widespread plagiarism in the black press. The date of his book suggests that Wolseley believed this to be true during the Vietnam War. He said the papers sometimes pasted up material lifted from various sources and published it without attribution or ran wire service pieces without giving the service credit for the material.[26] During the Vietnam War the black press did rely heavily on attributed wire service material for straight news items and some feature stories on the war, mostly supplied by UPI. Occasionally, items about the war appeared in black newspapers without attribution and may have been taken from other publications or a wire service without proper credit being given, but it is difficult to say with confidence how widespread the practice was.

The black press got out the story of the war in Vietnam by improvisation. It was unable to provide continuous on-the-scene reporting, but it managed to maintain a steady flow of news and commentary on the war, keeping its readers informed and engaged. The story never attained the dominant position in the African American press that it did in the mainstream media. The black press was far more interested in the ongoing struggle of black Americans to achieve full civil rights in America and gain a larger share of their own country's bounty. The war gained particular salience in the black press when commentary or reporting on it could lend power to the rhetoric of protest aimed at tackling the discrimination and deprivation experienced by African Americans at home.

2

Vietnam and the Great Society

The Two-Front War

If I left the woman I really loved—the Great Society—in order to get involved with that bitch of a war on the other side of the world, then I would lose everything at home.—Lyndon Baines Johnson

The black press frequently dealt with the competing demands of the Southeast Asian war and the Great Society as both clamored for the government's money and attention. Lyndon Johnson pushed hard for an ambitious program of reforms designed to redress the centuries-old grievances of African Americans, even as he led the United States into an escalating war in Vietnam. The theme of competing priorities grew out of the president's own inner struggle with the most intractable dilemma facing his administration. Johnson told Doris Kearns, his former aide and biographer, that early in 1965, he felt trapped between the inherently incompatible goals of lavishing resources on his Great Society and pursuing an expensive, and politically risky, war in Southeast Asia. He feared that all his cherished plans "to feed the hungry and shelter the homeless . . . to provide education and medical care to the browns and the blacks and the lame and the poor" would be swept aside by the war. "But if I left that war and let the communists take over South Vietnam, then I would be seen as a coward and my nation would be seen as an appeaser and we would both find it impossible to accomplish anything for anybody anywhere on the entire globe."[1]

Johnson's quandary mixed an emotional personal component with hard-nosed geopolitical calculation. He seemed to feel an almost adolescent fear of being "seen as a coward," as he told Kearns, a need to face up to the play-ground bully so he would not be seen as chicken. Johnson felt a strong need to be as tough as his political opposition in Congress, and hawks generally, inside and outside his administration. This made him particularly susceptible to the advice of hawks within his administration, as well as to the pressure from outside his circle of foreign policy advisers.

Johnson, like his predecessors and successors, also exemplified—and pursued in the jungles of Vietnam—a commitment to two interlocking articles of American faith in the cold war era, up to and including the Vietnam War: that expansionist communism would topple weak allies if the United States failed to help them and that central to the success of U.S. interests abroad was maintaining credibility. The latter required bolstering the confidence of allies that the United States was a strong, reliable friend and demonstrating to potential foes that America would be a formidable opponent of any threat to U.S. interests in the world. Except for adhering to these principles, nothing else was really at stake for the United States in South Vietnam. It was unimportant economically to the United States. It was insignificant militarily. Its sole importance was that it became the testing ground of America's resolve and hence of its credibility as the bulwark against the expansionist designs of communism in Southeast Asia.

Johnson's commitment to this worldview made it impossible for him to abandon Vietnam to save the Great Society, even if weakening the cause of reform was the price for persevering in Southeast Asia. Nor could Johnson abandon the Great Society, despite the pressures of his commitment to Vietnam, because of his deep faith in his program of domestic reconstruction.

Johnson's desire to launch the Great Society became as fervent as his fear of losing to the communists was deep seated. On the evening of Kennedy's murder, Johnson and several aides gathered at The Elms, LBJ's private Washington residence, to sort numbly through the day's events and to talk about future plans. One of Johnson's intimates, Jack Valenti, remembered that during the meeting LBJ laid out elements of what was to become the Great Society. Two days after the assassination, Johnson was emphatic about Vietnam as he spoke to aides at a White House meeting: "I am not going to be the President who saw Southeast Asia go the way China went."[2]

Then, three days later, Johnson addressed a joint session of Congress and told the assembled legislators and a national television audience of his resolve to bring to fruition Kennedy's social vision: "And now the ideas and the ideals which he so nobly represented must and will be translated into effective action."[3] These were the seeds of the Great Society. Whatever nuanced delineation Johnson used to separate himself from his predecessor, he placed himself squarely in a domestic and foreign policy tradition that incorporated an expansive vision of domestic reform with an assertive international activism. This conjunction of ideas was typically Democratic and one that, in the long shadow of FDR and the brooding menace of Stalin and his heirs, led almost inevitably to the simultaneous pursuits of the Great Society and the containment of Asian communism in Vietnam. A kind of terrible predestination was implicit in Johnson's domestic and international ideology, which both foreordained the Vietnam War and doomed the Great Society. Johnson felt compelled to pursue both, but in the end he could have neither victory in Vietnam nor the full promise of the Great Society. They were quite simply incompatible. But he would try (see figure 1).

Even after his sweeping victory at the polls in November 1964, military involvement in Vietnam held special political perils for Lyndon Johnson. It would jeopardize his personal political standing, endanger support for the Great Society, in which he firmly believed, and tarnish his legacy as a great reformer in the mold of President Roosevelt and his New Deal. Johnson was keenly aware that he had an opportunity to summon the nobler impulses that still lingered in the aftermath of Kennedy's death and the political muscle from his landslide election to get the legislation through Congress. But he also realized that he would lose that opportunity if he persisted, as he felt compelled to do, in enlarging the U.S. commitment to the war in Vietnam.

LBJ did not think he had much time to enact his cherished domestic policy goals into law. He told his vice president–elect, Hubert Humphrey, "I figure we have got about nine months to get our way in Congress, no more." The urgency felt by Johnson, never famous for his patience, led to what some critics viewed as a haphazard approach to domestic reform, laws mandating imaginative programs but not spelling out the details of how the programs should be organized and function.[4] He was a man with a mission and a man in a hurry. At least some of his haste, particularly as Congress labored on his programs well into 1965, grew out of his anxious realization that building the Great Society would be increasingly difficult as he led the country deeper into the uncertain conflict in South Vietnam.

As the war in Vietnam heated up, the political dangers he faced were never far from Johnson's view as he conceived and nurtured the Great Society. In February 1964 members of LBJ's staff had learned more of the outlines of the Great Society during a dip in the White House swimming pool. As he pon-

Figure 1. Double Date

President Johnson, trapped between infatuation and commitment. (Cartoon by
Tom Floyd, *Chicago Defender*, February 2, 1966. Courtesy of the *Chicago Defender*.)

derously treaded water with Bill Moyers and Richard Goodwin, the president
elaborated on his vision of a program that would build upon, but move beyond, Kennedy's social vision, a "Johnson program, different in tone, fighting and aggressive." The name of the program was self-consciously designed
to give the new administration a unique and catchy slogan, one that would
identify Johnson's presidency as a force for good for a nation still mourn-
ing the loss of John F. Kennedy. Fittingly, it was Goodwin, a former aide to
JFK and now a speechwriter for Johnson, who gathered ideas and gave them
the rhetorical wings, including the name, that would forever identify the
cluster of social initiatives as the Great Society. LBJ had used the phrase in

several speeches in the spring of 1964, but it was Goodwin who invested the phrase with the formalized status that allowed it to take its place in the lexicon of grand historical initiatives that defined presidencies in the manner of Franklin Roosevelt's New Deal.[5]

Johnson's formal introduction of his vision of a Great Society would come on May 22, 1964, when he addressed more than eighty thousand in the University of Michigan football stadium in Ann Arbor. He was there to speak to the graduating class and to receive an honorary doctorate. In twenty minutes LBJ spelled out his hopes for the kind of society the United States could become for all its citizens. He was interrupted by applause numerous times as the audience responded warmly to the president and appeared to sense that he was saying something momentous. It seemed an auspicious beginning.[6]

He had begun work on a major component of his ambitious social program, the War on Poverty, months earlier. On the evening of November 23, 1963, the day after President Kennedy's assassination, Walter Heller, an economic aide to Kennedy, told Johnson that JFK had asked for a plan to help the 22 percent of Americans who lived below the poverty line. Kennedy had been touched by the spectacle of American poverty when he visited West Virginia shantytowns and saw undernourished children plainly suffering from hunger during the 1960 presidential primary campaign. Later Kennedy had been moved by Michael Harrington's provocative book *The Other America*, a probing study of poverty in the nation, and in December 1962 had asked Heller to begin thinking of ways to attack poverty in the United States. Other staffers got involved and ideas slowly began to form, but no legislation was being drawn up. On November 5, 1963, Heller sent a message to various departments, seeking to develop "imaginative new programs" for a concerted assault on poverty to be mounted, if possible, in 1964. The national struggle against poverty, it appeared, might finally be picking up momentum.

Two and a half weeks later Kennedy was assassinated in Dallas.

The next evening, when Heller told Johnson about JFK's dream of an assault on poverty, LBJ quickly embraced the Kennedy initiative. The War on Poverty became one of the first pieces of Kennedy's unfinished business taken up by Johnson.[7] Within days some of his closest advisers were saying publicly that the president planned to make the reduction of poverty a top priority in his administration.[8]

Johnson himself provided the rhetorical basis for regarding the struggle against poverty as a war. In his first State of the Union address in early 1964, Johnson announced dramatically: "This Administration today, here and now, declares unconditional war on poverty in America." Later, in his message to Congress, he asked the lawmakers to approve an ambitious legislative program designed to produce "total victory" in the freshly declared war on poverty.[9] Johnson was invoking the inspiring tradition of America girding for war, summoning the nation's vast resources and the galvanized will of the people to fight for lofty ideals—and to fight until total victory was achieved.

His soaring language also helped produce one of the most powerful and persistent metaphors used by the black press to describe the impact of the Vietnam War on the struggle of African Americans for equal rights and economic justice: the two-front war.

The motif of a war fought on two fronts, or two separate wars, one at home and the other in Vietnam, was soon was embedded in the way many African Americans articulated the intersection of Vietnam and their own struggle. The *Baltimore Afro-American*, on March 2, 1968, published a poignant poem written by a black marine in Vietnam:

My battle is home, in my
native land,
The war that I know, and
understand.
Where the black must fight
if he wants to be free.
If he wants his civil rights
and equality.
This is the kind of war that
I am prepared to fight
The one that will make me
equal to the white.
Send me back to the battle
at home.
Because this one here is
not my own.

For the marine poet the important war was at home, where the sources of black despair were waiting to be located and overcome. The marine did not live to fight that battle. He was killed in combat in Vietnam.[10]

The metaphor of the two-front war owed its durability in the black press to its aptness in evoking the struggle that was so much a part of African American life and its ability to express the dimensions of that struggle as it related to the Vietnam War. The phrase also contained echoes of the Double V campaign during World War II, when much of the black press, led by the *Pittsburgh Courier*, linked the war in Europe and Asia with the war against racial discrimination in the United States and expressed the determination to achieve victory in both wars. The campaign was an effort to garner Americans' support for sweeping aside the injustices of discrimination and segregation. It was also a drive to motivate African Americans to support the war effort, despite the persistence of racial injustice experienced by black Americans on the home front.[11]

There were, of course, significant differences in the realities behind the metaphors in the two wars. World War II aroused a powerful national will to win the war overseas but little inclination in white society to fulfill the dreams of black Americans for a domestic victory over Jim Crow. During the Vietnam War the national will to go to war was never aroused and sustained, and indeed the country became sharply divided as the conflict dragged on. But a liberal consensus already had aligned itself with African American aspirations, sweeping aside the legal basis for segregation, and had begun enacting laws designed to improve the social and economic life of black Americans, progress that now seemed threatened by the war in Vietnam. However, in both cases the black press sought to connect the war abroad in the public mind with the black struggle at home to attain equal civil rights. During World War II the objective of the black press was to create a national determination to attack and overcome racial discrimination at home, an aspiration that was not realized. During the Vietnam War the goal was to sustain and strengthen the national political impulse toward reform until the project was completed and victory over discrimination and poverty at home finally was achieved.

In a dazzling display of his mastery of the ways of Congress, Johnson rammed ambitious bills through the House and the Senate, including legislation enabling his cherished war on poverty. In August 1964 he signed the Economic Opportunity Act, the legislative embodiment of the poverty program. Richard Strout, writing under his pseudonym, TRB, in the *New Republic*, said of LBJ's program, "He has proposed a 'war on poverty,' which—even with superlatives drained off—remains a splendid bundle of beginnings."[12]

Proposing this "splendid bundle of beginnings" was one thing. Pressing the attack on poverty and attaining results was quite another. Johnson wanted the program to be viewed by Congress and the American people as something that would benefit everyone, not just the poor. The president had told Congress the antipoverty crusade would give poor people "a chance." But, he added, "We do it also because helping some will increase the prosperity of all." He was concerned that the antipoverty program not be seen as just another form of welfare, with national resources consumed by idle poor who would not become productive members of society. Privately, Johnson had passed word to his aides that nothing in the program should be construed as a dole. It should be a "hand up," not a "hand-out."

To lead the War on Poverty Johnson chose the irrepressible and relentlessly optimistic Kennedy brother-in-law Sargent Shriver. He had headed the Peace Corps and had used that organization to translate highly idealized concepts into practical programs that helped impoverished third world countries and also caught the imagination of the American people.[13]

The War on Poverty was in the early stages of implementation in 1965, as the war in Vietnam was escalating and the nation's attention was turning to that distant conflict. Increasingly, the war was becoming the most absorbing concern in the Johnson administration, requiring sustained attention from the president and an increasingly burdensome allocation of national resources.

Even at this early stage, concerned African American leaders were recognizing the developing conflict between the two wars. When James Farmer, national director of the Congress of Racial Equality (CORE), stood to deliver the keynote address to its annual convention in Durham, North Carolina, on July 1, 1965, his discerning eye had already noted the shape of an ominous threat to all that CORE was trying to accomplish. As he spoke of past victories and future challenges, Farmer talked about what he called "this major war now confronting us," the war "to alter meaningfully the lives of the black Americans." Then, barely two minutes into his speech, with undisguised alarm and indignation, he said: "Further, it is impossible for the government to mount a decisive war against poverty and bigotry in the United States while it is pouring billions down the drain in a war against people in Vietnam. The billion dollars available to fight poverty is puny compared with the need and insignificant compared with the resources expended in wars."[14]

During the early weeks of the winter of 1965–66, Johnson wrestled with how to balance the war in Vietnam and the War on Poverty. According to the Johnson biographer Robert Dallek, LBJ knew that the Vietnam War would preoccupy his administration for the next year and that his domestic program would "have to take a back seat to the war."[15] Nonetheless, the president was determined not to acknowledge publicly the subordination of the War on Poverty to the war in Southeast Asia.

As Vietnam began to concern domestic policy makers in mid-1965, Congress, under intense pressure from Johnson, passed the historic Voting Rights Act. At the signing ceremony in the Capitol Rotunda, the president hailed the legislation with military language and metaphors that, consciously or not, evoked his role as the nation's commander in chief. It seemed to suggest that Vietnam was very much on his mind and already was shaping his domestic rhetoric, if not yet his policy, on the home front. Johnson had already agonized privately about the necessity to push reform legislation through Congress before the economic and political pressures of the Vietnam War made further domestic reform difficult, if not impossible. Now, as he signed the Voting Rights Act, Johnson said the political achievement it represented "was a triumph for freedom as huge as any victory that has ever been won on any battlefield." The black "fight for freedom" would have to "move now toward a different battlefield," entering an enforcement phase that would establish the rights of African Americans in fact as well as in law.[16]

Johnson's speechwriters clearly sought to cast him in the role of triumphant leader by adorning the moment with the imagery of a stirring military victory. But the president's military allusions in domestic contexts were more than the rhetorical swagger of a leader fresh from a great triumph and ready to press the attack further against problems at home. The imagery was also a call to arms designed to build determination for the fight on two fronts that he intended to lead as commander in chief.

Early in the Vietnam War, when there was a measure of optimism that both wars could be won, they could be seen as noble crusades, both led by a commander in chief whose compassion and expansive determination would bring victory. Such optimism could not long survive the relentless logic of unfolding events.

Despite the historic victory represented by the Voting Rights Act, the black press continued to express anxiety about the government's ability to deliver on the promise of the Great Society while managing a growing military commitment in Vietnam. The nagging fears about the threat of Vietnam to the cherished goals of massive and costly government intervention on behalf of the underprivileged, especially blacks, were not self-indulgent paranoia. Even as the African American press warned of the dangers to Great Society programs, Johnson wrestled with how to do the impossible and maintain the momentum of domestic reform in the face of rising war costs. He struggled with how to reconcile the competing demands of expensive domestic programs to fight the war at home against discrimination and poverty and what he and his planners knew would be a dauntingly high price tag for significantly increasing America's involvement in Vietnam.

Johnson realized that if Congress knew what the war in Vietnam was likely to cost, he would have a full-scale assault against the Great Society on his hands. To pay for the war his legislative opponents would demand a reduction in spending for domestic programs, which many in Congress were itching to slash anyway. Johnson's short-term remedy grew out of his natural secretiveness and soon hardened into a determination to end-run congressional critics and opponents by concealing the widening of the war in Vietnam. This, he hoped, would buy time until the domestic social legislation, which he envisioned as his legacy, was more firmly entrenched. The Vietnam War, Johnson believed, was an inescapable international commitment that had to be fulfilled. The Great Society, on the other hand, was not only an indispensable part of the war on discrimination and want but a social obligation of the nation to its less fortunate citizens.[17]

In the run-up to the State of the Union address on January 12, 1966, the black press began to get an inkling of the shift in national priorities and sounded the alarm. An editorial in the *Milwaukee Star* four days before Johnson's speech wondered in its headline "War Turned Skirmish?" The piece responded firmly to the rumors that the new U.S. budget would scale back funding for the War on Poverty to pay the costs of war in Vietnam. The editor wrote, "We find it hard to believe that President Johnson can take his much-heralded 'Great Society' program, which a year or so ago was recognized as vital to the interests of our country's poor and minority groups, and put it on the shelf as easily." He went on to excoriate Johnson for scaling "the domestic 'war' back . . . so that we can fight a bigger and better war against the peoples of Vietnam." In a final, bitter thrust the editorial wondered whether "the 'Great Society' [is] just so much talk to gain public sympathy left over from the 'New Frontier' [and is] now to be conveniently discarded to enable 'us' to kill Vietnamese peasants."[18]

Johnson and his staff anticipated just such concerns and sought to defuse the anxiety expressed with such uncharacteristic rancor by a member of the black press. In his State of the Union address Johnson spoke to the capacity of the national government to prosecute both the antipoverty war and the war in Vietnam.

The speech triggered a relieved editorial in the *New York Amsterdam News*. As the paper noted approvingly, LBJ had confidently asserted that the United States had sufficient resources to fight and win "the war on poverty and the war in Vietnam." Of those who would shortchange domestic programs to finance the war, the president had asked: "Whom will they sacrifice? Will they sacrifice the children who seek learning, the sick who need care, the families who dwell in squalor now brightened by the hope of home?" Then Johnson promised that the nation would not "wring that sacrifice from the hopes of the unfortunate in a land of plenty." In a glowing review of the president's broad vision, the editorial said, "Mr. Johnson's approach to the war abroad and the war at home is humane and aimed at bringing about the greatest good to the greatest number of people on both war fronts."[19]

The *Pittsburgh Courier* joined the New York paper in applauding the State of the Union address, also picking up on the rhetorically useful imagery of a two-front war. The newspaper worried that, confronted with the mounting costs of the war in Vietnam, Johnson would face irresistible pressures from opponents of liberal social legislation "to cut down spending on the home front." Noting that "what we are spending on poverty is negligible in comparison with what we have spent, are spending, and will spend in Vietnam," the editorial expressed the fervent hope that the president would not yield to pressures calling for a reduction in appropriations earmarked "to combat poverty."[20]

Another editorial in the *New York Amsterdam News* was headlined "Two Wars" and hearkened back to "the 'double victory,' which Negroes sought and popularized during World War II," but "never actually won." Citing the unfairness that placed an excessive number of blacks on the battlefield in Vietnam, the editorial suggested that, "while we deplore the disproportionate number of our sons on the battlefronts of Vietnam, we must at the same time redouble our efforts at home to see that the system which gives rise to such unfairness is corrected." Now, the piece told its readers, it was necessary "to strengthen Negro families, to cut down on the number of Negro school dropouts, to get rid of job discrimination and to train more Negro men for the specialized skills" they would need to achieve the American dream. The editorial concluded: "This is the war which Negroes must fight on the home front. It is as important as the war 'over there.'"[21]

Fueled by black frustration and anger, and exploding into unproductive paroxysms of destruction, riots broke out in a number of U.S. inner cities during the summer of 1966. When President Johnson "quietly cautioned" black Americans that the mayhem in the inner cities could put at risk "a great many of the gains" so recently won in the civil rights struggle, an editorial in the *Milwaukee Star* rebuked the president for what it called a "double standard": "The presidential brand of non-violence employs an interesting double standard—warning American Negroes to 'cool it' at home to spare antagonizing the whites while ordering the more than 40,000 American Negroes currently in Vietnam to 'burn, baby' against the yellow-skinned native population."[22]

The *Star* saw a moral incongruity in deploring violence by black Americans while condoning—indeed, ordering—it in Vietnam. As in most such incongruities involving blacks in overwhelmingly white America, the connecting thread was racism. If Johnson deplored violence in the inner city, he should deplore it in Vietnam. As the editor saw it, what made the violence in Vietnam palatable to the administration was that it was directed against a nonwhite populace.

However the argument was constructed, the issue at stake was the moral superiority of blacks' claim to a national commitment to eliminate privation. In the almost universal view of the black press and African American leaders,

America needed to redirect its energies and resources from the Vietnam War, which was both immoral and materially voracious, to fight the war at home against the causes of urban violence.

After watching months of political struggle over the president's domestic initiative, the *Chicago Daily Defender* pointed an accusing figure at the obstructionist Republican Party, which was intent on defeating Johnson's domestic programs that would benefit the poor and underprivileged, most notably, African Americans. The headline on an editorial about the Republican plan in the *Defender*, on January 12, 1967, was "The GOP Offensive." The objective of congressional Republicans, the editorial said, was nothing less than to "smash the Great Society and bring a halt to the war on poverty." Alas, the editorial noted, "the strategy may work." Then, continuing the militaristic imagery and summoning the familiar metaphor, the piece concluded: "The critics are saying that the Administration cannot finance two wars at once: the one in Southeast Asia and the war on poverty at home. President Johnson does not share that view. He believes that it is imperative to wage the twin fights on both fronts, and what's more, win them."[23]

Lending special urgency to the need for an aggressive offensive in the War on Poverty was another summer of rioting in a number of cities up and down the East Coast and in the Midwest. Urban riots had been a plague, principally in inner cities, for several summers, but the upheavals, which swept through ghetto after ghetto during the summer of 1967, culminating in the six-day riot in Detroit, were particularly violent. In *Ebony* Lerone Bennett Jr. described the sequence of uprisings as "a black fury, as elemental as a natural disaster," likening it to an avalanche that occurred after "great chunks of discontent" accumulated "in the steep mountains of black despair." Bennett endorsed the calls of senators Robert Kennedy and Charles Percy to transfer national resources of personnel and money from "the costly and demoralizing war in Vietnam to the crucial war in the cities of America."[24]

Martin Luther King Jr.'s was the most prominent in a chorus of voices calling for massive redeployment of resources to fight poverty. At a news conference, in remarks reported in the *Chicago Defender*, King chided Congress for "issuing an open invitation for the violence and riots" that had swept through several major cities. He blamed the rioting on cutbacks in funding of antipoverty programs, the type that would have alleviated precisely the problems that had touched off the riots that summer. King called the congressional assault on poverty funds "the worst economic holocaust ever to be experienced in the nation" and said Congress had "voted out rent subsidies, cut down on the model cities program, and voted $35 billion a year for fighting in Vietnam." Then King added: "They have declared a war against poverty, yet only financed the skirmish." Material written by King and distributed by the Southern Christian Leadership Conference promoted the assault on poverty and declared that the war in Vietnam "is being used by the American establishment against the poverty-stricken people of Vietnam and the poor people here at home."[25]

Here, the metaphor of the two-front war, or the two wars, one in Vietnam and the other on the home front, is given yet another twist. What began as a metaphor suggesting the United States was fighting an idealistic war for freedom and democracy in Vietnam and an equally idealistic war against poverty at home became a depiction of an expensive war in Vietnam that was absorbing vast American resources, depleting the War on Poverty. That imagery in turn had become a metaphor describing a malevolent U.S. power establishment that was simultaneously fighting both the threadbare peasants of Vietnam and poor Americans at home. The war had changed everything. In the metaphor the generous American spirit had transmogrified into an engine of devastation in Vietnam. And at home it was no longer a war against poverty, but a war against the impoverished.

One of those who had consistently opposed even a skirmish against poverty was U.S. Representative L. Mendel Rivers. The *Baltimore Afro-American* could scarcely contain its contempt for the Democrat from South Carolina when it reported his pious words on its front page: "What is a victory in Vietnam worth if veterans come home to charred and burned cities?" In citing his unfailing effort to end programs designed to alleviate urban poverty, the source of so much of the seething discontent that festered in the ghettos, the newspaper implicitly rebuked Rivers for his hypocrisy.[26]

Rivers was not the only white person to respond uncomprehendingly to the urban violence. Following the rioting that broke out in the Watts section of Los Angeles in 1965, sympathy for the plight of black Americans began to sag among whites. Even Lyndon Johnson was puzzled since, during his presidency, so much was being done for blacks. He was upset at what seemed like ingratitude on a grand scale.[27]

It was not that the president had been inactive in bringing the Great Society into being. Johnson's legislative achievements were legendary. During 1965 and 1966 Congress passed a flood of legislation rivaling that of the heady first two years of the New Deal. During the 1965 session Congress enacted eighty-four of the eighty-seven major bills proposed by the Johnson administration, including the historic Voting Rights Act, a tough law that cleared all the impediments that the South had so long thrown in the path of blacks who tried to exercise their vote. In 1966 Congress passed ninety of the 113 major laws proposed by LBJ. This was an astonishing feat of leadership by any measure and one that solidified the president's hold on the political backing of the black press.[28]

A major disappointment was the failure of Congress to pass Johnson's 1966 civil rights bill. While much had been accomplished in the civil rights laws enacted in 1964 and 1965, Johnson thought several areas—such as jury selection, housing, and expanded powers that would allow the U.S. attorney general to sue to enforce school desegregation—still needed strong federal legislation. The 1966 civil rights bill addressed all these areas. It immediately faced stiff resistance, particularly because of the sections on housing discrimination, which critics argued violated constitutional protections for property owners. After extended floor fights and behind-the-scenes negotiations, the House passed a somewhat diluted version of the bill, but the Senate blocked passage with a filibuster.

Roy Wilkins offered the most resolute comment on the legislative failure: "The problem is not going away. The Negro is not going away. . . . We will be back in this or another Congress." Other African American leaders expressed dismay and anger. CORE attacked the measure as "worthless in some sections, racist in others." King, who had been leading his troops in a dispiriting—and largely ineffective—campaign against segregated housing in Chicago, dismissed the bill with one eloquently disdainful word: "Worthless."[29]

Despite this loss, and a few others, the first two years of the Johnson presidency were a whirlwind of legislative achievement. There is no doubt that the shift of congressional power in the 1966 elections had much to do with slowing the momentum of the Great Society. But any assessment of the cascade of legislative achievements from 1964 to 1966 is inadequate if it does not give due credit to Johnson and his legendary powers to persuade and manipulate Congress.

When Johnson became president, he had moved quickly to break the congressional logjam that still existed when John F. Kennedy was killed. Johnson quickly put his stamp on an extraordinary period of legislative activism. If he was anything, Johnson was a savvy political leader, and he understood the political costs of escalating the Vietnam War. As his generals and members of his staff pressed him for another strike against North Vietnam late in 1964, the president mused to one of his aides how the war would likely give political opponents an excuse to torpedo the Great Society. "They hate this stuff," Johnson said. "They don't want to help the poor and the Negroes, but they're afraid to be against it at a time like this when there's all this prosperity. But the war—oh, they'll like the war."[30]

LBJ's quandary was genuine, the danger to his cherished social programs real. After the burst of legislative activity in 1964 and 1965, the black press would begin to sense more acutely the threat the Vietnam War posed to the Great Society.

As Congress assembled to resume work after its holiday recess in early 1966, one of the first things on its agenda was its third annual review of the poverty programs. Even before legislators settled in their seats in the U.S. Capitol, gloomy stories began appearing in the black press that alarmed the black community. The stories about pending congressional action to cut funding for the War on Poverty also prompted a flurry of pieces in the black press delineating the threat to the antipoverty programs posed by the rapidly escalating costs of the Vietnam conflict.

A UPI story ran in the *Defender* on January 6, 1966, under the headline "Vietnam War Expected to Cut Poverty Funds." The piece began grimly: "The 'War on Poverty' may find out in 1966 how it feels to be poor." Responding to rumors swirling through the halls of Congress, emanating from the vacationing president in Texas, the story reported that Johnson was determined to hold down costs and that "the 'War on Poverty,' although one of his proudest achievements, is regarded as a likely candidate for the budget scalpel." The *Los Angeles Sentinel* weighed in with a more complete version of the UPI story.[31]

Notably missing was any sense that Washington was considering holding back money appropriated for the Vietnam War so that the domestic programs could go forward at planned levels. If budgets had to be trimmed, all too many were eager to slash domestic commitments to combat poverty.

In the *Defender* of January 10, 1966, another editorial noted one of the potential consequences of such action. It quoted Martin Luther King Jr. as warning darkly that "a curtailment of commitment in the area of public aid would drive the civil rights movement into the peace movement." The editorial was adamant that step did not even have to be considered. "Must we equate the proliferation of the war in Vietnam with the war on poverty at home?" the piece asked. Then, answering its own rhetorical question, the editorial pointed to the vast and growing resources of the American economy and declared: "With such unlimited resources it would appear that there is no pressing necessity for weighing the imperatives of war against the responsibilities of public welfare. For the consequences of so unjust a curtailment would be to place the burden of fighting the war in Vietnam on the backs of the poor already bent by the yoke of economic vicissitude and broken dreams."[32]

Days later an editorial in the *Afro-American* bemoaned the choice that the government appeared to be making, to pursue an expensive and dubious venture in Southeast Asia and dash the hopes of Americans who had been promised assistance they sorely needed. "Having been led to the edge of an abyss," the paper wrote, "we are told the bridge we thought would be thrown across to secure passage to the other, and more attractive side, will be delayed because of other, more pressing matters." And later: "Instead of a shining hope, what will be left is despair, a feeling that the poor people of the country have been deceived again." No matter how eloquently the administration "defends the priority of Vietnam, the feeling will persist that another promise has been broken and that it was foolish to hope in the first place."[33]

President Johnson countered the mounting concerns by announcing that he was actually boosting the amount of money allocated to the poverty program by $2 billion. The *Defender* announced the president's plan in a news story headlined "LBJ 'Escalates' War on Poverty." The piece was a straight news story about the announcement, which was made by Secretary of Labor W. Willard Wirtz to a labor union audience.[34]

In his State of the Union message on January 12, 1966, Johnson sought to quiet fears that he was reducing his commitment to the Great Society. Still, in a phrase that must have sent a premonitory chill down the spines of African American leaders, the president began his speech by declaring that Vietnam "must be at the center of our concerns," since, as he would say later in the address, "the cup of peril is full in Vietnam." However, he said with equal determination that the communists in Vietnam could not be permitted to "win a victory over the desires and the intentions of all the American people. This nation is mighty enough, its society healthy enough, its people are strong enough, to pursue our goals in the rest of the world while building a Great Society at home." Later Johnson added: "I recommend that we prosecute with vigor and determination our war on poverty." He called on Congress to pass the third civil rights bill in three years, banning discrimination in jury selection and in the sale and rental of housing. Johnson also made a flurry of other proposals, including an urban slum rebuilding program "on a scale never before attempted," as well as addressing environmental issues, criminal justice, and consumer concerns, to name a few. His vision was bold, sweeping—and obviously very expensive.[35]

All these domestic programs were to be pursued even as the war in Vietnam continued. Johnson anticipated resistance to the cost of sustaining both efforts. He told Congress: "There are men who cry out: we must sacrifice. Let us rather ask them: whom will they sacrifice? Time may require further sacrifices. If so, we will make them." Then, echoing the thought—and addressing the fears—of the *Chicago Defender* editorial that had appeared just two days earlier, Johnson added: "But we will not heed those who will wring it from the hopes of the unfortunate in a land of plenty." He assured Congress and the nation that "we can continue the Great Society while we fight in Vietnam."[36] His words were meant as both an encouragement to those who feared that Vietnam would cripple his domestic reforms and a warning to those in Congress who might want to use the war as an excuse to diminish the Great Society.

Not unexpectedly, Johnson found broad support for his domestic policies in the African American press. After several months of watching the political jockeying in Congress, Clarence Mitchell Jr., a noted black columnist, had had his fill. In his June 18 column in the *Afro-American*, Mitchell cut through the thin veneer of excuses made by those who opposed the War on Poverty. He argued that those clamoring for reductions in funding for antipoverty programs were not truly concerned about funding the war in Vietnam. Instead, the antireformists were blocking the progressive agenda of the Johnson administration for their own narrow reasons; the war in Vietnam was convenient political cover for their miserly objectives. Mitchell wrote: "The war in Asia has become an alibi for foot-draggers and penny-pinchers in America. They want to scuttle legislation that will help build the Johnson great society."[37]

Mitchell's column appeared as influential forces in Congress were beginning to become increasingly vocal about the financial conflict posed by the need to fund both the Vietnam War and the Great Society. One form opposition to the Great Society took was opposition to any thought of raising taxes. Senator Richard Russell of Georgia, the influential chair of the Armed Services Committee, who was both a long-time ally of Johnson's in the foreign policy arena and a foe of progressive civil rights legislation, wrapped his prejudices in the cloak of budgetary restraint and rectitude. Senator Russell told the Georgia General Assembly in January that he was "one of those who has questioned whether this nation, for all its wealth and resources, can fight a war of the magnitude of Vietnam and carry on a broad range of domestic spending without a tax increase or a dangerous deficit."[38] Russell, in the view of the black press, was ignoring one obvious source of funds for the social programs: cutting back on the Vietnam War.

In September, in her *New York Amsterdam News* column, Gertrude Wilson vented her outrage at just this sort of thinking. "While we fight a two billion dollar-a-day war for democracy in Vietnam," she wrote, "the very existence, or need, for such legislation [i.e., poverty programs] is enough to make the devil himself cry." Then she used a staple of the black press, measuring what the costs of the Vietnam War could pay for in the war against poverty: "For two billion dollars a day we could tear down every Harlem in the United States of America, and rebuild them all in a year. For free rent if need be."[39]

Just before Christmas *Jet*'s "Words of the Week" feature quoted Martin Luther King's use of the same argument: "If our country can spend $800 a second, $2 billion a month, $24 billion a year to fight a war in Vietnam, and another $20 billion to put a man on the moon, it can spend billions of dollars to put God's children on their own two feet." Later, in his last speech to the Southern Christian Leadership Conference as its president, King offered the same formula but with a harsher judgment of the war, calling it "an unjust, evil war."[40]

In the meantime the Republicans gained forty-seven seats in the House and three seats in the Senate in the congressional elections of 1966.[41] While the Democrats retained sizable majorities in both houses, Congress had become distinctly more conservative, with potentially dire consequences for the president's ability to retain support for his domestic reform agenda, particularly while the United States was waging a costly war in Vietnam. This only deepened the concern of the black press that Johnson, despite his formidable legislative skills, would be unable to sustain the momentum of the War on Poverty.

Increasingly, the black press was criticizing Johnson for failing to exhibit the leadership required to defend the poverty program from attack. On December 3, 1966, an editorial in the *New Pittsburgh Courier* raised the issue, using the metaphor of the two-front war to dramatize its point: "Unless the President does take strong leadership in defense of the anti-poverty program it appears that in the next Congress it may well be scuttled. While the President has been leading an all-out war effort in Vietnam, the war against poverty has been in the nature of a holding operation, and in this domestic war its enclaves are in danger of being overrun by the conservative enemy."

In the end the *Courier* editor predicted the outcome of the president's weakening leadership would be that "the war on poverty will grind to a standstill, with the victims of poverty being asked to wait, wait, wait until 'times are better.'"[42]

Early in the new year the *Courier* columnist Adolph J. Slaughter was scarcely more optimistic, writing that "Vietnam, the war of death, intensified and escalated almost to the destruction of the anti-poverty war, the war of life. Cutbacks in poverty spending left a gaping hole in the hopes and aspirations of a disadvantaged segment of our own population." Slaughter conceded that while "the successes of the poverty war were nothing to write home about," at least "they were there."[43]

The pollster Stanley B. Greenberg, writing in the mid-1990s, saw a "flight from the Great Society" between 1964 and 1968: "In the 1968 presidential election, the American people rejected not only Lyndon Johnson and Hubert Humphrey but also a social contract premised on the needs of the most disadvantaged rather than on the needs of the people generally." The ultimate evidence of this defection was offered in the sheer magnitude of the collapse of support for Democratic presidential candidates: Johnson had pulled 61 percent of the vote in 1964, but Hubert Humphrey managed only a paltry 43 percent in 1968. As Greenberg wrote, "The great majority of Americans voted for candidates who opposed the Great Society: forty-three percent for Nixon and fourteen percent for Wallace."[44]

Civil rights leaders watched in dismay as national support for federal intervention in the area of civil rights dropped, while the public at large still was strongly behind the Vietnam War. The rise of the black power movement, which expressed anger and impatience with the pace of change domestically, also increasingly alienated many white reformers and antagonized many other ordinary white citizens.

At the same time there was a strong reaction against the large-scale urban violence that was becoming increasingly common in major cities, particularly during the long hot summers. By the summer of 1966, "white backlash" had become a political reality and the theme of law and order a political issue. In September 1966 pollster Greenberg's surveys found that "a majority of the public for the first time concluded that the federal government was pushing civil rights too far."[45]

Soon after 1967 began, the president went before Congress for the State of the Union address. As Johnson began, his tone was somber, almost defensive, as he grimly portrayed the difficulties the country was facing in waging the two-front war:

> I have come here tonight to report to you that this is a time of testing for our Nation.
>
> At home, the question is whether we will continue working for better opportunities for all Americans, when most Americans are already living better than any people in history.
>
> Abroad, the question is whether we have the staying power to fight a very costly war, when the objective is limited and the danger to us is seemingly remote.
>
> So our test is not whether we shrink from our country's cause when the dangers to us are obvious and close at hand, but, rather, whether we carry on when they seem obscure and distant—and some think that it is safe to lay down our burdens.

The president ticked off domestic achievements, then, almost wearily, laid down a challenge: "Now we must answer whether our gains shall be the foundations of further progress, or whether they shall be only monuments to what might have been—abandoned now by a people who lacked the will to see their great work through."

Johnson reminded Congress—and the country outside the walls of the chamber—that three years earlier he and Congress had joined "in a declaration of war on poverty, then I warned, 'It will not be a short or easy struggle— no single weapon . . . will suffice—but we shall not rest until that war is won.'"

He lumbered through an almost apologetic description of the fits and starts of the War on Poverty, expressing the hope "that we have learned from our own trial and error." Later, he again warned of the difficulty that lay ahead in both wars: "This war—like the war in Vietnam—is not a simple one. There is no single battle line which you can plot each day on a chart. The enemy is not easy to perceive, or to isolate, or to destroy."[46]

Two weeks later a bold headline in the *Atlanta Daily World* announced: "Johnson Gears Congress for Indefinite Viet War with $172 Billion Budget." The UPI story quoted Johnson as exhorting Congress not to retreat from Vietnam or from "modest progress toward the Great Society at home."[47] By this time Johnson's appeals to Congress to maintain support for the Great Society program were less expansive, a difference noted by the black press. There was a frantic element in the president's plea for at least "modest progress" at home, a call that was weakened by the overwhelming reality of the war and the strenuous opposition of Republicans, and some conservative Democrats, who objected to Johnson's proposal for a tax surcharge to fund the nation's commitments at home and abroad. The ballooning costs of the Vietnam War alone were sufficient reason to induce LBJ to go slow on the War on Poverty.

It seemed to many observers to be a desultory performance reflecting a deteriorating resolve by LBJ to prosecute the war at home aggressively. One listener who came to that conclusion was Martin Luther King, who was dismayed at what he thought were clear signs that the war in Vietnam had eclipsed the war at home against discrimination and want.

The White House was quick to respond to reports of King's dissatisfaction with the president's remarks. Cliff Alexander, an LBJ special assistant, spoke with King on January 11, the day after the speech, trying to quickly change King's mind. King told him that, "from what he heard, there was a retreat by the Administration." Alexander reviewed with King LBJ's record of progressive reforms and insisted that the president had been "particularly courageous . . . because so many people were saying that it would be politically smart to retreat." Rather, Alexander told King, the president had moved forward with his programs, despite the political risks and difficulties. According to Alexander, King seemed impressed by his arguments and promised to review the speech in greater detail.

Alexander then reported to LBJ on the defensive, remedial steps being taken to gain some protective cover from friends in the black press: "Louis Martin [editor and publisher of the *Michigan Chronicle* and an adviser to both Kennedy and Johnson] is talking to the Negro publishers in Miami; I have talked with the *Jet-Ebony* people here in Washington, and they are quite clear and should write an excellent story."[48]

Several key black newspapers quickly sprang to the president's defense. The *Baltimore Afro-American* injected some determined realism into the debate about Johnson's State of the Union, pointing out that the president's leadership would work but needed patience and time: "All the money we have cannot end the war in Vietnam or the war on poverty at home in one year or maybe even five. . . . President Lyndon Johnson should have the full support of the people in the New Year. He deserves it.[49]

The *Chicago Daily Defender* seemed sympathetic to the president's position as he sought to weather the criticism after his State of the Union address, although the editor observed that Johnson seemed to be off his game a bit, saying gently, "he refrained from giving it the emotional charge he has shown in the past." The editor then suggested that expectations may have been raised too high when the War on Poverty was first launched, that "the fanfare and hoopla surrounding the program have suggested a magic cure, a 'war' in which there can be 'victory' only a battle or two away. In fact, there can now be little more than a commitment and a start." The piece gave some realistic perspective to a tender subject: "No federal law can bring instant prosperity to the nation's festering urban slums; no magic wand can transform their residents overnight, and to suggest that it can is to invite trouble, when the gap between hope and reality becomes apparent."[50]

The *New York Amsterdam News* weighed in with a positive, supportive editorial. The editor noted that "many Negroes have voiced attacks on President Johnson . . . because of what, they believe, showed a growing lack of interest in the continuing fight against racial discrimination. . . . We believe those who spoke out against the President were premature and ill advised." After citing Johnson's record of achievement, the editor said, "So, think twice before belaboring a friend like Mr. Johnson. Stand by him. He has stood by you."[51]

The *Pittsburgh Courier*, in a brief editorial, said, "President Johnson shows fine statesmanship when he said in his State of the Union message that the Anti-Poverty Programme would not be curtailed as a result of the War. . . .

What we are spending on poverty is negligible in comparison with what we have spent, are spending and will spend in Vietnam. I hope President Johnson will not be pressured into cutting back the appropriations to combat poverty."[52]

There certainly was resistance in Congress to voting additional taxes to fund both the war and domestic programs. The president's economic advisers had been urging him for some time to ask Congress for a tax increase. Inflationary pressures from rising costs of the war and Great Society programs seemed to point to the need for new taxes to help foot the bill. But LBJ was reluctant to propose a tax hike and weaken political support for his top priorities: the war in Vietnam and his cherished Great Society. After dallying for months, Johnson finally relented and decided to propose a tax increase. He attempted to sugarcoat it by calling the increase a surcharge on corporate and individual income taxes and by proposing to limit the levy to two years.

Early in 1967, as Johnson was seeking the tax surcharge, the black press was reporting on the resistance to it in Congress. The *Atlanta Daily World*, in an editorial, noted that a poll of members of the new 90th Congress had revealed little willingness to levy new taxes to finance Johnson's two-front war. Eighty percent of the legislators polled said they opposed a tax increase but favored cutting spending on Great Society programs. The president would not get his tax surcharge until the summer of 1968.[53]

H. Carol McCall wrote in the *New York Amsterdam News*: "National attention has shifted to the war in Vietnam, Congress seems more and more distrustful of the community action program, and the money for the war against poverty is getting scarcer." An editorial in the same paper several months later said: "The President has stated that he thinks the United States is rich enough to handle its racial problems at home and still carry on the Vietnam War. We are sure it is rich enough. But is it interested enough?" And finally: "It hasn't been in the past."[54]

The kind of quiet resignation that closed the column said much about the waning confidence of some members of the black press in the power of the government's good intentions, as embodied in the Great Society, to overcome the inertia in the nation's will to deliver. As the country turned away from the needs of black Americans and focused its attention and vast resources on the needs of South Vietnam, African Americans could not help but see where they stood. The black press grasped the implications of that trade-off and made it a regular part of its assessment of the Vietnam War.

The Vietnam War was consuming both money and presidential attention. Supporters of the Great Society were confused about how programs should be implemented. And, of course, plenty of opponents were all too eager to sabotage efforts to maintain and expand the domestic effort. The war in Vietnam was eclipsing the struggle at home.

Johnson had often expressed pessimism privately to aides and confidants about the prospects of maintaining political support for his Great Society in the face of escalation in Vietnam. On November 9, 1967, in a speech honoring the labor leader George Meany, LBJ publicly criticized the foes of Great Society funding who were using the cost of the war in Vietnam as an excuse to slash domestic spending. Calling his opponents in Congress "the old coalition of standpatters and naysayers," he charged: "They never wanted to do anything. But this year they say they can't do it because of Vietnam. That is just pure bunk. This crowd was against progress before Vietnam. They are against progress tonight and they will be against progress tomorrow. And they will be against it when the war is over and when it is nothing but a dim memory."[55]

The black press frequently resorted to graphic depictions of the fierce struggle for resources of the Great Society and the war in Vietnam. Cartoons were a favorite device for dramatizing the competing financial demands. One cartoon in the *Afro-American* showed the quandary faced by the president himself as he struggled to sustain both the Great Society and the Vietnam War; the prodigious appetite of the war in Asia was devouring funds desperately needed for the War on Poverty (see figure 2).

As time passed, the bleak realization grew in the African American press that its community's needs were being ignored in favor of funding the Vietnam War.

The competition for food was a particularly evocative way to visualize the struggle faced by African American readers, a theme featured repeatedly in cartoons in the black press.

In two examples the Vietnam War is represented as a brutish bully, dominating the others at the meal, while the needs of the children at the table, who represent vital social programs, are ignored. Images like these emphasize the grim nature of the contest between the Vietnam War and the Great Society and the insatiability of the war as it devoured American wealth that could have been spent to alleviate poverty and hunger. It was a powerful way to depict what the black press perceived to be the imbalance in the attention and resources the government was willing to squander on the Vietnam War and the relative pittance the government was willing to spend to eradicate human need. It also was a survival metaphor, stirring primitive impulses of the pangs of hunger felt by the deprived in the face of the satiety and indifference of a well-fed society.[56]

Beginning as early as 1965, comparing the costs of the war in Vietnam and the War on Poverty became a standard part of the rhetoric in support of the

Figure 2. Struggle for Survival
The war on poverty goes hungry to feed the voracious appetite of the Vietnam War.
(Cartoon by T. Stockett, *Baltimore Afro-American*, January 15, 1966. Courtesy of the Afro-American Newspapers Archives and Research Center.)

Great Society and a means of shaming its opponents. The comparison almost invariably cropped up in arguments of any length in support of the administration's social programs. It was used by African American leaders and often was incorporated into opinion pieces in the black press. Even white liberals used the logic to reinforce their pleas for funding the Great Society, also finding it a useful way to reinforce their opposition to the war. When Johnson submitted a reduced budget for the War on Poverty, during the ensuing debate Robert Kennedy stood on the Senate floor in September 1967 and called for approval of the full $5 billion in funding originally requested for poverty programs, noting that with a gross national product of more than $750 billion, "we can surely afford this legislation, which would cost as much as a few weeks of effort in Vietnam."[57]

Even as the president was calling for a Great Society in 1964, Whitney Young, head of the National Urban League, had published a book of essays, *To Be Equal*. In the book Young calls for America to launch "an unprecedented domestic 'Marshall Plan.'" Young envisioned a massive investment to eradicate the blight of poverty and racism that had crippled African Americans. With sufficient investment Young believed the program could be phased out "as need for it diminishes over the next decade."[58]

Young had been thinking and talking about the need for "compensatory action" since the middle of 1963, the germ of an idea that eventually came to be called affirmative action. He knew he was swimming against a powerful tide of public opinion. One sampling showed that 97 percent of white Americans were against special preferences for blacks to compensate for past discrimination. Young gave a speech that year in his White Plains Community Unitarian Church that confronted this white resistance: "People, who all of these years have never said anything about zero quotas of Negroes and one hundred percent quotas of white people, now suddenly get awfully upset when we have to talk about numbers."[59]

The numbers Young was talking about for his domestic assault on poverty were breathtaking—hundreds of millions of dollars. It was bold and imaginative, and very expensive. By calling for a "domestic Marshall Plan," he was evoking memories of a generous past in the nation's history, when Americans had willingly shouldered the cost of rehabilitating the shattered countries of Western Europe, including their bitter enemy, Germany. By invoking that past, Young hoped to stir the same impulses of generosity toward the black inhabitants of America's crumbling ghettos.

Four years later his hopeful vision was still unrealized. In a January 1968 newspaper column Young would repeat his call for a "domestic Marshall Plan to do for the ghetto what we so willingly did for our allies and even for our former enemies in Western Europe." Young argued, "Wiping out slums, poverty, and racism should be our number one priority." Unfortunately, he noted, "our urban crisis doesn't rate the same priority as the war in Vietnam, not to mention such other costly programs like the space race." Young closed his column with a dire warning: "It is obvious that ending poverty is pretty low on the nation's scale of priorities. Until it gains a greater sense of urgency on the part of our leaders, urban unrest will remain at the top of the list of our national programs."[60]

In the four years between Whitney Young's first dramatic call for a "domestic Marshall Plan" in 1964 and his second call for the same national commitment in 1968, the nation's attention had become focused elsewhere. Young's renewed call for a domestic Marshall Plan in 1968 was more a lament for the nation's failure to respond than a realistic expectation that it would. During those four years the Great Society, which in many ways embodied Young's vision, never attained the sweeping scope Young had hoped for. It was weakened, it seemed, if not eviscerated, by the Vietnam War. In the same period, as the war in Vietnam came to dominate the American political and cultural scene, increasing numbers of black Americans came to oppose the war, many of them motivated by the impact of the conflict on the stalled War on Poverty.

During the last half of the 1960s, the war's erosion of Great Society programs became a regular part of the interpretation of the Vietnam War in the black press. It was apparent that, for whatever reason, the conflict in Southeast Asia was receiving a staggering commitment of American resources, while the War on Poverty was receiving a mere trickle. As the black press chronicled the war on both fronts, it often interpreted the war in Vietnam in the light of black struggle on the home front. The war in Vietnam served both as a metaphor for the domestic conflict and as a vehicle for affirming black entitlement.

The angle of vision the black press brought to the Vietnam War is apparent in the degree to which the struggle for equality and economic justice at home was incorporated into interpretations of the war. Black newspapers revealed a pronounced tendency to include aspects of African American experience and aspirations in editorial comment, opinion columns, and cartoons dealing with the Vietnam War. A few columnists appearing in black newspapers, like Henry Cathcart, tended to devote their opinion pieces on the war to a discussion of the ramifications of the conflict for international relations in purely geopolitical terms. More commonly, when columnists in the black press discussed the Vietnam War, they linked the war with black concerns and aspirations. This linkage allowed African American writers and cartoonists to serve a larger purpose than simply informing their readers about the war in Vietnam. It also provided impetus to the more critical task of waging the war at home: confronting and surmounting obstacles to black progress.

An exception to this tendency was the *Atlanta Daily World*. The paper was staunchly Republican, and, in keeping with the conservative traditions of the GOP, the newspaper was relentlessly hawkish in foreign affairs, including U.S. policy in Vietnam. While it opposed discrimination and bigotry, the newspaper placed a high premium on self-reliance and individual initiative in domestic politics. It was impatient with black radicalism when it collided with the paper's core Republican values. These predilections led the paper to maintain considerable separation between how it viewed the war and how it understood the domestic plight of African Americans. When the *Atlanta Daily World* made infrequent connections between the war and the black struggle, it was usually to observe and comment on relationships between the Vietnam conflict and the home front as other blacks saw or experienced them and to criticize the response of other blacks to the interaction of the two zones of conflict.

The metaphor of two wars would be a persistent way of framing the black response to the Vietnam War almost until the last American ground troops left Vietnam in the spring of 1973, although the use of the imagery slackened with a kind of weary resignation once the War on Poverty was reduced to a skirmish after Lyndon Johnson left the White House. The two-war metaphor, when it appeared, more often than not was a firm assertion that the struggle of black Americans at home ought to take precedence over the war in Vietnam—though it plainly did not. In the war at home the government was no longer seen as an ally of the poor and discarded but as a remote, even hostile, entity that had long since lost interest in the problems of American blacks. As a disillusioned black citizen in West Oakland, California, said, "The war? Man, there's a war right here in this country. I'm trying to feed my kids. And that's a war."[61]

In a *Newsweek* poll taken in 1966 African American sentiment already was reflecting considerable anxiety about the degree to which the Vietnam War was eating into the War on Poverty and civil rights enforcement. Forty-four percent of blacks said the war was weakening the nation's commitment to their community's needs. African Americans were growing restive about the nation's priorities.[62]

In the same poll 35 percent of all blacks and 22 percent of African American leaders believed that blacks should be opposed to the Vietnam War because they have "less freedom to fight for." In the survey 29 percent of black respondents would have liked to see the United States pull out of Vietnam, compared with 12 percent of all Americans.[63]

By the time a Gallup poll commissioned by *Newsweek* assessed African American attitudes toward the Vietnam War in 1969, black Americans overwhelmingly believed that the conflict was choking off the War on Poverty. By a margin of 7 to 1, blacks believed that the war was "directly pinching the home-front on poverty." *Newsweek* summed up black attitudes toward the impact of the war on their community: "Vietnam was their [African Americans'] own particular incubus—a war that depletes their young manhood and saps the resources available to healing their ills at home."[64]

As the war dragged on, it became clear that black Americans, including prominent leaders in the fight for civil rights, and eventually most of the black press, were impatient with official neglect of black needs and increasingly disturbed by the U.S. role in Vietnam, and they were being drawn to the ranks of those who openly opposed the war in Vietnam.

3

Fueling the Anger

The Draft and Black Casualties

It is not likely to give comfort to Negroes battling to gain equality on the home front to learn that they are being given more than an equal opportunity to die for their country on the battlefields in Vietnam.—*New York Amsterdam News*, January 8, 1966

During the buildup of forces in Vietnam, the initial response of the black press was generally supportive of the draft. Sometimes the support was effusive. An editorial in the *Baltimore Afro-American* during the spring of 1965 saw the draft and the military service that followed as an engine of progress for the black community: "Whether they wanted to or not, millions of men in the armed forces received the benefit of . . . travel, discipline and education which they could have gotten in no other way. It was in the Army that it was proved that a nation in peril cannot survive with segregation."[1]

A year and a half later, even after mounting black casualties had become an issue of wide concern, the *Afro-American* was still firmly committed, in principle, to the draft, saying editorially: "When our country needs us for defense, we should serve without quibbling."[2]

As draft notices multiplied and the induction net was cast more widely, the African American community began to feel its effects and increasingly came to see the draft as fundamentally unfair. As resistance began to coalesce around the drafting of black men, the September issue of *Jet* quoted a Detroit demonstrator who expressed the growing anger: "The draft takes black people to fight for abstract democracy in foreign lands when there is no complete democracy at home."[3]

Others called for more radical ways to confront an unfair draft.

On January 7, 1966, Clifford Alexander, a member of the White House staff, wrote a memo to the president informing him of "a distressing story" on the front page of the *New York Times* about a statement issued by the Student Nonviolent Coordinating Committee (SNCC) the day before. SNCC had assailed U.S. actions in Vietnam, opposed the draft, and urged "all Americans to seek work in the civil rights movement as a 'valid alternative to the draft.'" Alexander's memo then described a series of actions the White House was initiating "to negate the impact of this story." In addition to discussing the SNCC statement with selected civil rights leaders and some key black congressional figures, Alexander reported, Louis Martin, the publisher of the *Michigan Chronicle* and a Johnson adviser, had "talked to the Negro Publishers Association and has the feeling that they will strongly denounce the SNCC statements in their editorial columns."[4]

The *Chicago Daily Defender* reported on January 10 that John Lewis, chair of SNCC, had urged members to avoid the draft and, in a gesture of protest, to burn draft cards "if that is their desire." Lewis held a news conference at which he read a statement condemning U.S. policy in Vietnam and urged Americans to work for civil rights rather than participate in the war.[5] The *Defender* piece, a straight news story, alluded to Lewis's history as a freedom rider who had been badly injured, and jailed more than once, during civil rights demonstrations. The paper ran no editorial on the controversial statement, perhaps out of deference to the considerable stature Lewis enjoyed among African Americans.

However, the *Atlanta Daily World* castigated the SNCC position, saying, "We disagree with the SNCC . . . position on charges made against our government's policy in Vietnam and do not believe any young man should attempt to evade the draft. It is not rational nor logical to expect to enjoy rights and refuse to accept important responsibility such as defending one's country. There has never been any general doubt about our race's loyalty to our country, especially in time of war, and it should never be that way."[6]

Much of the black press said little about the SNCC statement. Part of the reason was that John Lewis's controversial statement on the draft was almost immediately overshadowed by a larger story stemming from a relatively obscure young black activist's comments about the same SNCC statement.

Julian Bond, SNCC's communications director, had been elected a state representative in Georgia by a landslide in 1965, capturing 82 percent of the vote in a large, predominately black district in Atlanta. Shortly before he was scheduled to take his seat in the legislature, Bond defended Lewis's controversial statement about the draft. Bond's fellow legislators promptly refused to seat him in the state assembly, judging Bond's views as fundamentally disloyal to the United States. Ironically, Bond's statements came as he performed some of his last tasks as SNCC communications chief before heading for the legislature. A reporter from a local radio station had called him a few hours after the SNCC statement was released and asked him if he endorsed it. Bond offered a thoughtful—if unrehearsed—answer. Among other things, he said: "I think it is sort of hypocritical for us to maintain that we are fighting for liberty in other places and we are not guaranteeing liberty to citizens inside the continental United States."[7]

Bond's spontaneity temporarily cost him his newly won seat in the legislature. According to Lewis, Bond had previously not made public statements about the war and had nothing to do with drafting the published policy.[8] Bond's comment to the reporter created an immediate uproar that led to a protracted legislative and legal battle. In the ensuing flood of publicity in both the mainstream media and the black press, which covered the story extensively, Bond gained prominence as a radical new African American voice. His often-controversial views were widely quoted, though seldom endorsed editorially, in the black press.

An editorial in the *Atlanta Daily World* skewered Bond, arguing that he "has hurt all concerned, and perhaps many innocent members of our racial group." The paper took issue with Bond's antiwar position and his opposition to the draft. The editorial, however, expressed disapproval of the legislature's action in barring Bond from taking his seat. However, the paper conceded that some "disciplinary action" might be called for, perhaps censure.[9]

None of the other black newspapers was as critical of Bond, preferring instead to focus on his right to dissent, which they defended vigorously, and on the right of citizens to elect representatives of their own choosing, however controversial their views might be about issues of the day. Most black papers argued that, since Bond was elected in a landslide and thus was the unmistakable choice of his constituents, the matter should end there.[10]

The *Milwaukee Star* saw more than Bond's dissent from national Vietnam policy at issue in his exclusion by the Georgia legislature. The thing that most infuriated and unsettled the legislators about Bond was that, during his political campaign, he and his SNCC supporters applied "the typical SNCC approach, unheard of in American politics." They "actually talked with constituents, asking them what they wanted done by their representative." Said the *Star*: "This dangerous person-to-person precedent, by a 25-year old Negro at that, lies behind the Georgia representatives' unfounded censure."[11]

The *Star* was on to something. Bond embodied the grass-roots political strength of emerging black leaders, who were a profound threat to the predominately white political structure so long taken for granted in the South. Recently enfranchised black voters were making their presence felt at the polls. Thus Bond's statement was not only a startlingly effective piece of political theater from a resourceful new politician with a solid game. It was also a brash young black man's uppity assault on the establishment. To a white southern political gentry steeped in a core set of patriotic, military, and social values, and unaccustomed to tolerating an affront to those values from a black man, Bond's statement seemed distinctly treasonous.

On December 5, 1966, the U.S. Supreme Court unanimously found the Georgia legislature's refusal to seat Bond to be unconstitutional. Chief Justice Earl Warren wrote the opinion for the Court, insisting, "Debate on public issues should be uninhibited, robust, and wide-open." The decision finally forced the Georgia legislature to seat Bond. The Supreme Court's ruling was uniformly welcomed by the black press, including the Atlanta paper that had been so critical of Bond's behavior but defended his right to express his controversial views.[12]

Even as the Bond story was playing out, opposition to the draft itself was mounting in the black community. In a front-page story in the *Afro-American* on May 21, 1966, U.S. Representative Adam Clayton Powell, D-N.Y., charged that a "disproportionate number of colored persons" would be sent "to the Vietnam slaughter house" because young black men were unfairly exposed to the draft because they did not qualify for deferment opportunities available to better-educated white men.[13] Powell's blast resounded with particular force in the black press, since he chaired the House Committee on Education and Labor. Powell also emphasized a connection between a discriminatory draft system and what would become a growing casualty list of African Americans in Vietnam.

The unfairness of the draft, which increasingly seemed to be linked to a fundamental racism, fueled the anger of African Americans, who felt the continuing burden of discrimination at home while watching young black men being caught in the draft, then sent to Vietnam to be maimed or killed. An expanding army of dissidents was beginning to form and refine a litany of protest, linking the draft and its consequences for blacks with the civil rights struggle at home.

A 1966 *Newsweek* poll caught the growing disenchantment of African Americans, particularly community leaders, with the draft. Twenty-five percent of all blacks in the survey and 58 percent of African American leaders in the sample thought that the draft was intrinsically unfair to blacks.[14]

In August 1966 Robert McNamara, U.S. secretary of defense, disclosed what would prove to be one of the most controversial elements of draft policy during the war: Project 100,000. The plan was to retrieve 100,000 of the 600,000 men who annually failed to meet induction standards and requalify them for military service. Ironically, the program was folded into the War on Poverty, because it was intended to yield benefits to underprivileged men—many of them African Americans—including jobs, both in the military and after discharge.[15]

Despite the high-minded rhetoric of liberalism used to introduce the plan, and McNamara's professed altruism as its champion, it was hard for many thoughtful African Americans to see the program as a constructive approach to improving the lives of young black men. Instead, it looked like a way to secure more bodies to satisfy the growing appetite for manpower for the combat units being bloodied in the rice paddies of Vietnam. Comment on the new program in much of the black press was unfavorable.

A week after McNamara introduced Project 100,000, the front page of the *Pittsburgh Courier* carried a story gloomily predicting that the percentage of blacks in the war zone likely would rise as a result of the plan to draft men who had already been sifted out, never mind that the combat force was already disproportionately African American in relation to blacks' representation in the U.S. population as a whole.[16]

Baker E. Morton, in his *Afro-American* column, "Baker's Dozen," maintained the pressure, leveling a barrage of criticism at the new policy: "Retrieving 40,000 military rejects to press into war is a pretty sorry way of curbing unemployment, but it's a great way to get about 12,000 colored males off the street, and perhaps permanently out of the way." He also quoted Adam Clayton Powell, who, in his characteristically blunt style, branded the plan genocide: "Nothing more than killing off human beings who are not members of the elite."[17]

Stokely Carmichael, the new chair of SNCC, charged that Project 100,000 was attempting "black urban removal" by drafting more black youths "to give them training." In a speech to more than a thousand students at the University of Wisconsin, Carmichael challenged the government: "If you want to train me, don't send me to Vietnam. Build a school in my neighborhood."[18]

The plan's implications were immediately apparent to a concerned black leadership increasingly alarmed by the war's mounting toll. It was past time for blacks to celebrate being given the opportunity to serve, as they might have in earlier wars. Now it seemed more and more like an opportunity to die.

During the life of Project 100,000, from its inception in 1966 until it was ended in 1972, the program scooped up more than 400,000 recruits, 45 percent of whom were black. Since so few of the men qualified for skilled positions in the military, most were placed in low-level positions, including in frontline combat. Only 6 percent received additional training, most of it in rudimentary reading skills to bring them to a fifth-grade level, hardly enough to qualify them for good civilian jobs after leaving the military. Eighty thousand of these inductees—20 percent—received undesirable, bad conduct, or dishonorable discharges. One hundred thousand more received general discharges. This amounted to a startling 45 percent that were recipients of less than honorable discharges, hindering them for the rest of their lives, particularly in finding decent employment. This dismal performance fulfilled the predictions of career military officers, who had responded negatively to the plan when it was first introduced. A study twenty years after the project ended showed that, as civilians, alumni of the program had underperformed their peers in every measure of achievement tested.[19]

Despite the criticism of McNamara's plan when it was first introduced, several black newspapers praised the defense secretary for his social commitment when it was announced in late 1967 that he would be leaving the cabinet. An editorial in the *Baltimore Afro-American* called McNamara "a gigantic force for social good," citing Project 100,000 as an example of his progressive vision. The editorial applauded his boldness and compassion in proposing the controversial program. If the newspaper had criticisms of the plan, it chose not to dim the luster of its praise by mentioning them.[20]

The editorial page of the *Pittsburgh Courier* echoed the sentiments of the *Afro-American* in describing the benefits to participants in Project 100,000: "The majority of these men will receive skills which they can use upon their return to civilian life. This kind of mass indoctrination with learning can only accrue to the good."[21]

The *New York Amsterdam News* recognized McNamara's various humanitarian contributions to African Americans in the U.S. military, including Project 100,000, "in which servicemen of limited skills can be trained so that when they return to civilian life they will have productive skills." The editor then expanded on the theme: "This is especially meaningful to black military personnel, many of whom are in the services simply because America's civilian society has no place for them." Next to the editorial was a cartoon by Melvin Tapley showing a slick, buttoned-down McNamara in a foxhole beside a black soldier. The soldier is holding a rifle while McNamara is heroically manning a machine gun with the words *anti-discrimination policy* inscribed on its barrel.[22]

Even without the boost of Project 100,000, the draft seemed to be skewed to induct higher percentages of blacks than whites. *Ebony* cited a 1967 report by U.S. Representative Robert Kastenmeier, a Democrat from Wisconsin, showing that the rate of black induction into the military was much higher than that for whites. While just 29 percent of black candidates passed the screening process for induction, 64 percent of those found acceptable were drafted. Of the white candidates who were tested, 63 percent were deemed acceptable, but only 31 percent of those men were actually drafted. For whatever reason, the induction system during the period of the report was biased in favor of inducting blacks and dismissing whites.[23]

It was becoming harder and harder for blacks not to believe that the draft was intolerably discriminatory and that it seemed to go out of its way to single out blacks for induction. The sheer number of black men qualified for combat roles in the armed forces was exacerbating the racial imbalance in front-line U.S. army units in the first years of the Vietnam War. Blacks accounted for about 11 percent of the draftee pool in the Vietnam era (about 250,000 of 2.2 million draftees from 1964 through 1973). However, blacks accounted for 31 percent of combat forces in Vietnam at the start of the war. Many blacks on the front line in Vietnam were there because they volunteered for hazardous duty—and extra pay—in units like the airborne. Many others were drafted. Many of these black draftees had limited job experience in skilled positions before entering the military and had educational disadvantages as well. These deficiencies among many African American soldiers gave rise to the judgment of military officials that a large proportion of black troops could serve only in low-skill functions. In Vietnam this often translated into assignment to rifle companies in combat units. Once casualty figures (and the attendant criticism) began to come in, the Defense Department set about reducing the combat exposure of blacks. The percentage share of combat duties shouldered by African Americans was reduced to 16 percent in 1966, then to 13 percent in 1968, and to 9 percent in 1970.[24]

One obvious reason for the apparent racial bias in the draft was the thousands of draft boards, many of which were either totally white or had only token representation from the black community. General Louis B. Hershey, head of the Selective Service, liked to call the local boards "little groups of neighbors on whom is placed the responsibility to determine who is to serve the nation." Few black leaders would accept Hershey's cozy characterization. Julian Bond made a cynical observation with which most of the African American press surely would have concurred: "Each draft notice begins: 'Friends and neighbors,' but none of my friends are on my local draft board."[25] Nor were any of his neighbors, in all likelihood.

As the United States geared up for deeper involvement in Vietnam and began increasing draft calls, the racial composition of local draft boards became an issue, one that would fester for years. The black press had little doubt that the racial makeup of draft boards, particularly in the South, contributed significantly to the overrepresentation of blacks on the battlefield in Vietnam. Often this was seen as discrimination directed against blacks generally, who were used to fill up draft quotas.

Sometimes the actions of draft boards were interpreted as a form of repression designed to silence particular blacks engaged in civil rights agitation. In a January 1965 editorial the *Afro-American* criticized the crusty head of the Selective Service, Hershey himself, for using the draft as a means of punishing activists who protested the draft. When previously deferred students engaged in what he characterized as unlawful demonstrations at Selective Service offices, Hershey announced they would be reclassified 1-A and subject to the draft. His action not only riled the black press but also raised a hue and cry from Congress, including an objection from House Republican Leader Gerald Ford, a supporter of U.S. involvement in Vietnam. More than one hundred law professors signed a letter of protest to the president.[26]

In November 1966 Stokely Carmichael was quoted as saying that because of "opposition to President Johnson and his war, we have been disrupted inside our organization and the government is trying to squash it. They are trying to draft all the young men in SNCC." *Jet* magazine, in a one-line item, reported in June 1967: "All-white draft boards in the South already are using induction as a weapon to punish civil righters."[27]

The editorial writers of most black newspapers would not go so far as to accuse the government of deliberately sweeping up large numbers of young black men in the draft as a means of repressing them and of depleting the supply of foot soldiers for the civil rights movement. But it was hard to dismiss the evidence of harassment against certain key black figures who were prominent in their opposition to the war and who directed their anger against the draft itself. Given the overwhelmingly white composition of local draft boards around the country, but particularly in the South, it was easy for blacks to generalize from the experience of individual militants and arrive at the conclusion that the draft system as a whole was used maliciously and systematically to draw disproportionate numbers of blacks into its web.

The sheer number of black men qualified primarily for combat roles in the armed forces was exacerbating the racial imbalance in frontline U.S. units in the first years of the Vietnam War. The presence of so many black soldiers in the combat zone required some explanation, and the prejudice of so many predominately white draft boards offered an easy institutional reason. But even more fundamentally, the black press believed that the presence of so many African Americans in the U.S. military during the Vietnam conflict resulted from the inhospitable quality of life and the lack of opportunity available to blacks in civilian society. That life of deprivation denied young blacks the educational opportunities that so many white young men of draft age used as a shelter from military service.

As the war in Vietnam escalated, a swelling number of African Americans were finding the draft inherently unfair and racially oppressive and were becoming a body of resistance. An increasingly vocal and active protest movement found the draft itself intolerable and galvanized protests against the draft as a means of expressing opposition to the war.

Voices in the black press began speaking out about the unfairness of the system of draft deferments, which systematically discriminated against the underprivileged, including many African American men who were unable to qualify for deferment. The editor of the *New York Amsterdam News* wrote: "Shouldn't patriotism belong to all levels of society? Should a prominent athlete be exempt from paying a personal price in the war effort? Should a college education enable a man to be a draft dodger?" Later the editor answered the questions: "We believe that the fighting should be done by the able bodied men of America who are best qualified physically and mentally to do it." Then he added that the phrase "able bodied men" encompassed "young men, college men, high school dropouts, educated, uneducated, laborers, craftsmen, professionals and non-professionals, black and white."

The editor likened the deferment system, which allowed the privileged to bypass service and forced the underprivileged to take their place, to the practice in ancient Rome by which Roman soldiers could hire someone to take their place and go off to war. In effect, the privileged in America were being permitted, under the prevailing system, "to hire the underprivileged to go out and fight the war in their place."[28]

Whitney Young, in a column in the *New York Amsterdam News* that ran on June 18, 1966, joined the chorus of columnists and editors in the black press calling for the nation to democratize the draft, to return to the concept of universally shared responsibility for the defense of the nation. The result of the existing system, wrote Young, was that "the burden of the service has fallen upon the shoulders of the poor"; because of persistent discrimination, blacks formed an unduly large proportion of the poor and underprivileged. Young pointed out that a black man "is more liable to be drafted—not because everyone else is being drafted, but because he is poor and because he is Negro."[29]

For the next several years various members of SNCC kept the organization at the center of agitation, using opposition to the draft as a vehicle for expressing opposition to the war in Vietnam. After he finished two days of physical examinations and mental tests to determine whether he was fit to serve in the military if drafted, Stokely Carmichael, head of SNCC, announced: "I'm not gonna go." Rather than enter the military, Carmichael stated bluntly, "I'd rather go to Leavenworth federal prison."[30] Later Carmichael elaborated on the basis for his refusal, placing the issue at the heart of a black assertion of power in the face of powerlessness: "We do not have the power in our hands to change the institution of war in this country—to begin to recreate it so that they can learn to leave the Vietnamese alone. The only power we have is the power to say, 'Hell, no!' to the draft."[31] There was no other way to stop an illegal, immoral war, in Carmichael's view. The political leaders in Washington held the levers of power. Those levers could be seized only by the resistance of a succession of individually powerless young men whose singular refusals to be drafted could accumulate, with other acts of defiance, to form a forceful, collective negation of the war.

Cleveland Sellers, a top aide to Carmichael, refused induction into the army on May 1, 1967, charging that the government was seeking to cripple the civil rights movement by drafting all civil rights workers. A story in the *Defender* speculated that Sellers was taking his stand because of "the urging of Carmichael." At the induction center, as Sellers refused to step forward and accept induction, Carmichael held a news conference to repeat his charge that the United States was waging a racist war against "colored people" in Southeast Asia. He went on to say that white people were "trying to draft black people to commit genocide."[32]

Another SNCC figure, the newly appointed chair, H. "Rap" Brown, announced what he called "a strong nationwide black anti-draft program." "We see no reason," Brown said, "for black men here who are daily murdered physically and mentally . . . to go kill yellow people abroad." In November yet another SNCC official, this time Fred Brooks, the chair of the Nashville chapter, refused to be inducted but did so without making a public comment. [33]

The SNCC leaders' refusals to accept induction into the armed services were public rituals intended to disavow the obligation of black men to obey the draft laws and participate in what was being castigated as a race war. The African American press reported these events, often placing them on the front pages of their newspapers, but did not devote much editorial space to SNCC's draft resistance, despite having much to say generally about the draft and about the war. It is likely that the somewhat conservative black press, which duly reported the SNCC antiwar actions as news, regarded the radical antics of Stokely Carmichael and his SNCC colleagues with an uncomfortable indulgence and chose, by and large, to ignore them editorially.

It is almost certain the silence did not signal agreement with the actions of the SNCC draft resisters. While the papers often complained editorially about the mechanics of the Selective Service apparatus and procedures, and often expressed those opinions vehemently, the papers generally did not approve of disobeying the draft laws. In fact, they were supportive of military service in general, acutely aware of the long struggle of blacks to attain equality in an integrated fighting force, and proud of the achievements of black soldiers, including those fighting in Vietnam.

Not all black resistance to the draft framed rejection of military service quite as starkly as the men from SNCC did, with their emphasis on the racist nature of the war in Vietnam. However, blacks who resisted the draft often recognized that their refusal to serve was uniquely grounded in their black experience, which gave their stance legitimacy. So long as their country refused to treat them as full citizens, it had no right to compel their service. Lenneal Henderson, a student at the University of California, Berkeley, was quoted by *Ebony:* "We resist on the ground that we aren't citizens. He who has no country should not fight for it." A similar justification for resisting the draft was offered in testimony before the U.S. Senate by two Howard University students, who argued that blacks who suffer in American ghettos should not be asked by their nation to "lay down their lives for the country."[34]

Muhammad Ali was the most famous black man to resist the draft. He first burst onto the sports scene as Cassius Clay, becoming Olympic heavyweight champion in 1960. Clay, the handsome and improbably skilled boxer, a heavyweight with lightning-quick hands and feet, was also a character. The combination of his artistry inside the ring and his irresistible, loquacious wit outside the ring made him a celebrity.

In 1964, shortly after Clay defeated Sonny Liston to become boxing's world heavyweight king, Clay proclaimed his allegiance to the Nation of Islam and took as his Muslim name Muhammad Ali. Sportswriters initially disdained his new name and insisted on calling him Cassius Clay. Oddly, much of the black press also found it hard to bring itself to use his Muslim name. When Ali's conflict with the draft became prominent news in early 1966, he was the subject of many stories and op-ed pieces in black newspapers. This was long after he had announced his name change, but they still frequently called him Cassius Clay. Sometimes the papers used both names alternately in the same piece.[35]

An editorial in the *St. Louis Argus* expressed the discomfort that much of the black press had with Clay's new name: "Cassius likes to be called by his Muslim name, Muhammad Ali, but we somehow can never get around to typing it out just like that. Frankly, it seems like an alias."[36] The black press dealt cautiously with the spirited Ali, and his new name expressed his religious preferences. His adopted moniker lacked the snappy alliteration of his old one. Worse, its intimations of controversy and non-Christian religious affiliation made a moderate institution like the black press skittish. The discomfort would persist until Ali's glory days in the ring during the late sixties made his Muslim name a household word for a swooning sports world.

Despite the apparent ambivalence that seemed to afflict the black press when it approached the Ali story, he would become the quintessential black man of the sixties. He was unabashedly proud of his blackness, unafraid to embrace a non-Western (and nonwhite) religion, and, eventually, would become fiercely staunch in his opposition to the Vietnam War.

When his draft board reclassified Ali as 1-A, after initially finding him unsuitable for military service because of his poor performance on an intelligence test, Ali quickly became a big story. The always talkative and quotable Ali found himself at centerstage. His early responses to his changed status were ambiguous. In January 1966 he was quoted in the *Baltimore Afro-American* as saying, "The Army is the boss and I respect the laws of the land."[37] Ali sounded compliant, but he was also looking forward to his next fight, despite his uncertain future in the draft. He was probably anxious to move on with his career and hoped the army would leave him alone.

The *Courier* referred to the garrulous boxer as "gaseous Cassius," "Louisville Lip," and "the loudmouth who talks like he had been vaccinated with a Victrola needle." The paper also insisted that he was as entitled to voice his impolitic criticisms of his draft board as senators Wayne Morse and J. William Fulbright were to criticize their government's Vietnam policies. The editor also guessed aloud that a white athlete popping off as Ali had would simply be indulged as colorful, while a black doing the same thing would elicit a very different, and harsher, response.[38] Despite his announced willingness to do Uncle Sam's bidding, Ali reached the conclusion that his vulnerability to the draft was unacceptable. He applied for conscientious objector status on religious grounds.

Some in the black press became more supportive of the embattled Ali. James Hicks, in his column, declared that Ali's problems stemmed from his flamboyant disregard of white protocol. So long as he was the clownish black man who "was too stupid to put on the uniform of his country," he was accepted as "the white man's colored boy." But once he had earned a million dollars by being an exceptional fighter, the military discovered he was smart enough after all; moreover, because he "was a Black Muslim speaking up for black manhood," he became a threat and had to be dealt with.[39]

As his induction neared, Ali's resolve hardened. The *Afro-American* carried his defiant words in a front-page banner headline: "I'D RATHER GO TO PRISON." As good as his word, in mid-April 1967 Ali refused induction.

With that, a number of critical pieces appeared in the black press. The *Daily Defender* was not inclined to give Ali much latitude. The headline for A. S. "Doc" Young's sports column called Ali's confrontation with the United States a "Black Day for Boxing." Young believed that Ali should have served his country or abdicated his title. Instead, he shirked his duty. Young described his supporters as "the small band . . . of Black Muslims; the draft-card burners," as well as "thoughtless members of my race who believe that any 'embarrassment of whitey' is important and symbolizes courage; enemies of this—the greatest though certainly an imperfect—nation; various and sundry misfits and malcontents."[40]

The *Atlanta Daily World*, no surprise, was also critical: "With our country actually involved in war, we cannot sympathize with anyone who refuses to take the oath of serving in the armed services." It muted its criticism somewhat by acknowledging that "Cassius Clay" (as the paper still called him) performed a service in calling attention to the unfairness of the existing system of draft boards with their insufficient black representation.[41]

As a consequence of his refusal to be mustered into the army, Ali instantly became the most visible symbol of resistance to the draft. On a front page of the *Afro-American* that prominently displayed no less than three Ali items, a William Worthy feature article recognized the importance of the champ's stand: "The historic day when Cassius Clay gave a firm 'no' to the U.S. Army, a lily-white Houston draft board had a single tiger by the tail." Worthy predicted that, inspired by Ali's example, "a small army of youthful, organized, buoyant tigers" would soon be defying the draft. The author further predicted that Ali's action would be seen "in tomorrow's history books" as a vital impetus to speeding up "the hitherto slow development of 'a second front,' that is, an organized all-out resistance to the war in Vietnam."[42]

An editorial in the *New York Amsterdam News* deplored the haste with which the New York State Boxing Commission and the World Boxing Association "stripped Muhammad Ali of his heavyweight crown," charging that the speed of their action showed the two governing bodies in boxing "had prejudged the champion even before he made his stand." The conclusion of the editorial declared, "To us, and to many more, Muhammad Ali is still heavyweight champion of the world."[43]

Even the staid *Defender*, hardly a fervent Ali supporter, deplored the haste of the decision to take away the champ's title, seeing it as evidence that the lords of boxing "were eager and glad to find an occasion to lift the crown from the brow of boxing's most colorful and morally clean fighter since Joe Louis' days." The newspaper went so far as to applaud a certain bravery in Ali's decision to face prison, if necessary, for his beliefs: "Viewed from the point of morality and personal conscience, the choice is scarcely different from that faced by civil rights activists in their demonstrations against unjust laws upholding racial segregation."[44]

In June the *Defender* printed a UPI story about the rejection of Ali's request to be reclassified as a conscientious objector. When the boxer heard about the denial of his request, he set off yet another furor when he said, "I ain't got no quarrel with them Viet Cong." The statement quickly got Ali into more hot water. According to the *Defender*, he found himself in conflict with veterans groups and others and was forced to move his next fight to Toronto because of the pressure. The story reported that "the loquacious Clay" had been taking steps to shore up his image among Americans and to avoid make more public statements about the draft.[45]

After a jury in Houston, Texas, declared Ali guilty, and the judge imposed a five-year prison term and $10,000 fine in mid-1967, the *Afro-American* headline trumpeted the disapproval expressed by Floyd McKissick, head of the Congress of Racial Equality (CORE): "Clay's Sentence Termed 'Incredible.'" The subheading of the piece was "CORE Chief 'Ashamed of My Country.'" The focus of McKissick's outrage was the total disrespect shown Ali for his religious convictions: "A black man exercises his right to protest an immoral war and white America's reflex is to sever five years from his life. A black minister honorably and peacefully refuses to serve in the armed forces and Jim Crow sits in judgment."[46]

An editorial in the same issue deplored the lack of consideration given to Ali's professed religious beliefs, which he had cited as his basis for defying the draft. The piece also argued that the severity of Ali's penalty was a racist reaction to his open defiance, likening the white establishment's response to Ali to that given to an equally unrepentant Adam Clayton Powell, the New York representative whom the 90th Congress refused to seat because of various allegations of personal and financial misconduct. Had either Ali or Powell "faced his tormentors with hat in hand and a 'Yassuh, Boss,' he would be today a free man, respected by all—except himself."[47]

After a federal judge ruled in 1970 against the arbitrary action of the boxing commissioners in withdrawing Ali's license to fight, editorials applauded the action and the boxer's anticipated comeback. When the U.S. Supreme Court, in June 1970, unanimously reversed Ali's conviction, permitting him to claim exemption as a conscientious objector, the *Daily Defender* approved: "The High Court's action is a healthy reaffirmation of a fundamental legal principle which needed to be articulated." The editor proclaimed that Ali had "scored a haymaker against Uncle Sam."[48]

Meanwhile, as the radical insurgency at SNCC against induction into the draft continued, and as Ali's resistance to the draft provided diverting and

extensive copy in the black press, others sought to work within the system
to make the draft boards color-blind. For black leaders this effort became a
continuing struggle. In the path of the reformers stood congressional powerhouses like South Carolina's Mendel Rivers, chair of the House Armed
Services Committee, and Louisiana Democrat F. Edward Hebert, who preferred to keep things just as they were.

An editorial in the *Afro-American* in the summer of 1967 noted the opposition of key southern political leaders, who were successfully resisting changes
suggested by President Johnson's special commission on the draft. The commission had found that the draft as presently operated, in the words of the editorial, "places a grossly unfair burden on the backs of black boys." The report
cited the educational disadvantages of young black men that made it difficult
for them to qualify for deferments and discrimination that tended to exclude
them from National Guard units and limited their access to officer training
programs. "But the most galling discrimination," the piece noted, "particularly in the Confederate states, is the widespread prevalence of lily-white draft
boards."[49]

In South Carolina, Mendel Rivers's home state, the president's commission
found only one black draft board member out of a total of 163 in a state where
African Americans comprised 34.5 percent of the population. Georgia, where
more than 28 percent of the population was black, had only five black draft board
members out of five hundred. Mississippi, where blacks accounted for 42 percent
of the population, and Alabama and Louisiana, where blacks comprised 30 percent or more of the population, had not a single black draft board member. The
result of the systematic exclusion of blacks from southern draft boards was that
30 percent of qualified young black men were "snatched for the armed services,"
while only 19 percent of qualified white men were summoned.[50]

Important reforms in the draft selection process were not far off. In
February 1968 the main headline on the *Atlanta Daily World*'s front page
announced the abolition of most draft deferments. On February 16, 1968,
a day affected students called "Black Friday," the Johnson administration
abolished draft deferments for graduate students except for those in some
medical specialties. The National Security Council announced that keeping
students in nonmedical fields out of uniform was not vital to the national
interest. Hershey, who still headed the Selective Service System, justified the
move by saying that the deferments being eliminated were inherently unfair because they allowed the educated elite to avoid military service while
young men from the working class were obliged to fight in Vietnam. Many
of those working-class sons were African Americans.[51]

As efforts to reform the draft process continued, a more drastic solution
was the subject of a presidential commission: dismantling the draft altogether

and producing an all-volunteer armed force. The commission concluded unanimously that the interests of the nation would be better served if its military needs were met entirely through the recruitment and induction of volunteers.[52] (The implementation of this recommendation would have to await 1973 and another president.)

The consequences of the draft were apparent in the combat losses of black troops in Vietnam. As the war heated up and raged on, many more black soldiers would become part of the grim and mounting statistic of African American deaths in Vietnam. By the end of American combat in Vietnam, 7,115 black troops were dead.[53]

Early on, the black press called attention to the scandalous treatment of blacks fighting for justice in the United States while other blacks were dying in Vietnam. In February 1965 Louis Lomax, an author and former *Afro-American* staffer, wrote scathingly of this in a commentary that ran on his old paper's front page under the headline "What They Say." His angry treatise anticipated many similar statements that would appear regularly in the black press: "We are dying in Vietnam to bring freedom there and at the same time 3,000 of our own people are in jail in Alabama for trying to vote. That makes us the laughingstock of the world."[54]

When the president stood before Congress on March 15, 1965, to deliver his historic speech at the signing of the Voting Rights Act, his remarks included a stirring invocation of uncommon service and common obligation: "As we meet here in this peaceful historic chamber tonight, men from the South, some of whom were at Iwo Jima, men from the North who have carried Old Glory to far corners of the world and brought it back without a stain on it, men from the East and West are all fighting together without regard to religion, or color, or region, in Vietnam." What lay before Congress and the nation now, according to the president, was nothing less than the vindication of these sacrifices, made by all Americans, conspicuously including black Americans, "to make good the promise of America."[55]

The black press soon noticed another element in the mounting black losses in Vietnam that lent an angrier, more urgent, tone to the discussion of black combat deaths: African American soldiers were bearing a disproportionate share of the fighting and therefore a disproportionate share of the dying. An editorial in the *New York Amsterdam News*, on January 8, 1966, presented recent Pentagon statistics that showed that the fighting force in Vietnam was getting blacker. The piece observed pointedly that it was precisely because young black men had been "denied equal opportunity at home" that they wound up in the army and became "prime cannon fodder."[56] African Americans comprised just over 9 percent of members of the U.S. military but

15 percent of the infantry in Vietnam. Between 1965 and 1967 they suffered about 20 percent of battlefield casualties.[57]

Two months after the piece appeared in the *Amsterdam News,* an editorial in the *Sentinel* cited the disproportionate casualty rate for black soldiers, noting that the Pentagon attributed the high death rate among black GIs to "the valor of the Negro in combat." However, the editor of the *Amsterdam News* was not seduced by that explanation, which flattered the black soldiers in battle for their bravery. What the paper wanted for disproportionate black casualties in Vietnam was proportionate justice for African Americans on the home front. "Nothing appears more anachronistic than the current resistance of bigots at home to the civil rights movement," declared the editorial.

The newspaper then went on to claim an entitlement to "first-class citizenship" for African Americans at home based on the disproportionate sacrifices of black Americans on the battlefield. Since the black soldier was dying at a higher rate than other Americans in Vietnam, it was "a crime for anyone to try to deny what is rightfully his as a citizen. Man can give no more for his country than his life and, in the jungles and rice paddies of Vietnam, Negro GIs have made the ultimate sacrifice over and over for the United States." The editorial concluded that the black soldier's "valor and courage in combat should embarrass and render absurd any organized effort to block the progress of the civil rights movement in our land."[58]

The *Pittsburgh Courier,* prompted by the same Pentagon figures that sparked comment over several months in other black newspapers, ran an editorial headlined "Negro Deaths Exceed Whites' in Vietnam." The editorial was dotted with statistics drawn from the military report on casualty rates and noted the high death rate among black troops in Vietnam. It concluded: "Negroes are serving their country with distinction, some having made the supreme sacrifice. Therefore, Negro-phobes should think twice about denying Negroes the full rights of American citizenship guaranteed under the Constitution."[59]

The *St. Louis Argus* viewed the problem as a "challenge to democracy":

"With the Negroes being only 10% of the population, why do they represent about 27% of the casualties in Vietnam. The Negro in America would also like to know why this differential?"[60]

Protests by the black newspapers and by African American leaders were effective. The rate of African American deaths in Vietnam in relation to blacks' representation in the U.S. population declined as the war went on. Thomas A. Johnson, writing in the August 1968 issue of *Ebony,* reported that after the African American death rate in Vietnam reached almost 25 percent in 1965, "the Pentagon ordered a cutback in the participation of black troops."

He quoted an unnamed army general in Vietnam as saying, "We deliberately spread out Negroes in component units at a ratio pretty much according to the division total." Then he added: "We don't want to risk having a platoon or company that has more Negroes than whites overrun or wiped out. It's a precaution easily taken."[61]

Johnson reported that Pentagon figures put the current death rate for blacks at 14 percent of total American fatalities. A Department of Defense study released in 1971 reported that between 1961 and 1966, 16 percent of those killed in hostile action in Vietnam were African Americans. The figure fell to just under 13 percent in 1967, remained about the same in 1968, fell to 11 percent in 1969, and declined further, to 9 percent, in 1970. For the years 1961 through 1970, 12.5 percent of those killed in action in Vietnam were African Americans. By the end of June 1971 a total of 45,353 Americans had been killed in combat, of whom 12.4 percent were blacks. The percentage of African Americans who died in Vietnam as a result of "non-hostile" causes was considerably higher. Among the 9,645 U.S. military personnel killed accidentally in Vietnam through June 1971, 1,419, or 14.7 percent, were black. Of the total of 54,998 Americans who died in Vietnam of all causes through June 1971, 7,033, or 12.8 percent, were African Americans.[62]

African Americans accounted for 11 percent of the U.S. population and about 10 percent of U.S. personnel serving in Vietnam as the war wound down, so the Defense Department's statistics still reflect a disproportionate death rate for blacks in Vietnam, though not on the scale of 1965 and 1966.[63]

What is particularly troubling is that during the years of peak African American casualties in Vietnam, which approached, then briefly exceeded, 20 percent of U.S. forces in the war zone during the midsixties, the percentage of blacks in all the U.S. armed services worldwide never exceeded 9.5 percent, the rate in 1965.[64] Obviously, during the early years of the massive U.S. combat commitment in Vietnam, blacks in the U.S. military proportionately were far more likely than whites to find themselves on the battlefields of Southeast Asia and far more likely to die—even though African Americans during the period were slightly underrepresented in the armed forces relative to their proportion in the U.S. population as a whole.

The theme of excessive black casualties as a basis to claim entitlement to the full rights of citizenship continued to crop up in the black press as the war dragged on, as casualty lists lengthened, and as the aspirations of African Americans for full participation in their nation's life remained deferred. Excessive casualties was regularly used as a rhetorical device to demonstrate the legitimacy of African American claims to their proper place as first-class citizens.

The opening words of an editorial in the *Defender* on January 19, 1967, published long after the magnitude of black casualties became a subject of editorial discussion in the black press, went straight to the heart of the matter: "While white America is engaged in the sordid business of denying the Negro his full citizenship rights . . . the war in Vietnam is taking an unprecedented toll of American black soldiers." The editor called the effort to block the full realization of black civil rights a "national conspiracy to keep the American black man in 'his place' as a second-class citizen." The writer noted that when the war finally ended in Vietnam, whatever its outcome, "the black soldier . . . will return home to the old slums, the depressing ghettos which delimit his social mobility and force him back into the black night of anguish and despair."[65]

An editorial in the *Milwaukee Star* suggested that those who struggle for liberty embrace the cost of bloodshed on the battlefield as an acceptable sacrifice for freedom if it in fact earns that freedom. But the bloody sacrifices of the American black, as far as the *Star* could tell, had not earned him the rights of full citizenship. Then the piece said: "What other price, besides his life and his blood, must the Negro pay to be able to live where he wants, get the job he wants, if qualified, or go to the school of his choosing?"[66]

A cartoon in the *Pittsburgh Courier* (see figure 3) applied the same logic to a black soldier who had been wounded in Vietnam but then faced having to deal with the bigotry of an ungrateful white society back home. Just over two years later, the *Courier* ran the cartoon again, a move that testifies to the durability and power of the idea that black casualties had earned full citizenship for the community.

Lyndon Johnson was aware of the statistics. On February 14, 1967, Cliff Alexander sent LBJ a memo informing him that, as of September 30, 1966—"the latest Pentagon figures"—Negroes made up 10.2 percent of U.S. forces in Vietnam, while black fatalities were 16.3 percent of all deaths from January 1 through November 30, 1966.[67]

These data apparently prompted a request for more information, because the next evening the stack of papers for the president to review before going to sleep included a memo from Cyrus Vance, deputy secretary of defense. Vance put the percentage of African Americans in the U.S. military in Vietnam as of September 30, 1966, at 10.2 percent and the percentage of blacks among the enlisted ranks at 11 percent. The 1964 U.S. Census reported the percentage of blacks in the total U.S. population to be 11 percent, with black males of draft age accounting for "about" 12 percent of draft-age Americans.[68]

When the president sent Congress an extensive new civil rights program on February 15, 1967, his accompanying message included a lengthy passage arguing passionately for equality for black Americans who were performing the

"Say baby, you reckon they goin' to allow me to eat in one of their restaurants if I make it back to Mississippi?"

Figure 3.
Bootsie (Cartoon by Ollie Harrington, *Pittsburgh Courier*, May 6, 1967, and May 31, 1969. Courtesy of the *Pittsburgh Courier* Archives.)

duties of citizenship on the bloody battlefields of Vietnam. It also included some of the statistics Vance had passed along to LBJ. Said Johnson:

> In our wars Americans, Negro and white, have fought side by side to defend freedom. Negro soldiers—like white soldiers—have won every medal for bravery our country bestows. The bullets of our enemies do not discriminate between Negro Marines and white Marines. They kill and maim whomever they strike.
>
> The American Negro has waited long for first-class citizenship—for his right of equal justice. But he has long accepted the full responsibilities of citizenship.

If there were any doubt, one need only look to the servicemen who man our defenses. In Vietnam, 10.2 percent of our soldiers are American Negroes bearing equal responsibilities in the fight for freedom—but at home, 11 percent of our people are American Negroes struggling for equal opportunities.

The bullets at the battlefront do not discriminate—but the landlords at home do. The pack of the Negro soldier is as heavy as the white soldier's—but the burden his family at home bears is far heavier. In war, the Negro American has given this nation his best—but this nation has not given him equal justice.

It is time that the Negro be given equal justice. In America, the rights of citizenship are conferred by birth—not by death in battle.[69]

The same day the Pentagon sent the White House a brief summary that offered insight into what officials had come to believe were the principal reasons for the disproportion in the statistics of black casualties:

Pentagon officers say the high proportion of Negro combat deaths in Vietnam is related to the high proportion of Negroes serving in fighting units.

A new Defense Department study showed yesterday that while the proportion of Negro enlisted men among all U.S. troops in Vietnam dropped to 11 percent last year, Negroes accounted for nearly 18 percent of the combat deaths.

The high concentration of Negroes in combat units—up to 25 percent in some airborne brigades—is not due to discrimination of any kind, [the] Pentagon officer said.

The number of Negroes in such units is high, these sources said, because Negroes:

- re-enlist at much higher rates than whites.
- volunteer more readily for elite combat units such as special forces and airborne divisions that offer more prestige and more pay.
- enter the service with more educational deficiencies, sharply limiting the number and type of armed service jobs available to them.[70]

Whatever the reason that put blacks in units such as the airborne brigades in unusually large numbers, their presence in those combat groups was a matter of common knowledge, according to Johnson's article in *Ebony*. He reported that officers in the airborne brigades had said black paratroopers usually represented about 25 percent of the men in those elite combat units, but he noted that "personal observations lead correspondents to suggest that the percentages are much higher." He said that observers had often seen airborne rifle platoons made up almost entirely of blacks during combat operations.[71]

The columnist James L. Hicks, writing in the *New York Amsterdam News* in March 1966, accepted the explanation that black troops were dying in larger numbers, proportionately, than whites because of their enthusiasm to join elite units and guessed that they did this to prove their mettle in combat. Hicks remembered how he and his buddies in segregated units in World War II were eager to prove in combat that they "could fight like any other Americans." This memory led Hicks to think about the black soldiers now "being given their chance to fight and die" in the integrated army in Vietnam. He wrote of being saddened by the image of all those "good Negro soldiers" who "were lying over there dead, who would still be alive if they had not been recklessly trying to prove something to somebody." Yet he also confessed to a feeling of pride "as an ex-Negro GI" that blacks were being recognized for shouldering more than their share of the burden of fighting and dying in Vietnam.[72]

It was not uncommon for the black press to find—as Hicks did—that disproportionate black casualties in Vietnam were a basis for both concern and pride. African American soldiers in Vietnam were bearing too much of the burden of combat and sacrifice, but they were also distinguishing themselves in ways that allowed the black press to extol their bravery and achievement.

Still, there was the gnawing sense that racial discrimination had something to do with the presence of so many black GIs in the battle zone. In discussing the Pentagon's statistics showing excessive black casualties, the *Defender*'s editor noted the Defense Department's denial that discrimination had anything to do with battlefield assignments, then asserted that the figures "fail to support that assertion."[73] However, the editorial writer did not follow up on the implication that bias in fact was involved in assignments that put black soldiers in harm's way.

Two days after the *Defender* refused to lay the issue of discrimination aside as a cause of disproportionate black casualties, the *Afro-American* splashed a story on its front page, under the lead headline "Congressmen Seek Investigation of Higher Vietnam Death Rate." The story was about the efforts by two African American representatives from Michigan, John Conyers and Charles Diggs, to get the Defense Department to answer questions about its report about the combat death rate among black Americans in Vietnam. When Diggs was asked whether he thought racial discrimination might be the cause of the high casualty rate for blacks, he replied that he had heard "no evidence that colored soldiers were being exposed to arduous and vulnerable duties," especially because of their race.

Diggs went on to speculate that one reason for the inflated numbers was that disadvantaged black youths had found better opportunities in the military than they could find as civilians. He also noted that lack of academic qualifications made young black men much more vulnerable to induction into the armed services than white youths who could qualify for deferments.[74] The implication, though unspoken in the news story, was that while official discrimination was not to blame for the high black death toll, the systemic discrimination that denied opportunities to young black males at home often created conditions that ultimately led them into the jungles of Vietnam.

As the war lengthened and the service commitments of soldiers began to expire, another phenomenon began to have an impact on the black casualty rate: blacks were reenlisting at a rate twice that of their white counterparts. In the U.S. Army the differential was even higher. This inevitably swelled the ranks of blacks who became available for service in Vietnam. By 1968 this tendency was sufficiently pronounced to merit an article in the August issue of *Ebony*. According to the piece, during 1966 and 1967, when the Vietnam War was being escalated rapidly and increasing numbers of U.S. soldiers were being killed in combat, about 49 percent of blacks eligible to leave the army chose to reenlist, whereas only 16 percent of white soldiers elected to sign up for another hitch.[75]

Some observers, black and white, viewed the high reenlistment rate of African Americans positively. It was variously seen as irrefutable proof of the high morale and patriotism of black soldiers and an affirmation of the quality of life the integrated armed forces provided for its black members. The *Ebony* article quoted the columnist Roscoe Drummond as saying, "Negroes find the U.S. armed forces just about the most productive, rewarding, and racially congenial experience that they can have." Critics, however, took a different view, arguing that "equality with the white man in predominately white institutions" could be negative for the black community. The article cited as an example of just such a negative consequence the disproportionate casualties that resulted from the overrepresentation of blacks in combat units in Vietnam.[76]

The article went on to explore the reasons for the high black reenlistment rate and concluded that it was rooted in both "economics and psychodynamics." The economic motivation was twofold. First, the pay and benefits available to a black GI were an attractive inducement to reenlist to a man coming from a community with high unemployment, an absence of academic opportunities, few dependable civilian jobs, and a future with little economic promise. Second, the Pentagon was paying attractive cash bonuses, ranging from $900 to $1,400, to troops who reenlisted. As one air force member said upon reenlisting, "That's an awful lot of money to a young black cat who's never had more than $150 at one time in his life."[77]

The other major reason for black reenlistment, the article argued, was a psychological one. The *Ebony* piece, citing the conclusions of the psychiatrist Alvin F. Poussaint, argued that young black men, particularly those from socially and economically deprived backgrounds, suffered from low self-esteem and were attracted to the opportunity to prove their manhood in the military, even in combat. This, according to Poussaint's psychological analysis, helped account for the large number of blacks who volunteered for elite units that bore the brunt of combat.[78]

Whitney M. Young Jr., head of the Urban League, had gone to Vietnam in 1966 to see firsthand how African Americans were faring in the battle zone and found evidence to support Poussaint's view. During his visit Young talked to many black soldiers, among them, men who had volunteered for combat units. Young concluded from these interviews that many young black soldiers had volunteered for frontline units to overcome feelings of inferiority, to "show the other guy and themselves that they are men."[79]

Whatever the reasons behind the unusually high rate of reenlistment among black military personnel, it contributed to the disproportionate black presence within the combat units in Vietnam and was at least one factor in the high rate of battlefield deaths among blacks during the first two years of large-scale combat operations by U.S. troops.

Occasionally, more sinister explanations were reported. Some were anecdotal, coming from soldiers in the field. *Ebony*, in an article on the draft, discussed the vulnerability of the black soldier on the front in Vietnam, citing the story of David Parks, a black soldier who kept a journal, later published as *GI Diary*. Parks described how his white NCO, a Sergeant Paulson, was responsible for assigning his men to various duties and assigned only "Negroes and Puerto Ricans to the hazardous job of forward officer." According to Parks, the "odds are against" the forward officer. The implication of the story was unmistakable. Out in the field, away from public relations officers and the eyes of prying media, discrimination was still a fact of life and could cost a black soldier his life as he was ordered into situations of special danger precisely because he was black.[80]

Firsthand accounts like this were rare in the black press, although accusations of such bigotry in combat were published from time to time, usually arising from more radicalized elements within the African American community. Late in 1966, after the story about the death toll among blacks in Vietnam had been prompting editorials and other comment for most of the year, the *Defender* picked up a UPI story about a youthful black nationalist leader, Alvin Harrison, a member of the Afro-American Unity Movement. Harrison pointed the finger at President Johnson, accusing him of "using the war in Vietnam to kill Negroes." As the *Defender* story characterized it, Harrison "put a raging end" to an antiwar rally by saying that the president "keeps sending Negroes to Vietnam so they'll get killed . . . and eliminate the civil rights problem."[81]

Al Flowers wrote a column in the *Milwaukee Star* that urged his readers to question American involvement in Vietnam. The piece, which ran in mid-December 1969, made some incendiary charges and was intended to arouse black opposition to the war: "With the war raging, the government has used the draft to force Blacks off of the street of the ghettoes, taking many of the rebellious young men and channeling their energies against a helpless country—Vietnam, rather than against the very society that has the Blacks in bondage—America. While forcing the Blacks to fight an immoral war, the United States in the meantime conducts acts of genocide against the Blacks giving them all the hazardous duties by putting Blacks unproportionately to whites in combat action."[82]

Generally, the African American press avoided such extreme explanations for the death rate among blacks in Vietnam. But the press acknowledged the issue, sought explanations for the phenomenon, and connected it, in one way or another, to the pervasive discrimination that still routinely denied blacks their full rights as citizens of the United States.

The deep and sustained interest of the black press in the disproportionate black casualty rate in Vietnam was seldom expressed in terms of a hostile or malevolent federal government, nor did the press view the problem as being chiefly one of military manpower policy. In fact, a *Baltimore Afro-American* editorial with the provocative headline "Cannon Fodder in Vietnam" argued that black representation was highest in combat units because large numbers of highly motivated blacks volunteered to serve in them. The reason for their heavy representation, the editor said, was a discriminatory society that failed to offer "equal educational opportunity" and good job prospects to African Americans. The result, the editorial observed, is "our youngsters find their only outlet in the armed services." The piece concluded by citing the sad irony "that, proportionately more of our boys are paying with their lives for 'freedom' in Vietnam, largely because they were never allowed to enjoy it in their native land."[83] While it may not have pinned the blame directly on specific actions of the national government, by making this argument the editorial was indicting the nation for its failure to eradicate the pervasive racism that still affected the way America dealt with its black citizens.

In all the attempts to decry or explain the high African American death rate in Vietnam, the black press ran the risk of deflecting attention from the bravery of the black soldiers who fought in the war with distinction. The "Cannon

Fodder" editorial in the *Afro-American* recognized this when, in the midst of a discussion of the problem, it saluted the valor of the black soldier, which, it insisted, was unquestioned.[84]

The ultimate indignity, which occasionally faced the families of black soldiers killed in action, was racial discrimination that barred their burial in certain cemeteries. An early instance of this was reported in the black press in 1966. After an enemy grenade killed Private First Class Jimmy Williams, nineteen, his grieving mother was told that her son could be buried only in a pauper's grave in his hometown of Wetumpka, Alabama, thirteen miles northeast of Montgomery. Private Williams, a Green Beret paratrooper, was the town's first Vietnam casualty. The case caused a sensation in the black press. The *Baltimore Afro-American* made it a front-page story on June 4, with a headline evoking the nativity story: "No Room in the Cemetery." The paper quoted the dead soldier's mother's tearful reflection on her son's fate: "My son died fighting on the front for all of us. He didn't die a segregated death and he'll not be buried in a segregated cemetery."

With burial in the local cemetery blocked, after a crowded funeral service Private Williams's body was taken to the Andersonville National Cemetery, one hundred miles from Wetumpka, where the dead GI was buried with full military honors.[85]

A week later the *Afro-American* continued its coverage of the episode with two editorials in the same issue. The first one began: "It is hard for a mother to see her son go off to the confused, controversial war in Vietnam. . . . What then, in the midst of this sorrow and uncertainty, must have been the feelings of the Alabama mother who was told by the mayor of her town that there was no room for her son in the white-only cemetery—except in a pauper's grave—no space for the town's first Vietnam fatality who died wearing the Green Beret."[86]

In the other editorial the paper described the racism that excluded the soldier from proper burial in his hometown and noted the irony that his final resting place would be among soldiers in the Union Army who had sacrificed their lives in the Civil War a century earlier to defeat the South and slavery.[87]

Another black casualty of Vietnam who was denied burial in an all-white cemetery became the center of the first formal lawsuit filed in federal court demanding equal treatment after death. Before he was killed, Private First Class Bill Terry Jr. had written a letter home telling his young wife that if he died in battle, he wanted to be buried in the lovely, prestigious Elmwood Cemetery in his hometown of Birmingham, Alabama. The grieving family sought to fulfill his wish but was turned away by cemetery officials, who explained that racial covenants in all the deeds to the plots explicitly excluded blacks. So Private Terry's body was laid to rest with full military honors in an all-black cemetery, Shadow Lawn.[88]

Afterward, his widow and his mother consulted their parish priest, who contacted the NAACP and asked for legal help. The upshot was a lawsuit filed on the basis of an 1866 civil rights law that protected former slaves. In a seventeen-page decision a federal judge ruled in the family's favor. A headline in the *Afro-American*, on January 3, 1970, celebrated the decision: "GI Lost Life in Vietnam, Won Ala. Cemetery Battle." The young soldier's casket was exhumed, and he was memorialized in his boyhood church. Then his coffin was carried to Elmwood Cemetery in a procession that included twelve hundred exultant mourners singing "We Shall Overcome." He again was laid to rest with full military honors.[89]

An editorial in the same issue of the *Afro-American* applauded Private Terry's belated victory and lamented the racist climate that continued to poison American life: "It is a shame that at the end of the 60's a black family has to go into court in democratic America to win the right of burial in a cemetery open to any white person." A week later the *Afro-American* picked up a UPI feature by Glenn Stephens and placed it prominently on its front page. The story related the victory by Private Terry's family in securing a grave for the black soldier in the cemetery of his choice. It was a fitting coda to a poignant saga.[90]

However, the court's decision in the Terry case did not immediately erase the problem of discrimination for bereaved African American families seeking burial in other federal districts. Several months after Terry was buried in the previously all-white cemetery in Birmingham, a front-page story in the *New York Amsterdam News* reported that authorities in Fort Pierce, Florida, had blocked the burial of another black soldier killed in Vietnam, Pondexteur Eugene Williams of Fort Pierce, in an all-white cemetery his family had chosen. Local authorities remained adamant even after a compassionate seventy-two-year-old white woman donated a gravesite for Williams in the cemetery.

An editorial in the same issue of the *New York Amsterdam News* summed up the injustice: "The total inconsistency of a 20-year-old black man dying in Vietnam fighting for his country; and, in death, being denied a narrow, 6-foot piece of his country's earth for his body's reposal is sufficient evidence of the stench of bigotry that follows blacks from birth until death— and beyond. . . . Blacks can pass physical examinations, be shuffled off to Vietnam and be killed side by side with their fellow corpsmen; but to repose in death within the same cemetery is not their right" (see figure 4).[91]

Figure 4.

A black soldier, in death, is denied his "narrow six-foot piece of his country's earth," as an editorial in the August 29, 1970, edition of the *New York Amsterdam News*, eloquently described it. (Cartoon by Melvin Tapley. Courtesy of the *New York Amsterdam News*.)

These dead black soldiers bore on their spent frames the aching aspirations of the whole community of African Americans. Their claim to equality in the life of the nation, purchased at the cost of their lives, was morally irrefutable but still stubbornly resisted.

An editorial in the *Defender* on November 22, 1966, described "the thoughtless, who make a fetish of decrying civil rights demonstrations and marches, and who feel that the Negro citizen is demanding more than he is entitled to have." Such people, the editor said, should look at the grim statistics showing the disproportionate number of blacks killed was "increasing with each debarkation of fresh troops in the theatre of the Asian war." It concluded: "These black men are spilling their blood in the defense of freedom they scarcely enjoy at home. On the battlefield, they are U.S. soldiers; at home, they are plain Negroes. The distinction is insufferable."[92]

4

African American Opposition
to the War in Vietnam

But looming darkly . . . is the long fattened and still grinning evil of Jim Crow, the American demon we have never chosen to exorcise with the self-preening righteousness we brandish as we pursue the ragged peasants of the Viet Cong.—*New York Amsterdam News*, May 6, 1967

When Martin Luther King Jr. was released from jail in Selma, Alabama, on February 5, 1965, he confided to reporters that he would be meeting with President Johnson to urge the passage of strong voting rights legislation so African Americans like those in Selma, for whose cause King had gone to jail, would be guaranteed their rights as American citizens. The very next day the Vietcong staged an assault on the U.S. base at Pleiku in Vietnam's central highlands. The attack killed seven Americans, wounded more than a hundred others, and precipitated a full-scale bombing campaign against North Vietnam.

The assault also riveted the attention of the administration and the nation on events in Vietnam. With the president preoccupied, King's visit was postponed. Although he finally got in to see Johnson a few days later, the delay was an intimation of the shift in priorities that ultimately would diminish, then marginalize, the civil rights movement. The focus of national concern was shifting inexorably to Vietnam.

If the attack on Pleiku failed to make the change in priorities apparent, the progression of events would. On March 8, a day after Alabama state troopers waded into a peaceful column of demonstrators in Selma on what came to be called Bloody Sunday, clubbing and teargassing the marchers, U.S. Marines landed on the beaches of Danang. The turmoil in Selma still held national attention, but the deployment of marines moved the Vietnam War higher on the nation's agenda.[1]

The civil rights movement was beginning to lose what it needed to be successful in the long run. The president was allowing his calendar to be monopolized by the Vietnam War, and the far-off war was pulling the attention of the American people away from the vivid stories of the civil rights struggle. With the escalation of the war came a fundamental shift in the political situation, an erosion of presidential political capital available for domestic initiatives, and demands on Johnson's time and attention. This shift made African American leaders increasingly uncomfortable and caused the black press to raise frequent alarms decrying the disproportion in the vast commitment of financial resources to the war and the relatively modest allocation of resources to fund the Great Society. Johnson's fundamental desire to further the cause of equal rights and economic opportunity for African Americans remained strong but could not withstand political opposition that arose, in part, on the strength of its assertion that LBJ could not have both "guns and butter," as he believed he could. Perhaps Johnson meant well, but one consequence, whether direct or indirect, of his decision to pursue a policy of escalation in Vietnam was the weakening of federal support for the reform agenda of blacks.

Several black leaders lashed out at the U.S. government for its misplaced priorities. John Lewis, whose skull was fractured on Bloody Sunday, was angry at the president's shifting priorities. Just before the leader of the Student Nonviolent Coordinating Committee (SNCC) checked out of the hospital, his head wrapped in bandages, he said in evident frustration, "I don't see how President Johnson can send troops to Vietnam . . . and can't send troops to Selma, Alabama."[2]

According to *Jet* magazine, the customarily mild-mannered head of the NAACP, Roy Wilkins, usually deferential to LBJ, observed with uncharacteristically salty language that if the administration could send the marines into Vietnam, then, "dammit, they can send somebody to Alabama and defend the government right here."[3]

In his column in the *Afro-American*, Whitney Young elaborated a more complex argument: "The people and the soil of Alabama ought to be as precious to us as the people and the soil of Vietnam, where we have only in the past week dispatched 3,500 Marines. If we cannot protect our own citizens in Alabama, how can the world expect us to protect the Vietnamese in Asia?"

Later in the column Young became even more pointed: "Make no mistake about it: if we, the people of America, lose in Alabama, we will never win in Vietnam." Young argued that, unless the United States successfully resolved its domestic racial crisis, American boys would be called upon to fight and die in the unforgiving jungles of Vietnam "because the communists can point to Alabama as a shining example of American hypocrisy against people of color." If the situation at home did not change, it would be impossible for the United States "to rally and inspire the uncommitted peoples of colored nations to the cause of the Free World."[4]

This argument lifted the issue from a question of the tactical feasibility of attending to both domestic and foreign concerns simultaneously to a strategic assertion that America's long-term international standing depended upon eradication of its domestic racial problems.

Johnson, though distracted by events in Vietnam, was not as unmoved as some black leaders supposed. What they did not know was the mounting indignation that stirred the president as he absorbed the images of black Americans being beaten by state troopers on Bloody Sunday only because they wanted the right to vote. On Monday, March 15, Johnson went before a joint session of Congress and gave one of the most moving speeches of his presidency. "I speak tonight for the dignity of man and the destiny of democracy," he began. He embraced the cause of the Selma marchers as his own. And he urged the lawmakers and the American public watching the speech on television to make the cause theirs as well. To repeated ovations the president laid out the case for justice long deferred and placed on the American conscience the plight of black citizens: "Their cause must be our cause too. Because it is not just Negroes, but really it is all of us, who must overcome the crippling legacy of bigotry and injustice." And then the president, the southern cadence of his voice steely with determination, invoked the words of the African American anthem: "And we shall overcome." Watching in Selma, where he had just delivered a eulogy for James Reeb, a slain civil right worker, Martin Luther King Jr. found his eyes welling up with tears.[5]

As black civil rights leaders initially were confronting the uncomfortable confluence of the Southeast Asian war and the domestic struggle to achieve equal rights for African Americans, a few were going so far as to declare themselves in opposition to the war. On April 17, 1965, a major antiwar protest was staged in Washington, D.C., organized mainly by the largely white Students for a Democratic Society (SDS), perhaps the most prominent organization in the emerging New Left. The executive committee of SNCC supported SDS at the rally. A featured speaker at the event was Robert Moses, a revered figure among the young black activists at SNCC and one of the first black civil rights leaders to publicly denounce the war. Moses said, somewhat obscurely, to the crowd of fifteen thousand clustered at the foot of the Washington Monument: "Use Mississippi not as a moral lightning rod, but if you use it at all, use it as your looking glass."[6] He seemed to be challenging the smugness, the moral superiority of Americans beyond the reach of his voice, even as he appealed to the highly motivated civil rights faithful gathered at his feet to begin their protest against violence, whether in Mississippi or in Vietnam, by seeing their own complicity in America's frailties.

The civil rights movement reached its zenith just as the war in Vietnam was beginning to really take off. The momentum generated by Bloody Sunday and the leadership of the president led finally to a bill securing the ballot for black Americans. On August 6, after several months of frenzied negotiation and determined arm twisting, Lyndon Johnson signed into law the historic Voting Rights Act.[7] It was, one observer said, "the most impressive single civil rights ceremony of the Johnson Administration, the President under the Capitol dome with the area there filled with the nation's leadership," including those of the main civil rights organizations.[8] It was the last major civil rights bill directed at dismantling the legal structure of segregation in the South, and the most important one.

The epochal signing of the Voting Rights law occurred just days after Johnson, on July 28, approved General William C. Westmoreland's request to send forty-four more combat battalions to Vietnam, to join the eighteen already there.[9] The war was heating up, and the United States was shouldering the major burden of fighting it. With continuing escalation came a gradual, relentless, but initially almost imperceptible, shift in the focus of the government's attention. The war's steady ascendancy as an issue continued to vie with the freedom struggle of American blacks until the war ultimately became the single item dominating the national agenda.

In the black press and among African American leaders, the degree to which the Vietnam War had become the central focus of the federal government, at the expense of the Second Reconstruction, raised deep concerns. The fear that the Vietnam War would displace civil rights as the top priority was not without foundation. One high-ranking official in the Johnson administration framed the problem tersely, if somewhat imprecisely: "There are less than twenty men in the government who can get something new done, and they really have to work and fight to do it; with Vietnam building up, they just had to drop this other thing."[10]

The anxiety the black press felt about the dwindling official attention to civil rights matters and the looming competition of the Vietnam conflict as a concern could scarcely have been eased by mounting evidence that public attention was making the same shift. Some of the evidence was as subtle as the anthem adopted by antiwar activists. In April 1965 antiwar protesters clotted together outside the White House fence and sang "We Shall Overcome." But they added a new stanza to the civil rights anthem: "We shall live in peace."[11]

The Gallup organization's polling numbers first captured the Vietnam War as a distinct problem of national importance in November 1964. Until then civil rights had, for several years, registered as the dominant social issue in most of the polling data. Shortly after mid-1965 Vietnam became the number one issue and would remain so through the rest of the decade (indeed, until 1971, when anxiety about the economy became the most pressing concern). In contrast, civil rights became a secondary issue and declined markedly in importance relative to Vietnam.[12]

Even as the sympathetic consensus of moderate and liberal white Americans about the importance of advancing the civil rights agenda was beginning to fray in the mid-1960s, the tactical and strategic consensus that had black leaders firmly aligned with the liberal white establishment on civil rights was starting to come apart. This tendency was exacerbated by black fears that the growing preoccupation with an increasingly costly war would siphon resources away from social reform. Although the president gave frequent assurances of his commitment to social justice and produced significant legislative victories for the cause, doubts still gnawed about his ability to continue to deliver the kind of expensive programs needed to implement the Great Society.

In remarks in the Capitol Rotunda, King raised the subject of Vietnam during the ceremonial signing of the Voting Rights Act. He urged Johnson to focus his administration's attention on the nation's ghettos, rather than on the war in Vietnam. The president was visibly upset by what he clearly viewed as King's meddling in foreign affairs.[13]

King found the administration's policy in Vietnam at odds with his own ideas of nonviolence. He began to build an antiwar philosophy organized around the core principles that had long animated his calls for social transformation at home. In U.S. military actions in Vietnam, he saw what he came to perceive as the same calloused indifference to the rights of nonwhites that he had seen in the darker corners of American society. Even as the president's civil rights legislation was being put safely in place, with despair in the ghettos careening toward violence and the war in Vietnam escalating rapidly, King began to move away from his old White House ally.

King's growing apprehensions about Vietnam created considerable anxiety among key associates in the civil rights fraternity. The concerns were, as often as not, pragmatic, not philosophical. A white attorney who counseled King about the finances of his Southern Christian Leadership Conference warned that important donors might defect, crippling SCLC poverty programs.

Bayard Rustin, an ardent pacifist and King's close confidant, cautioned the civil rights leader about alienating important allies in the federal government. Other leading blacks, such as Roy Wilkins and Whitney Young, urged King to temper his antiwar sentiments for the sake of the movement.[14]

But King was determined to come down on the side of peace in Vietnam. He was motivated by a profound moral critique of the Vietnam War in particular, and of war in general, that overwhelmed his practical concerns about the loss of presidential and congressional support. He undoubtedly was also emboldened by his new international stature as a man of peace; he had recently been awarded the Nobel Peace Prize. In his first overt step in opposition to the war, King began promoting a halt in U.S. bombing and peace talks, offering to mediate negotiations personally.

The *Atlanta Daily World* carried a UPI story about a King peace initiative, aired in a speech at Howard University on March 2, 1965, in which he based his actions on his personal philosophy of nonviolence. He said it left him "no choice but to urge negotiations." At Howard, King asserted that war had always been negative but with the advent of nuclear weapons had become completely unacceptable. "The war in Vietnam," he told his university audience, "is accomplishing nothing."[15]

King's call for a negotiated peace in Vietnam was the subject of reporting and comment in the press, including the black press, for several months. On July 2, 1965, at an event reported in the *Pittsburgh Courier*, King spoke to a rally at Virginia State College during an SCLC convention. He told the audience that the war in Vietnam had to be stopped and that the way to accomplish that would be an immediate settlement. He went on to say that he was "as much concerned about destroying communism as the next person" but that "we aren't going to defeat communism with guns, bombs and gasses, but rather by making democracy work and showing it to the world." Envisioning a redemptive example as an alternative to using force to defeat communism, King assumed a Gandhian stance while sounding like the theologian that he was. Then, offering a clue to the substance of his expanded agenda, he told the audience that society has three fundamental evils: racial injustice, poverty, and war.[16]

In a somewhat more provocative version of the event, a UPI story in the *Afro-American* item began: "Dr. Martin Luther King, Jr., and his Civil Rights movement have moved squarely into the foreign policy field, urging negotiations with the Viet Cong, if necessary, to stop the fighting in Vietnam." According to the UPI piece, King warned that unless the administration did something at the bargaining table to end the war, he might incorporate "peace rallies" in his civil rights activities. Then he told the cheering crowd: "I'm not going to sit by and see war being escalated without saying anything about it."[17]

King's threat to fuse the issues of peace and civil rights echoed the calls that Rev. James Bevel, King's close associate in the SCLC, had been making. But King stopped short of Bevel's vision of an alliance between the antiwar and civil rights movements. Bevel saw both a common methodology and a common purpose in such a partnership that made tactical and strategic sense. King was not yet prepared to go quite that far, fearing the loss of the old alliance of civil rights leaders and the liberal establishment, which controlled both purse strings and political power.[18]

The reaction within the civil rights fraternity was swift. *U.S. News and World Report* noted King's remarks in Petersburg and observed that his public stance put him at odds with James Farmer, director of the Congress of Racial Equality, and Roy Wilkins, head of the NAACP. The magazine reported that Farmer had to put down an effort to pass an antiwar resolution at the Congress of Racial Equality (CORE) convention after King's remarks. Wilkins, during a radio interview, was asked whether King would now attempt to shape foreign policy, using "moral force." Wilkins replied, "We think we have enough Vietnam in Alabama to occupy our attention. We will leave foreign policy to the United States."[19]

An editorial in the *Philadelphia Tribune* in mid-July 1965 probably spoke for much of the black press when it ventured the view that King was moving outside his realm of expertise in presuming to give advice to the president on foreign affairs. It suggested that King was a babe in the woods of foreign policy: "The chances are that Dr. King, despite his scholarship and competence, knows very little about the total Vietnam situation. . . . If there are those close to him, to whom he occasionally turns for advice and whose opinions he respects, they ought to caution him against spreading himself too thin."[20]

Even as King spoke out publicly about the war, urging peace negotiations to end the conflict, he was unwilling to make a complete break with the president and sought to soften the impact of his criticism of the Johnson administration. A few days after the Virginia rally, King spoke by phone with Johnson about a pending civil rights bill in Congress and sought to downplay his remarks. "In the last few days . . . I made a statement concerning the Vietnam situation," he said. "This in no way is an attempt to engage in a criticism of (your) policies," King assured Johnson, then trotted out a time-worn piece of political spin: "The press, unfortunately, lifted it out of context."[21] However passionately King felt about the war in Vietnam, he still clearly wanted to avoid antagonizing the president upon whose political leadership so much depended in advancing the cause of civil rights.

The call for negotiations with the Vietcong was too much for allies of the administration to stomach. In the next issue of the *Afro-American*, Senator John Sparkman, Democrat of Alabama, was quoted as saying of the proposal:

"Dr. King is just as wrong as he can be in calling for a negotiated settlement regardless of what the other side might demand." Then, addressing King's proposed new negotiating partners, Sparkman said: "We have no choice but to continue to wipe out the Viet Cong." George Weaver, the black assistant secretary of labor in the Johnson administration, spoke out from a convention dais against unnamed civil rights leaders who dared to venture into foreign affairs.[22] His words were unmistakably aimed at King.

Even his own organization rejected King's proposal. King's Vietnam initiative, proffered as the SCLC was meeting in convention, sparked discussions among the organization's members and officials. Benjamin Hooks, a member of the SCLC board, spoke for many black leaders in the group when he said, "I question whether it is wise for us to go too far in the international arena."[23] Hooks and others recognized the peril of dabbling in foreign affairs, particularly in opposition to Johnson's Vietnam policy, at a time when the support of the administration was vital to the continued development of programs important to African Americans.

Bayard Rustin, King's close adviser, fashioned a resolution to avert a convention split on the war—and "to restrain King," Adam Fairclough pointed out.[24] A front-page story in the *Afro-American*, in August 1965, described the resolution in which the SCLC announced it would not get involved in the growing debate about the Vietnam War unless a "perilous escalation" of the conflict occurred. The resolution went on to say: "The primary function of our organization is to secure the full citizenship rights for colored citizens of this country." Arguing that it simply lacked the resources to pursue an antiwar agenda, along with its civil rights agenda, the resolution urged that SCLC's efforts "be confined to the question of racial brotherhood."[25]

During the summer black newspapers weighed in. The *Dallas Express* published a blunt appraisal of King's peacemaking efforts, drawing a line between private citizens and the government in terms of proper authority to conduct negotiations: "Rev. Martin Luther King is out of bounds on his efforts to secure peace in Vietnam. His intentions may be good, but the effects of his peace move may be harmful to the U.S. effort in that war-torn country." Only the president or someone given the responsibility by him can negotiate properly for U.S. interests in Vietnam, the writer asserted.[26] Later, in December, an editorial in the *Express* continued to insist that private individuals ought to back off and let the administration seek an end to the conflict, grounding the assertion in geopolitics: "Every sane American wants peace in Vietnam. But as Americans, we feel that we do not have the right to try to pressure the administration into accepting a peace treaty that would not have adequate safeguards to prevent a complete communist takeover in South Vietnam."[27]

The *Afro-American* reported that, despite the position of some of the black press and his own SCLC, King was persisting in his efforts at international peacemaking. In September he renewed his call for a negotiated settlement of the Vietnam War, adding for good measure the suggestion that Red China be admitted to the United Nations. He announced his intention to write personal letters to Ho Chi Minh, North Vietnam's president, and the leaders of communist China. King also expressed his resolve to continue speaking out on the issue of peace, both "as an individual and a minister of the gospel."[28]

By characterizing his peacemaking efforts as arising from his personal actions and not his official capacity as head of the SCLC, King was attempting to maintain separation in his roles. This presumed that the public could make such careful distinctions about a public figure whose words and actions had defined him as the dominant leader of the civil rights struggle and whose larger-than-life popular image long ago had swallowed up the private man.

As King's announced intentions became more ambitious in the field of international diplomacy, he came under some intense political pressure behind the scenes. President Johnson let King know privately that urgent peace negotiations were underway through back channels with some prospect of success and appealed to him to avoid further public statements about the war while these delicate talks were continuing. Privately, the president was seething. According to a piece written by Dan Day and circulated by the National Newspaper Publishers Association (NNPA), the African American news service, "President Johnson almost blew a fuse" when he learned of King's "recent expedition into the field of foreign policy." The president was "particularly upset because the president of the Southern Christian Leadership Conference projected his civil rights image into the controversy over U.S. policy in South Vietnam." The piece attributed its information to "sources close to the White House."[29]

To attempt damage control the administration arranged a private meeting between King and Arthur Goldberg, U.S. ambassador to the United Nations, on September 10. King was told that peace was within reach and any talk of unilateral U.S. reductions in force would encourage the other side to hold out for an even better deal.[30]

The pressure from Johnson and the talk with Goldberg shook King's confidence and resolve. King decided to ease back on his explicitly political and diplomatic antiwar activity but to continue to speak out against the war as a minister of the gospel. King's invocation of his status as a minister in his campaign against violence in the Vietnam War added a curious and revealing element to his crusade. As an individual—particularly one who had won the Nobel Peace Prize—with gifts of oratory and persuasion, and as a renowned civil rights leader, King could and ultimately did wield enormous influence in the debate swirling around U.S. involvement in Vietnam. In this statement, however, he explicitly invoked his calling as a minister of the gospel, infusing his cause with the aura of a divine calling and thereby lending authority to his moral pronouncements. He seemed to be deliberately taking on a prophetic role in which he would open himself for use as a vessel of God to speak out against evil. King's avowal of his status as God's mouthpiece undoubtedly rested on a foundation of sincere conviction. It also was a natural outgrowth of his deep roots in the African American church.[31]

Whatever the moral underpinnings of King's stance against the war, it represented a striking departure from the focus of most previous civil rights leaders, which almost always had remained tightly trained on issues directly affecting African Americans. Not only did King venture away from this long-established model of propriety, but he persisted in his opposition to the war even when it was clear that this threatened to erode his influence in national domestic policy.[32]

For this he was subjected to considerable criticism even from old friends. Carl Rowan, a prominent African American who was both a columnist and a Washington insider with strong ties to well-placed political figures, recalled that he had cautioned his friend King to cool his antiwar rhetoric, which Rowan believed was threatening the momentum of the civil rights movement. Rowan was sympathetic with King. He had also earned the ire of LBJ, who earlier had made him head of the USIA. After leaving that post, Rowan had used his syndicated column to criticize America's role in Vietnam. This earned him a place on the list of people no longer welcome at the White House.

In late September *Jet* reported that Senator Thomas J. Dodd, the Connecticut Democrat, had accused King on the Senate floor of meddling in foreign policy, suggesting that King was dabbling in matters well beyond the limits of his competence. Dodd's condescending criticism brought a swift rebuttal from another senator, Stephen Young of Ohio, who noted sardonically that Dodd, who had attended only one of thirteen recent meetings of the Senate Foreign Relations Committee, on which he sat, could hardly claim superior experience to King in matters of foreign affairs.[34]

The growing tension between King and other leading members of the civil rights coalition was evident during an outing on the Potomac River. On board the presidential yacht *Honey Fitz*, at a gathering of civil rights leaders and administration figures led by Vice President Hubert Humphrey, a potentially awkward moment occurred when someone raised the subject of King's recent peace initiatives. With King himself in attendance, Whitney Young stepped into the discussion and pointedly asserted that "plenty needed to be done at home by civil rights organizations before going overseas." The account of the episode in *Jet* magazine reported that Young's bluntly expressed view was "apparently a majority view since the conversation shifted to domestic issues."[35]

A few weeks later the *Afro-American* described how Whitney Young had spoken out on the King controversy, parsing his comments carefully to reinforce the point he had made on the *Honey Fitz* but also giving King some wiggle room. During a news conference before a speech at the Iowa State Educational Association convention, Young had asserted that civil rights organizations should not be embroiled in the growing antiwar movement. However, civil rights leaders have the right to speak out as individuals so long as they make clear they are speaking "as citizens" and not as civil rights spokesmen. "When the two are tied together," said Young, "it does a disservice to civil rights."[36]

Soon King began to find some support in the black press, usually in defense of his right to dissent from administration policy. The *Afro-American* wrote editorially: "King may be right about Vietnam, and he may be wrong. However, he had every right to speak out on the issue." The piece noted accusations that King's comments threatened to weaken support for the civil rights movement. The paper dismissed such charges as an "expression of a hostility to King that probably existed long before he made his statements." Then the editorial suggested that the strong criticisms may have been nothing more than attempts to weaken King by opponents happy for a chance to mount "a flanking attack" designed to reduce his "effectiveness in other areas."[37]

After Senator Jacob K. Javits, a long-time friend of the movement for black rights, delivered "a broadside against civil rights leaders who dared to ventilate their views about the war in Vietnam," the *Defender* weighed in with a lengthy editorial asserting King's freedom of expression. The tone of the piece was measured outrage: "The right to express oneself on issues of national concern apparently does not extend to Negro citizens. The American black man, it seems, must limit his activity to a narrow sphere of racial grievances beyond which he becomes suspect and intolerable." The editorial chided Javits for being blind to the double standard implicit in his comments, since he apparently saw "no impropriety in the opposition voiced by some members of Congress" to the war.

Having said all that, the *Defender* added a cautionary note: "For the civil rights movement, as an entity, to veer toward the crisis in Vietnam would result in much needed energy being siphoned away from our main objective."[38]

After a few months King quietly abandoned his efforts to initiate negotiations to end the war. The simple fact was his peace initiatives had gone nowhere. Civil rights organizations, including his own SCLC, were decidedly cool to his proposals. The political and diplomatic pressure from the White House and Ambassador Goldberg had also made their mark. Stung by the largely negative response to his efforts and isolated within the civil rights fraternity, even within his own SCLC, King backpedaled and wearily abandoned his peace feeler. "I really don't have the strength to fight this issue and keep my civil rights fight going," he confessed to his aides. A bug planted by the FBI duly recorded his dispirited words. Two years later, referring to his abortive peace efforts, he told his staff self-deprecatingly: "My name then wouldn't have been written in any book called 'Profiles in Courage.'"[39]

For its part the administration largely ignored the antiwar position of King and other black leaders in its public statements, but the drift of several key civil rights leaders toward open opposition to U.S. policy in Vietnam privately worried some within the White House. In November 1965 one White House aide voiced his concern in a memo to Bill Moyers: "I am increasingly concerned over the involvement of the civil rights groups with the anti-Vietnam demonstrators. . . . Negro leadership involvement with the anti-Vietnam groups will set their progress back substantially."[40]

Three days later the same aide wrote to Moyers again, this time suggesting that the prominent labor leader Walter Reuther "talk turkey" with King to get him back in the fold on the administration's Vietnam policy. Recent polling numbers gave the staffer reason for alarm. The number of Americans who believed that the United States should get out of Vietnam immediately had risen sharply, to 28 percent from just 8 to 13 percent in recent surveys. When the pollster analyzed the latest poll's respondents by race, he discovered that most of those who wanted the United States to "get out now" from Vietnam were blacks, low-income people (many also black), and young females. The memo writer then argued that it was "in the Negroes' interest . . . to disassociate from the anti-Vietnam movement." To do otherwise, the aide reasoned, would alienate those in the population blacks needed most, saying: "For the civil rights groups to join the anti-Vietnam demonstrations will severely hurt their cause." Despite a desire within the administration to reverse the slippage in black support for the war, blacks continued to view it negatively. Opinion polls showed that, by 1969, a majority of blacks opposed the war and 80 percent believed that the war had been a mistake.[41]

Given the heavy and disproportionate black casualties in Vietnam between 1965 and 1967, which were widely and frequently reported in the black press as the war was escalating, and the perceived conflict of the war with domestic programs advantageous to African Americans, it should not be surprising that support for the war among blacks dropped as steadily and decisively as it did. In the five years between May 1965 and April 1970, Gallup polling data show that support for the war among black men fell from 55 percent to 27 percent, while among white men the decline was from 58 percent to 41 percent, a much less severe drop. Among black women, support fell from 31 percent to 19 percent, compared with a drop from 48 percent to 30 percent among white women. The drop for black women was less severe than that for white women, but support among black women was much weaker to begin with.[42]

Though King ultimately dropped his peace initiative, it substantially increased his prominence in the growing peace movement. As important, his abandonment of the traditional single-issue focus of the civil rights movement was a portent of more ideological experimentation to come. In early 1966, following King's brief antiwar offensive of the year before, the youthful iconoclasts in SNCC decided to go public with an official ringing denunciation of U.S. involvement in Vietnam. The statement skewered the U.S. government for failing to guarantee "the freedom of oppressed citizens" and said that the crusade in Vietnam was "a hypocritical mask behind which" the United States "quashes liberation movements."[43]

The SNCC position was particularly dangerous because it threatened the movement's cohesiveness, because it was so disquieting to many of the civil rights struggle's less militant elders. It also risked offending the white authority structure it was challenging.

King was not entirely alone within the SCLC in his dissent on the war. During 1966 James Bevel continued to press King and the others within the organization to move toward an open disavowal of U.S. policy in Vietnam. He was increasingly distressed about the violence in Vietnam, which was directed against Asian peasants by a powerful white nation. Bevel was pushing King in the direction he was already heading, accelerating King's movement toward a complete break with the Johnson administration over Vietnam.[44]

When the SCLC finally took a stand on the war, it undoubtedly helped King move toward a resolution of his dilemma. Perhaps SCLC members were emboldened by the SNCC move, goaded by Bevel, shamed or inspired into action by the example of their leader, or finally galvanized to act by the impact of the escalating war on the prospects of the Great Society. King's SCLC ended its annual meeting in Miami in April 1966 by taking what the *Afro-American* characterized as "a tersely worded and indignant slap at the official U.S. position in Vietnam." The resolution it adopted declared that "the immorality and tragic absurdity" of the American stance in Vietnam "is revealed by the necessity to protect our [citizens] from the [Vietnamese] population and army we were told were our cherished allies and toward whom we are benefactors." Referring to the succession of military juntas in Vietnam, the resolution stated, "American policy has become imprisoned in the destiny of the military oligarchy."

Then the resolution turned to what ultimately would move so many concerned African Americans to oppose the war. The resolution charged that the war was wreaking havoc with the domestic aspirations of blacks, draining the economy, and moving the Great Society to the top of "the casualty lists of the conflict." The SCLC said that, "as an organization committed to nonviolence," it "must condemn this war on the grounds that war is not the way to solve social problems."[45]

King himself punctuated the resolution with a statement urging the president to reconsider the involvement of the United States in the Southeast Asian war. "It is imperative to end a war that has played havoc on our domestic destinies," King said. "Our first consideration is still civil rights."[46]

The SCLC resolution developed a theme at the heart of the moral argument against the war and for the validity of the civil rights movement. Both were rooted in the view that America was a land built on a love of liberty. King, in his "Letter from Birmingham Jail," had argued from this principle in defending African Americans' pursuit of civil rights: "We will reach the goal of freedom in Birmingham and all over the nation, because the goal of America is freedom. Abused and scorned though we may be, our destiny is tied up with America's destiny." And then he said: "We will win our freedom because the sacred heritage of our nation and the eternal will of God are embodied in our echoing demands."[47]

The moral underpinnings of the civil rights movement became, for a growing number of black leaders, an argument for opposing the war, because the war was both denying Vietnamese the freedom to choose their own destiny and undermining the progress achieved in the United States to secure the civil rights of black Americans.

Many civil rights leaders were not yet prepared to accept the moral connection, which King and others saw, between the war in Vietnam and the black struggle in America. With the SCLC's resolution the civil rights movement was now in disarray. King and his organization, along with the firebrands at SNCC, whose manifesto King quietly supported, soon to be joined by CORE, were now positioned firmly to the left of the mainstream civil rights organizations and their respective leaders. An ideological and generational gulf opened between the two clusters of groups, but the defining line between them was where they stood on the war. Administration policy in Vietnam, not just racial realities in America, was allowed to become a salient part of what defined alliances and loyalties within a movement that clearly was at odds with itself.[48]

The contour of these fissures was plainly visible when Johnson assembled a White House conference, "To Fulfill These Rights," in early June 1966. Twenty-four hundred people attended the session, but SNCC boycotted it, an absence certainly unlamented by the president. While Johnson's contempt for the young Turks at SNCC was understandable, his undisguised annoyance with Martin Luther King led the president into an astonishingly inept effort to exclude King from the conference. First, King was left off the list of invitees. Then, in the unkindest cut of all, Johnson's aides suggested King was disloyal, citing FBI reports identifying the civil rights leader as a subversive. However, the president finally invited King after many leading figures in the movement informed Johnson that no one would attend if King was not invited.[49]

Once the conclave assembled, the president pointedly ignored King, whose aides were urging him to walk out of the conference to protest what seemed to be Johnson's snubbing of King. King's allies at the SCLC were not surprised by LBJ's behavior toward King. Andrew Young, a King loyalist, told an interviewer that the Johnson administration had been doing everything it could to bring the civil rights leader back into line, including bringing black editors together to encourage them to oppose King's antiwar position and doing the same with African American clergy.[50]

While the black press never mentioned administration pressures on editors to oppose King's antiwar views, the administration's efforts to tamp down opposition were only thinly disguised. LBJ's efforts to hush King and secure the support of other civil rights leaders for the administration's policies were partially successful—at least temporarily. Most of King's colleagues at the White House meeting reacted lukewarmly or with hostility to anyone attempting to express disapproval of the war in Vietnam. Whitney Young, for example, was colorful and blunt in his support of LBJ, telling the press, "The Negro was more concerned about the rat at night and the job in the morning than they are about Vietnam." Vice President Hubert Humphrey brought the delegates to their feet with a rousing keynote address that called on all sections of American society to do more to advance the cause of civil rights. Humphrey also scolded black extremists for seeking separation and exclusion as the path to racial justice.[51]

The president made an unscheduled appearance to introduce U.S. Solicitor General Thurgood Marshall, who then delivered an enthusiastic endorsement of LBJ's leadership in civil rights reforms. Johnson's appearance was met with frequent applause and even a standing ovation. Harry C. McPherson, from the president's staff, was there, along with "thirty observers," as he cryptically identified them, and reported later to LBJ that all had pronounced the response of the delegates "unanimously favorable." This assessment conveniently ignored the active minority dissent from the antiwar group in attendance.[52] An antiwar resolution introduced in committee at the meeting by CORE's recently elected head, Floyd McKissick, was easily defeated, maintaining a semblance of ideological solidarity between black leaders and Johnson.[53]

In an oddity of scheduling at the *Afro-American*, an editorial was written days before the White House conference was held on June 1 and 2 but was published two days after the session closed. The editorial's warnings about the negative consequences of the unseemly ideological jockeying that could mar the meeting sounded eerily prescient after the event had ended and participants—and readers—could contemplate the significance of what had just transpired.

The piece spoke of the dangers to the civil rights movement of dissension. The struggle to advance human rights, said the editorial, was "far too important to be overshadowed by the action of any individual or individuals who for reasons they deem right and proper, choose not to participate, but to stand outside and protest."

After defending the right to disagree in a movement founded on dissent, the editorial slapped SNCC's wrist for dragging Vietnam into a conference devoted to domestic issues and for sullying the reputation of a president who had done so much to advance the cause of equality. As the editorial closed, it recognized the imperfections of the conference's format: "It is not perfect—there should have been provision for freer discussions, a more representative sampling of people—but it will be worthwhile, it will serve to hasten the day when the walls finally come tumbling down."[54]

The *Defender* also devoted an editorial to the conference and did its utmost to paper over the differences that were exposed by the ideological clashes at the meeting and by the absence of those who had elected to boycott it. The editorial applauded the "impressive consensus" emerging from the conference despite intimations of dissension beforehand. The one sour note was the abortive effort of McKissick to get his antiwar resolution passed. As the editorial reported it, the McKissick proposal "rested on the premise that money needed to implement the civil rights program is being dissipated on the war in Vietnam." Acknowledging that "funds for a number of highly essential domestic programs have been drastically curtailed," the piece argued that the cuts had been made because of the "stern necessity of a conflict to which the United States is committed by word of honor and by preventive strategy."[55]

Many delegates who voted resoundingly against McKissick's resolution ultimately would find themselves reluctantly compelled to oppose the war precisely for the reason the resolution cited. But in the early summer of 1966 many still could not bring themselves to oppose their president on the war, which they—and the *Defender* editorial—already recognized was forcing cuts in funding for key Great Society programs.

Shortly after the White House meeting ended, a white gunman shot and wounded James Meredith as he trudged along a roadway crossing from Tennessee into Mississippi. He was marching to promote black voter registration. After the shooting the heads of the major civil rights organizations patched up their differences and converged on Memphis to continue the march. However, what began as a demonstration of unity soon exposed a fault line in the movement. A pronounced militancy and contempt for the passivity of King's doctrine of nonviolence surfaced in the frequent and sharp debates between King and the fiery proponents of black power.

During the march the phrase became part of the common coin of the movement. At a rally Stokely Carmichael, who had just been released after spending several hours in jail following an arrest for trespassing, spoke to the crowd of marchers from the back of a flatbed truck. He was clearly agitated and told the crowd, "This is the twenty-seventh time that I've been arrested. I ain't going to jail no more. The only way we gonna stop them white men from whuppin' us is to take over. What we gonna start sayin' now is Black Power!" Soon he was leading the aroused crowd in a raucous chant. He would yell, "What do you want?" And the crowd would shout back, "Black Power!" With each repetition the chant grew louder, more feverish. An emerging ideology had its name and militancy had its mantra.[56]

The next day, at another rally during the march, King pushed his way through an adoring crowd to a makeshift platform, clambered up on the stage, and addressed the crowd. He assailed SNCC's infatuation with violence and black power and said the only way to conquer the enemies of black Americans was to meet their hate with love, their violence with patient suffering. The crowd began responding to King, calling out encouragement, hoarsely giving its adoring assent. "Listen, listen," people said. "Speak on," they urged, and averred, "Can't he talk, Lord, can't he talk."

The SNCC members in the crowd were not among his vocal supporters. One white civil rights worker remembered how odd and unsettling it was to hear a SNCC worker mock King as "Gee-zuz" and "de Lawd" when most blacks still idolized the charismatic King. From the edge of the crowd a SNCC member yelled derisively, "Blessed Jesus!" No one laughed, and some in the crowd, taking his words at face value, seemed to approve of this adoration.[57]

One SNCC leader tried to maintain a common purpose with King. John Lewis, sensing King's isolation from SNCC members, who were now enamored with their heady new direction, sought to become the voice of unity, bringing his associates in SNCC back into the fold of nonviolence. Lewis climbed onto a wobbly box and began speaking: "Fellow freedom fighters, the whole man must say no nonviolently, his entire Christian spirit must say no to this evil and vicious system." As he spoke, his listeners slowly melted away. His style was too mild, his message lacked punch, and his speech fizzled. Lewis sensed his moment had passed. A month later, on June 25, 1966, a headline on the front page of the *New York Times* read "Lewis Quits SNCC, Shuns Black Power."[58]

The departure of Lewis and the ascendancy of Stokely Carmichael at SNCC marked the formal end of the organization's adherence to King's model of nonviolent protest, which was anchored in religious faith. Later Carmichael would remember the rift this way: "[We] had one simple definition that separated us. He saw nonviolence as a principle, which means it had to be used at all times, under all conditions. I saw it as a tactic. If it was working, I would use it; if it wasn't working, I'm picking up guns because I want my freedom by any means necessary."[59] Carmichael soon abandoned nonviolence even as a tactic; it just did not seem to work, so far as he was concerned.

White Americans who viewed the emergence of black power warily could take comfort only temporarily in the apparent split in the ranks of black radicals. The militant wing of the civil rights movement was just beginning to find its unsettling voice. A young radical expressed the growing impatience of SNCC with the stodgy moderation of King: "It's not important who's got the Bible. It's important who's got the guns."[60]

The ascendancy of black power loosened the movement's already weakening grip on the heart and purse strings of the liberal white establishment. It also provided convenient cover to former champions of civil rights in high places who had already been alienated by the more extreme antiwar sentiments of the new radicalism and were looking for an excuse to distance themselves from the cause. Black power was altering the conversation between liberalism and black activism and threatened to eclipse the dialog entirely.

Black power was also driving a wedge between the black civil rights organizations and their high-profile leaders. This time the issue was civil rights protest tactics, not the war, and it was dividing those committed to nonviolence and moderation and those crackling with the newfound militancy of SNCC and CORE.

When escalating urban violence was the most vivid language of protest during the long, hot summers, and the black power movement was advocating its own brand of uncompromising militancy, moderates were seeking a way to regain the initiative in the struggle for the soul of the civil rights movement.

The advent of the black power movement as an alternative to the traditional civil rights movement, the goal of which was to assimilate and integrate, was evidence for some that the civil rights movement had lost momentum and purpose. To advocates of black power, as well as its opponents, the swift ascendancy of the new model of black awareness and pride as the basis for the realization of African American dreams was an indication that the traditional movement was losing its hold on the hearts and minds of black Americans, especially the young.

Black power was, in effect, seeking to reverse the ideological direction of the civil rights movement by affirming the distinction between black and white rather than seeking to escape or ignore it. Color blindness had to give way to an intense color consciousness. Blackness was to be celebrated, not blurred into a kind of gray assimilation. Liberalism, both the ally and ideological home of the moderate civil rights organizations, sought to resolve the dilemma of racial discrimination by absorbing black Americans into a predominately white society with laws protecting the rights of African Americans and gradually breaking down old barriers between the races. Black power sought to empower black Americans with a valuation of their own cultural distinctiveness that would no longer rely on the goodwill or good intentions of whites but would itself define the terms of black life in America.

Carmichael said essentially the same thing—and bluntly—when he wrote: "Whites will not see that I, for example, as a person oppressed because of my blackness, have common cause with other blacks who are oppressed because of blackness. . . . It must be the oppressed to whom SNCC addresses itself primarily, not to friends from the oppressing group." A UPI piece about Carmichael in the *Baltimore Afro-American* drew on an interview with him as well as an essay by him in which he expounded on what was, in effect, the organizational corollary of his views. As he told the UPI reporter, civil rights organizations should be "black led, black controlled and black dominated."[61]

Black power was an affirmation of the value of being black, a recognition of the particular history of black Americans, a foundation upon which to build pride—and a concession to the reality that race was an inescapable category in differentiating the elements of American society. Better, then, for blacks to make race the basis of self-affirmation and militant action. So appealing was this perspective that within a relatively short time the influence of black power's model of cultural pride and black initiative would become widespread, even normative, among African Americans.[62]

A *Time*-Louis Harris poll published in 1970 found that black pride was "solidly entrenched." Eighty-five percent strongly supported black studies programs as "an important sign of black identity and pride." Almost

60 percent of young blacks and those in the upper-middle and upper classes supported the wave of interest in African culture. The prevailing social and political system needed complete revamping, the survey found. Only 17 percent thought they could ever rely on the federal government to establish and defend their rights. Not surprisingly, values of assertiveness and militancy in pushing for full civil rights were valued far more than notions of cooperation and understanding between blacks and whites. A majority continued to believe that civil rights could be secured without violence, though the size of the majority was shrinking, especially among blacks younger than fifty.[63]

Younger blacks were growing increasingly impatient with the pleas of civil rights leaders and with most voices within the black press, who continued to urge that social justice could best be achieved by nonviolent protest. When Martin Luther King and others championed nonviolence, the more militant black activists viewed the tactic as weak and ineffectual. When the white liberal establishment warmly embraced nonviolence as the appropriate way for African Americans to seek the fulfillment of their aspirations for full civil rights, many blacks saw hypocrisy, given the nation's resort to violence to secure its purposes in Vietnam. Nonviolence also seemed like a suspiciously convenient way for the white power structure to stifle the demands of black Americans and curb their more extreme expressions of disaffection.

With its emphasis on blackness as well as the exercise of power, black power also came to embody a uniformly unfavorable interpretation of the Vietnam War, which was seen as an expression of America's fundamental racism, a genocidal assault on a nation of peasants struggling to rid themselves of the vestiges of white colonialism. A corollary to this point of view was the effort to create an identification of American blacks with the people of color in Vietnam. One SNCC field worker was quoted as saying, "You know, I just saw one of those Vietcong guerrillas on TV. He was dark-skinned, ragged, poor and angry. I swear, he looked just like one of us."[64]

The racial affinity of black Americans with the Vietnamese, both friend and foe, was complicated. In an article in the November 1965 issue of *Ebony*, Simeon Booker described the strange predicament of black soldiers who found themselves in Vietnam, a society of color, facing racial blandishments from Vietnamese bar girls. The women "point to their skin as a sign of brotherhood in the worldwide order of darker people," while the radio carries communist propaganda praising the black soldiers in Vietnam for the "courage of the revolt back home." According to Booker, the black soldiers are "fully integrated GIs" and stubbornly "resist Viet Cong claims of brotherhood," even though they hear from home about the racial violence and injustice that still plague American society.[65]

The Vietcong frequently sought to exploit black discontent with the state of race relations in the United States. On Christmas Day 1967 the first of a batch of leaflets was found attached to a log raft floating down a river near the base camp of a battalion attached to the Seventh Marines, 20 percent of whom were African Americans. The leaflet said: "Colored American servicemen: Twenty million fellow countrymen of yours in the U.S.A. are being abused, oppressed, exploited, manhandled, murdered by racist authorities." The underlying theme was the commonality of the experiences of American blacks and the Vietcong, both groups presumably victims of U.S. racist oppression. The crude attempt to demoralize black marines and induce them to surrender to their communist brothers fizzled. Typical was the response of Corporal Tommy C. Taylor, twenty-four, of Jacksonville, Florida, reported in *Jet* magazine: "Personally, I think it's a waste of ink and paper." Private First Class Tyrone Brown, twenty, of Dixon, Illinois, agreed: "Our willpower is too strong. As long as I have the willpower to fight, I shall keep on fighting for my country."[66]

As leaders of the civil rights movement were staking out positions on the Vietnam War, black Americans generally were displaying notably weaker support for the war than the general population, just as they had tended to be less caught up in patriotic fervor during foreign wars as far back as the Mexican War in 1846 and including all the major wars of the twentieth century. Black Americans tended to identify nineteenth-century expansionism with slavery and to resent their own status as second-class citizens as the United States conducted foreign crusades in the twentieth century to support liberty and democracy for other peoples.[67]

African Americans tended to be sympathetic with the revolutionary aspirations of third world countries as colonial systems were crumbling and nationalism was asserting itself in midcentury. This was no less true when the United States was militarily involved in resisting these liberationist movements in the interests of containing communism. What's more, many black Americans felt alienated from the foreign policy goals of their country when their own domestic rights and aspirations as citizens still were not being met.

Martin Luther King was about to rattle much of the black press and many of the older and more conservative African American civil rights leaders by publicly announcing his solidarity with the international liberation movement and breaking openly with the Johnson administration over its policy in Vietnam.

5

Martin Luther King Jr. and the Globalization of Black Protest

A time comes when silence is betrayal.—Martin Luther King Jr., Riverside Church, April 4, 1967

Martin Luther King Jr. had been conflicted for some time about how directly he should challenge American policy in Vietnam. For two years he had actively supported efforts to find a peace that could be secured within the framework of U.S. regional interests through negotiations. But such negotiations would have legitimized those interests and implicitly sanctioned the resort to violence to protect them. This, despite private feelings that went much deeper, that loathed militarism itself, that viewed violence as a sin against humanity, and that had come to hold the United States, not its enemies, responsible for the bloodshed in Vietnam. He knew that he had to speak out against the war and call for America to end it.

King was also feeling the tug of a larger mission, a broader constituency. Just a little over a year before his death, he told his Atlanta congregation: "Our loyalties must transcend our race, our tribe, our class, our nation. This means we must develop a world perspective."[1] It was no longer sufficient to isolate the predicament of American blacks from the struggle of people of color in third world countries aspiring to shake off the yoke of oppression. King felt compelled to throw his lot in with all those who were part of a worldwide tide of revolution that was seeking liberation from the vestiges of white domination. Among those oppressed peoples he now counted the people of Vietnam.

With the civil rights consensus showing signs of disrepair, if not total breakdown, King was less encumbered by the burden of maintaining whatever caution he had displayed in spelling out his opposition to the Vietnam War. For almost two years associates within the civil rights leadership who were opposed to the war had been urging King to speak out with greater urgency. James Bevel, his close aide in the Southern Christian Leadership Conference (SCLC), had been the most persistent in making this pitch.

Among leaders in the African American press few would encourage King to break openly with the Johnson administration on Vietnam. An exception was Dr. Carlton B. Goodlett, publisher of the *Sun-Reporter* in San Francisco. Goodlett—a child psychologist with a doctorate from Berkeley and a pediatrician who earned his MD at Meharry, as well as a newspaperman—had been active in the international peace movement. He was an official of the World Peace Council and through his editorials in the *Sun-Reporter*, as well as through his affiliation with the council, he was a tireless opponent of the war in Vietnam, making his small paper's one of the earliest and most consistent antiwar voices among African American newspapers. For some time Goodlett had been pleading with King to take a strong, unequivocal stand against the war.[2]

King needed a catalyst that would bring him to act decisively on his developing vision. It turned out to be a magazine article, "The Children of Vietnam," in the January 1967 issue of *Ramparts* magazine. An SCLC staffer, Bernard S. Lee, and Coretta Scott King, who were vacationing with King in Jamaica, had read the *Ramparts* article and left it lying on the porch of the house where they were staying. King saw the magazine, began leafing through it, and was stunned and sickened to see the explicit color photographs accompanying the article. The pictures showed Vietnamese children who had suffered severe burns during a napalm attack by American jets. The pictures so unsettled King that he decided to step up his attacks on the war in Vietnam and take on the Johnson administration directly.[3]

In a series of crucial statements in early 1967, he began shedding all pretense of affinity with the Johnson administration and spoke out forthrightly and aggressively about the war.

On February 25 he gave a speech to the Nation Institute in Los Angeles that he titled "The Casualties of the War in Vietnam." He called the conflict "a war that mutilates the conscience" because of its wanton toll. But the real casualties of the brutal war were "casualties of principles and values," he said, among them, the moral stature of the United States, the self-determination of the

Vietnamese, and, more significantly for the aspirations of American blacks, the principles of domestic social reform. The *New York Amsterdam News* devoted two lengthy features, reproducing the full text of the speech and discussing King's increasingly outspoken position on what the paper called "this highly controversial subject."[4]

On March 25, 1967, King marched beside Dr. Benjamin Spock, leading a crowd of five thousand peace demonstrators in Chicago. Then King addressed the crowd, pressing his attack on the war: "We are committing atrocities equal to any perpetuated by the Viet Cong. The bombs in Vietnam explode at home—they destroy the dream and possibility for a decent America." He urged the crowd to "combine the fervor of the civil rights movement with the peace movement. We must demonstrate, teach and preach until the very foundations of our nation shake."[5]

According to an account of the march in the *Afro-American*, marchers carried the obligatory placards proclaiming "Make Love, Not War." Another sign called the president "Blood Finger Johnson." But one introduced a point much closer to King's heart: "Make War on Poverty, Not People." The *Afro-American* also reported that a small group of hecklers was present, chanting "We want white power" and displaying signs reading "Who's afraid of the draft?" and "Martin Luther Coon is a Commie."[6]

Jet magazine carried a picture of the Chicago march that showed King and Spock leading the parade, with a large banner behind them proclaiming "Men are not our enemies. If we kill men, with whom shall we live?" Beneath the message was a translation in Vietnamese. The sign evoked a sense of the human connection between Americans and Vietnamese and implied the wan hope that they might stop killing each other and live together in peace. *Jet*'s caption under the photo said the "crowd was orderly despite heckling."[7] The bland observation seemed to downplay the hostility of the counterdemonstrators and the racist vitriol reported in the *Afro-American*'s account.

At an early morning press conference on April 4 at the Overseas Press Club, King told the assembled reporters that he would urge all those who were against the war to avoid military service. He further called for clergymen, who were already exempt from the draft, to give up their exemption and seek status as conscientious objectors. He condemned the racism of the war, which was consuming a disproportionate number of black Americans. He called for teach-ins and preach-ins to "awaken the conscience of the nation" to the evils of the Vietnam War.[8]

These public statements were just a tune-up for what would be King's most detailed and devastating statement opposing the war in Vietnam. On the evening of April 4 he took the pulpit of Riverside Church in New York City to address an overflow crowd on the subject of the war in Vietnam. Although he had been speaking out on the war intermittently for more than a year, he would later recall his speech at the New York church as the time "when I first made public my opposition to my government's policy."[9]

"I come to this magnificent house of worship because my conscience leaves me no other choice," he began. As he laid the foundation for his indictment of U.S. policy in Vietnam, he gave several reasons for his stand. At the top of the list was seeing the poverty program, so full of promise for poor blacks and whites alike, "broken and eviscerated as if it were some idle political plaything of a society gone mad on war." The war was taking a disproportionate toll of the sons and husbands and brothers of poor black Americans. In addition, King noted the horrible spectacle of violence in the inner-city neighborhoods in the United States. Then he uttered perhaps the most famous line in his speech: "I could never again raise my voice against the violence of the oppressed in the ghettos without having first spoken clearly to the greatest purveyor of violence in the world today—my own government." He defended his vocal opposition to the war as an extension of the motto of the SCLC adopted in 1957: "To save the soul of America." To speak of Vietnam was to locate part of what had so debilitated the nation. "If America's soul becomes totally poisoned," said King, "part of the autopsy must read Vietnam."

King also cited the Nobel Peace Prize as a commission given to him to redouble his efforts for "the brotherhood of man." But even more fundamentally, he argued that his "commitment to the ministry of Jesus Christ" compelled him to speak out against the war and on behalf of all whom the war was harming: "Beyond the calling of race or nation or creed is this vocation of sonship and brotherhood, and because I believe that the Father is deeply concerned especially for his suffering and helpless and outcast children, I come tonight to speak for them."

In his speech King reviewed the tortured history of America's involvement in Vietnam, questioning both its geopolitical logic and its morality. He challenged the United States to abandon its support of a discredited imperialism and get on the right side of the world's liberation movements: "All over the globe men are revolting against the old systems of exploitation and oppression and out of the wombs of a frail world new systems of justice and equality are being born. The shirtless and barefoot people of the land are rising up as never before. . . . We in the West must support these revolutions."[10]

With the Riverside Church sermon King dramatically—and publicly—altered fundamentally the political tilt of his campaign for black rights, assuming an overtly adversarial posture in dealing with the national government. No longer would he speak and act in ways that assumed a partnership with the Johnson administration.

His fulminations over Vietnam rang with the moral outrage of an Old Testament prophet. Cooperation with the Johnson administration because of compatible domestic policy goals gave way to confrontation, prompted by King's perception of the fundamental solidarity between oppressed U.S. blacks and the racially oppressed people of color in emerging countries around the world, including Vietnam.[11]

By expressing solidarity with the revolutionary tide that was sweeping through the world of color outside the United States, King globalized the black struggle. This was a challenge to the projection of U.S. power in places like Vietnam where, in King's view, the United States was perpetuating the oppression of colonialism and stifling a local revolution under the guise of fighting communism. While King retained his image as the most important leader at the center of what had become a somewhat fractious domestic civil rights movement, the support he enjoyed was considerably shaken by the Riverside Church speech.

It shattered his relationship with the Johnson administration. If King had any bridges to the White House still standing before his address, they were burned beyond saving by his indictment of America's role in the war. Lyndon Johnson felt betrayed. It hurt him that, despite all he had done to advance the cause of civil rights, its leading spokesman would turn on the president and urge other blacks to oppose him.[12]

Overnight King transformed his into the most audible voice opposing the war and became the most visible opponent of U.S. actions in Vietnam. His national stature as a revered civil rights leader and his international prestige as winner of the Nobel Peace Prize placed him in the forefront of the antiwar movement. At the same time the linkage he saw between America's growing involvement in the war and the dwindling national commitment to social justice made King's position a vital part of action for social reform. By the time of the Riverside Church speech, King had concluded that the war had to be stopped if domestic reform was to go forward.

By taking his stand, King was threatening to create a fundamental realignment of the support structure upon which his cause had historically depended. He was isolating himself from many of his allies in the white political power structure, many of whom were bewildered and angry at the sheer vehemence of his denunciation of an administration that had accomplished so much for African Americans. At the same time he was unnerving many key moderate black leaders who wanted him to continue to supply the civil rights movement with single-minded inspiration and to avoid unnecessarily antagonizing the power elite. He also found himself at odds with many of the powerhouses in the black press.

In early April, during the same week as King's speech in the Riverside Church, his SCLC finally joined its leader in "bitterly condemning the Vietnam War." The day after the speech, the *Baltimore Afro-American* reported the story on its front page in a piece headlined "Dr. King Declares War on Viet War." King himself presided over the SCLC meeting. In what the paper called "a surprise change of policy," the SCLC board adopted a resolution that swaggered with "all the air of militancy of CORE-SNCC, and condemned the United States' war efforts in Vietnam." The statement repudiated the war, calling it "morally unjust" and committed the organization to fight "to end the war." The resolution noted that it was becoming tougher for the civil rights group to advocate "non-violence at home while our nation is practicing the very essence of violence" in Vietnam. Even as it adopted King's antiwar commitment, the SCLC recognized the possibility that King's activities could jeopardize the backing of crucial financial supporters and felt obliged to enclose with its fund-raising solicitations a defense of King's right to dissent.[13]

On April 15 King was back in New York City, this time to address a huge peace rally outside the United Nations building. The rally drew a crowd that was estimated at between 100,000 and 250,000, the largest peace demonstration the city had ever seen. On the dais was Spock, who lent his air of paternal indulgence to the proceedings. Also on the platform was Stokely Carmichael, whom King now regarded suspiciously as a rival for the hearts of the younger generation of blacks. King had agreed to speak at the rally with the understanding that Carmichael was not going to speak. King was not interested in lending his prestige to the volatile and charismatic Carmichael. Despite their generally congenial personal relationship, King still preferred to keep Carmichael at arm's length in public to maintain a distinction between their incompatible tactics of protest.

After King spoke, denouncing American actions in Vietnam—but sounding a little defensive, some observers thought—the rally organizers backtracked on their promise to King to keep Carmichael muzzled and gave the apostle of black power the microphone. Carmichael was anything but defensive, apparently relishing the opportunity to share the limelight with King and even to upstage him, if possible. Carmichael skewered U.S. policy in Southeast Asia, calling it "brutal and racist."[14]

The *Norfolk Journal and Guide*, in the lead story for its April 22 national edition, reported that King then antagonized the Johnson administration even further with a move whose symbolism was, at the very least, provocative. The gesture dramatized King's new internationalist perspective while surely annoying his detractors in official Washington. He presented a petition to Ralph Bunche, fellow Nobel Peace laureate and undersecretary of the United

Nations, formally protesting the U.S. role in the Vietnam War.[15] By presenting his protest against U.S. policy to the UN, rather than airing his grievances to Washington officials directly, King was explicitly stepping outside the bounds of U.S. civic protocol and identifying himself with that portion of the world community whose angry opposition to the Vietnam War often rang through the UN General Assembly and muttered down its corridors.

According to *Jet* magazine's Simeon Booker, the administration's reaction was desperate. After King went public with his break with American policy in Vietnam, White House aides feared a "runaway campaign" in response to King's appeal to young black men of draft age to boycott the war by declaring themselves conscientious objectors. Administration aides launched a frantic effort to enlist key conservative black leaders to support the president against the assault by King and other antiwar civil rights leaders.[16]

The same issue of *Jet* carried an item in Simeon Booker's "Ticker Tape U.S.A." feature section that contained a breezy assessment of the concern in the White House and the mood in the African American community that the administration's counteroffensive would find: "Administration bigs are in a tizzy about how to popularize the Vietnam war among Negroes. . . . When Martin Luther King, Jr., spoke out in New York City, he touched a sensitive nerve. Already angered by the high casualty and draft rate, Negroes are in no mood to be wooed about keeping quiet unless the Administration moves quickly on civil rights, anti-poverty . . . not to mention the reduction of Negro deaths overseas."[17]

The other black newsmagazine, *Ebony*, largely remained above the fray. It did not take an editorial position on King's antiwar views or his break with the Johnson administration on the subject. Even as the rest of the black press filled with stories and opinion pieces in the wake of King's Riverside Church address, *Ebony* said little about the controversy during that tumultuous summer. Stories about Vietnam appeared often in *Ebony*, but the story of King's opposition to the war was mentioned infrequently.

One person the White House tapped for help in its efforts to neutralize the impact of King's speech was Carl Rowan, the African American journalist and former director of the U.S. Information Agency (USIA) in the Johnson administration (1964–65), who left the agency to return to his career in journalism. George Christian, LBJ's last press secretary, sent a memo to the president on April 8, just four days after King's speech, reporting on his conversation with Rowan. According to Christian, "Everyone in the Civil Rights movement has known that King has been getting advice from a communist, and he [Rowan] is trying to firm up in his own mind whether King is still doing this. He wants to take out after King, because he thinks he has hurt the Civil Rights movement with his statements." Christian went on to report that Rowan believed "most Negroes disagree with King on this issue, but that many of the less educated will go along with him."[18]

Rowan did "take out after King" in a series of personal pleas to cool his rhetorical excess—and to watch his back politically. In one heated conversation Rowan chastised King for comparing "the greatest civil rights president in history with Hitler" and warned that, as a result, "millions of young blacks would suffer."

King replied, "It is simply a matter of conscience. I'm more than a civil rights leader; I'm a clergyman, charged with bringing Judeo-Christian ethics to bear on the sins of our time."

To which Rowan responded: "Goddam, Martin. Don't you have enough dangerous enemies without getting the Vietnam War zealots on your ass?"

"A good man never has enough enemies," King said.[19]

To those civil rights leaders who were alarmed by his newly assertive militancy, King seemed impervious to reason. He was not alone among prominent civil rights leaders in his full-throated opposition to Johnson. McKissick of the Congress of Racial Equality and Carmichael of the Student Nonviolent Coordinating Committee were already on record as opposing the administration, so Johnson aides believed they had to mount an urgent counteroffensive to forestall widespread black draft resistance. According to *Jet*, the result was at least one victory for the administration, when Whitney M. Young Jr., executive director of the National Urban League, publicly reaffirmed his support of the administration. Young announced that he "disagreed with King and said he strongly believed that issues of peace and civil rights should remain separate."[20]

The administration also received support from other stalwarts in the shrinking conservative wing of the civil rights movement such as Roy Wilkins and from a number of key figures in the black press.

The administration's behind-the-scenes efforts to control the reaction to King's controversial new position on the war served only to underscore the lack of consensus among black leaders. The diversity of points of views constituted a rich multilayered expression of black attitudes toward the Vietnam War. What made the interpretation of the war in the black press particularly interesting, provocative, and relevant was that it was rooted in the community's experience, frustrations, and aspirations. This was no less true of how the war was viewed and interpreted by the principal black leaders, whose voices were channeled and amplified by the black press.

The African American leadership establishment shared the belief that the struggle for racial justice was the central and defining issue in contemporary

American society. This issue was the principal reason for the existence of a black press and lay at the core of the commitment of every activist in the civil rights movement. And most black journalists and civil rights leaders came to believe U.S. involvement in Vietnam, in one way or another, posed a profound threat to the full attainment of the American dream for blacks.

They disagreed about the best way to attain reform. The pages of the black press resounded with black leaders squabbling about what to do and how to do it. At the heart of the debate was how to respond to the threat posed by the Vietnam War and whether accommodating the Johnson administration's Vietnam policy or opposing the war was the best way to achieve the domestic goals of the civil rights movement.

The NAACP board came out vigorously in opposition to King's new stance. The *Chicago Daily Defender* underscored the importance it attached to the debate by making the NAACP's decision the lead story in its mid-April edition. The bold headline read "NAACP Board Raps Linking of Rights with Viet Strife." and the accompanying story detailed the NAACP's sharp criticism of King for attempting "to weld the civil rights and peace movements" together.

The NAACP statement declared that the organization's board "knows that civil rights battles will have to be fought on their own merits, irrespective of the state of war or peace in the world." And the resolution concluded: "We are not a peace organization, nor a foreign policy organization; we are a civil rights organization." The *Defender*'s story characterized the statement as "a slap at the Rev. Dr. Martin Luther King." It also recognized how different leaders within the movement were lining up on different sides of the issue, with Stokely Carmichael and SNCC opposing the war and Whitney Young seeing the antiwar movement as distinct from the civil rights movement since they "had different goals."[21]

Although the *Defender* did not explicitly take sides, its sympathies lay with Wilkins and the NAACP. This is suggested in the prominent play given the story in the paper and the language of the headline, which implied that the rebuke from the revered civil rights group was tantamount to a tongue-lashing for King. The body of the story identified the NAACP as "the nation's oldest and largest civil rights organization," an invocation of venerability and importance that sharpened the group's rebuke.

King's reply also appeared in the *Defender*. He rejected the group's professed neutrality and called on "the NAACP and other critics of my position to take a forthright stand on the rightness or wrongness of the war." Although King was stung by the criticism, he obviously was not chastened by the NAACP's scolding and remained adamant in his opposition to the war, which he said was "hurting civil rights progress." He cited the "loud and raucous voices" being "raised in Congress and elsewhere suggesting that the nation cannot afford to finance a war against poverty and inequality on an expanding scale and a shooting war at the same time." King asserted, "It is perfectly clear" that the country had the resources to accomplish both goals, but the war gave civil rights opponents "the opportunity to pose a false issue." And now, King complained, his critics, including the NAACP, were "creating a non-existent issue."[22] King was telling his fellow black civil rights leaders that the war, not its critics, was hampering the progress of the struggle to achieve equal rights.

In a portion of his response to the NAACP that was not quoted in the *Defender*, he also affirmed his view of the interconnectedness of moral concerns: "I have always insisted on justice for all the world over, because justice is indivisible, and injustice anywhere is a threat to justice everywhere." This realization, he argued, compelled him to oppose the war: "I will not stand idly by when I see an unjust war taking place and fail to take a stand against it." In his reply to the board of the NAACP, King was repeating principles he had enunciated earlier in a speech at Howard University and that he traced to Gandhi. Said King: "There cannot be two consciences, one in civil and another in political life." He then quoted Gandhi: "The whole gamut of man's activities today constitutes an indivisible whole. You cannot divide life, social, economic, political, and purely religious, into watertight compartments."[23]

Wilkins was hardly impressed with King's attempts to justify his position. During a speech in New Haven, Connecticut, Wilkins launched what the *Defender* called "a bitter attack" on King and other black peace activists who had become vocal opponents of the war. Wilkins disagreed with those who defended the right of the peace advocates to merge their civil rights activities with the fight against the war. In fact, Wilkins argued, by taking up the peace issue, King was actually subordinating black aspirations to the war in Vietnam: "By involving himself in the peace movement, King indicates that Vietnam is number one on his agenda and civil rights is either number three, four, or five."

When pressed for his position on the Vietnam conflict, Wilkins refused to take the bait: "I don't speak as a hawk or a dove. I speak as a civil rights person and I don't want anyone to get in the way whether it be Martin Luther King or Lurleen Wallace" (wife of Alabama's segregationist governor; the pairing in itself was a searing rebuke to King). Then Wilkins asked: "Is it wrong for people to be patriotic? Is it wrong for us to back up our boys in the field? They're dying while we're knifing them in the back at home."[24]

In the midst of the stormy debate the noted African American psychologist Kenneth B. Clark invited the principal antagonists to his home to air their differences and to restore at least a facade of unity to the ranks of the movement's leadership. The meeting lasted a full day. Clark recalled it as "the first time I'd ever seen Martin angry." King and Wilkins went toe to toe, bringing into the room the considerable hostility that had fed the public debate between them about King's Riverside Church speech. After the emotions fueling the impassioned argument had somewhat spent themselves, Whitney Young moved between the two men, modifying his own position enough to take a mollifying middle ground. In Clark's recollection Whitney Young managed to pull King and Wilkins back to the ground they shared long enough for them to unite again behind their common goals.[25]

The brokered reconciliation of King and Wilkins hardly ended the furor about King's speech. The *Defender* reported other black leaders were piling on. Dr. J. H. Jackson, president of the National Baptist Convention, argued that "demonstrations against American foreign policy have no vital connection with America's effort to move toward self-fulfillment." Using Wilkins's metaphor, Jackson charged that antiwar demonstrators were "stabbing in the back every American soldier in Vietnam" by encouraging their enemies on the battlefield.[26]

According to the *Defender*, Senator Edward Brooke, the moderate black Republican from Massachusetts, defended the right of individual Americans to protest government policy but opposed any linkage between civil rights activities and the antiwar campaign. Brooke argued that "the civil rights movement is too important" to be entangled with other issues. The implication was that the only possible outcome of such entanglement would be to erode the status of civil rights as the preeminent issue in American society.[27]

Soon after King's speech at Riverside Church, Frank W. Mitchell Sr., publisher of the *St. Louis Argus*, responded to the debate with a series of statements that displayed a set of opinions very much in flux. At first he responded evenly to King's speech, choosing only to defend his right to speak out: "We neither condemn nor do we necessarily agree with Rev. King's controversial remarks. We respect his prerogative to express his views and the right to be heard."[28]

A week later the *Argus* publisher returned to the subject. He recognized the importance of finding a way to end the war in Vietnam so that the United States could return to the important business at home. His words had a note of optimistic contingency: "While we support the administration's efforts in Vietnam, we hopefully look forward to a just and quick conclusion of hostilities in Vietnam and an honorable peace acceptable to both countries."[29]

On May 19 Mitchell clarified what he viewed the proper end of the war to be. In the process he seemed to place himself squarely in Johnson's corner in the dispute with King: "We, who have taken the initiative in the war, must continue the initiative with defiant determination, proclaiming to an incredulous world that we are fighting the battle of freedom and of peace."[30]

But a week later the publisher of the *Argus* described the difficulties and misunderstandings inherent in grappling with the rising tide of nationalism and revolutionary stirrings in the third world countries of Asia, and he concluded wearily that the best policy might be less interference from the United States: "Perhaps, if we permitted the Vietnamese to work out their problems without U.S. involvement, it might serve as a better buffer to communistic penetration of Southeast Asia than the divided and warring two Vietnams."[31]

Meanwhile, as the *Argus* publisher's blitz of opinion pieces on Vietnam eased up, other newspapers weighed in with reactions to King's Riverside speech. The *Norfolk Journal and Guide* was horrified that King had "dropped a verbal bombshell into the ranks of Americans with his recent blistering criticism of the nation's role in the Vietnam War." The newspaper anticipated fallout: "Needless to say, the opponents of civil rights were delighted that they had been given this new opportunity to level heavy guns at one of the top leaders in the movement." Worse yet, the paper saw a yawning chasm opening between factions within the civil rights movement. The picture the editorial drew was of something much more dangerous for the black struggle than a minor tiff among rival factions. The fissure had created such "confusion and disunity" among civil rights leaders that, in the view of the editor, they "seem to have damaged if not destroyed the effectiveness of the movement." This was a somber view of the consequences of King's speech. The editor wrote bluntly: "Whatever his motivation or his purpose in speaking out so forthrightly on the Vietnam issue, the effect of his pronouncements was to split the civil rights forces right down the middle." Anticipating that violence would meet the massive campaign of civil disobedience that King threatened to use against the war, the editorial concluded: "It is not a pretty picture that Martin Luther King Jr. has etched."[32]

A series of columns by Gordon B. Hancock appeared in the *Journal and Guide*, skewering King for what Hancock viewed as the misguided, intemperate, and wrong-headed speech in New York. Hancock's columns bristled with angry charges based on a conservative set of geopolitical presuppositions that were consistent with classic cold war orthodoxy.

Hancock belittled King's position on the war, attributing it to his being "so completely brainwashed" by Russia and hence blinded to the dangers posed by communism in Vietnam. In Hancock's view, "We must meet the communists either in Vietnam or in California, and to surrender to them in Vietnam only postpones the meeting in California." A failure to stop the red menace was tantamount to the "surrender of our great country."

From this worldview flowed a series of attacks on King that became successively sharper. Hancock accused King of "following the communist line" and becoming "a stumbling block" in the path of black aspirations, rather than "a mighty steppingstone." In the process, Hancock said, King had failed to recognize the genuine threat that communist aggression in Vietnam posed to the United States. Hancock said: "King is showing great President Johnson just how ungrateful a man can be! In a critical hour he shows his benefactor his heels. It's pitiful." King's denunciation of the president's policy in Vietnam amounted to "a crime against the cause of better race relations." In the process, in Hancock's view, King's towering image was collapsing. Hancock called King's appeal to young black men to resist the draft during a time of "national emergency . . . a dangerous thing, if not indeed treasonable."[33]

The *Dallas Post Tribune* from Johnson's home state reacted in more measured terms, conceding King's right to disagree with the administration's Vietnam policy but taking issue with his views. In so doing the paper affirmed the essential solidarity American blacks should feel about their nation's foreign challenges, arguing that all citizens, black and white, were so obliged. Even more to the point, the paper insisted that Johnson had "done more to right the wrongs that exist than any other president." The piece ended by firmly invoking the theme of entitlement resulting from faithful service: "So we say, we must help our country fight this involved and tragic war. By so doing we will have done our part and we will have an easier battle when it is over in getting what is rightfully ours. We cannot expect to have rights without responsibilities that go with acquiring those rights. This is our position."[34]

The *Pittsburgh Courier* scolded King editorially for "preaching the wrong doctrine." The paper said King had "thrown the full weight of his influence and prestige into the struggle in Vietnam," using his "harshest terms yet." The piece recited a number of the points King had made in his Riverside Church speech, clearly implying that most were misguided or dead wrong. It took particular exception to King's statement, in the editor's words, "that he would no longer counsel young ghetto-locked Negroes to refrain from violence." This was a misreading of a key passage in King's speech. King had said: "I could never again raise my voice against the violence of the oppressed in the ghettos without having first spoken clearly to the greatest purveyor of violence in the world today—my own government." Once King *did* speak out, as he did in the Riverside speech, he had satisfied the condition in his statement and could continue to speak out against ghetto violence. In his speech King was establishing a justification for his outspoken opposition to the government's war policy, not announcing a cessation of his insistence on nonviolence in the fight against oppression.

The *Courier* went on to point out that black soldiers were disheartened by the antics of protesters at home: "Negro boys on the fighting front are reportedly dismayed at much of the draft-card burnings and other antiwar actions in this country." The editorial cited the reporting from Vietnam of the black war correspondent Ethel Payne, who had observed that the black GIs all "would rather be at home, but . . . to a man they are equally as determined to see this job through." This was an indirect, but sharp, rebuke of the civil rights leader.

Acknowledging that the war was draining national resources that might better be spent at home, the editorial suggested that King's assumption that, if the war ended, "a cessation of hostilities would automatically make a Congress lukewarm to this domestic program, reverse itself was blatantly naive." The writer lauded King for "raising the hopes and aspirations of American Negroes," and for his "firm courage and vision" that had sparked "the turnaround in civil rights during the past ten years or so." The piece then said sadly, "Yet we are moved to say that in this context, Dr. King is tragically preaching the wrong doctrine."[35]

In two cartoons by Sam Milai published in the *Pittsburgh Courier*, the depictions of King were distinctly unflattering. On May 6, 1967, a month after King's controversial speech, Milai imagined the civil rights leader as a substantially diminished figure. In one cartoon an African American newspaperman looks down disapprovingly at the tiny figure of King carrying an antiwar placard, signaling the negative response of the black press, and a black soldier looks over his shoulder at King, alarmed at the civil rights leader's pacifist diatribe. The GI's back implies his rejection of King's unflattering interpretation of the soldier's mission as well as pictorially representing King's antiwar activities as something done behind the back of African American soldiers and, in effect, undermining them. The following month, another cartoon by Milai pointedly interpreted the result of King's antiwar fervor: less focus on civil rights (see figure 5).

In an editorial published on May 6 the *Michigan Chronicle*, whose publisher-in-absentia was Louis Martin, deputy chair of the Democratic National Committee, took a very different tack. It granted the validity of King's charge that a disproportionate share of the fighting, and therefore of the casualties in Vietnam, was being borne by African American soldiers. It also shared King's concern with the shifting of national resources and attention away from issues critical to the fulfillment of black aspirations. But the piece took issue with blaming the war for the sagging fortunes of the civil rights movement: "Why blame the war in Vietnam for a civil rights struggle which is losing ground for want of clear purposes and unified leadership?

Figure 5.
A harried Martin Luther King Jr. is spread too thin. He is losing control of his civil rights responsibilities because his attention is consumed with opposing the war. (Cartoon by Sam Milai, *Pittsburgh Courier*, June 3, 1967. Courtesy of the *Pittsburgh Courier* Archives.)

Why blame the war in Vietnam for loss of white civil rights supporters whose once clearly envisioned civil rights goals of human equality and integration have been confused and beclouded by cries of black power and black nationalism?"

Then, later in the editorial, the writer brought up a consequential issue: whether the nation was able or morally bound to sustain "both the war against communist aggression abroad and the war against poverty and ignorance at home. We all seem to take it for granted that a choice must be made; that peace abroad and prosperity at home are not compatible."[36]

The sticking point for King, had he pondered the *Chronicle* editor's two salient observations, would have been that both statements presumed the necessity and moral legitimacy of the Vietnam War, a critical presumption that King would not have been willing to concede. While a key argument in King's jeremiad against the war was the damage it was doing and had done to the civil rights movement, he also believed that the war was profoundly wrong because it was a war against the legitimate revolutionary impulses of the Vietnamese people, who were seeking to rid themselves of the vestiges of white colonialist suppression.

After his paper had skewered King for his antiwar efforts, Benjamin Mays devoted one of his columns in the *Courier* to defending King's sincerity, if not his position, arguing that a civil rights leader should be free to speak out on more than one issue. Mays noted the ideological consistency in King's philosophy of nonviolence, which undergirded his civil rights campaigns, and the pacifism that animated his opposition to the war. Any disagreements with King, Mays argued, should be confined to his ideas, not his freedom to express those ideas.[37]

An editorial a week later continued the debate. It said the controversy swirling around King was "of unprecedented proportions since he switched his emphasis from civil rights to the unfortunate conflict in far-off Asia." The editor acknowledged that the paper had been critical of King's stand, believing it "a tragic mistake": "We do not believe that because Dr. King was the recipient of the Nobel Peace Prize that he has been handed a mandate to speak out on the war. . . . The issue with Dr. King, therefore, is not the rightness or wrongness of his position, nor is it whether or not the man is sincere. The issue is the impact of his stand on the country and the people whom he leads."[38]

Therein, of course, lay the rub. King believed he was compelled to speak out against the war, both because it was the moral thing to do and because the war was demolishing any chance for reform at home. His critics within the civil rights movement thought his antiwar activities would have precisely the same effect on the cause of domestic reform by antagonizing the president and splintering the civil rights coalition. The irony is that the fears of both sides of the debate were at least partially realized.

The *New York Amsterdam News* printed a cartoon offering its readers a troubling caricature of the perceived consequences of King's antiwar stand (see figure 6). The cartoonist, Melvin Tapley, viewed King's controversial stand as enabling the darkest forces of racism in America. By focusing on the war, Tapley charged, King was weakening the campaign for civil rights and thereby strengthening the forces of bigotry and racial violence.

Figure 6.

King is blamed for inflaming the angry passions of the foes of equal rights with his opposition to the war in Vietnam. (Cartoon by Melvin Tapley, *New York Amsterdam News*, April 15, 1967. Courtesy of the *New York Amsterdam News*.)

A banner headline on the front page of the *New York Amsterdam News* announced, "War-Rights Views Cause Split." The opening line of the late April story set the tone: "The annual blooming of the movement to end the war in Vietnam has sprouted new and controversial spokesmen this Spring." Heading the list was King, along with McKissick and Carmichael. Later in the story the reporter spoke of "the increasingly splintered civil rights movement," wracked by dissension "as other leaders hit Dr. King for going off on the peace tangent at the possible expense of the rights issue."[39]

The *New York Amsterdam News* recognized King's stand against the war could splinter the civil rights movement and compromise its future effectiveness. The newspaper was clearly uncomfortable with King's position while acknowledging that it grew out of his struggle against a racism that he saw as part of the immorality of American society and of the Vietnam War. The editor also pointed out King's risky call to action: "Thus the single most identifiable and honored leader of the civil rights movement risks that movement's future progress by taking a stand on conscience against an 'immoral war' and urging young Americans to become conscientious objectors."[40]

The *Atlanta Daily World* criticized King by firmly separating the issue of black rights from foreign policy. For the *Daily World* the wall of separation was not a tactical matter erected out of concern for the impact that combining the issues would have on the cause of domestic reform. The newspaper framed it as the responsibility of good citizenship: "We regret to see such a prominent member of our racial group such as Dr. King take such a stand on a foreign policy issue in which our country is actually involved in war over." Although the paper acknowledged that King had "a right to his opinion on this or any public question," it opposed his taking the drastic step of encouraging young men to shirk the draft.[41]

The *Afro-American* reported the dissension in the ranks of civil rights leaders in late April 1967 but sought to soft-pedal the bickering: "In keeping with the obvious campaign designed to create rifts where no rifts in the American social revolution exist, efforts have continued over the past several weeks to over-emphasize an apparent squabble between civil rights leaders." The editorial cited as an example the coverage of Roy Wilkins's New Haven speech expressing concern about King's linkage of the peace movement with the civil rights struggle.

The paper took comfort from the common goal that it said King and those who criticized his stance on the war shared: "The attainment of equal social, educational and economic opportunities." [42]

The newspaper's last observation was, of course, essentially correct. No one within the movement's leadership was disputing the goal of "equal social, educational and economic opportunities," as the editorial phrased it. The problem lay in determining how best to attain that goal and how the government's commitment of attention and resources to the Vietnam War was affecting that effort.

As King found himself beset by the opposition of much of the black press and of most conservative black leaders, the *Dallas Express* reported the Southern Conference Educational Fund (SCEF), an interracial civil rights organization, had come to his defense. At its semiannual meeting in Nashville, the SCEF announced its full support in language that could only have pleased the embattled civil rights leader: "America's denial of self-determination in Vietnam is cut from the same cloth as denial of Negro rights in Birmingham. Police brutality in Birmingham and the brutal bombing and napalming of villages in Vietnam are directed against fundamental change by and for the oppressed. We reaffirm our opposition to this war. We implore all groups working for human rights at home to join Dr. King and others in working for peace and human rights in Vietnam and elsewhere in the world."[43]

The Reverend Fred L. Shuttlesworth, the group's president, announced the SCEF's decision. The organization's close ties to King were embodied in Shuttlesworth, who was also an official of King's SCLC.

Later in the year a former executive director of the SCLC, Wyatt T. Walker, writing in *Negro Digest*, reflected on the hostile response to King's speech and detected "the fine hand of racism." King's critics, Walker charged, were simply parroting old racist sentiments about blacks when they, in effect, told King "he ought to stay in his place" and not meddle in national affairs outside the scope of civil rights. King was compelled to speak out against the war, Walker asserted, because it was a moral issue that knew no geographic limit: "The sum and substance of the King position on Vietnam and its connection with human rights in America is a question of the moral capacity of our nation. . . . If America has no morality beyond her shores, how can she be moral at home?"[44]

After King's open break with Johnson over the war, antiwar activists quickly began courting him to lead their movement, lend his considerable influence to the effort, and throw his hat in the ring as a presidential candidate. Word of this soon reached the White House. The *St. Louis Argus* said the rumors were "spreading like wild fire across a wide open prairie." To fight this fire the Democratic political apparatus promptly began to court key black leaders and the black press and induce them to stay with LBJ. An *Argus* editorial reported that a familiar African American publisher and political insider was spearheading the effort. According to the paper, an alarmed Johnson administration had tapped Louis Martin of the Democratic National Committee (DNC) to travel "all over the country working hard to persuade Negro ministers, publishers of Negro newspapers, labor leaders, civil rights organizations, and others to support the administration's Vietnam policy and civil rights record."[45]

It is apparent that the *Argus* was targeted in this blitz, along with other important regional and national black papers—and for good reason. The unambiguous support of the black press was crucial to the president. The *Argus* editorial also carries an almost palpable undercurrent of grim satisfaction that King had LBJ sufficiently off-balance to trigger a major effort to retain black political support. As the *Argus* editor saw it, the president's anxiety was well placed. King's position could weaken black support for Johnson, and the next election was barely a year and a half away. LBJ's fears handed a certain power to black opinion makers, and the *Argus* was not immune to the satisfaction of being wooed. For his part the president picked wisely when he sent

Louis Martin out to influence African American publishers. The owners of the *Argus* and other black newspapers knew Martin well as a colleague and fellow publisher, not just as a DNC official.

Martin was a logical choice because he was a familiar figure in the corridors of the White House, as well as among the fraternity of African American publishers. After all, he was publisher of the *Michigan Chronicle* and a longtime friend and business partner of John Sengstacke, publisher of the *Chicago Defender* and head of the largest group of black newspapers.[46]

The White House made a concerted effort to analyze the political risks posed by King's opposition to the war. In mid-May, just weeks after King's Riverside Church speech, Fred Panzer, a White House aide, pulled together some polling data measuring public attitudes toward King's aggressive new antiwar posture. On consecutive days—May 19 and 20, 1967—Panzer sent memos to the president laying out what the Harris polling organization had found and that Panzer had obtained in advance of scheduled public release on May 22.

Panzer's memo of May 19 said Harris had found wide divisions among Americans about King's antiwar views, with whites more opposed to King than blacks (73 and 48 percent, respectively), but the black support of King's views (25 percent) was sufficient to pose problems.

Harris stated speculatively that "Dr. King may well have within his power a capability of influencing between a third to one half of all Negro voters behind a candidate he might endorse for President in 1968." Assuming that Johnson would not be King's choice for president, and given King's expressed preference for either Robert F. Kennedy, a Democrat, or Charles Percy, a moderate Republican, "pressure from Dr. King could make the consideration of Kennedy for Vice President on a ticket with Mr. Johnson a significant factor, if it meant that 25% of the Negro vote might hang in the balance."[47]

Panzer forwarded more Harris polling numbers to the president on May 22. These showed that 34 percent of blacks believed that King was damaging the cause of civil rights, while the same percentage believed his antiwar views made no difference.[48]

On June 9 Panzer sent another memo to Johnson with polling data provided by the Gallup organization in advance of public release on June 11. The poll produced nationwide trial heats in two-way and four-way presidential races.

A two-way race between likely Democratic and Republican opponents showed LBJ with 45 percent and George Romney, GOP front-runner, with 48 percent, and 7 percent undecided. The same two-way trial heat three months earlier, in March 1967, had shown LBJ with 43 percent, Romney with 48 percent, and 5 percent undecided. Thus LBJ's numbers in the same pairing in June had improved slightly, though the president still was trailing, and the undecided pool of voters had increased slightly. In both two-way trial heats Johnson came up short.

In a four-way race that added George Wallace and Martin Luther King to the mix, the projected percentages were Johnson with 41 percent, Romney with 39 percent, George Wallace with 11 percent, and King with 2 percent, giving LBJ a small plurality in a tight race with Romney.[49] Despite gains for the president in a four-way race, the outlook for Johnson in mid-1967 was grim, although the King threat seemed to recede when he was viewed as a candidate. More problematic was King's potential influence on a race in which he was not on the ticket but was in opposition to the reelection of the president, a possibility that was not measured in this poll.

In August, when Sengstacke got wind of the efforts to draw King into an active political effort to oppose Johnson in the 1968 election, the publisher produced an editorial in the *Chicago Defender* that took dead aim at King's plunge into the political fray. Sengstacke set up his piece with King's announcement that if Johnson did not alter the course of his policy in Vietnam, King would "throw the full weight of his organization against the President." The editorial was aghast at King's move, calling it "a departure from the kind of entanglement, which Dr. King had heretofore meticulously avoided." In Sengstacke's judgment, before King decided to get involved in electoral politics, "his crusade for freedom and equality acquired greater breadth and gained a momentum that no other struggle of comparable character has ever achieved in modern social history." Now King's "premature decision" had threatened his lofty stature as a nonpartisan advocate for black aspirations.

"Should Dr. King do that," the editorial warned, "he will find himself engaged in two wars the consequences of which may well prove catastrophic to his already diminishing influence." Sengstacke warned that, should King "persist in his folly," he would further seriously impair his "diminishing influence."[50]

It was remarkable for a black newspaper to speak so bluntly of the dwindling moral reach of so towering a figure as King and to suggest that his public disavowal of the war could so disenchant African Americans that they would no longer follow his leadership. Sengstacke's denunciation is all the more startling in light of the fulsome praise his paper had heaped on King a scant eight months earlier: "Few men have so swiftly shaped the course of events . . . few have so deeply stirred multitudes. Dr. King's victories carry with them an awesome burden of responsibility and trust that grows larger with each new triumph over the forces that would keep the black man forever enslaved."[51]

The publisher's anger and disappointment as King went public with his political disenchantment with Johnson was a direct consequence of what Sengstacke's paper had earlier called King's "awesome burden of responsibility and trust." As King's antiwar militancy began to look like political insurgency, Sengstacke believed King was ignoring Johnson's singular contribution to the cause of ending racial injustice and creating economic opportunity for African Americans. In the process King was ignoring his own heavy responsibility as a leader and depleting the resources of trust he had accumulated as a single-minded champion of equal rights for the nation's black citizens.

After Sengstacke sent Johnson a copy of the August editorial, the president dashed off an appreciative note to the publisher: "I want to thank you for your recent editorial and for your thoughtfulness in sending it to me. The knowledge of your support and understanding helps more than I can say to lighten the burdens of office in these trying times."[52]

The quixotic groundswell to nominate a presidential ticket headed by King, with Dr. Benjamin Spock for vice president, continued unabated. A group calling itself the National Conference for New Politics actually met in Chicago in August 1967 to do just that. (For some time King and Spock had been prominently linked with the antiwar campaign. Earlier in the year, in an item about a peace rally in the Midwest, the *Los Angeles Sentinel* had called the pair the "two great doctors.") No sooner had the conclave assembled than it became a free-for-all, dividing along racial and gender lines. The racial divide was almost comical in its breathtaking abandonment of democratic process. The thirty-five hundred delegates included a vocal black caucus of four hundred that promptly demanded half of all committee seats and half the conference vote. Surprisingly, the black caucus succeeded in its demands, leaving a great deal of confusion and hostility in the aftermath.[53]

King's speech on the opening night of the conference reportedly was received lukewarmly, dissipating support for his presidential candidacy. He left the same night. Black and white radicals alike had concluded King was insufficiently militant and much too bland for their tastes. They were unable to coalesce around King and his vision for America, perhaps more than anything because he seemed to lack the revolutionary fire needed to lead them. The meeting's larger purposes petered out.[54]

King, for his part, after privately toying with the idea of mounting a presidential bid, had publicly distanced himself from the idea. During a television appearance in early August on NBC's *Meet the Press*, King spoke out on the issues of Vietnam and the domestic revolution, saying, "We are today engaged in two wars and we are losing both." Then he said that under no circumstance would he be a candidate for president in 1968. "Being a peace candidate is not my role," he said. "I feel I should serve as a conscience of all the parties and all of the people, rather than as a candidate myself."[55] Also, in purely pragmatic terms King's standing in the public mind had taken a hit after his polemic against U.S. policy in Vietnam.

According to public opinion polls, 73 percent of Americans disapproved of King's opposition to the Vietnam War. Blacks also were strong in their disapproval of King's antiwar insurgency. Much of this disapproval derived from the fear among blacks that King's antiwar stance was hurting the cause of civil rights. Sixty percent of those polled believed his stand on the war was damaging to the black freedom movement. Large numbers of African Americans were simply put off by King's attacks on the administration's conduct of the conflict in Vietnam. Forty-eight percent said his antiwar views were wrong.[56]

These figures show, at least in part, the influence of the black press on African American opinion, because much of the black press made clear its discomfort with King's public break with the administration over the war and viewed the conjunction of the antiwar and civil rights movements with considerable alarm. Even if he had been inclined to run for president—which he never really was—King would not have had the political support he needed, even within the black community, to mount a respectable candidacy.

King's fight against the war was largely rhetorical. He occasionally toyed with staging some sort of massive nonviolent direct action aimed at the war, but he never actually attempted to pull such an event together. While he did encourage young men to become conscientious objectors and led antiwar marches, most of his antiwar protests came from the stage and pulpit.

As King continued speaking out on the war, the black press continued commenting on the unfolding saga of his accelerating antiwar campaign. The *Courier*, which earlier had carried some distinctly unflattering commentary on King's insurgency, published a supportive piece. About three months after Milai drew his unflattering cartoons for the newspaper, Wilbert L. Holloway produced a cartoon that also appeared in the *Courier* and took an entirely different measure of the celebrated civil rights leader in August 1967. In Holloway's estimation King's stature was "looming larger and larger," as the caption asserted, precisely *because* of his denunciation of an "unjust, brutal" war and the way it was devouring the national resources better used to pay for badly needed domestic social programs. Rather than seeing an isolated figure, as many in the black press did when they looked at King in the spring and summer of 1967, Holloway discerned a man who regarded the brutality and waste of the war the same way a growing number of members of Congress did. Rather than viewing King as a marginalized figure who had lost touch with his proper constituency, the cartoonist saw him as a man who was building a growing reputation as a leader and statesmen.[57]

King was not immune to the criticism that the media, white and black, showered upon him for his open opposition to the war and administration policy in Vietnam. It hurt him deeply. He recalled how discouraging this was for him: "When I first took my position against the war in Vietnam, almost every newspaper in the country criticized me. It was a low period in my life." The papers attacked him incessantly, as he remembered it: "I could hardly open a newspaper. It wasn't only white people either; it was Negroes."[58] The barbs directed at him by other African Americans, whether by the black press or other leading civil rights leaders, stung King most painfully of all.

Representative Emanuel Celler, liberal Democrat from New York, had no doubt that the opposition of key black leaders to the war was in fact blocking the path of civil rights legislation in Congress. In remarks before a nationwide television audience, Celler had blamed King, McKissick, and Carmichael for the failure of civil rights legislation on Capitol Hill. The *Afro-American* called Celler's comments "the most absurd statement ever uttered by a member of the national legislature." The piece continued: "If this is the belief of a man who is supposed to be our 'friend,' we would fare better in the clutches of our enemies." The editorial interpreted Celler's statement to mean that "because these three civil rights leaders oppose America's involvement in the Vietnam War, 22 million other Americans of color must be penalized."

The editorial pointed out that no national leader had shown such indignation at the outspoken opposition to the war of Senator J. William Fulbright of Arkansas. The piece observed, "Mr. Celler, an old hand in the House of Representatives, knows full well that if Dr. King had not uttered a word, civil rights legislation would still have had rough sledding in this Congress."[59]

The editorial had a point. It was a frequent defense offered on King's behalf by writers in the black press who were resigned to the growing opposition to civil rights legislation within Congress, no matter where prominent blacks stood on the war. Still, whether voices in the black press were chastising King for his increasingly militant antiwar activism or defending his right to dissent, their general tone suggests that the black press found the whole controversy deeply unsettling.

Later that year, ironically, the *Los Angeles Sentinel* chose to barb its criticism of King's antiwar position by calling attention to the strange alliance that had implicitly united the civil rights giant and other activists with Fulbright, long a foe of civil rights legislation during his congressional career. "It must be embarrassing to them now to find themselves teamed up with a lifelong racist," the editorial suggested. The editorial held that critics of Johnson's Vietnam policy "were generally wrong," and it deplored "mixing the war issue with the civil rights issue." The piece concluded by saying, "Let's get on with the urgent job here at home and let the government take care of our foreign policy and conduct of the war."[60]

When a journalist from *Jet* sat down with A. Philip Randolph, the revered labor leader and civil rights activist, whom the magazine called the "dean of civil rights spokesmen," to discuss the foundering reform movement, he delicately avoided placing personal blame but acknowledged that "the civil rights movement is in a state of confusion" and unequivocally blamed "the Vietnam question" for doing most of the damage. "I am neither for nor against the war in Vietnam," Randolph said. "I am against plunging the civil rights movement into the controversy over that war." Then he added: "The most important front is the Alabama-Mississippi front."[61]

According to Andrew Young, King and his SCLC staff believed that Johnson was attempting to influence the black press to denounce King for his opposition to the war. To counteract these administration pressures, and presumably still the criticism that had already been generated in the black press, SCLC officials decided to induce African American publishers to invite King to address the annual meeting of the National Negro Publishers Association in Cleveland in the summer of 1967. According to Andrew Young, King had always enjoyed cordial relations with John and Robert Johnson, the publisher and editor-in-chief, respectively, of the Johnson Publishing Company, which owned *Ebony* and *Jet*, among other publications. King had also been a classmate of Robert Johnson and Lerone Bennett's at Morehouse College. Between *Ebony* and *Jet*, Johnson publications penetrated virtually every black community and gave the publisher and editors significant influence in the senior councils of the black press.

The Johnsons persuaded the publishers to invite King to address a luncheon meeting at the convention on the subject of Vietnam. As Andrew Young recalls the speech, King explained the moral and sociological basis for his opposition to the war and described the threat it posed to black aspirations to end poverty and usher in an era of economic justice. According to Young, King's "command of the facts and familiarity with all the issues turned the publishers completely around."[62]

Whatever the effect of King's speech on the publishers, it was not reported prominently in the black press. However, a measure of the somewhat uncomfortable relationship of King and the black press during the summer of 1967 is that he and his staff would have to go to such elaborate lengths to get an invitation for the most celebrated civil rights leader in America, the Nobel Peace Prize winner, to make a luncheon speech at a convention of African American publishers.

The biographer David J. Garrow reports that as King wrestled throughout that summer with the damage to his reputation within certain African

American leadership circles, he suffered recurrent bouts of self-doubt. This inner turmoil was scarcely reduced by the stinging personal rebukes from long-time personal friends and associates.[63]

In late summer one of those friends, Carl Rowan, the African American journalist and former USIA director, ratcheted up the heat on King. Rowan had an agreement to produce periodic articles for *Reader's Digest*. He wrote a scathing piece for the September issue that bore the headline "Martin Luther King's Tragic Decision." The article was even harsher in its criticism than Rowan had been in his telephone conversation with King shortly after the Riverside Church speech in April.[64]

In early September the *Dallas Express* summarized Rowan's strenuous critique of King in *Reader's Digest*. The *Express* piece quoted Rowan's charge that King was endangering "the well-being of millions of Negroes" by denouncing America's involvement in Vietnam. Rowan said that King's remarks had "created doubt about the Negro's loyalty to his country" and "alienated many of the Negro's friends and armed the Negro's foes," threatening any further progress in securing civil rights legislation in Congress. It also quoted Rowan as saying, "Beyond doubt, King's speech and his subsequent remarks have put a new strain and new burdens on the civil rights movement. He has become persona non grata to Lyndon Johnson. It is also likely that his friends in Congress will never again listen to or be moved by him the way they were in the past. This can make the difference between poverty and well-being for millions of Negroes."[65]

King told a reporter that Rowan was failing to distinguish between dissent and disloyalty. It was Rowan, not King, who was making "the tragic error," said King, referring to a phrase in the title of Rowan's article in the *Reader's Digest*.[66]

Despite the self-doubts, during the final year of his life King seemed liberated from whatever constraints had muzzled his outrage against the war. He spoke out often against the war and against the government that had been his partner in earlier, more congenial, days. During that year the black press alternately criticized him for spending the diminishing capital of goodwill he had accumulated during his single-minded pursuit of equal rights for black Americans; defended him against his critics, particularly those outside the black community; or stood by, puzzled and mute, as their hero of past civil rights struggles championed a new and bitterly divisive cause.

On February 4, 1968, at the Ebenezer Baptist Church in Atlanta, which he copastored with his father, the Reverend Martin Luther King Sr., the younger King stepped into the pulpit and delivered a sermon that crackled with moral outrage. He spoke of how nations were consumed with the desire for supremacy in the world. Among such nations, King said, he numbered his own. "I am sad to say that the nation in which we live is the supreme culprit. And I'm going to continue to say it to America, because I love this country too much to see the drift that it has taken." Then, like a fiery Old Testament prophet, King proclaimed: "God didn't call America to do what she's doing in the world now. God didn't call America to engage in a senseless, unjust war, as the war in Vietnam. And we are criminals in that war."

As he neared the end of the sermon, his tone softened. He spoke wistfully of what he would like to have someone say at his funeral. He asked his somber listeners to tell his eulogist not to mention the Nobel Peace Prize or his other awards or where he went to school. Then he said: "I'd like for somebody to say that day, that Martin Luther King, Jr., tried to give his life serving others."[67]

Two months later he stood on the balcony of the Lorraine Motel in Memphis, sharing a few genial moments with some of his associates. It had been exactly one year since his momentous speech at the Riverside Church. Since then he had been buffeted with criticism and estranged from associates from his long crusade for racial equality. His struggle to end the war in Vietnam had taken a painful toll.

But now, in the late afternoon, he was enjoying the quiet, reassuring company of his closest friends. It was six o'clock and cool in the early evening air. King said, "I don't know whether I need a coat." His sentence was punctuated by a sharp sound that ripped loudly through the retreating daylight. A hundred yards away a rifle barrel slithered back inside a bathroom window. Martin Luther King Jr. had been assassinated.[68]

After he was killed, Coretta Scott King requested that the haunting words her husband spoke from the pulpit of the Ebenezer Baptist Church that day in February be replayed at his funeral. As people wept, his disembodied voice floated eerily through the church, completing the eulogy he suggested: "I'd like for somebody to say that day, that Martin Luther King, Jr., tried to love somebody. I want you to say that day, that I tried to be right on the war question. . . . Say that I was a drum major for peace."[69]

After King was gunned down, the black press was filled with a flood of laudatory commentary on his life and accomplishments. It was natural to honor lavishly one of the most celebrated figures in the history of the African American struggle for equal rights. But how was the black press to deal with King's antiwar insurgency, particularly his revolt against Lyndon Johnson's war policies—and the president himself—during the last year? Much of the black press had criticized King, sometimes with considerable zeal, and described the fissures that had opened up between King and other key figures in the civil rights fraternity. The pages of the black press had carried stories about the harm being done to the cause of African American civil rights, buffeted by the storm swirling around King and his antiwar politics.[70]

What is remarkable is how little was said in much of the black press after King's death, in its voluminous tributes to the slain leader, about the very public way he fought against his government's policy in Vietnam and the sheer passion and energy he invested in that struggle. The virtual silence in much of the black press about his opposition to the war and his strident attacks on Lyndon Johnson's leadership abroad was all the more striking because the African American press had said a great deal about King's opposition to the war, much of it critical, particularly during the final year of his life. The black press displayed a pronounced tendency to downplay that part of King's contribution to America's public life when it wrote its memorials.

Perhaps black publishers' reticence was nothing more than avoidance of an awkward controversy. Until people had processed their raw feelings and the private anguish of the bereaved had spent its initial energy, perhaps silence about the war seemed the sensible response. King's grieving friends and admirers had plenty of common ground on which they could find solace and express themselves.

It seems more likely that the impulse in much of the black press was to reimagine the legacy of Martin Luther King Jr. and remove the dissonant note of his antiwar polemic. Part of the black press preferred the ideologically pure King, the tightly focused civil rights idealist whose boundless fervor for the cause was unalloyed by other passions. So, to preserve that Martin Luther King, the furious black prophet who challenged and inspired, who led his people with single-minded devotion to an idea, as they mourned his death and celebrated his life a number of African American newspapers and magazines ignored the loud dissent he brought to his fight against the war and muffled his noisy rage.

Not all the black press avoided comment on King's opposition to the war. The *Norfolk Journal and Guide* and the *Michigan Chronicle* dealt with King's antiwar ideology by reprinting an April 7 *New York Times* editorial eulogy, "He Had a Dream," which toned down some of King's more strident rhetoric about the war. Several lines two-thirds of the way through the editorial were about the derivation of King's antiwar views: "When the United States was honored by his Nobel Peace Prize, he felt obliged to extend his personal philosophy of nonviolence from the streets of Selma and Memphis to the rice paddies of the Mekong Delta and the jungles of Vietnam." The *Times* went on to describe how King viewed the war as a threat to the well-being of the civil rights movement and quoted pronouncements King had made arguing his point of view.[71]

The headline in the *Times*, "He Had a Dream," was framed in a static past tense, but in the two black papers the headline became "The Dream Is Closer." The dynamic present tense suggested a reality that was still evolving. The

Chronicle expanded its headline to add even more punch: "'The Dream' Is Closer to Reality through Him," embroidering the thought in language that sounded almost biblical. In both cases the modifications consciously placed emphasis on King's achievements as realized deeds. King was not only a dreamer but a doer whose triumphant actions in the field of civil rights were bringing African American dreams closer to fruition.

The *Times*'s reference to King's opposition to the war subtly distanced him from the conflict by citing his obligation, after "the United States was honored by his Nobel Peace Prize," to adapt his nonviolent philosophy to Vietnam as well as to Selma and Memphis. This argument of altruistic patriotism helped to soften King's rhetoric, making it more a philosophical and pragmatic objection to the war and less an attack on President Johnson. This made the statement more palatable to the two African American editors, who had disapproved of King's assaults on the president.

The editorial closed with a reference to the issue most African American publishers and editors had long since come to embrace: the war's consumption of resources better spent to alleviate hunger and poverty, especially rampant among the inner-city poor and rural blacks in the South. This argument, in one form or another, had been appearing in the black press for years.[72]

The two African American editors printed the *Times* piece to reshape the image of King, bringing his story into closer alignment with the values and expectations the *Guide* and *Chronicle* wished to convey to their readers. They chose the *Times* editorial—and rewrote its headline—because it supplied a balanced, well-calibrated interpretation of the martyred civil rights leader.

The *Dallas Post Tribune* and the *Dallas Express* each ran columns attributed to writers not on their staffs and who took opposite views of King. Both pieces mentioned King's antiwar activities. The *Post Tribune* published a column by Ray Zauber, the white editor of the *Oak Cliff Tribune*, a newspaper named after a town that had been annexed by Dallas and retained its small-town flavor—and its name—as a distinct neighborhood. The piece was a caustic assessment of King's legacy, including his opposition to the Vietnam War. Zauber wrote: "Martin Luther King was called an apostle of nonviolence. Yet violence followed in his wake. He was known as a man of peace. Yet disturbance and bloodshed, arson and looting resulted from his outcries." Zauber refused to "join with those who eulogize Martin Luther King as a man of peace. We rather thought his selection for the Nobel Peace Award was historical hypocrisy." Later in the piece, which ran with no explanation for why the *Post Tribune* decided to reprint it, Zauber charged that "Hanoi and Moscow were frequently comforted by the chaos created where he [King] lighted." The column continued in this vein and along the way eviscerated the Great Society and the aspirations of black Americans that LBJ was seeking to fulfill.

Zauber's column probably represented much of prevailing regional white sentiment at the time and was undoubtedly distasteful to the black editor of the *Dallas Post Tribune* because of its racist tinge and rejection of King's philosophy of nonviolent civil disobedience in domestic protest. A few days before King's death the *Post Tribune* editor probably would have agreed with Zauber's contention that King's merging of the civil rights struggle and the peace movement harmed "the Negro cause."[73]

After King's assassination the editor may have thought better of that position. The substance of this column likely offended the African American readership of the *Post Tribune*, not least because it appeared so soon after King's tragic death. It is hard to imagine that the editor would not have expected just that result. Zauber's rant was a caricature of the negative response to King that was common in parts of white America at the time. Publishing it must have aroused a distaste that both the editor of the *Post Tribune* and his readers shared.

The *Express* published a syndicated column written by Alfred Duckett, who had collaborated with King on a book and who contended that certain black leaders had hounded King for his antiwar ideology. Duckett likened this opposition to a lynching, using an image of violence that was visceral in the cultural memory of his African American readers. He closed the piece with the kind of plain talk that was vintage Duckett: "Maybe I am wrong. Maybe it isn't polite to tell it like it is when we all feel so bad. But I just wanted to say that, even though the great masses of black folks, I believe, never lost the faith in Dr. King, not all the killers of that dream was white. No sir."[74]

Before King was slain, the *Dallas Express* had criticized King's antiwar campaign against the president. But now the paper published the Duckett column, which protected the memory of King's pacifist position in the Vietnam debate by denouncing his more extreme African American critics for their attacks on King and for undermining his work. This may have been the Dallas paper's way of offering its own mea culpa for its criticisms of King, while he struggled against his prominent black critics, including many members of the black press.[75]

The *Philadelphia Tribune* published three pieces that dealt with King's antiwar views. Two were letters to the newspaper, published on April 9, and the third was a feature piece that appeared two weeks later. The Pennsylvania paper had no reticence about publishing multiple accounts of King's antiwar campaign just after his death, which sets the *Philadelphia Tribune* apart from most of the black press in the immediate aftermath of King's murder.[76]

Some black newspapers chose to affirm King's pacifist rhetoric in various ways and accord it a place in his legacy, even when they had criticized King in the last year of his life for his opposition to Johnson's war policies. But more of the black press chose to erase or subdue Martin Luther King's vocal opposition to the war in their post-assassination tributes to the slain civil rights icon.

The African American poet Carl Wendell Hines captured some of this comfortable amnesia:

> Now that he is safely dead
> let us praise him
> build monuments to his glory
> sing hosannas to his name.
> Dead men make
> such convenient heroes; They
> cannot rise
> To challenge the images
> we would fashion from their lives.
> And besides,
> it is easier to build monuments
> than to make a better world.[77]

The selective memories that afflicted some in the black press as they wrestled with the pain of losing their champion could not permanently suppress the stern message of his antiwar legacy. The passage of time and the growing consensus of disapproval of the war in the black press, and in the attitudes of most African Americans, ultimately gave King's views on the war broad credibility in the black community and in the black press. Ultimately, the totality of King's message, including his vocal opposition to the war, came to be an accepted part of a richly textured understanding of the nature of responsible citizenship for African Americans in a country still wrestling with the demons of racism, both in its domestic life and in its global relationships.[78]

Complicating the response of African Americans and much of the black press to the Vietnam War was the political and emotional bond they had formed with Lyndon Johnson. While Martin Luther King was their preeminent spiritual leader, African Americans found in Johnson the greatest champion of black aspirations ever to have occupied the White House.

6

"We're with You, Chief"

The Black Press and LBJ

Brickbat throwers notwithstanding, we take our stand with LBJ.—*Baltimore Afro-American*, December 23, 1967

Despite the increasingly sharp antiwar sentiments of certain African American leaders, most notably Martin Luther King Jr., and the parallel growth in opposition to the war among African Americans generally, political support for President Lyndon Johnson among blacks generally remained remarkably steadfast. Throughout his presidency he retained his personal standing among blacks because of his unwavering support of their domestic aspirations.

In the immediate aftermath of the Gulf of Tonkin affair in August 1964, Americans still were widely supportive of the Johnson administration's policy in Vietnam. The action in the gulf involved an unsuccessful attack by North Vietnamese patrol boats on a U.S. destroyer on August 2, 1964, and an imagined attack against two U.S. destroyers on the night of August 4 in the same waters off the eastern coast of North Vietnam. In the overheated political atmosphere after the naval incidents in Southeast Asia, Congress passed the Gulf of Tonkin Resolution, giving the president sweeping powers to meet communist aggression, and triggered the use of American ground troops in a vastly expanded war in Vietnam. The incidents in the Gulf of Tonkin caught the public's imagination, ignited a storm of patriotic fervor, and bolstered the president's poll numbers. Louis Harris reported that LBJ's approval rating for his handling of the Vietnam conflict went from 58 percent before the Tonkin Gulf incidents to a lofty 85 percent afterward. A plurality that had opposed taking the war to the North Vietnamese before the Tonkin Gulf engagement became a 2–1 majority in favor of all-out U.S. involvement.[1]

Despite the wide coverage in the mainstream media, the incident in the waters off Vietnam was not big news in much of the black press. One of the black newspapers that did engage the story, the *Chicago Defender*, supported the president editorially for ordering reprisals against North Vietnam. The *Defender* observed that the administration had "unquestioned justification for being tough" when faced with the threat "of the communists in Southeast Asia."[2]

The *Atlanta Daily World* put the skirmish on its front page on successive days, showing an early appetite for straight combat stories, a tendency the paper exhibited throughout the war. As was usually the case with such dispatches in the paper, these stories were attributed to UPI. An editorial in the *Daily World* took a line similar to the *Defender*'s, applauding the show of muscle in the Tonkin Gulf. The editorial ended with a triumphant note, almost gloating over the lesson presumably given to the ideological comrades of the Vietcong by the U.S. Navy: "We hope the communists of North Vietnam and China are now aware of the futility of their efforts to spread communism."[3]

When the Gulf of Tonkin Resolution, giving the president broad powers to involve the nation in military operations in Southeast Asia, sailed through Congress with only two dissenting votes, black newspapers largely ignored it.[4] U.S. involvement in Vietnam was still a low-profile foreign affair, not yet frequently reported or commented on in the African American press. Judging from the spotty coverage the black press gave to the Tonkin Gulf incident and the ensuing congressional resolution, at this early stage, in late summer 1964, African Americans were probably not particularly interested in events in Vietnam.

To be sure, some black civil rights activists had taken notice of the distant conflict. And there was an internal dissonance in an ideology that embraced nonviolence as a solution for domestic injustice, even in the face of violent repression, but condoned violence as a solution for foreign disputes. This incongruity ultimately would lead black advocates of radical pacifism to become vocal opponents of the Vietnam War. However, in August 1964 the complacent acceptance of U.S. foreign policy was more the rule in the African American press.

A key reason was Johnson's position as the "peace candidate" in the fall election. The president had the good fortune to find himself facing a Republican who made Johnson's occasional saber rattling seem docile. The aggressive fulminations of Barry Goldwater were easily and successfully caricatured in Democratic ads that portrayed him as a warmonger and likely to expand the small conflict in Vietnam into a larger war. After all, on May 24 Goldwater had immoderately suggested on national television that "low-yield atomic weapons" be used to defoliate the jungle along South Vietnam's borders where infiltration from the North regularly occurred.[5]

Such bluster so effectively painted Goldwater as the more extreme of the two candidates that Johnson's notorious—and short-lived—commercial showing a little girl picking daisies as an ominous voice counted down to a nuclear explosion proved unnecessary, indeed redundant, because of the Republican candidate's own self-portraiture. The *Defender* gleefully pointed out editorially that Goldwater had already been forced to eat some of his more extreme words, noting among other things, that he had backed away from his nuclear posturing somewhat after a wrist slapping by GOP elders.[6]

The *Afro-American*, in endorsing Johnson, characterized the choice as "between a policy of peace through strength and one of grave risk of war through brinkmanship, bravado and bombast."[7] That seemed to sum up nicely the distinction between Johnson, the sober man of peace, and Barry Goldwater, the reckless man whose aggressive public statements appeared to foreshadow an administration apt to plunge the nation needlessly into war. The newspaper gave the nod to Johnson.

The president also was the indisputable champion of civil rights and economic opportunity for black Americans and was squared off against a candidate who, it was widely believed, concealed a fundamental hostility to black aspirations under an ideological veneer of constitutional scruples about the precedence of states' rights. With such stark alternatives confronting black voters in the upcoming presidential election, the decision to support Johnson, even if it meant subscribing to administration policy in Vietnam, was no decision at all.

Among the major black newspapers, only the *Atlanta Daily World* failed to endorse Johnson, and it chose to sit out the election, endorsing neither candidate. So overwhelming was the conviction among most thoughtful African Americans that LBJ was an indispensable champion of black rights and should be elected to a full term that the *Pittsburgh Courier* endorsed him. It was the first time the Republican paper had endorsed a Democrat since it had made an exception and endorsed Franklin Roosevelt, in 1932 and 1936.[8]

By the time election day arrived in 1964, Johnson was firmly installed as the prohibitive favorite, with endorsements by almost all the major black newspapers. African Americans voted overwhelmingly for him, contributing to his landslide victory. They had not been disappointed by LBJ's steadfast commitment to civil rights since he took office after the assassination of John F. Kennedy. For a year he had been vigorously promoting legislation that would begin the long process of fulfilling black aspirations.

Despite the occasional disconcerting news from Indochina, to African American leaders and to the black press, Vietnam seemed little more than a faraway annoyance. The real arena of action was going to be in the nation's capital. To most black Americans, Johnson's sweeping victory in 1964 presented a unique opportunity to reconstruct the nation's social and political life and to dismantle, once and for all, the rotting edifice of racism and injustice.

Lyndon Johnson had not always been so popular with the black press. Soon after he took office, he got off on the wrong foot with Simeon Booker, the Washington bureau chief of *Jet* magazine. Barely a month after the assassination of John F. Kennedy, Booker wrote a column claiming that Johnson had refused to be photographed with black leaders who had called on him in the Oval Office but then was seen hobnobbing with "Southern guests." Booker wrote that when the new president was sworn in aboard Air Force One, "a wave of pessimism and dejection began to build" across black America. Booker said that Johnson, unlike Kennedy, did not have a "civil rights image" or a "wide clientele of Negro admirers" and, while serving as vice president, had "turned down suggestions for meeting with Negro reporters," begging off on the ground that Kennedy was the administration's spokesman. The unkindest cut of all was the assertion that Johnson "didn't get involved" in the battle for a civil rights bill.

The Oval Office taping system captured Johnson discussing Booker's allegations with Assistant Press Secretary Andrew Hatcher, the first black ever to serve in the White House press office. Johnson was stung by Booker's charges and insisted that, in fact, he not only met with the African American leaders but had his picture taken with them, contrary to Booker's report. LBJ asked Hatcher if he could get Martin Luther King, James Farmer, and A. Philip Randolph to set the record straight. To mollify the president Hatcher delivered a curious and rather stinging assessment of Booker. "He has to write this type of column that's supposed to be a smart-alecky type of Washington column," said Hatcher. "Everybody recognizes that this is sort of a controversial type of column that this fellow writes, and everybody that reads it knows how inaccurate he is most of the time." Immediately after he talked to Hatcher, the president called Roy Wilkins, head of the NAACP, and complained to him about Booker's piece in *Jet*, saying, "I had my picture made with every damn one of them." Wilkins assured LBJ that he would call the editor and the publisher of the magazine and point out the error.[9]

Booker was not the only African American who distrusted Johnson's commitment to the cause of civil rights. LBJ had given critics reasons to question his civil rights credentials. For eleven years after he was elected to Congress from his district in Texas in 1937, Johnson had voted against every piece of civil rights legislation brought before the House, including a bill that would have made lynching a federal offense. During his run for the Senate in 1948, he had opposed Harry Truman's civil rights program, calling it "a farce and a sham—an effort to set up a police state."[10]

When Kennedy picked Johnson as his running mate in 1960, some black leaders were uncomfortable with the selection because of this history of Johnson's and his deep roots in the South. For example, Farmer, founder and long-time head of the Congress of Racial Equality, remembered being against Kennedy's choice for vice president. Farmer told an interviewer that his image of Johnson in the summer of 1960 "was not good" because "he had, at least up through 1957, been negative on civil rights and . . . [I] felt that his voting record was very bad." Fearing that Johnson "would be a disaster," Farmer aired his misgivings in public speeches and private conversations during the campaign.[11]

Louis Martin, publisher of the *Michigan Chronicle* and long-time partner of John H. Sengstacke, head of a major group of black newspapers whose flagship was the *Chicago Defender*, became a one-man pipeline between the new Kennedy-Johnson ticket and the major black publishers. Martin would soon be named vice chair of the Democratic National Committee, where he would serve for eight years. He lobbied his associates and friends in the black press—"the most powerful newspaper guys," he called them. His message, as he described it in an interview, was "I do not want Lyndon Johnson lynched in these newspapers simply because he's from Texas." Martin was not asking for any favors from the black press, he insisted. "I only want this guy given a fair shake, and nobody ought to oppose him just because of the geography." Martin received assurances from the newspapers that they would be fair and treat LBJ objectively. Martin acknowledged that both Kennedy and Johnson were "somewhat vague" in their civil rights commitment in the summer of 1960 but stacked up well against their competition. After Martin twisted their arms, he said the black press promised to be fair and objective. "So this was the sort of . . . off-the-record commitment that I got from the keys to the Negro press," Martin said.[12]

What Martin was hoping to do was head off a repeat of what had happened when the *Pittsburgh Courier* had panned John Sparkman, the Alabama senator who was Adlai Stevenson's running mate on the 1952 Democratic ticket. According to Martin, the *Courier* "did a vicious job on Sparkman."

Martin speculated that the Republicans must have paid the newspaper to run the piece. "It was anti-southern . . . and literally killed [Sparkman] in the Negro eyes—at least it did a great deal of damage." The *Courier's* position was echoed in some other black papers, Martin recalled. The anti-Sparkman campaign hardly influenced the outcome of the 1952 election, which Dwight Eisenhower won by a landslide. But the 1960 election looked like a squeaker, and Martin and other Democratic operatives wanted to make sure the African American vote was nailed down. Getting the black press on board was vital.

Martin assiduously cultivated black publishers during the 1960 election campaign by assuring them of periodic full-page ads for the four weeks before election day, paid for by the Democratic National Committee (DNC). This commitment "would win them over to run our other stuff—releases, et cetera," Martin said. There were about 150 black newspapers at the time, according to Martin, of which twenty-five were "very effective."[13] To publishers of black newspapers, perennially strapped for cash, major ad buys over a period of time were rare, so the Democratic ads in the run-up to the election were a godsend. In all likelihood most of the papers would have supported the Democratic slate in any case, because that seemed to be in the best interest of the papers' readers. But the dependable stream of advertising revenue during the presidential campaign was an expedient way for the DNC to cement the support of the black press in a crucial election.

The publishers and editors of the major black newspapers were as good as their word and backed the Democratic ticket in 1960, including the man from Texas whose deep roots in the South were evident every time he spoke. Johnson suffered from what Ralph Ellison called "the Myth of the Flawed White Southerner," the presumption that a man who spoke with the honeyed drawl of a Texan could not possibly be free of the bias that made it so difficult for southern politicians of his time to embrace the cause of civil rights.[14] But the ticket received the support of virtually all the black press.

After Kennedy's assassination the new president had moved quickly to win over African Americans leaders, some of whom had harbored lingering doubts about LBJ's commitment to their cause, and established himself as an enthusiastic advocate of civil rights.[15] Days after Kennedy's death Johnson personally contacted top civil rights leaders. He called Roy Wilkins, then executive secretary of the NAACP, and invited him to a private meeting at the White House the day after Thanksgiving. Several weeks later LBJ called Wilkins again, saying to him, "I want to do anything that I ought to do. If you'll tell me what I ought to do, I'll do it. If you've ever had a friend in this place, you've got one now." Whitney Young, the National Urban League chief, received a phone call that was followed up by a meeting with the president in

Washington, D.C. Johnson also telephoned a very tired—and astonished—Farmer at home and asked him to meet him in the Oval Office. A. Philip Randolph remembered Johnson's calling him to the White House for a meeting with several other African American leaders soon after the assassination. At that meeting Johnson spoke passionately and at length about his plans for domestic reform.[16]

On December 3 Martin Luther King Jr. met with the new president and his civil rights adviser, Lee Wright, for forty-five minutes. They discussed pending legislation and the ongoing struggle in the South to secure voting rights for black Americans. King emerged from the meeting to tell the press that he was "impressed by the President's awareness and depth of understanding," and added that the talk had been "very fruitful."[17]

On January 28, 1964, Lyndon Johnson met privately with John H. Johnson, publisher of *Ebony* and *Jet*, the two leading news and social magazines for a predominately African American readership. John Johnson was a major force among black publishers. Carl T. Rowan, then head of the U.S. Information Agency, sent the president some talking points on the day of the meeting. The president was eager to secure the firm support of the publisher.[18]

He elicited unprecedented support from John H. Johnson. On September 2, 1964, the publisher sent the president two advance copies of the September 10 issue of *Jet* magazine, along with a letter, saying, "We normally avoid endorsing candidates and have not done so in twelve years. However, we felt that the issues were so important this year and your election so necessary that we departed from this policy." He directed LBJ to pages 4, 5, and 6 and the editorial announcing the magazine's endorsement of the president for election in November. The endorsement included an enthusiastic and thoughtful embrace of Lyndon Johnson's brief record as president and his ideals as a leader. The magazine pronounced the president "firm and prudent in foreign affairs, courageous and determined in domestic relations."

In his response LBJ wrote: "As one President and one Johnson to another —allow me to say 'thank you' for your warm endorsement of the national ticket. It is my fondest hope that we shall continue to merit your confidence and good will." The president's appreciation—and subtle flattery—continued LBJ's courtship of the powerful and influential publisher.[19]

Two days after his private meeting with John H. Johnson, LBJ met for an hour with the officers and board of directors of the National Newspaper Publishers Association (NNPA). This brought him face to face with the people who were in a position to shape the op-ed content of the black newspapers most influential in their markets. It also marked the beginning of regular meetings of the president and black publishers as a group at least once a year, usually early each year. The publishers also had regular contact with other officials within the administration, reflecting Johnson's desire to cultivate and maintain the support of a critical sector of African American leadership uniquely positioned to influence black opinion. The regular meetings with black newspaper publishers provided a forum in which they could convey the concerns of their readers to the president. It was an also an invaluable way for the president to stay in close touch with the black press and remain in a position to exert influence.[20]

Not all these meetings of the president and the NNPA were cordial. After the January 27, 1966, meeting, Carlton B. Goodlett, publisher of the *Sun-Reporter* in San Francisco, sent a peevish letter to LBJ, saying, "We are indignant at the rather cursory manner in which the Negro press was received by you at the White House." He then went on to describe the lecture the publishers received from the president about the "duties of the Negro press" in helping implement the recently passed Voting Rights Act. The publisher told the president, "The Negro press needs no instruction from any source on its responsibilities in the area of freedom and justice." He also noted that LBJ's aides seemed in an unseemly hurry to end the session, once Johnson had his say. Goodlett ended by saying he would suggest to the rest of the NNPA board that the group return to the White House only "when the Chief Executive will give the Negro press a proper audience."[21]

LBJ seldom took such a direct affront lightly. Despite his eagerness to cultivate black publishers, he declined to respond to Goodlett directly. Instead, LBJ passed the letter to a staffer for reply. Marvin Watson, a presidential assistant, wrote a perfunctory answer to Goodlett. Nothing further came of the incident.[22]

Lyndon Johnson also cultivated close personal ties with certain individual African American publishers. After his one-on-one meeting with John H. Johnson, LBJ continued to shower the publisher with invitations to White House social events and appointed him to influential administration positions, such as the National Advisory Council of the Office of Economic Opportunity, which oversaw the War on Poverty, and the National Advisory Commission on Selective Service. The latter gave the publisher input into draft policy, a ticklish area for African Americans because of problems with discriminatory practices in the execution of the draft, in particular, the racial composition of draft boards.[23]

Even after the early flurry of invitations and appointments, the president's personal attentions to the publisher continued. Throughout the rest of LBJ's presidency, John H. Johnson appeared, sometimes accompanied by his wife, in the President's Daily Diary, as a guest at affairs of state or at business or political meetings or as an appointee to public service. LBJ clearly considered the publisher an important person with considerable abilities to offer in the public sector, as well as a man of great influence in the African American community—and someone whose continued political support was crucial.[24]

The president was equally ardent in courting John Sengstacke, dean of black newspaper publishers, long-time owner and publisher of the *Chicago Defender*, cofounder of the NNPA, and ultimately head of a growing string of black newspapers. In addition to participating in the regular annual meetings of the president and the NNPA, Sengstacke received social invitations to the White House, and LBJ named him to two terms on the Board of Governors of the United Service Organizations (the USO), seeing "to the physical, moral, and spiritual welfare of the young men and women of the Armed Services." LBJ also sent Sengstacke a long letter commending him for his service on the Committee on Equal Opportunity in the Armed Forces, to which President Kennedy had appointed him in 1962. In the letter LBJ outlined the contributions of the group to the cause of full equality for all members of the U.S. military, regardless of race. It was a gracious statement by Johnson of the value he placed on Sengstacke's contribution to the national government—and a way for the president to reinforce his relationship with the publisher. The president also appointed Sengstacke to the National Alliance of Businessmen in January 1968, tapping his skill as a seasoned and influential business executive in the African American community and beyond.[25]

While LBJ was particularly attentive in his efforts to foster close ties with John H. Johnson and Sengstacke, the president also was assiduous in his attentions to others in the upper echelons of the black press. On at least one occasion the president sent a book containing all his 1967 messages to Congress to key figures in the black press. One recipient, T. C. Jervay, publisher and editor of the *Wilmington Journal* and a member of the NNPA board that year, wrote to Marvin Watson, of the White House staff, to express appreciation for the "wonderful volume, *No Retreat from Tomorrow*, which the President was kind enough to send us at Christmas time." Jervay then informed Watson: "In the meantime, we shall continue to carry on our front page, as we have for months—even when the polls were not encouraging—ALL THE WAY WITH LBJ!" He enclosed a recent copy of his newspaper showing the slogan prominently displayed on the upper righthand corner of the front page.[26]

After the March 15, 1968, meeting with the NNPA board, LBJ sent its chair, John Murphy, president of the *Baltimore Afro-American*, a letter thanking him and his group for meeting with him in Washington. Murphy responded with a note of his own and included a page from his newspaper. Not to be outdone by Jervay's newspaper, the Baltimore paper also published the president's campaign slogan every day: "All the Way with LBJ!"[27]

The key player in building and maintaining the goodwill of the black press was the same Louis Martin who had helped secure the support of the black press for the Democratic ticket in 1960 and who had remained an important adviser to LBJ on political as well as civil rights matters at the White House, as the publisher had been for JFK. [28] Martin's *Michigan Chronicle* was closely aligned with the Sengstacke group of black newspapers, and Martin was well connected in the tight-knit fraternity of black newspaper publishers. Martin quickly gained LBJ's confidence and was instrumental in maintaining the president's active contact with black publishers.

An example was a telling memo White House assistant Perry Barber sent to Jack Valenti, another key LBJ staffer, in August 1965. The memo contained Martin's recommendation that he arrange for the NNPA to invite the president to speak to the organization. This, Barber said, would keep the publishers revved up to inspire their readers to use "the new tools we're giving them—education, poverty program and civil rights act." Then Barber added significantly: "They could also get the Negroes solidly behind us on Vietnam."[29]

It had taken the Johnson presidency a few months to get all key White House domestic staffers aware of the importance the president attached to the black press. On September 8, 1964, LBJ received an internal memo informing him of Martin's request for an off-the-record meeting of the president with the board of the NNPA. The memo noted that these publishers "represent the influential Negro newspapers throughout the country." Valenti attached to the memo a note to George Reedy, White House press secretary, asking, "Would you please let me know who these people are?" Reedy fired back: "These are Negro newspaper publishers and we should set something up fast." The note of urgency was apparent. Reedy was well aware that it was important for the president to develop a close relationship with leaders of the black press.[30]

Except for the staunchly Republican *Atlanta Daily World*, which kept its political distance from Lyndon Johnson, the major African American newspapers were strongly in his corner in domestic politics.[31] Even black papers such as the *Baltimore Afro-American*, which consistently opposed American involvement in Vietnam during the Johnson administration, enthusiastically embraced the president politically.[32]

While the *Afro-American* held its nose over Vietnam, it defended LBJ against personal attacks from his political adversaries. In one editorial the paper scolded senators Wayne Morse and J. William Fulbright for their "brazen attempt to control the President or give our enemies the idea our country is divided."[33] The paper seemed to exempt its own criticisms of the war from this charge, perhaps because they were offered by a free, independent press and not by powerful politicians in the halls of the Senate. The *Afro-American* never allowed its criticism of U.S. policy in Vietnam to become personal attacks on Johnson, as it later would in assailing Richard Nixon for his conduct of the war.

For an explanation of the newspaper's kid-gloves handling of LBJ, one needs to look no further than another editorial in which the *Afro-American* declared its support for the president: "But notwithstanding our concern about the Asian posture of our country, at a time when many have declared open season on the man from Texas, we assert our belief that he has done great things since he entered the White House." The editorial then enumerated a long list of domestic achievements favorable to blacks that it credited to Johnson.[34]

Sometimes black newspapers argued editorially that Johnson's policy making in Southeast Asia relied on information known only to a handful of people in the administration, so the public should not second-guess how Johnson and his team were running the war. This argument was on display in an editorial in the *Philadelphia Tribune* in June 1965, as the tempo of the Vietnam War was increasing. The *Tribune* editor wrote: "Unfortunately for the average citizen who presumes to offer advice on Vietnam, he does not have all the facts that the President has." Warning that a person "giving advice on the basis of incomplete information would most likely reach another conclusion if he had all the facts," the piece ended by saying: "Whether the President and his advisers are doing what we think they ought to be doing or not, the hard, cold fact is that they have information we don't have upon which their decisions are based."[35]

While this argument was used in the black press to deflect criticism from President Johnson, it was not extended to his successor in the White House. Part of the reason for this lay in the very different view the African American community had of the two presidents. Another reason lay in the difference between the levels of public awareness about the war in 1965 and 1969. Since this argument was more common early in the war, when the public had much less information about the conflict than would be the case four years later, the argument would have carried little weight by the late sixties.

One African American paper that expressed early misgivings about the American role in Vietnam was the *Pittsburgh Courier*. In January 1965 the *Courier* found American involvement in Vietnam distinctly disquieting. As in Korea, unless the United States was willing to set off a cataclysm, it faced a stalemate in Vietnam. "We can't win a little war in that country without starting the big war which nobody wants," the paper declared. Faced with that disagreeable choice, the *Courier* concluded, "It therefore makes no sense for us to continue to send men and money to South Vietnam. The wise thing to do would be to find some face-saving way to get out—yesterday."[36]

In February 1965 the *Courier* found another compelling reason for the Johnson administration to abandon its growing involvement in Vietnam and focus all its energies on the home front: the urgent need for domestic reform. The newspaper called for the president to bring all his considerable energies to bear to introduce change "behind the 'Cotton Curtain.'" The paper said, "LBJ must call time on the stumble, bumble and fumble diplomatic game being tossed away in South Vietnam and return home."[37]

In a matter of months the *Courier*'s opposition to the U.S. role in Vietnam disappeared, replaced by support for Johnson's leadership on Vietnam. The newspaper recognized that the conflict was likely to continue for some time, given the intransigence of the enemy. In an editorial in May it summed up the unpleasant realities facing the United States in Southeast Asia. Seeing no acceptable alternative, the newspaper reluctantly acquiesced in the president's policy: "This and many other things must be taken into consideration before we condemn President Johnson and his cabinet."[38]

The *Courier* continued to offer support to a president who was increasingly beleaguered by a progressively vocal antiwar movement(see figure 7). In February 1966 the paper opposed calls for unilateral withdrawal from Vietnam, insisting that peace could come only through mutual agreement between the United States and North Vietnam. To abandon South Vietnam "would be a terrific blow to American prestige and would greatly encourage communist groups everywhere, especially those the U.S. is now opposing in Latin-American lands, [such] as Cuba, and Santo Domingo, and Venezuela." In view of its international stature and commitments, the piece said, "the U.S. isn't going to pull out of Vietnam except on agreeable terms and the majority of Negroes are going to stand by America until she decides to pull out."[39]

The *Courier* would continue to support the president's Vietnam policy through August 1967, when it declared: "The Vietnam conflict, at best, is a confused and complex matter. We have stood with the President in his position to resist the spread of communism in that part of the world. We continue to do so."[40] This would be the newspaper's last editorial supporting American policy in Vietnam before Johnson announced, in the spring of 1968, that he would not run for reelection.

The *Los Angeles Sentinel* similarly stood behind Johnson's Vietnam policy, but the paper's stance was expressed less as personal support of the president (though the paper was staunchly pro-Johnson) and more in terms of the le-

Figure 7. When a Feller Needs a Friend
Surrounded by the clamor of antiwar criticism and against the backdrop of American bombs raining on Vietnam, an embattled LBJ is assured of the strong support of the black community. (Cartoon by Sam Milai, *Pittsburgh Courier*, February 12, 1966. Courtesy of the *Pittsburgh Courier* Archives.)

gitimacy of the policy itself. The *Sentinel* accepted the generally prevailing view that the United States was fighting for freedom in Vietnam and that it was pursuing an honorable course there. The paper then argued that the moral corollary of that commitment abroad should be a national dedication to the task of extending "full freedom" to African Americans at home. A *Sentinel* editorial in August 1966 stated that black Americans were "fighting for our country against communist aggression in Vietnam," and they were "fighting for freedom," a freedom not fully available to them at home. Black soldiers fighting for freedom abroad "should have full freedom and equality here in 'the home of the brave and the land of the free.'"[41]

The newspaper was appalled at the disloyalty of certain radical black leaders who, in the editor's view, offered aid and comfort to the enemy: "It is nearly incredible that our country fails to fully realize that some Black Power leaders' involvement with foreign powers is indisputable." The paper point-ed to the shenanigans of Stokely Carmichael, who flirted with Hanoi as well as Castro's Cuba. However, the paper reserved its special wrath for Robert F. Williams, a deposed NAACP chapter president who had fled serious criminal charges in the United States and taken refuge in the embrace of Ho Chi Minh. Williams was broadcasting propaganda to black troops in Vietnam "implor-ing them to put down their arms." The editorial noted with satisfaction: "The troops clearly detest him. It is time the people here at home recognize him for what he is—a traitor." The piece ended by saying: "It is time for our Black Power leaders to begin working more assiduously for better education for our people, better jobs, and better housing."[42]

At the end of 1967 the *Sentinel* was still content to trust the government to handle the war in Vietnam. The paper was distinctly uncomfortable with the antiwar movement in general and was particularly edgy when Martin Luther King Jr. became prominently involved with groups opposing the war. The edi-tor wrote: "We wouldn't deny them their right to their belief, although we do believe they could devote their time and energy better to helping the cause of their people." The paper was eager to draw a boundary between the functions of the government in foreign affairs and the proper sphere of individual civil rights leaders—tending to issues of domestic reform: "Let's get on with the urgent job here at home and let the government take care of our foreign pol-icy and the conduct of the war."[43]

The *Amsterdam News* also gave strong early support to Johnson's conduct of the war. The paper was convinced that the president was firmly commit-ted to prosecuting with the same vigor both the war in Southeast Asia and the battle for equal rights and economic opportunity for black Americans. In the paper's words, "Mr. Johnson's approach to the war abroad and the war at home is humane and aimed at bringing about the greatest good to the great-est number of people on both war fronts."[44]

With an editorial in December 1966, the *Amsterdam News*, for the first time, exhibited serious doubts about the U.S. commitment to Vietnam. While the war was advertised as a fight to bring democracy to South Vietnam, the editorial contended that the real objective behind American exertions was to keep the communists from taking over South Vietnam. The news-paper noted that the claim that the American goal was to defend the free-dom of the nonwhite South Vietnamese was undercut by the way the United States was unfairly placing its own black soldiers at risk: "Since more than 20 percent of the American soldiers fighting and dying in Vietnam are American Negroes, the position of purity and high principle posed by the U.S. in this war is untenable."[45]

At times the paper waffled. In an editorial later in 1967 the newspaper applauded as Johnson gave a sturdy defense of his policy at home and abroad, promising to pursue the war on poverty even as he fought the war in Vietnam.[46] But scarcely two months later the paper cheered from the sidelines as Eartha Kitt scandalized guests at a White House luncheon, and visibly disturbed her host, the first lady, by speaking out against the war in Vietnam. The *Amsterdam News* noted the outrage of many at the event and in the media who thought the volatile singer's comments were rude but observed: "There are others [and the piece left little doubt the paper included itself among them] who think Miss Kitt was the only guest who added truth to the luncheon menu." The piece concluded with a defense of the singer's selection of that particular forum for her remarks: "Where else could one bring forth the most frustrating problems of our time and command the attention they so desperately warrant?"[47]

After LBJ announced he would not seek reelection, the *Amsterdam News* published an editorial lauding the president for laying aside political ambition and praised him for his many domestic achievements. Then it said: "As for winning the peace, even there we feel he has done everything possible this side of humiliating the country without surrendering; without success to be sure, but no one can surely say at this time that his way has been the wrong way. Only the unforeseeable future will bring in that verdict."[48]

It may have been the best the paper could muster, damning with faint praise, but it was a gesture of understanding and support at a difficult moment for the president.

No paper was more loyal to Johnson during his Vietnam ordeal than the *Chicago Defender*. Even when a note of anxiety about the war crept into the *Defender*'s editorial voice, the paper invariably gave Johnson personally the benefit of the doubt: "There is much apprehension about the increased tempo of military actions in Vietnam. The anxiety is admixed with a helpless feeling of not knowing what the war is all about." But, the paper added, "President Johnson cannot be held responsible for this mess. He inherited it and is doing the best he can to uphold the nation's commitment and integrity."[49]

Both the *Chicago Defender* and the *Pittsburgh Courier*, after Sengstacke purchased the Pittsburgh newspaper in 1966, loyally supported the president. The moving force behind this loyalty was Sengstacke, who had long been a force in Democratic administrations for civil rights reforms and could be counted on generally to support them in foreign affairs. He had lobbied President Franklin D. Roosevelt extensively on racial policy. The culmination of that relationship was Sengstacke's appointment to a presidential commission dealing with issues of discrimination in employment. After the war Sengstacke was one of seven people appointed by Truman to the President's Committee on Equality of Treatment and Opportunity in the Armed Forces, which led to the executive order mandating desegregation of the U.S. military. Sengstacke remained an important voice for domestic reform during the Kennedy and Johnson administrations. In an interview Sengstacke also said that he had been an acquaintance of both LBJ and Vice President Hubert H. Humphrey, the long-time senator and Democratic presidential candidate in 1968.[50]

Ethel Payne, the eminent African American journalist and Washington bureau chief and war correspondent for the Sengstacke papers, not only was well known in the White House pressroom but from 1962 to 1966 was also on the payroll of the Democratic National Committee, serving as assistant to Louis E. Martin, the deputy chair.[51]

With all those ties between key figures in the Sengstacke empire and the Democratic Party, it would have been surprising if the *Defender*—and the *Courier*—were not firm supporters of LBJ. The president's passionate support of the civil rights goals of black Americans would have been reason enough for both newspapers to support him, but the warm relations between key members of the Sengstacke group and Lyndon Johnson cemented the papers' political support.

Whether for ideological or pragmatic reasons, the *Defender* stoutly defended the president against his critics. The paper often was critical of those who openly opposed the country's policy in Vietnam. In one particularly pointed cartoon, the paper suggested that such opposition strengthened the hand of the enemy, not just in Vietnam but in the rest of Southeast Asia as well. Opposition to the war is caricatured by a shaggy, slouching demonstrator who is picketing the U.S. Capitol. Watching the disheveled antiwar protester is Chairman Mao, pictured in the cartoon as the leader of "Communism, Inc." in Asia and as saying gleefully, of the protester, "Him velly good for business!"[52]

Indeed, the domino theory drove U.S. policy in Vietnam. And the assumption that as Vietnam went, so would go the rest of the region underlay the thinking of many editorial writers, columnists, and cartoonists in the black press during most of Johnson's presidency. Chief among the president's supporters was the *Defender*.

Whatever concerns the *Defender* might have had about the administration's deep entanglement in Vietnam, the paper submerged them and sought to work from within the circle of the president's domestic allies to cultivate the long-term prospects of social reform. In doing so, the newspaper was in tune with other moderate voices within the black community that sought to keep civil rights and the Great Society at the top of the national agenda, even when pushing black priorities meant muffling criticism of U.S. policy in Southeast Asia. The result of this calculation for the *Defender* was remarkably sustained support of the president, even as his popular support wavered. Whatever its misgivings about the war, the *Defender* largely excused LBJ for his role in escalating the conflict.

Still, suspicion lurked that the president might be losing control of events in South Vietnam. A *Defender* cartoon published near the end of 1966 revealed considerable uneasiness with the war, though even as it expressed this anxiety, it seemed to place the blame for the predicament on the wily and demanding South Vietnamese. Drawing on the imagery of the fable *Gulliver's Travels,* the cartoon depicts the president as tied down by tiny, Lilliputian-like Vietnamese, who are warlike and greedy opportunists exploiting the generosity of the American government and its genial president.[53]

As the war dragged on, a predominant feature of the way the *Defender*'s cartoonists viewed the war was their sympathy for a president beleaguered by domestic turmoil and weighed down with the burdens of an unpopular war. When they wanted to criticize or poke fun at the administration's conduct of the war, the cartoonists often directed their jabs at Johnson subordinates. This allowed the paper to comment on a war that was becoming increasingly controversial, while leaving the president personally untouched. In effect, Johnson's underlings, who executed his orders, became convenient scapegoats for him.

A favorite subject was Secretary of Defense Robert McNamara. In one cartoon McNamara is a nerdy martinet who addresses his generals with a prissy self-assurance, making sure they understand just who is in charge of managing the war. The cartoon nails down the point that McNamara, not the president, was "running the war." This was a convenient way to shield Johnson from blame and lay it instead on the shoulders of the powerful secretary of defense, who seemed all too eager, in any case, to be the administration's most visible and articulate apologist for the war outside the Oval Office.[54]

A measure of the lengths to which the *Defender* would go to insulate Johnson from criticism of his handling of the war is that, in one case, when the newspaper chose to express its anxiety about the escalation of American involvement, it used Barry Goldwater, a celebrated hawk and one-time electoral opponent of the president's, as the critical foil. Since criticizing Lyndon Johnson ran the risk of alienating a key ally in the fight for social justice, the *Defender*'s cartoon instead linked the escalation to a politician who provided a tempting target; he was both hawkish on the war and an opponent of Johnson's Great Society.[55]

Still, paradoxically, such expressions of concern, even anger, about the war usually did not translate into an outright rejection of LBJ personally; he continued to enjoy strong support in the black community. However much they might deplore the neglect of the poor as the nation lavished its wealth on the war in Vietnam, black leaders and the black press almost uniformly continued to offer support to LBJ personally and politically. When they did chafe under the continuing burden of their community's needs, they frequently gave Johnson the benefit of the doubt, often blaming forces beyond his control for his absorption in prosecuting the war and his inability to deliver fully on his vision of the Great Society. Frequently, the blame came to rest on the intransigence of the president's domestic political foes or of the enemy in the jungles of Vietnam that refused every gesture of peace and persisted in aggression.

However, the black press viewed Johnson's stewardship as president with ambivalence. It supported LBJ for his commitment to the cause of ending segregation and fulfilling African American aspirations. But a growing number of black newspapers were either uneasy about the war or came to oppose it. These conflicting attitudes would sometimes override personal support for Johnson and produce sharp criticism.

Some African American newspapers embraced LBJ's domestic programs and supported him politically as enthusiastically as the *Defender*, but they were far less patient and supportive of him when it came to the Vietnam War. Among major African American newspapers, one that backed LBJ politically but opposed the war firmly almost from the beginning was the *Baltimore Afro-American*. Among the major black newspapers, the *Afro-American* was the most actively engaged editorially with the war. Editorials dealing with Vietnam were published in a third of the newspaper's issues. Most that expressed an explicit position on the war opposed it, which gave the paper a distinctly antiwar voice.

A much smaller paper, the *Sun-Reporter* in San Francisco, made the *Afro-American*'s antiwar pieces seem tame. The Bay Area paper maintained a withering assault on Johnson's war policies from the beginning, with an unrestrained vehemence that set it apart. The publisher, Dr. Carlton B. Goodlett, was an active opponent of the war, both in the pages of his newspaper and on the international stage through his membership in the World Peace Council, of which he was an officer; he served on the organization's presidium at the height of the Vietnam War. The paper had always had a left-wing tendency, which it made no bones about, and frequently exhibited a cozy regard for leftist causes in international politics. During the Vietnam conflict Goodlett worked tirelessly through his contacts in the international peace movement to promote an end to U.S. involvement in the war.

Eleanor Ohman, his secretary and a talented cartoonist for the *Sun-Reporter*, remembers attending a meeting of the World Peace Council and accompanying Goodlett as he met with North Vietnamese officials in Berlin in the late sixties to discuss the war. Ohman shared Goodlett's antiwar views and frequently used her artistic skills to draw stark images of the war. While she was a firm admirer and supporter of Johnson's for his support of civil rights goals, she did not allow this sympathy to extend to the president's handling of the Vietnam War. In her cartoons she sometimes saw an essential conflict between the benign intentions of the president and the practical consequences of his policy as it destroyed the countryside and villages of Vietnam, where even children were among the unintended victims of the war (see figure 8).[56]

Figure 8. The Great Society Meets Vietnam

Johnson's global vision of social welfare collides with the reality of the suffering in Vietnam caused by the war. (Undated cartoon by Eleanor Ohman, *San Francisco Sun-Reporter*. Courtesy of the *San Francisco Sun-Reporter* and Eleanor Ohman.)

Even when a number of black papers gave Johnson's Vietnam policy either open or tacit support, their editorials frequently discussed subjects related to the war that had negative implications for African Americans. For instance, an editorial might comment on disproportionate black casualties in Vietnam as a subject of considerable interest and concern to its readers without formally stating opposition to the war or even implying it.

Editorials discussing these negative implications for black Americans inevitably cast the war in a bad light. This almost certainly had the cumulative effect of creating the impression for readers that the newspapers either opposed the war or were curtailing their support if they had backed it in the past. These negative editorials were also likely to erode reader support for the war and produce or reinforce opposition among blacks to American participation, even though this was not the manifest intent of papers like the *Chicago Defender* and the *Pittsburgh Courier*, two of Johnson's strongest backers.

However much many members of the black press might have been disposed to excuse Johnson for the war, events soon conspired to bring him down. The Tet Offensive, which erupted on January 31, 1968, caught the administration and the American public by surprise and seemed to show that the enemy was far stronger and more capable of gaining the military initiative than the administration's battlefield assessments had let on.

In the fall of 1967. White House officials launched a campaign, headed by former Illinois senator Paul Douglas, to convince the public that the country was winning the war in Vietnam. Administration advisers supplied senators from both parties who supported the war with information to counter opposition from antiwar members of Congress. The Vietnam Information Group was formed to confront opposition as it arose. The president asked U.S. embassy and military authorities in Vietnam to report anything that could be construed as good news for use in moving opinion on the home front. The White House even arranged for prominent Americans to go to Vietnam to see progress being made in the war zone.

To cap off the administration's public relations blitz, General William Westmoreland, commander of U.S. forces in Vietnam, was brought home to spread a positive message on the home front about progress in the war. In a speech to Congress he put an optimistic spin on things, declaring: "We have reached an important point where the end begins to come into view." He even spoke of beginning withdrawals of U.S. troops within two years.

Westmoreland appeared on NBC's *Meet the Press* on November 19, 1967, and cited the attitudes of the Vietnamese people and their officials, declaring, "I find an attitude of confidence and growing optimism. It prevails all over the country, and to me this is the most significant evidence . . . that constant, real progress is being made." Later in the same interview he said, "We have evidence through our intelligence that the enemy has very serious manpower problems in the South. He is unable to recruit the guerrillas that he needs . . . and we have intelligence that he is having manpower problems now in the North." Two days later he told the National Press Club that victory "lies within our grasp—the enemy's hopes are bankrupt. With your support we will give you a success that will impact not only on South Vietnam, but on every emerging nation in the world."[57]

The Johnson administration's full-court press worked, reversing the steady erosion in the polls of popular support for the war. Opinion polls taken near the end of 1967 showed a 7 percent increase since August in approval of the president's handling of the war. The percentage of poll respondents who thought America was "losing ground" or "standing still" in Vietnam fell dramatically, while those who thought the United States was "making progress" in the war climbed from 34 percent to more than 50 percent.[58]

The Tet Offensive in early 1968 changed all that. It shattered public confidence and gave pause to official U.S. complacency, apparently contradicting the administration's upbeat assessments. Now it seemed apparent the enemy was not on the ropes but able to mount resounding attacks in all of South Vietnam's major cities simultaneously. Prominent voices in the mainstream media questioned whether the United States could ever prevail in Vietnam. In late February the iconic television anchorman Walter Cronkite announced solemnly: "It seems now more certain than ever that the bloody experience of Vietnam is to end in a stalemate. . . . To say that we are closer to victory today is to believe, in the face of the evidence, the optimists who have been wrong in the past. To suggest that we are on the edge of defeat is to yield to unreasonable pessimism. To say that we are mired in stalemate seems the only realistic, yet unsatisfactory, conclusion."[59]

The *Wall Street Journal*, which had previously supported the president's policy, asked plaintively if developments in Vietnam were "making a hash of our original, commendable objectives." Surveying the wreckage in Vietnam, the paper asked: "If practically nothing is to be left of government or nation, what is there to be saved for what?" The *Journal* warned: "The whole Vietnam effort may be doomed." *Time* magazine also saw the portents of disaster in Vietnam: "1968 has brought home the awareness that victory in Vietnam—or even a favorable settlement—may simply be beyond the grasp of the world's greatest power."[60]

According to the historian and Johnson biographer Robert Dallek, the mood within the White House in February was growing bleak. As aides prepared for the president's planned speech at the end of March on steps to end the war in Vietnam, they were, in the words of Joseph Califano, LBJ's assistant, "beyond pessimism. They sounded a chorus of despair. Secretary of State Dean Rusk appeared exhausted and worn down." Bill Bundy described South Vietnam as "very weak" and added, "Our position may be truly untenable." After a meeting with foreign policy officials, Califano described the mood among other White House staffers as "a state of depression." When he said, "This is crazy. It really is all over, isn't it?" Harry McPherson replied, "You bet it is."[61]

The Tet Offensive cast fresh doubt on the credibility of the administration and its invariably upbeat assessments of American progress in Vietnam. Senator Robert Kennedy declared that Tet "shattered the mask of official illusion with which we have concealed our true circumstances, even from ourselves."[62] These doubts nagged at the public's view of the president and eroded its confidence in the nation leader's just as the presidential primary season was beginning. In the weeks leading up to the Tet Offensive, Johnson had seen his dismal standing in national opinion polls recover somewhat. His approval ratings had improved to 46 percent in December, against 41 percent disapproval, and reached 48 percent in January, compared with 39 percent disapproval. He was expected to win two-thirds of the Democratic vote in the New Hampshire primary on March 12. However, the Tet Offensive sent his approval ratings slumping to 41 percent, with 47 percent disapproval. For LBJ it was a political catastrophe.[63]

When the New Hampshire vote in the Democratic primary was tallied, results showed Johnson with 49 percent to Eugene McCarthy's 42 percent. While it was a victory for the president on paper, the size of the vote for McCarthy was stunning. Johnson had failed to defeat handily a man who was generally dismissed as a weak opponent and who stood little chance of being elected in November. The New Hampshire vote was widely seen as a repudiation of the administration's war policy and a stinging personal rebuke to Johnson himself.

Three days later, on March 15, 1968, Johnson met for the last time with the leaders of the black press as a group. It was his annual meeting with the board of the NNPA. The president chatted both amiably and forcefully with the leading lights from the major black newspapers. He discussed ways to maintain momentum in building the Great Society and fighting poverty, and, inevitably, he also discussed Vietnam. Walt Rostow, his national security adviser, had given LBJ a two-page summary of talking points for the meeting. As the recently named head of the White House Psychological Strategy Committee, Rostow had a mandate to convey an upbeat message to the public about America's prospects for winning in Vietnam. It was a tall order, especially with an informed audience like the NNPA, painfully aware of the havoc wrought by the recent communist offensive.

Among other points, Rostow suggested to LBJ that he emphasize to the NNPA that the Tet Offensive had hurt the enemy badly and its position was deteriorating rapidly. He advised the president to emphasize that "if we lose our heads at this critical moment and listen to extremists, we might destroy the basis for the resistance to aggression in Southeast Asia" and "open the way to a new phase of communist expansion." If the dominoes began to fall in Vietnam, it would "bring us all much closer to a third world war." Rostow urged LBJ to appeal to his captive audience's sense of public purpose: "What we badly need is that the publishers and editors play their part in explaining in good balance to our people the critical issues we face, so that our democratic system can find the right answers."[64]

Just how many of these talking points came up in the session is unclear. What is clear is that the discussion generated some probing questions from the leaders of the black press. At least some of the publishers did not appear to have been eager to deliver Johnson's upbeat message about Vietnam to their readers. Over dinner that evening the president told two friends and major fund-raisers, Arthur and Mathilde Krim, that the publishers had fired about ten hostile questions at him about U.S. war policies during the afternoon session.[65]

After the session was over, Louis Martin called James R. Jones on the president's staff to tell him "the meeting with the editors and publishers was 100% successful" and that the leaders of the black press were "all going up to the hill today to carry out the suggestions the President made."[66] Martin was putting a very positive spin on the meeting, glossing over the somewhat rancorous exchanges that apparently took place about Vietnam. At the meeting the president was surrounded by people who deeply appreciated his commitment to the cause of equal rights. Vietnam was a discordant note, which Martin elected to omit from his summary.

Several days later Elizabeth Murphy Moss, vice president and treasurer of the *Afro-American*, wrote LBJ reflecting on the time she and other members of the NNPA had just spent with the president: "Ever since I left the White House on Friday I have been marveling that you were able to spend over an hour with our publishers' group. No one appreciates another man's burdens until he sits and listens to him as we did with you. This is my personal note to say, 'Special God's blessings on you.' Keep on pushing for the meaningful legislation we must have. You're doing the right thing."[67]

Moss was graciously displaying a genuine empathy with the president's heavy burdens of office—and also soothing whatever ruffled feelings may have lingered because of the rough questions some of her colleagues threw at him during the session. It was also a tactful way to steer LBJ's focus back to what the black publishers and editors all viewed as the major issues facing the nation: continued action to strengthen the Great Society and legislation to complete the Second Reconstruction.

As if tying up the last loose end in his ongoing relationship with the black press, LBJ wrote a letter to John H. Murphy III, president of the NNPA. It sounded suspiciously like a valedictory, written by someone who knew that change was coming. After saying how heartening it had been "to exchange ideas and friendships with a group as wholly committed to the national interest as your own," President Johnson wrote:

> Your members have consistently and constructively championed not only the freedom of the Fourth Estate, but human freedom everywhere.
>
> Your perseverance has brought valuable support to our efforts to free all men from the shackles of poverty and prejudice and bring them into the mainstream of our common prosperity.
>
> I salute the role that you have played in our resolute and encouraging march forward to the day when full equality of opportunity will be ours to share—as Americans—and regardless of race, creed, or color.
>
> Please accept my warmest wishes for the challenging months ahead.[68]

And they would be challenging indeed. LBJ's meeting with the NNPA was a brief respite spent with political allies before he made the final calculation of what he should do to salvage something positive for the country after the politically disastrous results of the primary in New Hampshire. His own assessment of the political realities finally forced his hand.

Johnson had been toying for some time with the idea of not standing for reelection. After months of private, personal deliberations, beginning as early as January 1967, Johnson finally broached the idea with several senior officials of his administration. On October 3 he met with members of his national security team for several hours to discuss the situation in Vietnam and the antiwar movement at home. An LBJ aide, Tom Johnson, was taking notes at the meeting, which was attended by Rusk, McNamara, Rostow, CIA Director Richard Helms, and Press Secretary George Christian. After a somewhat rambling discussion, the president said he did not want what he was about to discuss to leave the room, then dropped the bombshell that he was considering not running for reelection. Everyone who spoke up, in varying degrees of alarm, was adamant that the president should seek a second full term. In the end the matter was dropped without Johnson's announcing a decision to his staff.[69]

After the political debacle in New Hampshire, LBJ bowed to the mounting evidence that he had lost the support of the American people and announced his withdrawal from the presidential race in a televised address to the nation on March 31, 1968.[70] His decision instantly reshuffled the political deck by making the contest for the Democratic presidential nomination a wide-open affair.

Later, Lyndon Johnson would see the fierce opposition that forced him from office as a form of assassination. "The only difference between the Kennedy assassination and mine is that I am alive and it has been more torturous," he said.[71] The torture was largely self-inflicted, brought on by an unfortunate compulsion to pursue cold war ghosts into the gloomy jungles of Vietnam where destruction awaited him. Perhaps any other American president would have done the same, perhaps not. But, so far as most African Americans were concerned, with the political ruin of Lyndon Johnson came the likely extinction of their dreams that the Great Society would be fully realized. Those hopes may have been illusory in any case, but the debacle in Vietnam and the president's departure amid the political wreckage helped perpetuate the firm conviction among many African Americans that the fulfillment of their hopes was no longer possible with Johnson gone. For this, most of them believed, the Vietnam War was to blame.

At least one observer in the African American press had a different take on Johnson's fate. Gordon Hancock, writing in the *Norfolk Journal and Guide* two weeks before the Tet Offensive began and two and a half months before Johnson announced his withdrawal from the presidential race, saw the forces of opposition gathering around the president and likened his onrushing fate to the vilification and crucifixion of Jesus. Hancock compared the vitriolic opponents of the president to the baying mob screaming for the blood of Jesus before he was crucified. "In many ways," wrote Hancock, "it resembles a sentiment abroad in our land to crucify President Johnson. This sentiment is incubated in the anti-Negro South and is sweeping the nation. It has spread like an evil contagion and not only is still spreading, but intensifying as it spreads!"

In this overwrought view, the real reason for the opposition to Johnson was not the war but his embrace of the cause of black civil rights. "President Johnson's unpardonable sin," wrote Hancock, "has been his open declaration that the Negro's full citizenship is a part of the program of his proposed Great Society! And it is for this proposal that the prejudiced mob of this nation is crying with raucous voices, 'Away with him!' 'Crucify him!'" For Hancock the ultimate disgrace was that some blacks were joining in the opposition to the president, which was, at bottom, nothing more than a racist reaction to the Second Reconstruction: "It is all about the Negro! It becomes all the more amazing to see some Negroes join with the mob and in its wicked cry!" And later: "'Away with him!' 'Crucify him,' Negroes, that cry is about you!"[72]

At most black newspapers Johnson's decision to retire was a deep disappointment and a matter of deepening concern for the future. These papers had supported Johnson enthusiastically and admired him profoundly. Now, with the civil rights movement in disarray and the Great Society stalled, the future looked grim for progress toward the full realization of the black vision of domestic reform. It was impossible for the disappointment not to harden into disapproval in the commentary of those black newspapers that had either supported LBJ's policies in Vietnam or had stifled doubts out of deference to their greatest supporter in the fight for African American causes.

The sense of despair and longing in the black press and in the black community was palpable as they grappled with the numbing news of the president's decision. A Chester Commodore cartoon, which appeared in the *Defender* on April 2, mixed evident disappointment with the wan hope that somehow it might turn out alright in the end, that the champion of black America might not leave the fight after all. In the cartoon an African American getting a haircut turns to his barber and says, "Supposin' he comes on tonight an' says, 'April fool?'"[73]

The cartoon was a sad, gentle rebuke to Johnson, who had been the focus of the *Defender*'s dreams and who had accomplished so much early in his presidency to ease the burden of legal discrimination and infuse the black community with expectations of genuine economic progress. The president had accomplished a great deal for black Americans, but there still was so much to be done.

When the *Defender* editorialized about the president's pending departure, it did not cling to false hopes but exuded a gloomy foreboding about what the future might hold now for African Americans. As the newspaper took stock, it was grimly realistic. "As for black America, there is much to be worried about," the piece declared. Among the likely aspirants to the Oval Office, the only topic being discussed, the paper noted, was the Vietnam War, and no one seemed to have a clear idea how to end the conflict. Worse yet, no one was speaking out on the subject of civil rights. Once again, as so often before, it seemed that Vietnam was crowding out the aspirations and needs of black Americans.[74]

Still, there was little doubt in black leadership circles, including virtually all the African American press, that Hubert Humphrey was the only candidate in the race who was committed to the cause of full equality for black Americans. With the fall presidential election looming, the *Norfolk Journal and Guide* weighed in with an editorial about the choices facing the electorate. The editor noted that not even as ardent an opponent of the war as Julian Bond could seriously contemplate the election of either Richard Nixon or George Wallace; they were simply unthinkable options. The *Journal and Guide* quoted Bond's musings about the choices. While he could not, "in good conscience support" Vice President Humphrey because he had not opposed the war in Vietnam, Bond said, "The issue is whether you're going to build four more years of opportunity. I know George Wallace won't. I don't think Nixon will. I think Humphrey probably will."

The Norfolk editor, who had been receiving reports of the support Wallace was beginning to build, was eager to impress on African American voters the importance of turning out at the polls in November, despite the crushing disappointment so many blacks felt with LBJ out of the race. This election might be a squeaker and every vote was crucial, so the editorial was designed to motivate black voters to exercise their right and make a difference. The editorial hinted darkly at the threat posed by Wallace to the cause of equal rights, a sure way to send icy fear through any African American's veins. The piece ended with a flourish to get out the vote: "Seldom before in history has there been such motivation for black men to speak out with their votes for freedom. It is a matter of self-preservation. And in saving themselves they will save America."[75]

The election turned out to be a squeaker in the popular vote, giving Nixon a narrow plurality, 43.4 percent to Humphrey's 42.7 percent, and a popular vote margin over Humphrey of 499,704 out of just over 73 million votes cast. Wallace captured 13.5 percent of the vote. Other candidates polled just 239,908. The electoral college totals were Nixon, 301; Humphrey, 191; and Wallace, 46.[76]

For many in the black press the presidency of Lyndon Johnson effectively ended when he made his historic announcement that he would not seek reelection. The *Defender*, however, remained effusive in its praise of the president as he prepared to take his leave. In an editorial published on April 3, 1968, just days after Johnson's startling announcement, the paper paused to recognize him. The editor cited the president's remarkable record of success on behalf of black Americans, summing up his legacy: "Mr. Johnson is the greatest President who has ever occupied the White House." Johnson, the paper asserted, "has brought the Negro closer to the fulfillment of the dream of full citizenship than has ever been attempted before."

Despite the personal praise for LBJ, the paper bemoaned the way the war had deflected the administration's attention and blocked the "full utilization of the resources needed to fight poverty at home." This amounted to a criticism of the administration's war policy while softening its judgment by saluting Johnson personally for his other achievements in the field of civil rights. The statement permitted a criticism of the war while reserving personal praise for the president.

The editorial closed on a somber note. After praising the president for his contributions to the cause dearest to the hearts of black Americans, the paper observed: "It is doubtful that his successor will be as fully and earnestly committed to the cause of freedom as he." Then the paper closed the piece by chiding the president for abandoning the cause.[77]

This editorial marked a shift in the stance of the *Defender* on the war. Thirteen of the newspaper's previous fourteen editorials on the war since August 1964 had been supportive of American policy in Vietnam. After April 3, 1968, only four of thirty-eight such editorials could be construed as expressing support for administration policy in the conflict. The rest opposed America's handling of the war. The paper had long been uncomfortable with the war but had loyally maintained its support for Johnson's foreign policy leadership, including in Vietnam, and only indirectly displaying its unease with the course of events in Southeast Asia.

Once Johnson announced his intention to withdraw from the race, the political landscape changed drastically for African Americans and for those black editorial writers who had supported LBJ's policy in Vietnam. The strategic importance to the newspapers of maintaining support for Johnson's Vietnam policy, and thereby protecting and extending gains made in the area of civil rights and economic justice, now disappeared. LBJ, so admired by black Americans and by these black newspapers, had been fatally wounded politically by his unwavering commitment to the struggle in Vietnam. With him would likely go the best prospects for realizing the dreams for full equality and prosperity of a generation of black Americans.

Their loyalty to Johnson no longer constrained the African American newspapers in commenting on Vietnam. They would continue to admire the immense contributions of Lyndon Johnson to the cause of civil rights and economic prosperity for black Americans. But they would also express more freely their opposition to the war since to do so no longer risked compromising their domestic goals for reform.

The *Defender* expressed relief when talk of peace raised hopes that the war, at long last, might end, making "it possible for America to give undivided attention to the problems of poverty at home."[78] In expressing these hopes for a reallocation of resources to domestic needs at war's end, the paper was expressing a recurrent theme in the black press. Beyond its specific concerns for the impact of the war on black progress, the *Defender* also saw the political ramifications of the conflict, calling it "a massive political blunder which weighs heavily on the national conscience."[79] Twice, despite its deep respect for Johnson's domestic accomplishments, the paper referred to "President Johnson's obdurate war policy."[80]

But the paper tried to take Johnson off the hook for the fiasco in Vietnam. "The commitments to give military and technical assistance to Vietnam were made long before Johnson occupied the White House," the paper reasoned. How did this justify Johnson's role in prolonging and escalating the conflict? The paper insisted that the commitments he inherited "were so strong that he could not have disengaged himself from them without hastening a deterioration of the nation's prestige abroad." The president "was under moral compunction to carry on where his predecessors had led the country." The newspaper pointed out that it is often forgotten "that President Johnson was not the architect of the foreign policy in Southeast Asia." The *Defender* continued to be charitable to LBJ in assessing his handling of the war after the election of November 1968. As the president bent his efforts to finding peace, devoting his energies to what one administration insider called "an increasingly frantic chase after the will-o'-the-wisp of negotiations," the *Defender* was sympathetic. It recognized his desire "to leave office with the reputation of a peace-maker."[81]

The image of the Vietnam War that emerges from the pages of black newspapers was generally negative. Even papers that supported national policy during Johnson's presidency almost uniformly saw the war as damaging to the interests of African Americans but continued to hold LBJ personally in high esteem. Unlike the mainstream press, the black press was virtually unanimous in its praise of Johnson, despite misgivings or outright opposition to the war. The issue of credibility, which so bedeviled the president's relations with the white media, scarcely disturbed the loyalty the black press bestowed upon the president. The key to this loyalty, of course, was that Johnson was the unswerving champion of the aspirations of black Americans. Even a distaste for the war in Vietnam, which Johnson had presided over throughout the period of escalating troop levels and soaring casualty lists—including daunting numbers of black GIs—was not enough to loosen the strong bonds of political support and personal affection that African Americans felt for the president. Black newspapers often went to great lengths to inoculate Johnson from ultimate responsibility for the unfolding debacle in Vietnam. They found other reasons to explain continued U.S. participation in the war, reasons that absolved the president: commitments made to South Vietnam by previous administrations; the obstinacy of the enemy in refusing Johnson's many peace initiatives; the lack of maturity, stability, and performance in battle of South Vietnam's government and military; or lack of political support from people and politicians at home, which lengthened the war.

In an editorial published on New Year's Day 1969, the *San Francisco Post* looked back on the eventful year just ended and on the political calamity that had befallen Lyndon Johnson, whose ruined presidency was in its final days. The paper tried to make sense of how it, and the black community generally, were able to view the war with such distaste and still support Johnson politically, in contrast to the antiwar movement generally, which had managed to bring him down: "Negroes accepted this war as one of folly but being accustomed as they are to many frivolous acts on the part of the majority, they saw no reason to make this their principal issue when their stride for civil rights had reached such momentum." Instead the *Post* cited the unprecedented way President Johnson had accomplished things beneficial to African Americans. He had appointed blacks to high positions in his cabinet and in the judiciary. Even more significant were his legislative achievements that changed the domestic landscape for black Americans. Therefore, the piece concluded: "Out of gratitude for President Johnson's apparent sincerity in an effort to right the wrongs of hundreds of years of treason, as far as Negroes were concerned, the Negro saw no reason to embarrass him by collectively opposing his war in Vietnam."[82]

After Lyndon Johnson died on January 22, 1973, most black newspapers focused their memorials on his achievements in civil rights and forgave him for his messy war in Vietnam, often choosing to excuse him for the war by blaming it on his predecessors. The *San Francisco Sun-Reporter* was less forgiving. The paper saw in the Johnson presidency not one president but two. One would be remembered as the man who wrestled landmark legislation through Congress: historic civil rights bills that systematically dismantled the old system of segregation and intolerance that barred black Americans from restaurants, better schools, and, most important, the voting booth. He established agencies and laws to improve the quality of life for millions of African Americans.

But, said the *Sun-Reporter*, all those achievements, despite their importance, "pale from the catastrophe which Johnson brought to America at home and abroad when he pursued war in Southeast Asia. . . . Thus, Johnson's legacy will not be his work for poor and minority people, but his war in Asia."[83]

In the eyes of most of the black press and most African Americans, Lyndon Johnson's principal legacy despite the war would be his achievements in civil rights. *Crisis* magazine quoted Roy Wilkins as saying, "Never before in the history of the United States of America had this great goal of human equality been championed from the White House." *Crisis* recalled and embraced a phrase from Dean Rusk's eulogy in the Capitol Rotunda: Johnson was "Lyndon, the Liberator."[84]

To most black Americans he would remain the foremost champion of African American rights ever to occupy the White House. He was the man who swept away the legal basis of segregation and redefined the rights of the nation's black citizens. He would be celebrated as the president who, more than any other, finally set African Americans free from the tyranny of the Jim Crow laws that perpetuated their bondage long after the institution of slavery was overturned.

After Lyndon Johnson died, his body lay in repose for one day in his library in Austin, Texas, then lay in state in the Capitol Rotunda in Washington, D.C., for two days. Almost immediately, individual African Americans formed their own view of the legacy of Lyndon Baines Johnson. Thousands expressed their view silently as they joined the stream of mourners moving quietly past his casket. One observer estimated that 60 percent of those who came to pay their respects were African Americans. He overheard one black woman say to her little girl: "People don't know it, but he did more for us than anybody, any President, ever did." To the observer, "That was his epitaph as far as I was concerned."[85]

7

The Black Press and
Vietnam in the Nixon Years

There will be no honeymoon between the 37th President of the United States Richard M. Nixon and the black press.—*San Francisco Sun–Reporter,* January 18, 1969

With the notable exception of the redoubtably Republican *Atlanta Daily World,* African American newspapers generally viewed the election of Richard Nixon with sentiments ranging from disappointment to alarm. The *Chicago Daily Defender,* for example, greeted Nixon's election glumly. On November 7, 1968, the paper published a cartoon that took up the entire front page of the newspaper. The gloomy image of Martin Luther King Jr. crumpling a copy of his "I have a dream" speech spoke as eloquently of despair as his soaring words had evoked hope.

The *Defender'*s reaction was a visually poignant and apt response to the election that captured the mood of much of the black press, which saw the Nixon presidency as a time of peril for the African American agenda of reform. As Lyndon Johnson entered the waning months of his tenure at the White House, American society seemed poised to become something much different from what it had been during the hopeful, if flawed, years of the Great Society. To be sure, the Vietnam War had slowed the momentum of reform and distracted a president deeply committed to the cause of civil rights and an improved quality of life for African Americans. But at least blacks knew where they stood with Lyndon Johnson. He was with them, supported their aspirations, and would remain their champion.

Richard Nixon was quite another thing. He had won the election by courting the southern vote and had displayed little interest in the concerns of African Americans. The black press coped with its uncertainty and fear by trying to establish contact with the president-elect. An editorial in the *San Francisco Sun-Reporter* suggested that these efforts were largely fruitless. On January 18, 1969, the paper complained: "Ever since his election, Nixon has avoided a meeting with the National Newspaper Publishers Association, trade association of the black press in the U.S." The piece went on to recite a litany of slights that the black press had received from Nixon over several years. Nixon "has constantly avoided serious discussions with the black newspaper publishers," wrote the editor. "In 1960 he refused their invitation to address the NNPA [National Newspaper Publishers Association] Chicago convention and sent an assistant." In 1968 Senator Eugene McCarthy and Vice President Hubert H. Humphrey "both addressed black America via mass communications media from the NNPA convention in New York City," but Nixon turned down an invitation to do the same. Instead, he spent what the editorial called "a few meaningless minutes at an NNPA cocktail reception." Nixon, the paper believed, had snubbed the black press.[1]

The *Sun-Reporter* cartoonist Eleanor Ohman marked Nixon's inauguration by depicting him as a puppet of the Pentagon, dancing to the tune of the same war machine that ultimately had pulled the strings controlling Lyndon Johnson (see figure 9). Here Ohman reveals the disappointment she felt in Johnson's failure to exert his will and withstand the warrior impulses rampant at the Pentagon that led the United States into the Vietnam War.

Other black newspapers were somewhat more inclined to give the new president a little leeway before taking up partisan cudgels, though there was little enthusiasm for Nixon outside the editorial offices of the *Atlanta Daily World*, where the joy was unbounded.

The *Baltimore Afro-American* showed considerable restraint in its response to Nixon's election despite its evident disappointment: "Our reaction to the hairline victory scored by Mr. Nixon and Agnew can best be described as one of mixed emotions," said the editor. He then gave reasons for uneasiness: the indifference of the Republican ticket to the interests and needs of black Americans; the stirring of white backlash against urban unrest; the heavy-handed ideology of suppression of dissent rather than seeking to eliminate the causes of disaffection; silence on key issues like poverty, discrimination

Figure 9. The Presidents as Puppets
Two puppets, but the same puppeteer pulls the strings. (Cartoon by Eleanor Ohman,
San Francisco Sun-Reporter, January 25, 1969. Courtesy of the *San Francisco Sun-Reporter*.)

in housing, and employment; and the absence of a coherent strategy to end
the Vietnam War.

Then the editorial said: "Our apprehension notwithstanding, President-
elect Richard M. Nixon and Vice President-elect Spiro Agnew have won the
right to try their hand at running the affairs of the nation. They deserve our
support. . . . We extend our heartiest congratulations to President Richard M.
Nixon and Vice President Spiro T. Agnew."[2]

Despite its keen initial disappointment when Nixon was elected, the
Defender, like the *Afro-American*, seemed prepared to give him more leeway
than most black papers in 1969. One reason may have been an olive branch
Nixon extended to the *Defender*'s publisher, John Sengstacke, even before the
inauguration. On December 2, 1968, the president-elect sent Sengstacke a letter asking the publisher to help find suitable people to serve in the new administration—people who would be "the best minds in America to meet the
challenges of this rapidly changing world." Nixon told Sengstacke, "You, as a

leader, are in a position to know and recommend exceptional individuals." There is no evidence Sengstacke made any specific recommendations of individuals to Nixon's transition team, but perhaps the publisher wanted to keep his lines of communication open in the early going.[3]

Another reason for this moderation at the *Defender* was that the newspaper assumed the war would soon end. Only a few odds and ends were left to tidy up, it appeared. "It remains for Nixon to finish the job," said the paper. The imminence of peace seemed certain.[4] The *Defender*'s confidence that peace was at hand in Vietnam undoubtedly had been fed in the final days of the election campaign. Johnson had announced a bombing halt and hinted that peace was near. If this initiative was timed to influence the voting for Johnson's successor, it nearly succeeded. Despite a strong 301–191 victory in the electoral college, Nixon's popular-vote margin over Hubert Humphrey was only 499,704 out of just over 63 million cast for the two main candidates. George Wallace captured 13.5 percent of the popular vote and 46 votes in the electoral college.[5]

Nixon had also contributed to the peace hopes. The *Defender* apparently found the optimism exuded by the new administration contagious. As a candidate for the presidency, Richard Nixon brimmed with confidence as he told a group of journalists in July 1968 that he hoped to induce the Soviet Union to apply sufficient pressure on the North Vietnamese to bring the war to an agreeable conclusion.[6] In his acceptance speech at the Republican National Convention, Nixon solemnly intoned, "I pledge to you tonight . . . to bring an honorable end to the war in Vietnam."[7] In his inaugural address on January 20, 1969, Nixon said: "Let us take as our goal: Where peace is unknown, make it welcome; where peace is fragile, make it strong; where peace is temporary, make it permanent. . . . After a period of confrontation, we are entering an era of negotiation."[8]

As the new president settled into the Oval Office, talk of peace was in the cold January air. It lingered there briefly, flimsy as a wisp of frozen breath. All the talk of peace obscured Nixon's continuing effort to wring a victory of sorts out of Vietnam, combining negotiations with the continued application of military power to realize the U.S. goal of preserving the independence of South Vietnam and halting the spread of communism down the Indochina peninsula. The hope for an elusive peace with honor in Vietnam was another way of clinging to this objective, and the persistence of this goal assured the continuation of the war.

After the election Nixon met with several black leaders, including the president of the NNPA, but the *Sun-Reporter* was not impressed with what it called a "slight recognition of the black press," which it dismissed as "a mere afterthought."[9] *Ebony* was somewhat more impressed by Nixon's outreach at the meeting. An editorial, published in the April 1969 issue of the magazine, admonished in its title: "Let's Give Him a Chance." The piece described how Nixon invited six black leaders to meet with him in New York; the group included *Ebony*'s publisher, John H. Johnson, and the *Afro-American*'s publisher, John H. Murphy III, who was also president of the NNPA: "To these men, Mr. Nixon pledged that he would endeavor to surpass the efforts of his predecessor to improve the economic and social conditions of black Americans. He said that this meeting was the first of many meetings in which he hoped to develop communications between his Administration and black Americans. He said he was seeking advice from black leaders to give him 'direction, advice and criticism' in affairs that affect black citizens."

The editor concluded his piece with an appeal to the magazine's readers to "give him [Nixon] a chance to prove himself."[10] The wait-and-see restraint of both the *Afro-American* and *Ebony* after the election may very well have been influenced by the meeting of the president and the publishers.

After his inauguration the new president continued reaching out to important publishers in the black press during the first several months of his administration, inviting them to participate in events at the White House. Nixon sent a telegram to Sengstacke on January 26 asking him "to join with members of my cabinet, chief executives of America's leading companies, state governors, mayors of the nation's largest cities, and national labor leaders" to meet with the executive board of the National Alliance of Businessmen (NAB) on March 15 to help "provide permanent jobs for the hard-core unemployed and jobs for needy youngsters during the summer."[11]

Nixon sent Sengstacke another a telegram on January 31, the first anniversary of the NAB's founding, this time thanking him effusively for his service on the executive board of the organization. The president's words of praise for the publishers' contribution to the NAB's accomplishment were over the top: "It is obvious that this splendid record is the result of your exemplary effort in this unique cooperative enterprise uniting the private sector and the Federal government." The president offered Sengstacke his "personal assurance that the new administration is solidly behind the Alliance" and expressed his hope that "our mutual efforts will become even more productive in the future."[12]

On March 5, 1969, barely six weeks into his presidency, Nixon signed Executive Order 11458, designed to encourage the formation of new businesses by minorities. The president invited John H. Johnson, the eminent black publisher, to attend the signing ceremony. Johnson, who was one of the most successful African American entrepreneurs, lent his considerable prestige to the proceedings. The executive order led to the formation of the Office of Minority Business Enterprise (OMBE). The initiative came to be widely scorned among vocal black community leaders and Democratic members of Congress, who viewed it as a "cosmetic device to lull minority Americans into acquiescence while corporate America carves up the national pie." Only long after Nixon's departure from office would African American business leaders recognize the program as a positive force for economic development in the community.[13]

The president's courting of major publishers of the black press and African American leaders continued when he hosted a stag black-tie affair at the White House on May 12 to honor Whitney M. Young Jr. and the rest of the executive committee of the Urban Coalition. Both John H. Johnson and Sengstacke attended. At the time they were arguably the most powerful and influential figures in the black press.[14]

When Nixon went to the Liberian Embassy in Washington to attend a celebration of the sixth anniversary of the Organization of African Unity, he was joined by Lillian Wiggins, columnist for the Washington edition of the *Afro-American*; Ethel Payne, White House correspondent for the *Chicago Defender*; and Simeon Booker, the popular columnist for *Jet* magazine. The guest list also included an array of luminaries from all three branches of the government. The White House record of the event notes the affiliation of Payne and Booker with the Sengstacke and Johnson publishing empires, respectively, testifying to the importance the Nixon administration attached to the two top African American publishers and their respective companies.[15]

Nixon finally met with seventeen publishers, editors, and other leaders from the NNPA on May 28, 1969, in the Cabinet Room at the White House. One notable no-show was Sengstacke, who sent Payne in his place. John H. Murphy III led a three-person contingent from the *Afro-American*. Nixon came to the meeting armed with talking points supplied by staffers. Nixon's staff suggested particular emphasis on programs that had been part of LBJ's Great Society, including the Job Corps and Model Cities, and Nixon's own OMBE. The talking points also included the perennially controversial military draft, a particularly sensitive issue during the Vietnam War and a centerpiece of antiwar protest and resistance among many African Americans.[16]

Nixon's meeting with the black publishers and editors made little discernible progress in changing the black press's extremely negative view of the Vietnam War. Judging from the increasingly united front of the black press against U.S. policy in Vietnam, apparently nothing said at the meeting eased the mounting concerns among African American journalists about Nixon's stewardship of the war.

The president's early wooing of the black press could do little to counter his own history. Nixon's campaign rhetoric and electoral strategy, including his selection of the acid-tongued Spiro Agnew as running mate and designated attack dog, and Nixon's hearty embrace of themes designed to appeal to conservative prejudices, made it unlikely the black press would give him credit for much of anything, even programs with progressive goals, such as Nixon's own OMBE.[17]

By the fall of 1969 the *Defender* was taking on the war again, impatient with the failure of the Nixon administration to produce the promised peace. In an editorial in early November the *Defender*'s headline dismissed a Nixon speech on efforts to extract the United States from Vietnam as "The Same Old Stuff" and scolded the president for his failure to make good on his campaign promise that, if elected, "he would bring the boys back home and end the senseless war."[18]

Other black newspapers, which had avoided criticizing the war editorially during the Johnson years, opposed it actively once Nixon became president. Some of these newspapers began speaking out against the war after Johnson announced he would not seek reelection, or they did so in the early months of Nixon's first term.

For example, there was a noticeable about-face in the editorial position of four major black papers, which switched from offering general support to Johnson's Vietnam policy to opposing the war during the Nixon presidency. Three of these, the *Chicago Defender*, *Pittsburgh Courier*, and *Los Angeles Sentinel*, altered their positions after Johnson withdrew from the presidential race in the spring of 1968. The fourth, the *New York Amsterdam News*, first opposed the war in the summer of 1969 and consistently did so thereafter. In contrast the *Baltimore Afro-American*, *Milwaukee Star*, and *San Francisco Sun-Reporter*, to name just a few, opposed the war throughout both the Johnson and Nixon administrations, until the final U.S. withdrawal in the spring of 1973. The *Atlanta Daily World*, with its typical Republican hawkishness, supported the war throughout both administrations.

The *New Courier* in Pittsburgh joined its sister paper in the Sengstacke group, the *Defender*, in edging away from the lame-duck Johnson and began questioning Johnson's war policy, gently to be sure, by speaking of "the dubious merits of further intensification of military action in Vietnam." It did so in an editorial on the growing clout of the black vote in American politics, a power owing much to the exertions of Lyndon Johnson and liberals and moderates in Congress in passing the landmark Voting Rights Act of 1965, as well as of civil rights workers, particularly in the South, who worked tirelessly to galvanize blacks to register to vote and thereby strengthen African American clout on election day. The *Courier* viewed the black vote as the deciding bloc in the upcoming presidential election and imagined the leverage that new reality would place in African Americans' hands: "In the ebb and flow of the tides of politics, only numbers count. The Negro vote this year more than ever has the relevant density to tilt the scales on the side of the black man's choice. . . . Negro leadership must not fumble this golden opportunity to make its power felt."[19]

Once Richard Nixon was elected president, the *Courier* took on the administration's war policy in an editorial, "The Fight on Poverty." Using the familiar formulation in the black press of weighing the costs of the Vietnam War against the lesser costs of funding the war on poverty, the editorial made very clear how the paper viewed the overseas war effort: "The federal government . . . is spending some 33 billion dollars a year to carry on a foolish war in Vietnam. Less that half of this amount stretched through a five-year period would go a long way toward eradication of slums and its accompanying poverty in the United States."[20]

After supporting Lyndon Johnson's Vietnam policy consistently, the *Los Angeles Sentinel*'s patience ran out as the nation prepared for a new era under Richard Nixon. In November 1968 the newspaper signaled its new perspective on the war. The paper was no longer content to give the government's handling of the war uncritical blanket approval. In a Veterans Day editorial the paper quoted its hope from the same observance a year earlier, "that the day will soon come when the human race will 'study war no more.'" Now the paper observed, "That hope is still with us . . . so is the war." Despite a bombing halt by President Johnson, the violence continued unabated on the ground, with casualties mounting on both sides. "Underscoring the obvious," the paper observed somberly, "the only way to stop a war is to stop the fighting."[21]

A year later the *Sentinel* published another Veterans Day editorial. The war was still grinding on relentlessly, despite promises by President Nixon to end it quickly. In the face of overwhelming opposition to the war, as exemplified in the massive Vietnam Moratorium protests in late 1969, Nixon persisted in his refusal to heed the swelling chorus of protest. The people were making their feelings known but uselessly. The paper said: "The Vietnamese war is contrary to the wishes of the American people. If Mr. Nixon does not care to heed the wishes of the people who put him in office, then he may rest assured there will be another new resident on Pennsylvania Ave. in 1972."[22]

A week after the Vietnam Moratorium demonstrations in November 1969, an editorial in the *Sentinel* was unstinting in its praise for the moratorium's expression of popular opinion on the war and insisted that the message of the protesters be heeded. Failure to heal the fissures splitting the nation because of Vietnam could spell trouble for the country; what resulted would be the fault of a president out of touch with his people: "An America divided by a leader deaf to his followers, a seemingly unending drain of human life and spirit and tax dollars, can fell the mightiest of nations."[23]

When the U.S. space program finally landed men on the moon in July 1969, a flurry of opinion pieces appeared in the black press that used the event to remind readers just how distorted the government's moral values were in allocating billions of dollars to the space program—and to the Vietnam War—and in failing to devote the resources necessary to end poverty and heal crumbling inner cities. The space triumph was interpreted as just another expression of America's misdirected priorities and its failure to deliver on Lyndon Johnson's bold commitment to eradicate poverty.

The *New York Amsterdam News* was an early supporter of American involvement in Vietnam. As the war escalated in 1965, the newspaper saw the struggle as an ideological one, pitting the communist Vietcong against America's plucky ally, the South Vietnamese. Even as the Vietcong were seeking "to force [their] ideologies on the Vietnamese," however, the paper saw an even more "disgusting spectacle" in the ugly racism on display in the fawning adoration bestowed on three Klansmen accused of murdering three young civil rights workers in Mississippi. "It is most certainly true," an editorial in the *New York Amsterdam News* acknowledged, "that we do have problems to solve in Vietnam"; however, "it is equally true that we have some very serious problems to solve right in our own backyard."[24]

By mid-1969 the *New York Amsterdam News* had lost patience with U.S. policy in Vietnam. On June 28 the paper published an editorial headlined "Against the War," and cited the mounting combat losses of young black men (including a Brooklyn fifteen-year-old who somehow got into the service despite his age) as justification for the growing black opposition to the war, including the editor's own outrage. Pointing to the soaring poll numbers measuring African Americans opposed to the war, the editor ventured a guess that, if pollsters returned the next day, they would find the number even higher.

The following month an *Amsterdam News* editorial took on the "outlandish costs of the space race, coupled with the outlandish costs expended in the Vietnam War." The funds, the piece insisted, "that should have been spent resolving these immediate problems at home are exhausted in the race for the moon and the endless war in Vietnam."[25]

The *Oakland Post* was a vigorous opponent of the war and frequently criticized Nixon for what the paper perceived to be badly misplaced priorities. The manned moon landing in mid-1969 afforded an opportunity for the newspaper's editor to point out how American ingenuity, coupled with compassion, ought to be able to find a way to end the wasteful war in Vietnam and win the war on want in the homeland: "What the [space] program and its success really tell us is that man has the capacity to accomplish almost anything that he can imagine, given sufficient time and money." What was sorely lacking, the *Post* argued, was the kind of commitment to solve domestic problems that the nation had made to space travel and to the war in Vietnam: "We subscribe to the fact that man has the ability to accomplish that which he can imagine. . . . It is difficult to understand why our leadership cannot imagine what would happen if the money spent on the space program and the war were channeled into our domestic development."[26]

Across the bay in San Francisco the *Sun-Reporter* was relentlessly critical of U.S. involvement in the Vietnam War. When the National Mobilization to End the War in Vietnam planned a preinaugural meeting in Washington, D.C., the *Sun-Reporter* applauded and warned the incoming administration: "Millions of Americans are sick of the frustrating cancer, Vietnam, with its dangerous potentials which could even destroy the nation."[27]

The *Sun-Reporter* continued its barrage of criticism of the war and Nixon's stewardship of it throughout his first year in office, using such headlines as "Nixon's Tricky Dickering" and "Nixon's Madness" to dismiss his policies.[28] The newspaper kept up the pressure on Nixon, insisting that he produce the peace plan that he had dangled before the nation during the 1968 presidential campaign: "For many months we have waited for the birth of Nixon's brainchild after its long period of gestation. We have doubted over the months that Nixon has any new approach to Vietnam. Like Johnson, he speaks of an 'honorable' peace while his generals wage more intense and vicious war, threatening not only the survival of a tiny country ten thousand miles away, but also the moral fiber of our people here at home."[29]

To galvanize support for an antiwar march and rally scheduled for San Francisco on November 15, 1969, the *Sun-Reporter* urged African Americans to participate in the peace movement "to demand an end to the war in Vietnam." An editorial laid out the costs of the war to blacks: "Black soldiers are being killed and crippled at a higher rate than any others. . . . Whatever the causes of American militarism, it has always used minorities as cannon fodder. American militarism itself is one of the biggest forms of oppression against black Americans as well as against the Vietnamese."[30]

In a column in the *Afro-American*, John Lewis expressed anger but not surprise at the routine discrimination practiced by whites against blacks: "Who can be surprised in a country where we spend $30 billion to go to the moon and many billions more to suppress the struggle of the Vietnamese people for self-determination?" he wrote. Lewis saw further evidence of the indifference of the nation's white leaders to the needs of black Americans in the misdirection of government resources from Great Society programs to space exploration and the Vietnam War. In fact, Lewis called the government's failure to direct sorely needed funds to the War on Poverty "a harsh comment on the evil nature of the Federal government."[31]

In the fall of 1969 Whitney M. Young Jr. came out against the war in Vietnam. He was one of the last major civil rights figures to maintain a public silence while other black leaders denounced American policy in Vietnam. In June, before his public denunciation of the U.S. role in Vietnam, he had said privately: "I must confess, I have changed somewhat in my own thinking now and feel maybe Dr. King was more right than probably I was, because it is hard to separate the war from the domestic problems in terms of resources of the country and of manpower and all this."[32] It was an awkward statement revealing a distinct change in Young's thinking yet containing an unmistakable hesitance to disavow his long-standing practice of remaining publicly silent when he disagreed with the administration on foreign policy.

Young had been among those who had been squeamish about Martin Luther King's antiwar activities for several years before King's death and had been particularly uncomfortable with what he saw to be King's attempt to fuse the civil rights struggle and the antiwar movement from the spring of 1967 until his death a year later. Young was a moderate pragmatist who prided himself in his ability to maintain lines of communication with key members of the white political and business establishment.

In an interview with *Jet* Young finally dropped his customary caution: "Our involvement in this war on distant Asian soil has sharpened the divisions and frustrations among the people of this country." He called for an "immediate plan" for pulling U.S. troops out of Vietnam, charging, "The black is the victim of a backlash greatly sharpened by the tensions of the war." Young's words ironically established the same linkage between the war and black suffering at home that King had made two years earlier, saying, "The war has so increased Negro frustration and despair that urban outbreaks are now an ugly feature of the American scene."[33]

Nixon's response to his critics was a carefully honed speech on November 3, 1969, that went through twelve drafts by exhausted speechwriters before Nixon himself applied the final touches. He described in his memoirs how the run-up to the speech was accompanied by speculation that "reached fever pitch" before he appeared before the television cameras. He wanted the speculation to ignite interest and build a bigger and more avid audience. He also sought to counter protest and criticism of his war policy by going on the offensive and marshalling to his side an army of supporters whose quiet support, he believed, had been drowned out by the noisy protesters who inveighed against the war in Vietnam. Finally, Nixon went on television to address the nation: "I have chosen a plan for peace. I believe it will succeed. If it does succeed, what the critics say now won't matter. If it does not succeed, anything I say then won't matter. . . . And so tonight—to you, the great silent majority of my fellow Americans—I ask for your support. . . . Let us be united for peace. Let us also be united against defeat. Because let us understand: North Vietnam cannot defeat or humiliate the United States. Only Americans can do that."[34]

It seemed to some in the black press that one way President Nixon sought to muffle dissent—including black dissent—was to announce his much ballyhooed strategy of Vietnamization. *Vietnamization* was the term given to the policy of gradually withdrawing U.S. troops from South Vietnam and letting Vietnamese forces assume an increasing share of the fighting. The term was probably coined by Defense Secretary Melvin Laird in the spring of 1969, although a year earlier General Creighton Abram, as he succeeded William Westmoreland, who had retired as commander of U.S. forces in Vietnam, had spoken of "Vietnamizing" the war by turning more of the fighting over to the Vietnamese.[35]

The *Los Angeles Sentinel* lampooned the new policy after the president pitched it to the country in his speech. Rather than viewing the policy as a military strategy designed to shift the burden of fighting to the South Vietnamese and enable the systematic withdrawal of U.S. forces, the paper focused on the propaganda value of the policy. It regarded Vietnamization as a cynical attempt to manipulate and control popular sentiment about the war and to defuse the threat posed by vocal opponents of the U.S. role in Vietnam (see figure 10).

Whatever the basis of the policy of Vietnamization, it did have the effect of quieting protest significantly, though scarcely permanently. The speech produced an avalanche of responses. The White House switchboard was swamped with calls as soon as the broadcast ended. The mailroom counted more than fifty thousand telegrams and more than thirty thousand letters in response, the majority in support of the president's new policy.[36]

The speech also led to a dramatic upswing in approval ratings for the president's handling of the war, from 58 percent before the speech to 77 percent in its immediate aftermath. The figures for those who disapproved of his handling of the conflict dove from 32 percent to 6 percent. A few weeks later another poll found 74 percent of the American people opposed to an immediate withdrawal of U.S. troops from Vietnam.[37] By the time Nixon summoned his

Figure 10. Withdrawal Pains
Domestic pacification as a foreign policy strategy. (Cartoon by Clint C. Wilson Sr., *Los Angeles Sentinel*, November 20, 1969. Courtesy of the *Los Angeles Sentinel*.)

silent majority, he had already moved well down the path of gradualism in his effort to end the war. Vietnamization was a repudiation of the vocal minority who clamored for an immediate end to the war, and increased approval ratings seemed to validate Nixon's decision to go with Middle America, where he believed support for his policy of patience and tenacity lay. The silent majority, Nixon was convinced, wanted the war to end but wanted it done in a way that would not humiliate the United States.[38]

Vietnamization was the logical implementation of the Nixon Doctrine, which had been announced in July. It limited U.S. assistance to economic and military aid under treaty agreements but in most cases excluded the commitment of U.S. troops. The United States stood ready to help nations under attack, but the assistance would be directed toward enabling allies to defend themselves. The doctrine's primary application was clearly intended for countries such as Vietnam, which was located on the Asian mainland but not covered by firm treaty commitments.[39] The first application of the new doctrine was to the U.S. effort in Vietnam. The difficulty with that was that American troops had already been committed to ground combat there. The retrospective implementation of the strategy to Vietnam was a little like attempting to unscramble an omelet. Vietnamization was the name given to the messy attempt.

Withdrawal of U.S. forces from Vietnam began in August 1969 when twenty-five thousand service people were pulled out of the battle zone in what military public relations officers coyly called a redeployment.[40] This began the process of implementing a strategy that could achieve desirable domestic results for Nixon in terms of stabilizing political support and recovering popular backing for his handling of the war. It also seemed to be an inherently sensible idea: helping South Vietnam help itself. However, Vietnamization was a hopelessly contradictory strategy, containing in the very thing that made it attractive the inevitable precursor of failure. By setting in motion the process of withdrawal, the president simultaneously gave relief to war-weary Americans and hope to the North Vietnamese. At the heart of Vietnamization was the presumption that, in the foreseeable future, the last U.S. soldier would leave Vietnam and come home. This expectation was the very element of the policy that would arouse public support at home but would also steel the determination of the North Vietnamese in Hanoi and on the battlefield.[41]

Despite the inherent weaknesses of Vietnamization as a strategy, Nixon had little choice but to do something that offered the prospect of an end to the war. As the policy was being implemented with the first troop withdrawal in August 1969, the public's support for Nixon's Vietnam policies was steadily weakening. In a Lou Harris poll taken in June, a narrow margin of the public supported Nixon: 47 to 45 percent. In July the poll found only 44 percent of the American people supported Nixon's handling of the war. By the end of September the number had slipped to 35 percent.[42]

Nixon needed to shore up popular backing for his leadership in the war, and the announcement and implementation of his Vietnamization strategy appeared to have had the desired effect. After the realization sank into the public consciousness that the war in Vietnam might be coming to an end after all, Nixon's poll numbers began to climb, exceeding a majority by the time he gave his "silent majority" speech in November 1969, which in turn pushed them higher still. However, the effects were temporary. By 1971, 61 percent believed that American involvement in the war was a mistake, and 58 percent thought the war was immoral.[43]

The African American press and the larger constituency it served were decidedly not a part of Nixon's silent majority. Whatever goodwill the president might have purchased in the black press by public appeals for support, and by bringing some troops home as part of Vietnamization, was more than offset by the deep suspicions about Nixon's intentions for the nation's black citizens. After Nixon had been in office barely a year, these suspicions had already become part of the standard fare offered widely in the black press in evaluations of the new president.

An editorial served up in the *St. Louis American* on March 5, 1970, was a particularly caustic example of this viewpoint. The editor described the political environment fostered by Nixon and his combative vice president, Agnew. Despite the unifying theme of Nixon's "campaign promise . . . to 'bring us all together,'" according to the editorial, Nixon and Agnew were taking steps to foster a segregationist culture in the nation, with a law-and-order domestic strategy veiling the menacing shape of a "police state," buttressed by the nomination of two racist candidates to the Supreme Court and suppression of dissent against the Vietnam War.

The editorial closed with a bizarre and pungent example of polemic: "And pray for us all, if and when the bulk of those American black soldiers return from Vietnam! They are having troubles over there—and they will hardly swallow whole the Nixon-Agnew castor oil prescription for the Preservation of Segregation in the schools of this land! This is something more than a figure of speech—it is a forecast of some form of national diarrhea brought on by Doctor Nixon and Intern Agnew. . . . It can be just as ugly and fouling as that!"[44]

Not many of the op-ed pieces in the black press about Nixon at this stage in his presidency were as colorful in imagery, but the antagonism was virtually unanimous. Nixon's vaunted southern strategy, which the *St. Louis American* editorial referred to as the "Dixie strategem," had made any accommodation between the black press and Nixon virtually impossible.

At about this time the *New York Times* obtained a copy of a year-old memo from Daniel Patrick Moynihan, then a Nixon aide, to the president and published a story about it. In the January 1969 memo Moynihan had used an unfortunate phrase: "The time may have come when the issue of race could benefit from a period of 'benign neglect.' The subject has been too much talked about. The forum has been too much taken over by hysterics, paranoids, and boodlers on all sides. We may need a period in which Negro progress continues and racial rhetoric fades."[45]

The phrase "benign neglect" passed into political parlance, signifying what was widely viewed to be the Nixon administration's indifference to African American needs. The statement proved to be a colossal blunder, as it seemed to codify Nixon's executive actions as cynical and racist, and the president's relaxation of enforcement efforts in such key areas as school desegregation was all the confirmation the black press needed.

Moynihan's phrase was deeply offensive to African Americans. The customarily unflappable Sengstacke devoted an angry editorial in the *Chicago Daily Defender* to what he called the "Moynihan Memorandum." Sengstacke called Moynihan's statement "a grand prescription for inaction in those acute areas where the momentum on civil rights has been already altered." The memorandum applied "the rhetorical icing for the Administration's indefensible Southern strategy." Sengstacke scoffed at Moynihan's "obsequious tribute to the efforts of the Administration to develop 'programs that will be of help to blacks,'" which the publisher dismissed as "a classic instance of intellectual dishonesty."[46]

Nixon, in his memoirs, described a pattern of obstructionist policy that validated the suspicion among blacks that he was quietly retarding civil rights progress even as he offered lip service to lofty goals. After the Supreme Court, on October 29, 1969, handed down a unanimous decision that every school district must end segregation at once, Nixon regarded the edict "as unrealistic and . . . impossible to meet" with the speed the Court envisioned. He wrote: "I felt obliged to uphold the law; but I did not feel obliged to do any more than the minimum the law required. . . . One thing I was determined to ensure was that the many young liberal lawyers in HEW and in the Justice Department's Civil Rights Division would not treat the decision as a carte blanche for them to run wild through the South enforcing compliance with extreme or punitive requirements they had formulated in Washington."[47]

It seemed abundantly clear to African Americans that Nixon was in no particular hurry to push the South along the path toward full integration, even when it was the law of the land. Appeasing segregationists seemed to be more important to the president than redressing wrongs done to black Americans. A yawning chasm had opened between the president and the African American community, which felt abandoned. The mood of indignation drove Nixon's polling numbers among black Americans to abysmally low levels. The black community had virtually no hopes that the president would provide effective leadership on matters of race. Five weeks after the Moynihan memo became public, a *Time*-Louis Harris poll published in the April 6, 1970, issue of *Time* magazine showed that blacks had developed a deep antipathy toward the Nixon administration. While 63 percent of African Americans surveyed said they looked to Washington for a great deal of leadership on racial matters during the Kennedy and Johnson presidencies, only 3 percent said the same about the Nixon administration.[48] For blacks it seemed there was no longer any mooring for their hopes, no national political compact they could rely on.

In Vietnam things seemed to be going from bad to worse. The U.S. incursion into Cambodia in the spring of 1970 further squandered whatever goodwill the continuing troop withdrawals from Vietnam might have secured for the president among black Americans. The operation in Cambodia was ostensibly to destroy the Central Office for South Vietnam, which was thought to be the regional headquarters for the communist campaign in South Vietnam, and to otherwise interdict the chain of support. The Cambodia incursion, which ended in June, failed to achieve its objectives, except for interrupting briefly the flow of men and supplies from North Vietnam into the theater of operations in the south. The military action created a storm of protest and gave new impetus to the antiwar movement generally, which had been uncharacteristically quiet in the six months since Nixon's television appeal for support during implementation of his Vietnamization program.[49]

Then, on May 4, 1970, during student demonstrations at Kent State University in Ohio in the wake of the Cambodian invasion, National Guardsmen opened fire on student protesters, killing four students and wounding nine others. A wave of revulsion and anger swept the country, and campus protests became common. A national student strike grew spontaneously out of the angry reaction, briefly bringing the nation's university system to a virtual standstill.[50]

Ten days after the Kent State shootings Mississippi state police shot and killed two black students at Jackson State University, a predominately black college in Jackson, after a day marked by demonstrations. The edgy troopers fired at a dormitory, insisting during subsequent investigations that they did so in response to shots fired from the building. The exact circumstances of the tragic shooting were never explained to the satisfaction of African American leaders and the black press.[51]

In the immediate aftermath of the college slayings, black newspapers expressed dismay at the killings on both campuses. They deplored the official violence, of course, but the editorials also reflected simmering resentment that the national outpouring of sympathy and outrage that followed the Kent State shootings was notably absent after the similar killings at Jackson State. The *Michigan Chronicle* saw the deaths at the two colleges as a litmus test for the kind of progress America had made in its race relations: "Will the whites be as diligent in their investigation of the black killings as of the white, or as persistent in their protests? The record is not good. We believe . . . that the climate has changed."[52] But had it changed enough? Many other black Americans were sure it had not.

In a long editorial headlined "Death in Black and White," the *Dallas Post Tribune* described the divergent responses of white and black America to the two outbreaks of violence on campus. The different responses, the paper said, "underlined the persisting racial division in American society" as no other recent event had. According to the newspaper, when blacks saw the wide coverage given the Kent State shootings and the relatively skimpy coverage in the mainstream media given the Jackson State murders and other slayings of blacks, "most blacks could only conclude that the Kent students were mourned with such tremendous emotion because they were white."[53] President Nixon did not help matters by asking the Jackson State president, "Look, what are we going to do to get more respect for the police from our young people?"[54]

In a column written in late May the usually unflappable Roy Wilkins applauded the demonstrators who expressed indignation at the killings at Kent State but wondered why the same national "horror and revulsion over the taking of precious young life," which greeted the shootings at Kent State, were not expressed after the slaying of black students at Jackson State. Then he wrote: "Colored Americans, who have carried a lonely torch in an unseeing and generally unfeeling world, mourn with the nation over the Kent State tragedy. They would be much more heartened, however, so much better soldiers in the peace and freedom army, if concern for the spilling of young blood were just that, without Ole Debbil Race raising his ugly head."[55]

Meanwhile, for alarmed black leaders Nixon's incursion into Cambodia seemed to signal the administration's willingness to enlarge the war in Southeast Asia. This concern was widely reflected in the black press. An editorial in the *St. Louis American* in early May saw the "calculated design" of the invasion as the portent of a political and geopolitical apocalypse, which the editorial described in panicky hyperbole: "The danger is great. Richard Nixon may quickly metamorphosize into 'the Man on a White Horse'—and it will have happened right here in the U.S.A. Give him a 'military' victory with atomic weapons and a nation torn with internal strife—plus the ready strong arm of the military, and in the name of 'salvation' you shall have the first American dictator in the White House."[56]

Despite the individual efforts of prominent African Americans to generate opposition to the war, and the broad disapproval of the war in Vietnam among black Americans, few individual blacks participated in formal antiwar protest activities. Even those leaders who opposed the war saw clearly that their primary mission was to concentrate on the issues of civil rights and economic justice for African Americans and to focus the energies of black rank-and-file activists on the goal of fulfilling black domestic aspirations.

By the fall of 1969, when most of the black press was opposing the war, editorial writers were calling attention to the absence of significant numbers of African Americans from major antiwar protests and were lamenting that absence. The *Defender* wondered why this was the case, given the damage to the black agenda of reforms that preoccupation with the Vietnam War had presumably caused, and the large number of blacks who had become casualties in the conflict. The paper concluded that African Americans were focused on the totality of the threat to their well-being in American society and that wholehearted participation in the antiwar movement would exhaust their energies on too narrow a focus. The editor wrote: "Our fight is a total fight, not confined to Vietnam or the streets of Chicago. . . . When we rid ourselves of the monster which has created the dependency, that contemporary slavemaster who now controls his flock with a gun, then we will be able to rid ourselves of all the Vietnams which threaten our existence."[57]

In an editorial a few weeks later the *Defender* returned to the question of black participation in antiwar events. The writer was plainly disturbed that so few African American young people had joined the throngs of youth who participated in the massive Vietnam Moratorium only a month earlier, in mid-October. The *Defender* called the protest "an historic moment which was amplified by the greatest outpouring of young people that this nation has ever known."

The newspaper obviously was troubled by the absence of blacks from the huge antiwar demonstration: "Negroes have more justification for opposing this Asian war than anyone else. They are fighting and dying for the liberation of the people of South Vietnam, a struggle in which the blacks have not yet been able to disengage themselves at home."[58]

Oddly enough, even as the *Defender* decried the absence of blacks in public antiwar demonstrations, its editorial comments on opposition to the war generally played up the involvement of blacks in opposing U.S. policy in Vietnam, a tendency even more apparent in other major black newspapers.[59]

In discussing a proposal floated by a group of black churchmen to conduct a referendum on the war, the *Defender* had no illusions about how black opposition to the war would affect administration policy, even if it were to become apparent that blacks strongly opposed the war. The newspaper asserted that "the black masses should be a part of the movement against the war" but warned that African Americans "should not delude" themselves into believing that their opposition to the war "would cause the administration to show greater concern for the indigent who are wallowing in the mud of slum poverty." The editor, it would seem, was urging opposition to the war and support of the referendum for their own sake, despite the clear likelihood that this would leave Nixon unmoved and indifferent to the needs of the indigent for significant additional governmental assistance. It was not just a note of despair but a call to principled action.[60]

The *Defender* piece shows how different the objective of opposition to the war had become in the black press. Gone was any realistic expectation that, if the war ended, money and attention focused on the war would be diverted to meet the needs of black Americans. So long as Lyndon Johnson was president, the black press and the community it served believed that the administration cared about the cause of civil rights and the economic well-being of black citizens. Once the war ended LBJ could be counted on to resume his leadership in completing the Second Reconstruction. The black press was just as sure that Richard Nixon was indifferent, even hostile, to the aspirations of black Americans.

Opposition to the war in the black press during the Nixon presidency centered on the immorality of the war, including what was widely seen to be its essential racism, and the death and destruction the war was wreaking on both Vietnamese and American soldiers, including black soldiers, whose sacrifices had not lifted the burden of discrimination from the backs of African Americans back home. While Nixon was president, the black press still decried the way the United States squandered money on the war that should have been used to fight poverty in America, but there no longer was any real expectation that the end of the war would mean the investment of those resources in the improvement of the lot of underprivileged black Americans.

As the war spilled outside the borders of Vietnam, the black press gave wider coverage to what it saw as the racism inherent in American participation in the war.

This darker view of the war—and an accompanying sense of urgency to oppose it—was evident in an editorial in the *San Francisco Post* that appeared in the midst of the popular tumult that greeted the incursion into Cambodia. The editorial, "The Black Man's Stake," laid out the case for "black and brown people" to "reassess their position" toward the war, urging people of color to abandon their previous detachment and to get involved in opposing the war. The necessity for a heightened sense of urgency, the paper argued, was that a holocaust was "in progress" in Indochina. Poor blacks, who were overrepresented in the combat units fighting an expanding war, faced a heightened risk of dying and were being ordered "to kill little brown people in what must be interpreted as a white middle-class war." Later in the piece the editor implored blacks to become involved in speaking out against the war: "This condition points up the necessity of Negroes addressing themselves to international affairs and to the foreign policies of this country in order to bring weight to bear upon the ever-present need for change. In the short strokes, it is the Negro youth which is paying the highest proportion of the price in death and wounds in this war, which on the home front sends blacks into the streets daily as unemployed while economic chaos reigns."[61]

Black newspapers and periodicals began to focus more closely on the apparent racial component in U.S. policy in Vietnam and its bloody consequences. Whatever the ideological rationale for U.S. involvement, the targets of American bullets and bombs in Vietnam were Asians; white men were indisputably killing people of color.

Ralph Abernathy, successor to Martin Luther King Jr. at the Southern Christian Leadership Conference, identified two dimensions of the racism of the Vietnam War. In an article in the African American journal *Freedomways*, he wrote: "The war is an attempt to destroy poor people of color in Southeast Asia, at the expense of the black and poor at home and in the interest of maintaining the largest military-economic empire in history."[62] In Abernathy's view the war destroyed dark-skinned Asians even as it plundered the national treasury of the resources that could have eradicated poverty and decay, both the result of an insidious racism, in America.

While the proud tradition of civil rights progress that was the legacy of the Johnson years altered the surface of American life, beneath it was a visceral contempt for people of color that some thoughtful African Americans believed had helped plunge the United States into the war. During the Nixon years this contempt became much more evident, so far as black Americans were concerned.

Black newspapers found the war's brutality, and its racism, played out in the grim disclosures of the My Lai massacre, which occurred in March 1968 but did not become public knowledge until November 1969. The response of the *Pittsburgh Courier* was typical. Almost as disturbing to the paper as the atrocity itself was the response of white Americans to the massacre and its aftermath, expressed in their ambivalence toward issues of race and racial violence at the 1970–71 trial of Lieutenant William Calley, one of the officers responsible for leading the raid. An editorial in the *Courier* saw the public reaction to the guilty verdict in late March 1971 as another piece of evidence that "the agony of Vietnam has torn this country apart." A nation that four years earlier was insufficiently outraged by the gruesome murders of three civil rights workers in Mississippi was once again displaying a certain callous disregard for atrocities when the victims were people of color. The *Courier* regarded a presidential pardon of Lieutenant Calley as almost inevitable, so once again the guilty would go unpunished.[63]

The *Afro-American* likewise found the popular objections to the guilty verdict in Calley's court martial "chillingly disturbing." It was equally appalled by how this "illegal, immoral and unwinnable war" could so deaden moral sensibilities as to lead Calley to testify that "wasting" those civilians was almost routine. "It wasn't any big deal, sir," the newspaper quoted him as saying. Calley was not alone in expressing such inhumanity at the trial. Another participant who testified considered the Vietnamese to be almost subhuman, saying, "When you shot someone you didn't think you were shooting at a human. They were a gook or a Commie and it was okay."[64]

Even some African American troops, dulled by their experience in combat, excused Calley's actions. One such soldier said, "This dude, Lieutenant Calley, really didn't do nothing, man. I know, because I use to be in the field. He didn't do that on his own to My Lai. He was told to do that. We killed a whole lot of innocent gooks by mistake, because they were not supposed to be there."[65]

The savagery of the conflict was something more than the brutality of war. So far as the *Afro-American* was concerned, it grew out of a racism ingrained in the U.S. approach to the nonwhite world. When the newspaper took President Nixon to task in April 1972 for failing to end "the brutal conflict," it observed editorially, "There is no white nation in the world in which the U.S. would have waged such a war." The war was seen not simply as a geopolitical mistake but as a violation of humanity and profoundly racist. Will America, the editorial wondered, allow the war to continue "until uncounted millions on both sides have been killed or mutilated? The answer to that question, is that it is possible, but only because the victims on both sides are other than white."[66]

The *Afro-American* reported that officials of the General Baptist State Convention of North Carolina, which had a membership of more than 350,000 African Americans, had condemned U.S. policy in Vietnam, calling on Nixon to "call for immediate withdrawal." The statement castigated "the recent escalation of the war by the President of the United States," stating: "Too many black folk have died there for nothing. . . . We feel it is a senseless war."[67]

Beneath America's lofty protestations of geopolitical orthodoxy, the *Afro-American* argued, the world saw U.S. involvement "in a racial light." It was hard to believe that the United States would wage such a vicious war "against a white nation if the vital interests of the U.S. were so blurred," as the paper plainly believed they were in Vietnam: "Every day and every bomb further poisons the air of the world through a kind of racial pollution that is more dangerous than any good we ever thought gainable in the costly Vietnamese war."[68]

The *San Francisco Sun-Reporter* went so far as to call the violence visited upon Vietnam "American genocide." The paper was troubled by the lack of interest displayed by most Americans in what it viewed as the wanton destruction of the country and its people: "Genocide in Vietnam hardly affects the complacent American, whose main concerns are rising food prices, an increased cost of living and the crime problem. The American apathy cuts across all socio-economic lines. Someday this apathy will come back to haunt the complacent American public."[69]

In its assessment of his stewardship of the war, the black press subjected the president to stiff criticism. A favorite rhetorical device was to recall Nixon's campaign assurances that he would extricate American troops from Vietnam, then to show that the war, if anything, was being intensified, despite gradual troop withdrawals. A 1971 editorial in the *San Francisco Post* was an example:

> President Richard Nixon was elected on his promise that he would grind the war to a halt in Southeast Asia and get us out of Vietnam. When we reflect on this pledge, we must be quick to add that he didn't say how he planned to accomplish this terribly desirable feat. Recent Administration decisions—first to go into Cambodia and second, to push a revitalized South Vietnamese army into Laos with unlimited American firepower from the air—have made it clear to all thinking Americans that if the President had any intention of getting out of Vietnam by the end of his four-year term, it was by carrying American troops deeper into an Asian war. Any thought that his activities would involve bringing American troops home was purely a misunderstanding of the deviousness to be found in the exercise of presidential discretion.

The *Post* editorial went on to call the war in Vietnam "America's greatest mistake in the 20th century."[70]

In the next issue the *Post* continued its assault on Nixon's stewardship of the war with an editorial brusquely headlined "Fact vs. Fiction: Who's Kidding Whom." Challenging the president's assurances to the contrary, the newspaper said bluntly, "We are losing the war in Southeast Asia. We have failed in our efforts to acquire a military victory or to bring about successful negotiations in Paris. The Paris peace talks have continued to disintegrate." The Vietcong, the editorial asserted, were winning the war on the ground in terms of territory under their control. The United States had "given up on the possibility of containing their movements or of developing any stabilized government under our auspices."[71]

By the spring of 1972 the *Defender*'s opposition to the war had produced one of its most pointed editorials. As "tides of anti-war demonstration" swept across dozens of American universities in the wake of expanded bombing assaults on Hanoi and Haiphong, the newspaper took its place beside the students inveighing against "the indefensible war in Southeast Asia." The *Defender* again lamented black leadership in opposing the war as "too passive and too timid in this crucial matter." In contrast to its earlier jitters about Martin Luther King Jr.'s speaking out against the war, the *Defender* now proclaimed: "All the civil rights organizations should be loud in their denunciation of the escalation of the war. They should register in no uncertain terms their commitments to peace. They have much at stake." The editor was contemptuous of Nixon's policy of Vietnamization, which was, in the paper's view, nothing more than the president's strategy "to continue to commit this nation to the defense of a corrupt, unrepresentative South Vietnam government," even if it meant "dragging America into a third world war." The editorial was unambiguous in its assessment of Nixon's policy: "It is equally evident that the so-called Vietnamization process is a scandalous failure."[72]

Two days later the *St. Louis American* announced, "The Vietnamization policy itself has already 'blown up.'" With more vehemence than literary finesse, the paper said: "President Nixon has turned the clock back 50 years on civil rights. . . . Instead of pulling the nation together on racial matters he has set going a positive polarization." Four months later, with an eye on the approaching election, the *American* declared: "Whether we like it or not, history will hold us accountable for what is being done in our name in Vietnam. Every people must accept responsibility for what they really are. Try as hard as they will, there is no way of escaping this ultimate responsibility. In this election of 1972, the American people have a date with history."[73]

An editorial in the *San Francisco Sun-Reporter* was equally critical of Vietnamization. The piece was savage in its assessment of the policy and its consequences: "The 'Vietnamization' policy, with the gradual withdrawal of U.S. ground forces, has been a hoax thrust upon the American people by a cynical Nixon, only interested in re-election to a second term in the White House. An exposed Nixon has been incited to reckless, arrogant and extremely dangerous measures, to wit, bombing of Hanoi and Haiphong, with an open-end[ed] threat to allow no part of North Vietnam as a sanctuary against massive air attacks." The editorial characterized the president's state of mind, as reflected in his wartime leadership, as psychotic and closed with a warning that if Nixon persisted, "he and he alone will be recorded in history as the massacrer of the whole Vietnamese people."[74]

An editorial in *Freedomways* found another reason to denounce Vietnamization. The piece asserted that Vietnamization "simply means Asians killing Asians which is the old divide-and-rule policy, which is as old as colonialism itself" and an expression of the "benign neglect" in Nixon's foreign policy that was so evident in his domestic policy toward African Americans. The editorial called for Nixon to "bring the troops home. . . .Cut the military budget and use the money to finance the rehabilitation of American cities."[75]

By the spring of 1971 the country as a whole shared the frustration of the black press with the seemingly interminable and draining struggle in the jungles of Vietnam. This was evident in a measurable decline in the willingness of the American people to fight other wars to defend third world countries from outside aggression. A Gallup poll published in April 1971 found that only 45 percent of Americans would support the use of U.S. troops to help defend Mexico if it were attacked by a communist-backed enemy.[76] Clearly, Americans were no longer buying the domino theory. It was also apparent that Nixon would have to find a way to extract the United States from Vietnam.

The black press generally continued to oppose the war throughout Nixon's stewardship. Black popular opinion had also solidified into an overwhelming opposition to the Vietnam War. In a Gallup poll published in May 1971, 83 percent of blacks opposed the war. This compared with 67 percent of white respondents. A higher percentage of blacks opposed U.S. policy in Vietnam than any other group in the poll, which also measured opinion by gender, age, and educational level. The next-largest group opposing the war was women, 72 percent.[77]

On October 26, 1972, with the election barely twelve days away, Henry Kissinger announced to a press conference that "peace is at hand." It was hardly necessary to play the peace card. Nixon buried the Democrat, George McGovern, in a landslide; McGovern managed to win only Massachusetts and the District of Columbia. But Kissinger's remarks had the effect of exciting hopes that American prisoners of war would be home for Christmas.[78]

When these hopes were dashed, the *Chicago Defender* wrote an angry editorial headlined "Viet Peace, A Cruel Hoax." The paper saw the public intimations of peace as blatant electioneering to ensure Nixon's reelection. Now, with Christmas over and the war "just as bitter and intense as ever," the American people, in the view of the editorial, would have "to be resigned to the unpalatable fact that they have been deceived and that they are dealing with an administration that is more concerned with its own self-accommodation than with the anxieties and discomfort of the people." It was not just a matter of the war now; for the *Defender* it was a fundamentally "grave moral question: Whether a government that deceives its people is entitled to their confidence." The newspaper was sure it was not: "A leadership that is founded on deception is built on sand. The war in Southeast Asia may expose the moral bankruptcy of the present administration."[79]

As 1972 came to a close, the tumult of antiwar activity was matched by expressions of outrage in much of the black press as American bombers pummeled North Vietnam in an operation called Linebacker II. The air campaign was launched on December 18 after the peace talks broke down in Paris, and the bombing continued until December 29.[80]

The *San Francisco Sun-Reporter* was struck by the incongruity of fighting a widening war with more ferocity than ever—but mostly from the air—barely three months after Kissinger announced, "Peace is at hand." Against the backdrop of the bombing assault on North Vietnam, the paper wrote, "Kissinger's optimistic comment . . . has been shown for what it was; a ploy to dupe the naive American public." Troubled by what it interpreted as an "apathetic system" that blithely reelected Nixon despite his failure to end the Vietnam War during his first term, the newspaper observed, "The public must like what it sees in its leader or be too lazy to care." Now, with the election behind him, "Nixon has a mandate from the voters. What is Nixon's first act? Nixon scuttles the peace talks, drops the bombs and makes ready for a gala inauguration ceremony."[81]

In the same issue of the *Sun-Reporter*, a lead editorial by Eleanor Ohman, who usually appeared in the paper as its cartoonist, served up one of the sharpest personal attacks directed at the president during the Christmas bombing offensive. Both Carleton B. Goodlett, publisher, and Thomas C. Fleming, editor, of the newspaper shared her passionately antiwar views. The editorial was an open letter to Nixon:

> *Mr. President:*
>
> *Please stop the bombing. You have made our beloved country a big bully, a mafia, a brutal, computerized extortionist—a force so evil it is inconceivable to realize it is the United States of America.*
>
> *With Christmas so near, how could you pour tons and tons of death upon the people of Vietnam, while you pray in your sequestered White House "church" for the safety and well-being of American prisoners of war?*
>
> *How could you? How can your wife sleep at night beside a man so vastly cruel as you? Does pretty Trisha even once wake up from her sleep with her eyes wide staring into the dark with a sudden awareness of what it would be like to be under a falling bomb from a B-52, miles in the air? Do you ever wonder what the world will find out about you when the asbestos curtain of war is opened one day and the first outsiders come to see the smoking ruins of Vietnam?*

The letter continued in this vein for several more paragraphs, a passionate screed that progressively intensified its personal attacks on Nixon, who, the writer was sure, could find forgiveness for his cruel sins only from "the god of war and destruction, the high priests of the Pentagon and the war industry."[82]

Stanley O. Williford, writing in the *Los Angeles Sentinel* in late 1972, summed up what he viewed as the Nixon administration's duplicity in Vietnam in an item with the heading "Promise and Refusal to End the War in Southeast Asia." It was the lead item in a year-end summary: "Perhaps more than any other event, the Vietnam War has dominated the news pages. There was a promise of peace . . . then it was cruelly withdrawn. It would seem that few issues could be more important than halting the destruction, the crushing terror of American bombing in Vietnam."[83]

The brief but ferocious bombing campaign was specifically aimed at breaking the will of North Vietnamese leaders and forcing them back to the conference table. In that limited objective, the "Eleven-Day War" succeeded. On January 23 they agreed to a ceasefire and four days later signed the Paris peace accords effectively ending U.S. involvement in ground combat in Vietnam.[84] Later Nixon would point out that, because of his toughness, American prisoners of war were brought home from North Vietnam "on their feet rather than on their knees," another way of giving the U.S. retreat the gloss of a peace with honor.[85]

President Richard Nixon ended the controversial draft system and began the era of the all-volunteer military the day after the peace agreement was signed in Paris in January 1973 and all U.S. ground troops were scheduled to leave Vietnam. The echoes of the protests against the impact of the draft on the young African American men who fought and died in the suffocating dampness of the Vietnam jungle had long since faded, replaced by other issues and other political leaders.[86]

In early January, just days before the peace agreement was signed, Melvin Laird, the outgoing secretary of defense, delivered a final report to Congress. In it Laird preened with satisfaction at what he judged to be the success of Vietnamization: "Vietnamization . . . today is virtually completed. As a consequence of the success of the military aspects of Vietnamization, the South Vietnamese people today, in my view, are fully capable of providing for their own in-country security against the North Vietnamese."[87]

It would be two years—the "decent interval," as some cynics called it—before South Vietnam was finally overrun by the military forces of the North.[88] Vietnamization had been a success in providing cover for extracting American forces from Vietnam. It had been an utter failure in preparing the South Vietnamese to fight a war that they never seemed to want to embrace as their fight.

In one of the stranger coincidences of the Vietnam era, Lyndon Johnson died at his ranch in Texas on January 22, 1973, and was lying in state in his library in Austin the next day, when a cease fire was declared in Vietnam. The formal peace agreement followed four days later. He did not live quite long enough to see the end of the war that had brought down his presidency and consumed his dreams.

In an editorial memorializing LBJ, the *Los Angeles Sentinel* wrote of "the tall Texan whose dreams of ending poverty and social injustices in a 'Great Society' were shattered in the national anguish over the Vietnam War." In a tribute filled with his domestic accomplishments as "the President who led this nation to a new plateau of humanity and decency," the only other mention of the war was this: "He will be remembered because he hated the Vietnam War and all its horrors."[89] It was a poignant, if hopeless, attempt to detach Johnson from the war he fanned into a conflagration and would not extinguish. Balanced against all of LBJ's stunning achievements in advancing the cause of civil rights and equal opportunity for African Americans, it was enough for the *Sentinel* that he hated the war and the horrors that it unleashed. This was a sentiment shared by virtually all the black press.

A month after Johnson's death the *Sentinel* published a deeply pessimistic editorial, "Aftermath of Peace." In the piece the paper reflected on Nixon's second inaugural address and found nothing in its exegesis of the speech that offered much hope for black Americans. The editorial quoted the president as saying, "In the challenges we face together, each of us must ask not just how can government help, but how can I help?" This echo of John F. Kennedy's famous inaugural address, the *Sentinel* suggested, "was said with a solemnity that added emphasis to a sinister implication. It seems beyond doubt that Mr. Nixon is laying the foundation for an escape by the government from its moral responsibility to the masses. How can the poor, the hungry, the neglected help themselves?"

The editorial then resorted to a variation of a familiar formula, one that the black press had used for years to criticize Vietnam War expenditures. In earlier attacks on war costs editorial writers often compared the billions being spent on the war in Southeast Asia and the relatively paltry sum being spent on the war at home to fight poverty. Now the *Sentinel* introduced a new twist: "Billions will be spent for the reconstruction of Vietnam, to put the natives back on their feet, while the poor and the hungry at home must continue begging to keep body and soul together."[90]

The editor was not speculating idly about American intentions. President Nixon had begun making noises about putting together an aid package for North Vietnam to help it recover from the ruinous U.S. bombing campaign. The president's intentions had been rumored in Washington for some time. A scant few weeks after the *Sentinel* editorial appeared, the president ordered Kissinger, his national security adviser, along with Secretary of State William

Rogers and Attorney General Elliot Richardson, to begin lobbying Congress to approve an aid program for the reconstruction of North Vietnam. Nixon wanted them to use the Marshall Plan as a model, evoking all the historic altruism of that program to stir Congress to action.[91]

This was precisely what the *Sentinel* editor had feared. Instead of Whitney Young's grand vision of a domestic Marshall Plan to eradicate hunger and destitution at home, America was opening its coffers to help North Vietnam. A government that seemed to find it impossible to meet the needs of its own population of black Americans, devastated by centuries of harsh bigotry and economic neglect, would somehow find the means to repair the damage it had caused in a distant, exotic land to people who had been its enemy.

With the end of American involvement in Vietnam, *Ebony* assessed Nixon's stewardship of both the war and the less fortunate of his nation's citizens. It was a lengthy editorial, but its point was plain: "During his first term, Nixon moved slowly both on ending the war and in putting an end to the social welfare programs started by Kennedy and Johnson. It took him just about four years for each. To all extents and purposes, he ended the war just before reelection and he scuttled the Great Society in his announcement of the fiscal year 1974 federal budget shortly after his inauguration."[92]

The solidly Republican *Daily World* made it clear that it did not support a retreat in Vietnam. In April 1968 the paper had embraced, in almost giddy terms, Richard Nixon's assurance that he would end the war if elected, comparing Nixon's gambit with the promise of Dwight Eisenhower to go to Korea if he were elected: "There is one thing certain we can all believe, and that is that Mr. Nixon will never sell this country short to the communists. Nor will he surrender to them."[93]

After Nixon's policy of Vietnamization began to take shape, the *Daily World*—virtually alone among black newspapers—continued to stand by his side, agreeing that peace must be achieved but only if it were an honorable one. The *Daily World* even praised Nixon's incursion into Cambodia in spring 1970 as "wise and courageous."[94]

So grateful was Nixon for the newspaper's support that he wrote a letter of thanks to the editor and general manager, C. A. Scott. "The majority of Americans support what we are doing to stop the fighting and, because of this, the world is aware of our resolve," Nixon wrote. "Such a display of national purpose will, I believe, hasten the day of peace." Then, singling out the Atlanta paper for praise, Nixon wrote: "The *Atlanta Daily World*'s editorial, with its own forthright support, plays an important part in this effort, and I am grateful for it." The letter was published on the editorial page in late May 1972, along with an accompanying editorial expressing the paper's pride in being honored with a letter from the president.[95]

The relationship between the Scott family and the Nixon administration had been further solidified a year earlier when Stanley S. Scott, a one-time member of the *Daily World's* editorial staff, was named an assistant to the president's communications director, Herbert Klein. At a meeting of black publishers in Atlanta in mid-1971, Klein had introduced Scott to the publishers with a flourish, a gesture undoubtedly designed to impress a generally hostile black press but also to show appreciation to C. A. Scott for his steadfast support of the president's Vietnam policy.[96]

To the *Daily World* linking the war and demands of the black community for more governmental assistance, which was so commonplace in other black news publications, was an affront to black pride and self-sufficiency. An editorial sheds considerable light on why the Atlanta paper, unlike most other African American papers, was uninterested in the issue of the diversion of funds from social programs beneficial to blacks to pay for the Vietnam War.

During the 1972 presidential campaign the *Daily World* bridled at Democrat George McGovern's suggestion that African Americans were demanding that money being wasted on the war be used instead to help them: "In reference to the Senator's idea [to] quit spending in the war and spend more on the needy, apparently he thinks our people always want a handout. We want freedom and security of this nation above all else and at any cost. We oppose the Senator's plan to surrender to the communists."[97]

Here the newspaper's conservative 1960s-era Republican stance was on display. In the paper's view social programs were usually nothing more than handouts, stifling individual incentive, wounding the pride of recipients, and damaging the chance of the underprivileged to develop independence and self-sufficiency. What is more, national security was paramount and deserved whatever resources it required. Anything less was to risk surrender to the menace of international communism.

Right up to the end the *Atlanta Daily World* remained convinced of the rightness of America's mission in Vietnam. Long after the last U.S. ground troops left Vietnam on March 29, 1973, leaving the South Vietnamese armed forces to continue the fight alone, the *Daily World* did not slacken in its support of what America had tried to do in Southeast Asia. In this the paper was virtually alone among the black press.

8

Race Relations in an Integrated Military

Black soldier and white fought to survive a war they knew they would never win. . . . And often, they fought each other.—Wallace Terry, *Bloods*

The black soldiers who fought through the sporadic firefights and long stretches of tedium were also foot soldiers in the larger battle for human rights in which all black Americans were desperately engaged. The risks the black soldiers endured, the wounds they suffered, and the deaths they died became part of the currency used to animate the rhetoric and purchase the advances made in the freedom struggle of all African Americans.

The two-front war was waged throughout the Johnson administration and through most of the Nixon presidency, from the beginning of direct U.S. combat operations in Vietnam in early 1965 until the evacuation of the last American troops from the war zone in the spring of 1973. So tracing the history of race relations in the military in Vietnam, as seen through the eyes of the black press, belongs properly at the end of this account. It illuminates and clarifies the intersection of the African American battle for freedom at home and the simultaneous struggle on the battlefields of Vietnam.

In Vietnam, for the first time in American history, the United States entered a war with armed forces that were fully racially integrated from the beginning of their engagement. So, for many black Americans, who had long fought for racial equality in the U.S. military, Vietnam was a unique opportunity to fulfill the objective of serving their country alongside whites and others in a multiracial community of warriors and citizen soldiers.

Early in Lyndon Johnson's first full term as president, when the war began in earnest with the arrival of thousands of U.S. combat troops in Vietnam in 1965, there were optimistic expectations of the benefits and prestige that would be available to African American soldiers in a fully integrated military that offered equality to all members of the armed forces. The black press found reason to celebrate the realization of the dream of full participation of African Americans in all aspects of the U.S. military and to focus attention on the exploits of black soldiers in a racially harmonious combat force.

As late as August 1968 Thomas A. Johnson would write a line of striking irony for *Ebony* magazine: "The Negro has found in his nation's most totalitarian society—the military—the greatest degree of functional democracy that this nation has granted to black people."[1]

The black press often celebrated an idealized image of the American military as an outpost of racial harmony, an image that contrasted sharply with a turbulent civilian society crackling with racial tensions. At the outset of the war the egalitarian environment the military offered inevitably created a tension between pride in the military achievement of African Americans in Vietnam and disappointment, even despair, at the continuing realities of black life in a predominately white society at home. This tension produced an interpretation of the war in the black press that tended to idealize aspects of the experience and achievements of African Americans in the battle zone and to use these idealized images as models for urging the reform of American life.

An example of this, especially early in the war, was the recurrent theme in the black press of the brotherhood that developed between black and white soldiers on the battlefield, a harmony that stood in sharp contrast to the racial animosity that so often characterized the relationship between the races back home. Images and descriptions of battlefield brotherhood were used as a rebuke to a society that found it impossible to achieve racial harmony.

During the 1960s race riots became commonplace in the United States, particularly in the cities, which ruptured along the fissures where heightened black frustration and assertiveness collided with stubborn white resistance and racial antipathy. Meanwhile, on the battlefield in Vietnam the black press saw the possibilities of racial reconciliation playing out, with black and white soldiers in an integrated military appearing to form a harmonious community of shared interests and needs, united against a common danger.

Images of battlefield brotherhood in the black press countered the racial tensions so often evident back home. An editorial in the *New York Amsterdam News* in the spring of 1967 used a UPI combat photograph to illustrate the editor's lament of the state of race relations in the United States. In so doing, the editorial transposed the photographer's snapshot into an idealized image to make its point. The photo shows two black soldiers and two white soldiers carrying a wounded comrade after heavy fighting near the Cambodian border. The caption under the picture was "Equality in Vietnam." The headline above the picture was "But Not at Home." However illogical the visual sequencing, the pointed contrast is unmistakable.

The editorial beside the photograph referred to "the dramatic photo" and said it showed "the equality some Americans can find only on the battlefield." Then the piece declared: "While these four men can fight and sleep together, while they can be shot at, wounded and even die together, they would still find themselves separated on their return home to these United States."[2]

Episodes of black heroism in battle, often celebrated by the black press, could become lessons of battlefield brotherhood designed to affirm the possibilities of racial reconciliation in U.S. society. The apotheosis of black heroes in Vietnam was an eighteen-year-old paratrooper named Milton Olive III. On October 22, 1965, Olive and four other troops were on patrol when a hand grenade bounced onto the jungle trail in the middle of the unit, endangering all five men. Olive dove onto the grenade, smothering it with his body; he died instantly in the blast, saving the other four soldiers. For his act of supreme heroism Olive became the first of twenty African Americans to be awarded the Medal of Honor in Vietnam.[3]

Olive's designation as a Medal of Honor winner received wide coverage in the black press. On two consecutive days Olive's story was on the front page of the *Atlanta Daily World*.[4] A front-page story in the *Afro-American* told of how President Johnson presented the young hero as a role model: "He taught those of us who remain how we ought to live." The president read a letter written to him by the soldier's father. It was a plea for international goodwill and domestic racial and religious harmony, a fitting memorial for a young man who died for his buddies, including his white lieutenant from Texas.[5]

A Brooklyn reader of the *New York Amsterdam News*, in a poem titled "Integrate," used the heroism and selflessness of Private Olive to bring together the themes of battlefield brotherhood and black valor to draw a lesson for American society on racial harmony:

Let each color play its part
With sincere love within
the heart.
Like the young Negro,
Milton Lee Olive

Who proved his love by
throwing himself
On a grenade, to save four
other men.
He didn't think of color
then (his concern was)
Let me save four men.[6]

An editorial in the *Pittsburgh Courier* also transformed the intrepid deed of Milton Olive into a call for social justice, quoting approvingly the words of Olive's father at the award ceremony. He said it was not the time for "tears of self-pity—but for renewed dedication to the principle of equality of all Americans." The editorial then expanded on the meaning of Private Olive's act of valor; his "heroism is basic proof of the Negro's loyalty and dedication to the principles of democracy for which this country is supposed to stand." That loyalty, the editor said, is at the heart of the black struggle "for our civil rights within our own land and throughout the world."

This expansive interpretation was carried a step further by placing this struggle at the center of Olive's motivation at the moment of his heroic act: "Private Olive must have had this in mind as he fell on the grenade to sacrifice himself so that his buddies could live to carry on the fight for the rights of all people."[7]

The sense of brotherhood on the field of combat was not just the realization of some ideal of interracial harmony. It was also a real and natural response to the shared exigencies of war, a view also noted by the black press as it sorted through the implications of life at the front in an integrated army. A story in *Ebony* captured a sense of the limitations to the idealized image of interracial brotherhood in Vietnam. In the piece a black soldier was not being cynical, just pragmatic, when he said, "There is no segregation or discrimination when GIs hold live ammunition. It's only after the battle is over and the men get back to town."[8] This black paratrooper was simply reflecting the daily reality of life in Vietnam and the differences between camaraderie in combat and social life in the rear.

Mike Davis filed many stories for the *Afro-American* while he was on assignment in Vietnam in 1967. The paper ran one major feature on Page One under the headline "They Couldn't Care Less What Color You Are." The subhead contained a wistful recognition of the way things really were: "Mixed Viet Units Concede It Won't Be Same at Home." The story featured snippets of interviews of men in Vietnam, one of whom was a white trooper from Alabama. "I never had much to do with colored guys back home," he said, "but I'd rather go into battle with them than anyone else." He described how he ate and slept with black troops, then got up and went into combat with them. "It's something the people back home just won't be able to understand," he added. He conceded that once he got home, he probably would have little to do with black people again.[9]

One of the later examples of stories of battlefield comradeship between blacks and whites ran on January 27, 1968, in the *Pittsburgh Courier*. The headline evoked the theme of interracial brotherhood: "Negro Dies but Saves White Buddy." A wounded white marine from Macon, Georgia, told his story from his home, where he was on leave from treatment at the Charleston Naval Hospital. Steve Ford, immobilized in a cast, told an interviewer that he wished he knew the full name of the black marine who had saved his life but sacrificed himself. Ford said he and the other guys in the outfit called the black leatherneck "French" or "Boss Man." Said Ford ruefully, "He was a Negro and I never knew his whole name."

During a fierce firefight French and Ford had both scrambled for a foxhole. French dove in first, then watched in horror as Ford was shot in one leg, then the other, and in an arm. The black marine crawled to his wounded comrade and dragged him into the foxhole. After pulling the wounded man into the trench, French removed his own flak jacket, covered Ford's head with it, then flung his body over the white marine as a shower of hand grenades fell on them. The black marine died instantly. The story ended with the young white southerner's words: "I just would like to know the full name of the Negro GI who saved my life."[10] This story offered readers both a feeling of intimacy in the sacrificial brotherhood displayed in the foxhole and a sense of the fleeting quality of battlefield relationships. They were buddies, but the white guy did not know the black marine's name.

By the summer of 1968, only six months later, the theme of battlefield brotherhood between black and white soldiers had virtually disappeared from the black press. The theme had persisted long after stories of racism and racial unrest among U.S. soldiers in Vietnam had created new realities and made the old vignettes of camaraderie outmoded. The imagined racial harmony in the military began to disappear as the cultural turmoil in the nation at large became common in the U.S. armed forces as well.

As the war dragged on into a new administration in the late 1960s, racial animosity in the military was heating up, threatening the old paradigm. And it was spilling over into the battle zone. Black soldiers were embracing unique expressions of African American culture in grooming, clothing styles, and greeting rituals to proudly distinguish themselves from white GIs. These expressions of black culture tended to alienate white soldiers and were frequently suppressed by unit commanders.

White soldiers, for their part, often flaunted their bigotry, resorting to racial epithets and frequently displaying the Confederate flag (see figure 11). This was particularly galling to black soldiers. A group of black soldiers told *Jet* magazine in a signed statement that whites were permitted to fly the rebel flag without interference from white officers, celebrating a southern heritage rooted in black slavery, while African Americans were not allowed to use symbols that expressed pride in their African origins.[11]

It is hardly surprising that, in the black press, the ideal of battlefield brotherhood gave way to the notion of a brotherhood of black soldiers, banding together to confront the searing indignities of racism. By the late 1960s,

Figure 11.
The Vietcong prisoner fastens on an unspoken irony: he is the prisoner, but his captor is imprisoned in a cultural reality that is just as confining—and far more humiliating. (Cartoon by Chester Commodore, *Chicago Defender*, March 20, 1968. Courtesy of the *Chicago Defender*.)

as often as not, combat in Vietnam not only pitted American soldiers against a common enemy but also arrayed blacks and whites against each other. Brotherhood was expressed in the solidarity of black soldiers, who found the most relevant community to be the cultural affinity that linked them to each other within the larger context of the functionally integrated, but fundamentally hostile, armed forces.

Despite the occasional anecdotal record of instances of interracial brotherhood on the battlefield in Vietnam after 1968, the black press seldom found them typical enough of life in the combat zone to write about, much less idealize. The image simply no longer adequately represented the reality of much of what was occurring in Vietnam. Battlefield brotherhood had lost its power as a staple in the journalistic rhetoric of the black press as it confronted deep racial problems at home and sought other ways to inform, inspire, or shame a culture that was so flawed in its interracial life.

This change could be seen in observations made two years apart by Wallace Terry, an African American journalist. Terry went to Vietnam for a brief visit in 1967 and later returned for a two-year assignment that ended in 1969. In 1967 Terry spoke glowingly of the positive attitude of black soldiers toward the war and said: "I have observed here the most successfully integrated institution in America." In 1969 Terry described a very different situation, with black troops alienated from white soldiers and expressing strong opposition to the war. Even in the heat of battle, the old patterns of interracial harmony seemed to have shifted. As Terry put it, "The spirit of foxhole brotherhood I found in 1967 had evaporated."[12]

As they went into battle, black GIs often felt exploited. The proportion of blacks seemed to be much higher on the firing line than elsewhere in Vietnam. And everywhere a sullen chasm seemed to be opening up between whites and blacks.

Increasingly, the African American press was seeing the war as a chaotic place of violence in which, all too often, the identity of the enemy became blurred. For the black GI it sometimes seemed as if the enemy in Vietnam could have been white American soldiers as easily as the brown-skinned Vietcong peasants. The interracial tension in the American ranks was part of an ideological and cultural migration into the U.S. military in Vietnam of attitudes and behavioral norms from the civilian society back home. Blacks in the military were meeting racial stereotyping and persistent discrimination by whites with greater militancy. Plainly, there was what the *New York Amsterdam News* would call a new breed of African American GI.[13]

For some time after physical clashes between blacks and whites became commonplace in the United States during the struggle for equal rights, first across the segregated South, then in northern cities, racial violence had continued to be a rarity in the structured and highly integrated U.S. military. African American soldiers in Vietnam often were alarmed at the first outbreaks of violence in major cities back in the States during the sixties. In August 1967 the *Baltimore Afro-American* carried a feature story by Mike Davis, on special assignment in Vietnam. The headline expressed the sense of uneasy bewilderment felt by some black GIs in the war-torn country: "GIs Shocked by U.S. Riots."

"Most colored troops in Vietnam interviewed by the *Afro* this week expressed shock, horror and disappointment over the recent rash of disturbances that have plagued major U.S. cities," wrote Davis from Saigon. The response of Private First Class Roland Sherwood was typical: "I don't know what they are trying to prove with violence. I know that everything isn't what it should be as far as race relations are concerned, but rioting is no way to set things right." Marine Corporal James Davis from Detroit, which had been hit by major rioting, was equally incredulous: "It doesn't make any sense. I'll bet that some of the same boys I went to North Eastern High School with, some of the same ones who don't want to come to Vietnam because of all the violence over here, are the ones that are rioting and burning back home." One after another the black troops expressed similar dismay and shock at the riots that were breaking out in inner-city neighborhoods in major American cities.[14]

The *Afro-American*'s Davis noticed, as others had, that racial harmony was most evident among troops who had shared the rigors and dangers of battle. Behind the lines Davis observed that men tended to separate along racial lines. "It is not uncommon," he wrote, "at an enlisted men's mess to see large groups of colored servicemen eating at one table together, or to visit the Khanh Hoi Street section of Saigon and find that all of the bars are frequented exclusively by colored servicemen." One black GI from Indiana explained it this way: "I don't have nothing against the Chucks (white soldiers), but they just ain't down with it. I like to be around the guys that speak my language and know what's happening."[15]

Ethel Payne, in a long feature about the same famed Saigon haunt for black soldiers, Khanh Hoi, nicknamed Soulville, found that the African American GIs who socialized in the district congregated there not because they were not allowed to enter bars in other parts of town but because they preferred the company of other black soldiers. "It's just more comfortable," said a young private first class from Alabama, "and besides, ain't it got a railroad track down the street just like back home."[16]

More than a year later another *Defender* reporter took a very different view of Soulville. Donald Mosby wrote: "'Soul City' is the result of out-and-out social segregation. That it exists in Vietnam is an insult to the black GIs fighting and dying there. 'Soul City' didn't spring into being just because the black GIs wanted a place of 'their own.' 'Soul City' is in Saigon because of the prejudice that Americans couldn't leave at home. America must stop taking its social institutions to war with it."[17]

While part of the difference between the two descriptions of Soulville may have owed to a natural divergence in the way the two writers interpreted what they saw there, it seems more likely that the difference represented an evolution in the nature of race relations among black and white troops in Vietnam.

In the supposedly color-blind military the stain of discrimination, which American soldiers carried with them into Vietnam, was reflected in the preponderance of black soldiers, sailors, and marines in the lower ranks who were performing lower-status duty because of inadequate educational qualifications and undeveloped skills, the result of discrimination in civilian society back home. That lack of preparation grew out of institutional biases, deep and long-lived individual prejudices, and thwarted social development that distorted the way black and white Americans in the military perceived each other as they attempted to relate across an increasingly uncomfortable racial divide.

By late 1968, as the United States went through a tumultuous year of political dislocation, assassinations, and the most widespread urban riots in the nation's history, black soldiers were impatient with the military's overwhelmingly white power apparatus. Many came to believe that attaining promotions or coveted assignments within the armed services would not be possible if they relied on or appeased the white military establishment, which the black GIs saw as fundamentally unfair, even hostile. Instead, they found the path to fairness in relying upon solidarity with other blacks.

Even a black American who had attained officer rank was emboldened to speak out about the racism that kept him and others like him from rising even higher. The *Norfolk Journal and Guide* reprinted an editorial from the *Defender* that recounted the story of Major Lavelle Merritt, who had denounced the military services as "the strongest citadels of racism on the face of the earth." In an eight-page statement he described instances when he had been called nigger and "treated as an inferior." He complained that he had been unfairly passed over for promotion and that other able African American officers were experiencing the same treatment. Those blacks who were promoted, according to Merritt, were a "collection of identifiable accommodationists," or "Uncle Toms."[18]

The editorial was strong stuff, filled with bitterness and expressed with a degree of pungency that was becoming common among blacks in the U.S.

military in the late 1960s. Discrimination was no longer accepted as a commonplace evil. A new militancy was replacing accommodation.

On March 20, 1968, the *Defender*'s lead story bore the banner headline "Threaten Race Riots in Viet." The story featured a taped letter that a black Seabee named Barry Wright had sent home to his mother in Chicago. The voice of the young navy man described for his mother a U.S. military that was infested with racial discrimination. He said that the black soldier in Vietnam was fighting three enemies: the Vietcong, the South Vietnamese, and the bigoted white soldiers within his own ranks. "Whitey has lost no time in teaching the Vietnamese to hate Negroes," he said. "Although they can't speak English, they can say 'Nigger' quite clearly."[19]

The story reported that Confederate flags were flying in "most barracks" and on many official U.S. vehicles. According to the young man, this was the most visible symbol of a culture of racism that pervaded relations between blacks and whites in Vietnam. A common slogan, scrawled on washroom mirrors and barracks walls, was "Nigger go home." Then Wright's voice described a cheerless prospect: "What could be more devastating than an all-out race riot in Vietnam?" He went on to predict that this would soon occur if authorities did not step in.[20]

The Navy Department responded to Wright's allegations by sending its undated and unsigned report on the charges to the *Chicago Defender*. The navy said that Wright had exaggerated when he said Confederate flags were flown everywhere, adding that "a blanket prohibition against all such displays could prove to be unenforceable." The report criticized Wright for failing to take his concerns up the proper chain of command, and his complaints were waved off.[21]

Displays of the Confederate flag had been a recurrent source of irritation to black soldiers in Vietnam. In early 1966 an NAACP official had petitioned Robert McNamara, the defense secretary, to order disciplinary action against any soldier who flew the rebel flag. Philip Savage, tristate director of the NAACP in Philadelphia, was prompted to act by a report that white GIs had waved the Confederate flag on Christmas Day in Vietnam during a Bob Hope performance. The black soldier wrote: "I should not have been upset, but I was." Several white officers and noncoms posed with the flag and had their pictures taken. "I felt like an outsider," the black soldier confessed. "No one in authority stopped to think what effect this had on the morale of the [black] GIs. No one there knew that perhaps the very next day or the next week, many of those same guys would give their lives for America."[22]

In early 1968 a young black officer, a Lieutenant Kitchen, wrote a letter to his mother, and enclosed a copy that he asked her to get to Senator Robert F.

Kennedy and to give copies to President Johnson and anyone else who could help. Kitchen's mother pushed through a crowd at a Kennedy rally and shoved the letter into the senator's hands.

In the letter Kitchen told his mother that Confederate flags were being flown by white soldiers in his unit, "mounted on many vehicles," and displayed at "some installations." The lieutenant, whose unit included forty-five black GIs under his command, described an environment fraught with racial tensions. The letter said, "We are fighting and dying in a war that is not very popular in the first place, and we still have some stupid people who are still fighting the Civil War."

Later in the letter he said that he did not think black soldiers should "serve under the Confederate flag, or with it. We are serving under the American flag and the American flag only." Kitchen said he had complained to his superiors and had gotten no effective response. He ended his letter by saying, "The Negroes here are afraid and cannot do anything." Then he promised to send a picture of a Confederate flag with his next letter.

Three days later he was killed in action in Vietnam. The story appeared in *Jet* on April 4, 1968, the day Martin Luther King was murdered.[23]

While there had been episodes of racial tension and even violence in the military before, King's assassination in April 1968 seemed to mark the beginning of a new, more explosive, period of racial unrest in Vietnam. The first response to King's slaying was often racially primal and raw. Staff Sergeant Don F. Browne, a black airman stationed at an air force base in South Vietnam, remembered his gut reaction: "When I heard that Martin Luther King was assassinated, my first inclination was to run out and punch the first white guy I saw." Browne recalled hearing a white soldier, who had tired of the television coverage of King's death and funeral, say, "I wish they'd take that nigger's picture off." Browne and two other black airmen within earshot reacted by giving the soldier what Browne euphemistically called "a physical lesson" to refine his choice of words.[24] It was a season of deeply hostile emotions that were ready to erupt into violence in the U.S. military in Vietnam—and in the ensuing weeks and months did so altogether too often.

King's assassination evoked responses from angry blacks and jubilant whites that defined and amplified feelings of estrangement and hostility between the races. Even whites who were not openly disrespectful of black feelings at the loss of their leader were put off by the spectacle of rampaging blacks setting fire to block after block in major American cities in the worst rioting in the nation's history. For their part many black soldiers became convinced that white GIs simply had no understanding of the cost of being black in a predominately white culture, including the military, that persistently ignored the legitimate claims of African Americans for equality.

What was apparent to the black press was that, even in the officially integrated armed forces of the United States, social and institutional racism continued to thrive. The largely white command system was lethargic in responding to, and remedying, the interracial problems that always simmered just below the surface and occasionally ignited into racial violence. Discrimination against African Americans continued to be a significant problem in a military that had prided itself on being a model of social enlightenment.

Increasingly, the racial tensions and fault lines that marked life along the boundaries of color back home, were mirrored in the U.S. military in Vietnam, despite its officially mandated integration. The new recruits and draftees that filled the ranks in the 1960s came into the military from a civilian world that was still trying to come to terms with issues of civil rights and economic opportunity for African Americans. U.S. society was sundered by the widening racial divide between the legitimate, and often clamorous, demands of black voices for a more equitable participation in the American dream and the recalcitrance of a Congress and public increasingly weary of the tumult and distracted by the political uncertainty growing out of an unpopular war.

In December 1969 the *Chicago Daily Defender* and the *Baltimore Afro-American* both published a story based on a UPI feature. According to the story, after examining the issue of racial unrest in Vietnam, L. Howard Bennett, an acting deputy secretary of defense for civil rights at the Pentagon, wrote: "We found problems, problems which are really a reflection of the turbulence of the American community. We are now finding that as the turbulence in American society begins to subside, it's manifesting itself with some degree of increase in the military because we're now taking into the service young men who are the products [of] and who have experienced violence in American urban communities."[25]

Twice within a month the *Pittsburgh Courier* ran an editorial echoing that theme, connecting racial confrontation and violence within the U.S. military in Vietnam with "the black revolution and general civil unrest at home." However, the *Courier* went further, foreseeing a worsening of racial violence in the United States because of the bitter experiences of African Americans in the military. The paper warned that the cycle of violence might become worse if the armed forces were not decisive and forceful in altering the culture within the military that fostered racial animosity, because black veterans would bring back with them all the accumulated grievances, "the hatred and frustration," and "swell the army of black discontents, the stuff of which riots are made."[26]

In late summer 1968 an editorial in the *Afro-American* on the subject of racial violence in Vietnam began with a note of resignation: "The more things change, the more they stay the same." This was a startling measure of just how commonplace interracial violence in the war zone was becoming. The editorial was prompted by a racial clash between white and black GIs in Saigon that left sixty-five wounded and two dead. The editorial offered no additional details about what had happened. Attempting to explain such outbreaks, the editor wrote: "Trouble arises in zones where men live a wild life far removed from the social controls that their own civilization and culture impose. They are lonesome, often bitter, short tempered and responsive to the slights that might be overlooked were they existing in a more harmonious and peaceful circumstance. The mystery is not that riots flare up, but that as few riots break out as do."[27]

The motif of a two-front war, in an odd and disturbing way, sometimes seemed applicable to the experience of the African American military in Vietnam, who sometimes felt they were facing enemies both across the firing line in the lurking Vietnamese enemy and within their own ranks among the white troops. A story on the front page of the *Afro-American* on June 14, 1969, introduced the metaphor to describe the state of interracial relations in the U.S. Marine Corps in Vietnam. According to the feature, 105 leathernecks of the Third Battalion, First Marines, signed a six-page statement describing a combat force that was far from the harmonious interracial community sometimes idealized in the black press earlier in the war. Instead, the marines described a unit wracked by discrimination. The piece said of the marines: "They currently are fighting two wars—one against racial prejudice and the other against the Viet Cong."

The story included a response from Major General J. M. Platt, assistant chief of staff of the marine corps, who quickly denied the allegations, citing the firm antidiscrimination policy of the service and arguing that the infrequent individual instances of discrimination were dealt with promptly. For its part the *Afro-American* stated without elaboration: "Allegations about racial prejudice in the three branches of the services reach the editorial office of the AFRO frequently. However, this is the first time that such allegations were made by such a large number of Marines."[28]

Barely a month later a bloody race riot tore through the complacency of the corps and set in motion a reexamination of marine corps policies and practices in the area of race relations. The riot occurred the night of July 20, 1969, at a nightclub at Camp Lejeune, a marine base in North Carolina, and landed on the front pages of a number of newspapers, including the *Afro-American* and the *Pittsburgh Courier*.

Before the mayhem was over, dozens of people had been injured, including two marines who were hospitalized after being slashed with knives and a third who suffered severe head injuries. A nineteen-year-old white corporal from Mississippi, who had just returned from Vietnam, was dead with a fractured skull, according to the *Courier*. During the evening other violent confrontations occurred, though none with the deadly consequences of the main free-for-all outside the club. In the confusion and darkness it was not clear just how all the separate incidents began or just who was responsible. When racial passions were added to the mix of bottled-up energy and high-spirited nerves characteristic of a predeployment environment, the stew proved to be volatile.[29]

In the *Afro-American*'s account the picture that emerged was of a culture of violence at the base that had produced 190 assaults involving Camp Lejeune marines during the first seven months of 1969, including those on the night of July 20.[30] After the tumult at Camp Lejeune, the marine commandant, General Leonard F. Chapman, conceded the corps had unresolved racial problems. He disclosed there had been a rash of racial clashes that, in the language of the *Afro-American*, had "erupted on an unusually large scale recently at Camp Lejeune." Chapman said the racial clashes "began in April and continued through July." Then he added: "We thought we had eliminated discrimination in the Marine Corps, and we are still determined to do so. If anyone brings a complaint to me, I will have it investigated and corrected if the complaint is valid."[31]

How could what had once been viewed as the most integrated institution in America—the military—later appear as a place simmering with racial hostility?

At least some of the answer lay in the heightened consciousness of blacks in the military, as African Americans in the services embraced the principles of black pride. Conflict often occurred when black soldiers sought to express their cultural pride and met with resistance from white soldiers and their usually white commanders. The suppression of black cultural expression was a frequent irritant in the relationship of black GIs and their white fellow soldiers and superiors.

Jet magazine published a statement signed by a group of unhappy black airmen at a base in Pleiku who described acts of individual racial harassment and official disapproval of expressions of their black heritage. The men stated that acts of prejudice had occurred in Vietnam since the beginning of U.S. involvement there but said that since the summer of 1968, the incidence of overt racial discrimination had become intolerable. "These people don't try to hide their feelings or their prejudices any longer," the airmen wrote, then went on to complain of a pattern of verbal abuse, including threats of physical harm. The black airmen described official distinctions made between white and black behavior, with the former indulged and the latter suppressed:

"White men may wear their hair almost any length and style they choose. On the other hand, neatly worn naturals that are evidence of our ethnic pride are taboo and are dealt with as evidence of an inevitable belligerence or a rebellious nature."[32]

A few months later *Jet* magazine published another brief item on the same subject: "The flood of letters reaching *Jet* and points all over the U.S. [is coming] from black Vietnam soldiers who are complaining that they are banned from wearing the Afro-bush hair styles. The black GIs say white commanding officers in certain Vietnam military units look the other way when shaggy-haired white soldiers pass, but dish out the severest penalties the book will allow when long-haired black GIs are involved."[33]

The ban on Afro hair styles extended to other forms of African American cultural expression, including black wristbands, or "unity bracelets"; the clenched-fist black power salute; black power flags; and soul handshakes, which whites found annoying. As a piece in *Jet* pointed out, many black soldiers found these forms of cultural communication reassuring and reinforcing, whereas white superior officers often viewed them as a sign of black militancy that threatened morale and cohesion in a military unit. Some white commanders even viewed them as incipient insubordination. When these cultural gestures and symbols were suppressed, black GIs seethed with resentment, which sometimes boiled over into overt racial conflict and violence.[34]

The persistence and occasional severity of attempts by military authorities to suppress the use of black cultural symbols and modes of communication seemed to be an expression of both their racism and their anxiety when confronted by individual acts of black nonconformity and the larger perceived threat of collective solidarity among potentially rebellious black soldiers. African American soldiers, for their part, saw gestures of racial identity as a way to express not only their cultural distinctiveness but also their manhood. The military response therefore came across as not only discriminatory but as a challenge to black self-esteem. The *Chicago Daily Defender* quoted a recently discharged black veteran: "If you're black, wear a natural and act like you're a man, you're automatically discriminated against and charged with all kinds of things."[35]

The first branch of the U.S. military to address these sources of friction was the marine corps, perhaps because so many of the episodes of violence involved marines. In early September 1969 Chapman issued an order to all commands that for the first time sanctioned the wearing of Afros by black marines. His message included guidelines to ensure some uniformity in the styles of Afros to be worn. Chapman also opened the door to the informal use of other "actions, signs, symbols, gestures and words" but excluded them from official corps ceremonies because they were "contrary to tradition." In an effort to address other elements of persistent institutional racism, Chapman ordered all marine commands to review such matters as promotions, military justice procedures, and duty assignment routines to ensure fair treatment of black marines.

The black press greeted the initiative warmly. The *Afro-American* wrote: "Now, the Marine Corps is at last taking some steps to make life easier for its black men and at the same time trying to heal the racial friction on and off base."[36]

On the heels of the marine corps commandant's initiative, Army Secretary Stanley Resor began actively addressing continuing problems of racial friction in his branch of the service. An editorial in the *Afro-American* commended him for saying that "one way to minimize racial tensions in the Army is to make the Army as responsive as it can be to the needs of all of its men." The editorial also applauded Resor's recognition of the special cultural backgrounds of black soldiers and their need to express their unity with other black servicemen. The editorial noted the secretary's call for army commanders to "recognize slogans such as 'Black is beautiful' as a gesture of pride, comradeship, and solidarity." However, the paper demanded that the army move beyond such cultural adjustments and eliminate "every vestige of inequality based on race."[37]

For its part the *Chicago Daily Defender* kept up the pressure. Months after the encouraging initiatives taken by the marine corps and the army, the *Defender* was still concerned with what it viewed to be a continuing climate of racial discrimination and harassment in America's armed forces. The paper noted that blacks "are unable to communicate up the chain of command without their communication being adulterated." The *Defender* urged that "all services follow the Marine Corps in permitting such overt expressions of black pride as the clenched-fist, black-power salute, and the Afro hair style." Unless the military did something to change the continuing climate of discrimination, the consequences might manifest themselves in alienated black veterans joining the swollen ranks of disillusioned blacks in America and adding to the highly combustible mix of broken dreams and angry young men.[38]

Racial tension, which continued to erupt into violence from time to time, plagued the U.S. military in Vietnam throughout the rest of the war, even though the number of reports on the subject in the black press declined after they reached a peak in 1969. As the American presence in Vietnam steadily dwindled during the Nixon years, so did the incidence of racial violence in the battle zone. However, the black press continued to carry reports of outbreaks of violence among American troops.

Black newspapers also periodically published reports of various studies aimed at diagnosing and finding solutions for the problem of race relations in the U.S. military. The proliferation of studies was evidence of concern about racism in the military and showed an active interest on the part of high-level officials in reducing the causes of racial friction. The strenuous exertions directed at resolving the issue were a testament to its intransigence and longevity. And, as often as not, both the black press and African American leaders were cautious in their assessments of these studies, having been disappointed for so long by official pronouncements brimming with high purpose.[39]

For some time the black press had been reporting concern that black soldiers, embittered by racism in the armed forces and confronting continuing discrimination at home, might use the violent skills they had learned in the military to vent their rage. Once racial violence became commonplace in Vietnam, some saw the outbreaks as a storm that might sweep across the Pacific and engulf the homeland in greater racial conflict than it had already experienced. Johnny Bowles wrote in the *Baltimore Afro-American* of the "gathering storm," differentiating between dissident soldiers who sought to expand their "constitutional and civil rights" and others moved by darker, revolutionary impulses. He cited instances of weapons stolen from military installations that had turned up at mail facilities in the San Francisco Bay Area and reported that U.S. Customs officials were concerned that "many GIs in Vietnam are sending weapons home to be stockpiled by revolutionaries."[40]

Another concern was the spread of drug addiction among the troops in Vietnam. A leading African American prosecutor, quoted in a *St. Louis American* editorial, feared that the problem of dope addiction in Vietnam would be used to explain the worsening drug epidemic in the inner cities and that returning black veterans would be singled out as scapegoats. The prosecutor, speaking at a meeting of the National Bar Association in Atlanta in the summer of 1971, voiced his fear that "with the urban ghettoes already the cesspools of the dope hustlers" and the incubators of so much teenage crime, the next major outbreak of violent civil disorder in the inner city might be "charged to the black Vietnam returnees" who had added even more drugs to the volatile mix of poverty and despair.[41]

In fact, organized uprisings spearheaded by angry black Vietnam veterans, the subject of persistent fears and warnings in the black press, never materialized. A piece in *Jet* magazine in the summer of 1968 proved to be an accurate gauge of the likely response of black vets returned from Vietnam. *Jet* observed: "Contrary to black extremists' beliefs, most black veterans are not coming home from the war to lead riots." UPI found that black soldiers who had faced death in Vietnam were "disillusioned on their return home to find that they are still subjects of discrimination." However, as one black vet said, "Rioting has done more harm than good. You don't prove anything with rioting." Most returning black veterans bore their frustrations with remarkable restraint. As Ponchitta Pierce and Peter Bailey wrote in *Ebony*, "When they return from the war, black vets have been disciplined to keep their mouths shut."[42]

The black press frequently reported on the travails of black veterans who faced special difficulties as they reentered civilian life. In disproportionate numbers they were turned out of the military with "bad discharges," often resulting from overly severe sanctions for relatively trivial infractions—that frequently grew out of the racial tensions that sometimes shaped the interaction between culturally assertive black troops and their white superiors. A piece in *Jet* called the recipients of these discharges "branded men" who would be haunted by an inescapable "social stigma." These less-than-honorable discharges from the service blemished the records of these men and often doomed their hopes for a reasonably successful transition to civilian life and meaningful employment. Other vets came home hooked on drugs, often heroin.[43]

Most black veterans returning home were not these hard cases. They were young men who had either enlisted, often to escape economic hardships, or were drafted and wound up in Vietnam, enduring the boredom and terror of an incomprehensible war. They suffered combat casualties in disproportionate numbers. Those who were fortunate to return home unscathed—or at least alive—found they were in a society that was generally as inhospitable to blacks as the one they had left when they went off to serve their country. This central irony, as much as anything, defined the plight of the black veteran. He had answered the call, done his duty, gone to a far corner of the world to fight for someone else's freedom, only to have his own still circumscribed by the harsh realities of life on his side of the racial and economic divide in American society (see figure 12).

Two years after the last American POWs came home from Hanoi and the last U.S. troops were flown out of the battle zone, the war in Vietnam finally approached its end. In the spring of 1975 President Gerald Ford, Nixon's successor, could not persuade Congress to provide additional funds to the besieged South Vietnamese government. As he read the first draft of a speech to a joint session of Congress, the president saw these words: "And after years of effort, we negotiated a settlement which made it possible for us to remove our forces with honor and bring home our prisoners." Ford was not prepared to go that far. He crossed out the words *with honor*.[44]

Figure 12.

The returning black GI, despite his sacrifices, finds himself a second-class citizen, his government apparently indifferent, and the U.S. capitol a far-off, inaccessible place, remote from his needs. (Cartoon by Chester Commodore, *Chicago Defender*, February 19, 1968. Courtesy of the *Chicago Defender*.)

As the black press presented its obituary for the conflict, two distinctly opposite perspectives emerged. The *Atlanta Daily World* cringed at the shame of the final debacle in Vietnam. The paper believed in what America had sought to do there. Even after the collapse of the South Vietnamese army and the fall of Saigon in the spring of 1975, the paper believed that the cause had been just. In an editorial headlined "A Tragedy in Vietnam," the paper described the fall of America's hapless South Vietnamese ally as "a tragedy that will go down in history." The *Daily World* remained unrepentantly hawkish about the U.S. role in the struggle: "But we hasten to disagree with those who say we had no business in Vietnam."

In the tattered remnants of American policy in Vietnam, the newspaper was still able to discern the shape of destiny: "So we had a right and a duty in Vietnam and despite the cost of the conflict to us in lives and injured and billions in dollars, we do not believe we invested in vain."[45]

Most of the black press could not share this assessment at war's end, for in the wreckage of America's effort in Vietnam also lay the dashed hopes that so many American blacks had struggled to realize.

Vernon Jordan, in his column in the *Los Angeles Sentinel*, listed some of the nonfinancial costs of the war: heavy damage to U.S. international prestige and national self-confidence, and the destruction of the Second Reconstruction, by gutting its key economic and social programs.[46]

In her column in the *Chicago Defender*, Shirley Lens made it more personal, describing the United States as "a land torn by tragedy" in the wake of the Vietnam War's gloomy end, where "thousands of young men sit in veterans' hospitals minus an arm or leg, or permanently paralyzed from the chest down, wondering why their lives were wasted in a useless and ignoble cause."[47]

Jet magazine looked back at the conflict after the fall of Saigon and recognized the relevance of Martin Luther King's vision and the prescience of his denunciations of the war. The brief article revisited King's contribution to the antiwar debate and granted his ideological insurgency the recognition hindsight seemed to have earned it. The piece quoted a statement made by Henry Kissinger, who acknowledged in an interview that the United States "probably made a mistake" by getting involved in Vietnam. In so saying, one of the national policy makers who had helped shape the U.S. role in the war had arrived at a realization that "finally caught up with Dr. Martin Luther King's prophetic revelation," *Jet* said. Later in the article, *Jet* quoted King: "There are those who say that I should not mix the war in Vietnam with civil rights. I have fought too hard and too long against segregation to end up at this point in my life to segregate my moral concern. Power asks the question, 'Is it safe?' Expediency asks, 'Is it politic?' Vanity asks, 'Is it popular?' But conscience asks, 'Is it right?' It is now necessary for me to take a stand that is neither safe, nor politic, nor popular but I must do it because it is right."[48]

9

The Black Press and the Vietnam War

The war and the civil rights struggle moved with a kind of ironic symmetry, as
if each had become a metaphor for the other. —Arnold R. Isaacs, *Vietnam Shadows*

The interplay of the war in Vietnam and unrealized African American expectations fundamentally defined the way the black press viewed the conflict. The war came to dominate the national agenda just as the civil rights
movement appeared to be on the brink of realizing long-deferred black
hopes for full equality. America seemed poised to yield, at long last, to the
legitimate claims of its black citizens. The greatest explosion of civil rights
reform since Reconstruction came just before the peak of U.S. involvement
in the war. The U.S. Supreme Court had struck a body blow to segregated
public education in *Brown v. Board of Education* in 1954. By the late 1950s
and early 1960s an energetic civil rights movement had galvanized a growing constituency, often dominated headlines and evening television broadcasts, and enjoyed wide moral support.

As President Lyndon Johnson led Congress in enacting a flurry of legislation that expanded the rights of African Americans and finally established
in law the right of the nation's black citizens to vote, the legal basis of segregation was crumbling. The president also vigorously threw his apparently boundless energy into the task of addressing the long-standing social and
economic needs of black Americans, putting in place the legislative and institutional architecture of a Great Society.

Despite these momentous changes, African Americans still faced vexing problems, and the black press and civil rights leaders continued to call for further ameliorations of the conditions facing blacks in the United States. Johnson's messages to Congress and the nation still rang with a note of urgency as he challenged America to complete the work of reform. Much had been done, but there was still more to do. Still, as the war in Vietnam escalated in 1965 and beyond, the conflict became the nation's top priority, supplanting the issue of civil rights. Progress toward the Great Society stalled.

At that moment, when the Second Reconstruction seemed tantalizingly close to achieving what the first one had failed to do, the Vietnam War elbowed it aside. It is likely that the momentum that had carried so much progressive legislation through Congress already was faltering and might have ended even if the Vietnam conflict had not siphoned national resources and attention away from the Great Society. Some isolated commentary in the black press acknowledged as much. But the nearly simultaneous escalation of the war and lessening of political support for further domestic reform gave rise to the widespread conviction in the black press that the war was responsible for denying African Americans the last measure of moral and financial commitment that would have fulfilled their dreams.

When congressional opponents of Johnson's reform initiatives explicitly used the cost of the Vietnam War to argue against further funding of Great Society programs, it was easy for African Americans to assume that, without the war, that opposition would not have existed, or at least would not have been strong enough to block the president's programs. The correlation they perceived was a powerful impetus to the black press in developing its interpretation of, and response to, the Vietnam War. Almost inevitably, the war came to be viewed as a critical moment in the history of the civil rights struggle, a fulcrum upon which the fate of the Second Reconstruction turned.

From the perspective of the black press, any measure of the domestic consequences of the war would have to take timing into account: the greatest opportunity for transformation in civil rights since post–Civil War Reconstruction disappeared when the attention and resources of the United States shifted from domestic issues to fighting the war in Vietnam. While most of the black press gave Lyndon Johnson plaudits for his commitment to civil rights and the Great Society, and overwhelmingly supported him politically, it agreed that the Vietnam War blunted full civil rights reform and drained away the resources needed to ensure economic freedom and opportunity for most African Americans.

The theme of a struggle between competing national priorities became a staple of black anger directed against the war. This grew out of the realization that the cause of civil rights had been supplanted by the war in Vietnam as the number one issue in official Washington and, according to Gallup polls, in the public mind as well. The civil rights movement seemed to be losing the undiluted support of the president and Congress, and the attention and concern of the American people. These were vital to enacting further civil rights legislation and funding major reform initiatives to sustain and expand the Great Society.

The battle for resources, which deeply troubled the black press, led to the development of a powerful metaphor that appeared often in the African American press: the two-front war. This metaphor was a compelling vehicle for imagining the struggle between these two fronts as they fought for the means needed to achieve victory. The black press rhetorically established a relationship between the two spheres of conflict and then sought to measure and compare the resources committed to one or the other. During the first year or so after the large-scale escalation of the war began, some optimism was expressed in the black press that the war on both fronts could be waged successfully and that both could be viewed as noble crusades led by a determined, energetic, and compassionate president, Lyndon Johnson. This optimism was short lived.

Once it became apparent that the war was siphoning off vital resources needed at home, the black press sought strenuously to maintain the momentum of the struggle for racial equality and to fend off attempts to diminish gains already made. This shaped an interpretation of the Vietnam War that saw the conflict through the prism of black experience. The theme of the two-front war was one of the most enduring manifestations of this persistent hermeneutical tendency. The war in Vietnam served both as a metaphor for the domestic struggle and as a vehicle to affirm entitlement.

The black press often used the theme of the two-front war in criticizing the power elite (sometimes Congress but often the president, especially during the Nixon years) for its failure to provide adequate resources to fight the battle at home against discrimination and poverty. The emphasis was no longer on a collaborative national effort but on the desperate struggle between the voracious appetite for resources of the Vietnam War and the urgent needs of domestic reform. As the black press realized that the competition between the war and the Great Society was an unequal struggle, and that black dreams for reform would have to be deferred, the tone of the commentary and the imagery of the cartoons became grimmer, more caustic. The swelling anger was palpable.

Another motif of the black press grew out of observations of the interracial harmony on the battlefields of Vietnam. The achievement of brotherhood between black and white men as they faced combat together often was seen in the black press as the ultimate realization of racial reconciliation and brotherhood. Battlefield brotherhood became a template used to sketch the shape of what the ideal civilian society should look like but seldom did.

Despite the power of these idealized images, the black press often acknowledged that racial discrimination sometimes crept into military life behind the lines, away from the stern realities of shared danger. By the late 1960s the racial tensions that had been exploding into violence all too frequently in America had become a growing problem in the U.S. military as well. Black consciousness had been elevated in the battle zone, as it had back home, and with it came a new assertiveness. African Americans were no longer content with functional integration in the military. They began demanding respect and recognition from their fellow soldiers and the mostly white command establishment.

As the realization dawned that the quality of life for blacks in the military in Vietnam was not that far removed from that in the rest of American society, with racism a persistent reality in both spheres, the theme of interracial brotherhood virtually disappeared from the black press. It was replaced by a new construct. Brotherhood in the military would now be seen as a bond uniting black soldiers in a community of shared experience, within the larger context of the functionally integrated, but fundamentally hostile, armed forces still dominated by whites. Racial justice for African Americans would be a goal to pursue in both the civilian and military arenas with unrelenting vigor.

Another tendency prominent in the interpretation of the Vietnam War in the black press was the use of descriptions of African American exploits in combat to point out the continuing injustices that blacks routinely faced on the home front. These accounts were often both celebratory and hortatory. Even as they provided opportunities to express pride in African American achievement, they were used to inform and confront a society that continued to treat blacks with indifference or even hostility.

Black casualties in combat offered a particularly persuasive means for the black press to claim for its constituency all the rights and economic opportunities granted to other Americans. The irony of blacks' fighting and dying for the freedom of the South Vietnamese while black Americans were not enjoying full rights of citizenship at home made the argument for entitlement all the more potent. The connection of these ideas would appear often in opinion pieces in the black press.

Adding more urgency to the claim of entitlement based on sacrifice was the revelation by the Pentagon that blacks were dying in disproportionate numbers in Vietnam. The subject of excessive black casualties quickly became an important theme used in the black press to call for social reforms in

America. So useful was the subject as a lever of social reform that its rhetorical uses overshadowed discussions of the subject itself as a problem to be solved. Questions of causation and remediation were raised but took a back seat to the more pressing needs of the campaign for domestic reform.

The black press built the war in Vietnam into its interpretive framework of major issues confronting African Americans, sensing it was an obstacle to the realization of black aspirations. Even those black newspapers that continued to support President Johnson's international policies, in deference to his domestic leadership in pursuing programs beneficial to blacks—and out of fear of losing that leadership—saw the war as a threat to important reform goals.

Despite the growing antiwar sentiment in the African American press, when Martin Luther King Jr. openly broke with the Johnson administration over the war in a landmark speech in April 1967, shudders of apprehension rippled through much of the black press. King's opposition to the war was built around a direct assault on the legitimacy of U.S. geopolitical assumptions. He argued that America was ignoring the true nature of the revolutionary impulses that were stirring in much of the third world and were driving the people of Vietnam to throw off the vestiges of colonialism. The United States, King believed, was on the wrong side of this revolution, mistakenly seeing the struggle of oppressed peoples for self-determination and independence as the product of international communism's expansionism rather than the homegrown stirrings of nationalism. By ignoring its own revolutionary roots, King argued, America was fighting against powerful currents of international change, aligning too often with corrupt, oppressive regimes against popular yearnings for freedom, and, in so doing, was strengthening, rather than weakening, the allure of communism as the champion of revolutionary change.

The ideological nuances of King's attack on U.S. policy were not of particular interest to the black press. But the potential political consequences of his stance caused great anxiety and considerable controversy. The discomfort of the black press and other black leaders centered on what was broadly seen as King's de facto merging of the civil rights movement into the antiwar movement. They instinctively sensed the considerable peril to the cause of domestic reform if the black agenda for change were to become identified too closely with the raucous antiwar movement. This danger quickly became apparent as long-time political allies of the civil rights movement began distancing themselves from King, roundly criticizing him for his controversial pronouncements about the war in Vietnam. Even members of King's inner circle were concerned that key political support might evaporate and funding sources would scurry for cover, abandoning the inconveniently controversial civil rights leader.

As anxiety increased over the adverse political consequences that might ensue from King's denunciation of Johnson's Vietnam policy, many members of the African American press criticized the civil rights leader directly for putting the movement at risk. Throughout the balance of King's life, much of the black press remained unsettled by his antiwar ideology, preferring to see him focus on the cause of equal rights and economic justice for African Americans.

Even when the black press was not explicitly opposing the Vietnam War editorially, it viewed the war as a threat to the interests and welfare of African Americans. This was because, in the view of the black press, the war threatened the very existence of the Great Society, which provided structural support to the black goal of reforming American life and creating an equitable, prosperous national community. It took the lives of young black men in disproportionate numbers and wounded countless others in body and soul, without altering the fundamental inequities at home, where African Americans were still treated as second-class citizens. It created deep fissures in the United States, as antiwar sentiment grew, solidified into a movement, and attracted the support of key black leaders. Their opposition often brought down the wrath of powerful whites whose support had been critical in advancing the black agenda. Many leaders of the political establishment came down hard on African Americans who challenged the nation's entanglement in Vietnam. To make matters worse, the functionally integrated U.S. military began to come apart at its racial seams.

Even during the Johnson years, when a number of black newspapers supported—or at least acquiesced in—the president's policy in Vietnam, they presented their readers with a view of the war that tended to be at odds with black interests and hostile to blacks' aspirations. This negative perspective was significantly strengthened in these papers when they began explicitly opposing U.S. policy in Vietnam. Taken together, most of the editorials, columns, and cartoons about the war in the black press built a negative interpretive framework within which they discussed the Vietnam War. When they did not explicitly oppose it, they linked the war with themes, such as threats to Great Society funding and disproportionate black casualties, that presented particularly negative conceptual images to African Americans. The black press had a persistent tendency to view the war through the lens of black experience and aspirations, and that view was shaped by the negative, even threatening, implications for black Americans of much of what the black press presented.

Throughout the Johnson presidency members of the black press and civil rights leaders were uncertain how to respond to the Vietnam War. It became apparent in 1965 and beyond that the war was pushing aside the African

American agenda for domestic reform at the top of the nation's priorities. Black leaders began assessing their own feelings about the conflict and the impact of the war on the prospects for continued progress in implementing and expanding black equality and opportunity. As they did so, fissures began to open between those who chose to oppose the president's handling of Vietnam, such as King and other, younger civil rights leaders, and more conservative establishment civil rights leaders such as Roy Wilkins, who continued to support the president. The same demarcations were visible between those African American newspapers that opposed the war during the Johnson administration and others in the black press that continued to support Johnson's Vietnam policy, or at least avoided openly opposing the president's actions in Southeast Asia.

Much of the support Johnson received for his Vietnam policy from the black press was halfhearted and restrained, especially after the initial flush of patriotism faded into the grim reality of fighting an increasingly controversial war. Few black voices strongly backed U.S. involvement in Vietnam. When they did support it, their support, more often than not, seemed to be driven by personal and political loyalty to LBJ, not by geopolitical imperatives. The way much of the African American press responded to King for breaking with the Johnson administration in 1967 over Vietnam grew out of fear of the consequences to the civil rights struggle of King's insurgency. The visceral reaction was not because of any great enthusiasm for the national effort in Vietnam. Instead, it was a defensive crouch designed to avoid taking a position on a controversial public issue in a way that might risk the president's displeasure and jeopardize support for domestic reform beneficial to African Americans. The president's continued goodwill was particularly important, since he was the one national leader most likely to produce results for blacks in the field of equal rights and economic opportunity.

Johnson's announcement in 1968 that he would not run for a second term changed the implicit ground rules for those members of the black press and black leaders who had kept their doubts about Vietnam to themselves in deference to the president. The election of Richard Nixon completed the process of liberating conservative black protest against the war. Since Nixon was assumed to be unsympathetic to black goals for domestic reform, and would be supported in that distaste by a Congress that seemed increasingly indifferent, or even hostile, to African American aspirations, blacks had little to lose in expressing their misgivings or outright opposition to the Vietnam War.

African Americans lost their most effective champion in the U.S. government when Johnson withdrew from electoral politics, but his retirement also removed an obstacle to the free expression of black opposition to the Vietnam

War. Consequently, one result of Nixon's election was the amplification of official black opposition to the conflict in Vietnam. This was reflected in the virtual unanimity of editorial opposition to the war in the black press and in the now unrestrained criticism of U.S. policy in Vietnam among prominent civil rights leaders who had expressed support for Johnson's leadership in the war or had remained silent during his presidency.

Even as editorials in black newspapers became more critical of the U.S. role in Vietnam after the departure of Johnson and the arrival in office of Nixon—the unrepentantly hawkish *Atlanta Daily World* was a notable exception—ironically, the war as a news story began to recede in the black press. One reason for this change was Nixon's deliberate strategy of pushing a balky South Vietnamese ally to assume a greater role in fighting the war. As Nixon noisily implemented his policy of Vietnamization and began drawing down American forces in Vietnam, a corresponding reduction occurred in U.S. ground combat activity and casualties, and the conflict became less prominent in the black press as a news story. Both the number and prominence of news stories about the war diminished.

However, even as the Vietnam story began to recede somewhat, it began to take on a harder, grittier tone. Where once the black press had run pieces hailing the racial integration achieved in the military, particularly in combat in Vietnam, the prominent emphasis, as the 1970s approached, was on the pervasiveness of racial tension and strife in the U.S. armed forces. The new cultural self-awareness of African American troops, fed by the assertiveness of the black power movement, which bolstered the pride and morale of black GIs, soon collided with the entrenched prejudices and fears of white troops and produced interracial stress and outbreaks of racial violence in Vietnam.

From the beginning, the black press subordinated stories about the war to pursuit of the realization of equal rights and economic justice for African Americans. The black press quickly incorporated its interpretation of the war into its central reformist vision. It used black experience in Vietnam to bolster its argument that African Americans deserved equal treatment as full-fledged citizens. Black sacrifices in Vietnam were adduced repeatedly as a means of establishing that entitlement.

Despite their essential moderation and geopolitical orthodoxy in the early stages of the Vietnam conflict, most black newspapers ultimately were driven to oppose the war, frequently linking the conflict with the deferment of black aspirations. In contrast, the *Atlanta Daily World* made no effort to relate its commentary on the war to issues of particular importance to African Americans. This was consistent with its support of American involvement in the war and its support of the Republican approach to issues of social entitlement, including a generally skeptical view of the Great Society, an approach that reduced the rhetorical utility of the black experience in Vietnam as a basis for demanding domestic reform.

The interpretation of the Vietnam War in the black press was firmly rooted in black experience and often assumed the coloration of that experience. The vicissitudes of the domestic African American struggle affected the perceptions of the war in the black press and the expression of those perceptions in the positioning of the story and in shaping commentary about the war. As issues of race determined the reality of African Americans at home, so they often determined the way the war in Vietnam was covered and interpreted. Most publications gave preeminence to those stories about the war that either reflected the nature of the black struggle for equality or provided a basis for strengthening the African American claim to the entitlements of first-class citizenship.

Commentary on the Vietnam War in the black press was enriched by argument drawn from the intersection of the war and African American experience. The conflict in Vietnam became both a mirror in which black Americans saw reflections of their own suffering and a lens that magnified and clarified black demands for change.

Notes

Introduction

1. I am indebted to the definitive account of the incidents in the Gulf of Tonkin in early August 1964 that appears in Moise, *Tonkin Gulf*. The book describes the two incidents in the gulf (73–93; 106–41), evidence as to the nature and details of what happened (143–207), as well as the geopolitical and military consequences (208–55). An insider view from the Pentagon is provided by Daniel Ellsberg's provocative book *Secrets*; Ellsberg began a new assignment in the Defense Department on August 4, 1964, and found himself handling the action reports telegraphed from Herrick. See, especially, Ellsberg's account of the reported "action" in the waters off North Vietnam, then the rush to passage of the momentous Gulf of Tonkin Resolution, which marked the beginning of the long slide into the morass of Vietnam and gave LBJ virtual carte blanche to prosecute an expanded war in Vietnam (7–20; 48–64).

2. Weisbrot, *Freedom Bound*, 99.

3. Ibid., 113; Bennett, *Before the Mayflower*, 573.

4. For an account of what Bob Moses said at the memorial service, see Branch, *Pillar of Fire*, 473.

5. Moses's use of the mirror metaphor is quoted in Hayden, *Reunion*, 177.

6. Henry Lee Moon, "The Role of the Negro Press," *Dallas Express*, December 18, 1965. Moon was director of public relations for the NAACP. For a good summary of the birth of *Freedom's Journal*, see Pride and Wilson, *A History of the Black Press*, 3–16. The first issue of *Freedom's Journal* appeared on March 16, 1827, and laid the foundation for the mission of the black press: "We wish to plead our own cause. Too long have others spoken for us." The paper enumerated other principles and goals: to nurture and develop children; foster character development and personal improvement, and thus elevate the conduct of free blacks; guide readers to a full realization of their civil rights; and lead readers away from publications that were frivolous and time wasting. By recommending useful and educational books, the *Freedom's Journal* also sought to offer ways for readers "to enlarge their stock of useful knowledge." As Pride

and Wilson summarize its role, " the new publication proposed to be a teacher, prod, unifier, and defender and to pursue a reformist program." (13).

7. Simmons, *African American Press*, 9, 10.

8. Frank L. Stanley, "Negro Press Heartbeat of Freedom," *Dallas Express*, March 18, 1967. Metz T. P. Lochard, associate editor of the *Chicago Daily Defender*, produced a manuscript in 1967 titled "Why the Black Press?" He posited that learning what the black press is requires first answering the question "Why the black press?" Lochard expanded his thesis, saying: "Posed in this manner, the question would bring to the surface the failings of the American democracy and the indifference of the white press to the woes and grievances of the black masses." This approach brought Lochard back to what the founders of the *Freedom's Journal* had said nearly a century and a half earlier. Lochard wrote: "The Negro Press was born out of stark necessity . . . as a voice crying out in the wilderness for social justice for the black people of America." The typewritten documents (there are two) in the Abbott-Sengstacke Family Papers present a curious puzzle of provenance. One document, under the byline of John H. Sengstacke, publisher of the *Defender*, appears to be the earlier of the two. It is a rough draft, with cross-outs and corrections. The name Metz T. P. Lochard is handwritten next to Sengstacke's name. The second manuscript reproduces the more roughly typed manuscript exactly and is assigned to Lochard's authorship. The index to the Abbott-Sengstacke Family Papers has a single entry for the document attributed to Lochard. Sengstacke probably drafted the piece, then gave it to Lochard to publish under his name. For the manuscripts see Lochard, "Why the Negro Press," 1967, box 95, folder 8, Abbott-Sengstacke Family Papers.

9. Moon, "Role of the Negro Press." For more on the pressures the U.S. government brought to bear on the black press during World War I, see the fine book by Jordan, *Black Newspapers and America's War for Democracy,* 110–68. For accounts of similar issues during World War II, see Finkle, *Forum for Protest*, 62–87, 108–28; and Washburn, *A Question of Sedition*, which examines the unsuccessful attempt by the FBI to impose wartime censorship on the black press during World War II. It was thwarted by Attorney General Francis Biddle, a passionate supporter of civil liberties.

1. Bringing the News Home

1. The number of reporters is given in Laurence, *Cat from Hue* 481. Also see Pach, "And That's the Way It Was,": 533, 534; and Prochnau, *Once upon a Distant War*.

2. The paucity of black reporters in Vietnam is noted in "Press: Beyond Ghetto Sniffing," 89.

3. Ethel L. Payne, "Proposed Coverage and Assistance Needed," December 28, 1966, memo to Barry Zorthian and John Stuart, box 1 of Vietnam materials, containing Payne's correspondence and other materials by Payne, Payne Papers, Howard University.

4. Payne interview, September 24, 1987, 94–97.

5. "Conrad Clark in Final Army Hitch," *Baltimore Afro-American*, December 2, 1967.

6. Mosby's reports from Vietnam, published in the *Chicago Defender*, included "Our Reporter Tells It Like It Is in Saigon," May 6, 1968; "Saigon Slayings Leave Our Man a Little Scared," May 7, 1968; "Black GIs in Viet Accuse U.S. of Betraying Them," May 8, 1968; "What's This? Jim Crow Found in Saigon Brothels," May 13, 1968; "Young and Old Vietnamese Wish Black GIs Would Leave Country," May 21, 1968; "Hate Found behind Front Lines in Viet: Black Doctor," May 22, 1968; "Our Man Mosby Finds No Prejudice in Viet Combat," May 23, 1968; "Filth, Bias, Prostitutes in Saigon's 'Soulville,'" May 28, 1968; "Black GIs in Viet Won't Wait for Their Freedom," May 29, 1968; "Woman Reporter Tells of Race Hate in Viet," June 5, 1968. The titles of Mosby's Vietnam dispatches convey something of the passion he brought to his writing about the war in the *Defender*. Written in the immediate aftermath of the slaying of Martin Luther King Jr., the columns are suffused with an understandable pain and anger at the racism confronting black GIs in the war zone. The same sort of energy and idealism led Mosby to publish a twice-monthly newspaper called the *Struggle* in the mid-1960s. The paper was devoted to civil rights advocacy and politics. See Mosby Papers.

7. "Courier Reporter on Way to Vietnam," *New Pittsburgh Courier*, December 24, 1966.

8. "*Jet* Washington Bureau Chief Going to Vietnam," *Jet*, July 29, 1965, 25; series of articles by Simeon Booker: "Negro GI Heroes in the Vietnam War," "*Jet's* Booker Narrowly Escapes Vietcong Sniper," "Vietcong Flops in Effort to Put Race Wedge between GIs," *Jet*, August 19, 1965, 14, 17–21; "Predict Many More Negroes Will Be Killed in Vietnam War," *Jet*, August 26, 1965, 20, 21; "*Jet* Newsman Views Vietnam War from Copter," September 9, 1965, 45–47.

9. *Ebony* was issued monthly and had a circulation of 1,176,375 in 1970. *Jet* was a weekly and had a circulation of 414,555 in 1970. During its first twenty years of existence *Ebony* was devoted to the celebration of black achievement and focused on positive elements of African American life. By the 1960s it had evolved into a more serious magazine than *Jet*, featuring in-depth pieces on all aspects of black life, including the struggle for equal rights. *Ebony* was directed toward a more sophisticated readership that was looking for lengthy, probing pieces about the major issues of the day, including the struggle to achieve black empowerment. *Jet* featured a breezier approach to news, human-interest stories, and issues; its relatively brief segments were prepared for an audience looking for news, comment, and features in easily digestible servings. The content of the magazine was geared as much toward entertainment as the presentation of weightier news stories. For the publication data on the two magazines, see Wolseley, *Black Press, U.S.A.*, 13. For a summary of the evolution of *Ebony*, see Henry Lee Moon, "The Role of the Negro Press," *Dallas Express*, December 18, 1965.

10. Payne, "Review of Vietnam and the Far East, with Some Recommendations," memo to John H. Sengstacke, March 30, 1967, box 1, in Payne Papers, Howard University.

11. For Payne's work in Washington, D.C., see Payne, "Loneliness in the Capital," 158; unnamed information officer, "Media Representatives," October 5, 1966, box 2 of Vietnam materials, Payne Papers, Howard University.

12. Joshua Brown, "Cartooning," 118. An article by David R. Spencer provides the history of the use of cartoons in the press to mold American attitudes toward using war to project national power. Spencer's focus was on nineteenth-century developments in the role of cartoons as a vehicle for education and persuasion as the United States became an international player. During this period Americans were generally congenial toward "American military adventures" but viewed "warfare waged by others as a form of immorality" (Spencer, "Visions of Violence," 47). The perspective Spencer describes as characteristic during the nineteenth century remained largely intact until the Vietnam War, when the black press overwhelmingly, and the mainstream press frequently, came to view the U.S. role in Vietnam as immoral. The same moral judgment against U.S. involvement in the war became the motivation that propelled many thoughtful Americans into the antiwar movement.

13. William G. Jordan cites both cartoons—and a number of others—produced by the black press during the First World War to document a boldness of protest that was quite daring, given the pressure by the government on the black press to maintain national solidarity in the face of a common enemy during the war. See Jordan, *Black Newspapers*, 74, 91.

14. "Courier's Milai Top NNPA Winner," *Pittsburgh Courier*, July 9, 1966.

15. "Biographies: Oliver Harrington," n.d., www.pbs.org/blackpress/news_bios/harrington.html; Turner, "Reflections of a Black Cartoonist," 165; Nelson, *Black Press* For the date of Bootsie's first appearance, see Inge, *Dark Laughter*, xix, xx. For Harrington's recollection of his stint as a war correspondent, see Harrington, *Why I Left America*, 101.

Harrington's Bootsie was part of a tradition of wartime cartoon characters who became fixtures during World War II. Among these were the Bill Mauldin characters Willie and Joe. Mauldin's World War II strip appeared in the military newspaper *Stars and Stripes* and was syndicated to hundreds of U.S. newspapers. The weary, sardonic wit of Willie and Joe kept their war human, accessible, and poignant. Willie and Joe were not above poking fun at the military brass, but there was a grimy earnestness about their dissatisfaction that kept their grumbling from seeming unpatriotic. Among other memorable cartoon characters produced during World War II were George Baker's Sad Sack, described by Baker as "a bewildered civilian trying to be a soldier," and Sergeant Dave Breger's G.I. Joe, who appeared first in the *Saturday Evening Post* on August 30, 1941, as Private Breger. When the war started, the character was renamed G.I. Joe but remained "a freckled, bespectacled naïf" (Michael E. Haskew and Douglas Brinkley, eds., *The World War II Desk Reference* [New York: HarperResource, 2004], 478, 479).

16. Ohman interview, July 13, 2004; Fleming interview; Thomas C. Fleming, "Carlton B. Goodlett: Champion of the People," *Reflections on Black History*, part 77, June 4, 1999, www.freepress.org/fleming/flemng77.html.

17. The Vietnam War was first the subject of the question posed to individuals by the "Inquiring Photographer" in the *Defender* on January 6, 1966. when the "Inquiring Photographer" wanted to know whether Johnson's efforts to achieve peace in Vietnam would be successful. The *Los Angeles Sentinel* devoted only one of

its "Inquiring Reporter" columns (in the July 1, 1971, issue) to a war-related matter: a question about the U.S. Supreme Court's recent vacating of Muhammad Ali's
draft evasion conviction. For an example of the "Poets' Nook," see *Baltimore Afro-
American*, March 25, 1967.

18. "AFRO in Vietnam," *Baltimore Afro-American*, July 1, 1967; "GIs Greet Our
Man," *Afro-American*, July 15, 1967.

19. Pride and Wilson, *A History of the Black Press*, 229, 230. The flow of black reporters and other journalists from the black press to mainstream media was encour-
aged further by the Kerner Report, published in 1968, which urged the mainstream
press to hire more blacks because of their underrepresentation on the staffs of the
predominately white traditional press. See National Advisory Commission on Civil
Disorders, *Kerner Report*, 382–86.

20. The Sengstacke memo is in the Payne Papers, Correspondence General File,
box 4, Library of Congress. For Payne's recollections see the transcript of her interview, September 24, 1987, 101, 106–10.

21. For a lengthy list of the various black news services that came and went, see
Pride and Wilson, *A History of the Black Press*, 160–62; for the name change of the
NNPA in 1955, see Pride and Wilson, 194. For an account of the collision between the
ANP and the NNPA, see Hogan, *A Black National News Service*, 215–33. Hogan's book
is a full treatment of the history of the founding and history of the ANP through the
peak of its influence during World War II.

22. For Barnett's words see Hogan, *A Black National News Service*, 270. Arnold
Rampersad describes Jackie Robinson's literary relationship to Alfred Duckett in
Jackie Robinson: A Biography, 362. For Duckett's purchase of the ANP, see Pride and
Wilson, *A History of the Black Press*, 166.

23. Wyatt, *Paper Soldiers*, 133, 135.

24. Braestrup, *Big Story*, 33.

25. Payne interview, September 17, 1987, 57.

26. Wolseley, *Black Press, U.S.A.*, 310–12.

2. Vietnam and the Great Society: The Two-Front War

1. Kearns, *Lyndon Johnson and the American Dream*, 251, 252.

2. An account of Jack Valenti's report of the meeting at Lyndon Johnson's Washington
home appears in editorial notations in *Lyndon B. Johnson*, 1:85. The president's White
House meeting with aides on November 24, 1963, is described in Newman, *JFK and
Vietnam*, 487.

3. The full speech is in the *Public Papers of the Presidents of the United States: Lyndon
B. Johnson*, 1:8–11.

4. Elba K. Brown-Collier, "Johnson's Great Society: Its Legacy in the 1990s," *Review
of Social Economy* 56, no. 3 (1998): 259.

5. Dallek, *Flawed Giant*, 80–82. Richard Goodwin's own account of the gestation of
the Great Society is in his book *Remembering America*, 267–92.

6. For the text of the speech see *Public Papers of the Presidents of the United States:*

Lyndon B. Johnson, 1:704–7. For a description of the circumstances of LBJ's speech, see Rulon, *Compassionate Samaritan,* 202–8. See Dallek, *Flawed Giant,* 81, 82, for a good description of the development of the Great Society concept and the Ann Arbor speech introducing it.

7. Unger, *Best of Intentions,* 65–69.

8. Dallek, *Flawed Giant,* 60–62.

9. For the text of the president's address to Congress, see *Public Papers of the Presidents of the United States: Lyndon B. Johnson,* 3:112–19. For Johnson's development of this theme, see Robertson, *American Myth,* 324.

10. "Marine Puts War Lament in Verse; Dies in Action," *Baltimore Afro-American,* March 2, 1968.

11. "The Courier's Double 'V' for a Double Victory Campaign Gets Countrywide Support," *Pittsburgh Courier,* February 14, 1942. Patrick S. Washburn published an important study of how the black press labored under recurrent pressure from the U.S. government, including visits by FBI agents to a number of African American newspapers, particularly early in the war. Some in the federal government, including FDR himself, perceived an incipient threat to national wartime cohesion stemming from African Americans' criticisms of the unfair treatment they frequently experienced. The Double V campaign during World War II, with its implicit equation of war and the repression inherent in black life in a predominately white U.S. society, could easily have led to severe official reprisals were it not for the enlightened attitudes expressed by U.S. Attorney General Francis Biddle. With the active encouragement of Biddle, President Franklin Roosevelt ultimately resisted impulses to impose severe restraints on the freedom of the black press when it called for social reform. See Washburn, *A Question of Sedition,* 81–104, 203–8.

12. TRB, "LBJ Isn't JFK," 470.

13. Dallek, *Flawed Giant,* 74–77.

14. James Farmer, "Annual Report to the National CORE Convention," in Williams and Williams, *Negro Speaks,* 170.

15. Dallek, *Flawed Giant,* 299.

16. For the text of the president's comments, see *Public Papers of the Presidents of the United States: Lyndon B. Johnson,* 4:840–43. For Johnson's strong use of military language and symbols during the event, see Dudziak, *Cold War Civil Rights,* 237.

17. Mann, *A Grand Delusion,* 379, 380.

18. "War Turned Skirmish?" *Milwaukee Star,* January 8, 1966.

19. "A Firm Hand," *New York Amsterdam News,* January 22, 1966. For the president's remarks see *Public Papers of the Presidents of the United States: Lyndon B. Johnson,* 5:4. The full text of the speech is on pages 3 to 12.

20. "LBJ Anti-Poverty Stand Is Fine Statesmanship," *Pittsburgh Courier,* February 5, 1966.

21. "Two Wars," *New York Amsterdam News,* January 8, 1966.

22. "Double Standard," *Milwaukee Star,* November 30, 1966.

23. "The GOP Offensive," *Chicago Daily Defender,* January 12, 1967.

24. Lerone Bennett Jr., "How to Stop Riots," *Ebony,* October 1967, 29–35.

25. Betty Washington, "King Assails Congress for 'Inviting' Violence," *Chicago Daily Defender*, July 27, 1967. The SCLC literature is quoted in Yglesias, "Dr. King's March," 268.

26. "What They're Saying," *Baltimore Afro-American*, December 30, 1967.

27. Dallek, *Flawed Giant*, 412, 413.

28. O'Brien, *No Final Victories*, 194, 195.

29. For Wilkins's response see Sundquist, "Building the Great Society," 202–6. For the reactions of the Congress of Racial Equality and King see "A Symptom of Anger," 59.

30. Langguth, *Our Vietnam*, 328.

31. Arnold B. Sawislak, "Vietnam War Expected to Cut Poverty Funds," *Chicago Daily Defender*, January 6, 1966; *Los Angeles Sentinel*, January 20, 1966.

32. "Vietnam vs. Public Aid," *Chicago Daily Defender*, January 10, 1967.

33. "Poverty War and Vietnam," *Baltimore Afro-American*, January 15, 1966.

34. "LBJ 'Escalates' War on Poverty," *Chicago Daily Defender*, January 10, 1966.

35. *Public Papers of the Presidents of the United States: Lyndon B. Johnson*, 5:3–12. The *Washington Post* on January 13, 1966, headlined its story of the speech "U.S. Can Continue the 'Great Society' and Fight in Vietnam—LBJ Hands Congress Massive Work Load."

36. Quoted in Barone, *Our Country*, 411.

37. Clarence Mitchell Jr., "Chiselers Seize upon Vietnam as Opportunity to Scuttle President's 'Great Society,'" *Baltimore Afro-American*, June 18, 1966.

38. Dallek, *Flawed Giant*, 307.

39. Gertrude Wilson, "$2 Billion a Day," *New York Amsterdam News*, September 10, 1966.

40. "Words of the Week," *Jet*, December 22, 1966. For the quote from King's last speech to the SCLC, see King, "Where Do We Go from Here?" 248.

41. Dallek, *Flawed Giant*, 339.

42. "Anti-Poverty Program in Danger in New Congress," *New Pittsburgh Courier*, December 3, 1966.

43. Adolph J. Slaughter, "Here's Hoping '67 Has More to Offer," *New Pittsburgh Courier*, January 14, 1967.

44. Greenburg, *Middle Class Dreams*, 114, 115.

45. For the statistical data on the shifting political fortunes of civil rights, see Greenburg, *Middle Class Dreams*, 115.

46. "Annual Message to the Congress on the State of the Union," January 10, 1967, *Public Papers of the Presidents of the United States: Lyndon B. Johnson*, 7:2–4.

47. Robert M. Andrews, "Johnson Gears Congress for Indefinite Viet War with $172 Billion Budget," *Atlanta Daily World*, January 25, 1967. The full text of the president's message to Congress is in *Public Papers of the Presidents of the United States: Lyndon B. Johnson*, 7:2–14.

48. Clifford L. Alexander, memo to President Johnson, January 11, 1967, Name File, WHCF, box 127, LBJ Library.

49. "The New Year," *Baltimore Afro-American*, January 14, 1967.

50. "A Moral Commitment," *Chicago Daily Defender*, January 18, 1967.

51. "Unwarranted Attacks," *New York Amsterdam News*, January 21, 1967.

52. "LBJ Anti-Poverty Stand Is Fine Statesmanship," *Pittsburgh Courier*, February 5, 1966.

53. "Congress and Taxes," *Atlanta Daily World*, January 15, 1967.

54. H. Carl McCall, "Shapeup for Opportunity," *New York Amsterdam News*, April 22, 1967. The later editorial in the same paper was "Spreading Madness," *New York Amsterdam News*, August 5, 1967.

55. Lyndon B. Johnson, "Remarks in New York City at the Jewish Labor Committee Dinner Honoring George Meany, November 9, 1967," *Public Papers of the Presidents of the United States: Lyndon B. Johnson*, 8:1009.

56. The two examples are in the *Chicago Daily Defender*, January 5, 1967, and the *Pittsburgh Courier*, November 25, 1967.

57. "RFK Fights Administration Cut in Anti-Poverty Budget," *Chicago Daily Defender*, September 28, 1967.

58. For Whitney Young's 1964 statement, see the excerpt from his book *To Be Equal*, 26–33.

59. Quoted in Josh Pawelek, "An Informational Essay on Whitney M. Young, Jr.," Unitarian Universalist Association (Fall 1996), 3, 4, http://archive.uua.org/programs/justice/antiracism/twsunday/wyessay.html.

60. Whitney Young, "The New Year: Hopes and Doubts," *New York Amsterdam News*, January 6, 1968.

61. "Ron Dellums and the Politics of 'Niggers,'" *Ebony*, May 1972, 95.

62. "Crisis of Color '66." In a 1967 study Sidney Verba and colleagues confirmed the importance of race as a predictor of attitudes toward the war. They found that race was the strongest predictor of opinions about the war in counting those who supported U.S. policy in Vietnam versus those who did not; as a predictor, it was stronger even than gender or political party affiliation. Blacks were more likely than whites to oppose the war (Verba et al., "Public Opinion and the War in Vietnam," 325). Data presented by Edward M. McNertney suggest that the war cost the Great Society more in attention and political commitment than in actual dollars. He points out that from 1965 to 1969, the period when U.S. involvement in the conflict reached its peak in terms of manpower commitment, total federal government spending increased by $65.4 billion while defense costs rose $31.9 billion. McNertney concluded from this "that the defense buildup was not being financed by reductions in other parts of the budgets" (McNertney, "U.S. Economy and the War," in Tucker, *Encyclopedia of the Vietnam War*, 113).

63. "Great Society—in Uniform," 46.

64. "Report from Black America." 16–35.

3. Fueling the Anger: The Draft and Black Casualties

1. "What the Army Does," *Baltimore Afro-American*, April 24, 1965.

2. "Why Quotas on Our Defense of Our Country?" *Baltimore Afro-American*, October 8, 1966.

3. "Word of the Week," *Jet*, September 30, 1965.

4. Clifford L. Alexander Jr., memo to President Johnson, January 7, 1966, Name File, WHCF, box 144, LBJ Library. The full text of the January 6 SNCC statement to which the White House and the *New York Times* were reacting may be found in Grant, *Black Protest*, 393–94.

5. "SNCC Leader Urges Flock Avoid U.S. Draft," *Chicago Daily Defender*, January 10, 1966.

6. "SNCC Leader's Statement Is Deplorable, Misleading," *Atlanta Daily World*, January 8, 1966. Ironically, Julian Bond had been on the staff of the *Atlanta Inquirer*, a paper formed in 1960 to offer a strong protest voice as an alternative to the more staid—and very Republican—*Atlanta Daily World*. For the *Inquirer*'s founding objective to provide an alternative to the *Daily World*, see Wolseley, *Black Press, U.S.A.*, 103.

7. Whittemore, *Together*, 65, 66. For what Bond told the reporter, see David Hudson, "NAACP's Julian Bond Speaks on First Amendment and his Supreme Court Triumph," *Freedomforum*, August 23, 2001, www.freedomforum.org/templates/document.asp?documentID=14675.

8. John Lewis, *Walking with the Wind*, 360, 361.

9. "Harm to All," *Atlanta Daily World*, January 12, 1966.

10. Examples of editorials dealing with the Bond story and the issue of free speech can be found in *Pittsburgh Courier*, February 5, 1966; *Chicago Daily Defender*, January 17, 1966; *Baltimore Afro-American*, January 22, 1966.

11. "Seat Julian Bond," *Milwaukee Star*, January 22, 1966.

12. Taylor Branch briefly describes Bond's ordeal, culminating in the Supreme Court's ruling, in *At Canaan's Edge*, 563. For examples of editorials applauding the decision, see *Atlanta Daily World*, December 7, 1966; *Chicago Daily Defender*, December 8, 1966; *Baltimore Afro-American*, December 17, 1966. The case is *Bond v. Floyd*, 385 U.S. 116 (1966).

13. "Tan Recruits Sent to 'Vietnam Slaughterhouse,'" *Baltimore Afro-American*, May 21, 1966.

14. "Great Society—in Uniform," 46.

15. A description and evaluation of Project 100,000 can be found in Appy, *Working-Class War*, 32, 33. The McNamara biographer Deborah Shapley offers a more personal treatment of Project 100,000, including insights about the program drawn from her interviews with McNamara, who remained proud of the program even after leaving the Pentagon in early 1968. See Shapley, *Promise and Power*, 384–88.

16. "Pct. of Negroes in Vietnam Could Rise," *Pittsburgh Courier*, September 3, 1966.

17. Baker E. Morton, "Change in Drafting Could Be Biased," *Baltimore Afro-American*, September 10, 1966.

18. "Don't Send Me to Vietnam, Build a School in My Area," *Baltimore Afro-American*, February 18, 1967.

19. Nicosia, *Home to War*, 301.

20. "Hon. Robert S. McNamara," *Baltimore Afro-American*, December 9, 1967.

21. "McNamara's Leaving," *New Pittsburgh Courier*, December 9, 1967.

22. "Good Man Gone," *New York Amsterdam News*, December 16, 1967.

23. L. Deckle McLean, "The Black Man and the Draft," *Ebony*, August 1968, 62. The data in *Ebony* are repeated in Schomburg Center, *African American Desk Reference*, 287.

24. Overall draft data for the Vietnam era may be found in Baskir and Strauss, *Chance and Circumstance*, 3–8, 277, and Appy, *Working Class War*, 28–38.

25. Spector, *After Tet*, 31.

26. "Abuse of the Draft," *Baltimore Afro-American*, January 15, 1966.

27. Ann Mohr, "ACLU Attorneys to Ask Courts Prevent Operation of Draft Boards Barring Negro Members," *Atlanta Daily World*, May 3, 1967; "SNCC Sees Conspiracy in Draft," *Chicago Daily Defender*, November 17, 1966; Simeon Booker, "Ticker Tape U.S.A.," *Jet*, June 1, 1967.

28. "The Draft," *New York Amsterdam News*, June 11, 1966.

29. Whitney Young, "Democratizing the Draft," *New York Amsterdam News*, June 18, 1966.

30. Stanley Scott, "I'd Rather Go to Prison," *Baltimore Afro-American*, November 5, 1966.

31. Stokely Carmichael, "Black Power," *American Rhetoric: Top 100 Speeches*, www.americanrhetoric.com/speeches/stokelycarmichaelblackpower.html.

32. "Carmichael Aide Refuses Army Induction," *Chicago Daily Defender*, May 3, 1967.

33. H. Rap Brown's statement is in "New SNCC Head Promises 'Business as Usual,'" *Jet*, June 1, 1967, 10. The Fred Brooks episode is recounted in "SNCC Chairman Steps Back at Army Induction Center," *Baltimore Afro-American*, November 25, 1967.

34. McLean, "Black Man and the Draft," 62.

35. For an example of the shifting name usage, see "Cassius Clay No Draft Dodger," *Baltimore Afro-American*, February 26, 1966. Ali is called "Cassius Clay" in the title, then the text refers to him variously as "Muhammad Ali (Cassius Clay)," "Cassius Clay," "Cassius," and finally "Muhammad Ali."

36. "One Man's Religion," *St. Louis Argus*, May 5, 1965.

37. "Clay Says Army Is Boss, Calls Terrell a 'Bandit,'" *Baltimore Afro-American*, January 8, 1966.

38. "A Smart Fish Keeps His Mouth Closed," *Pittsburgh Courier*, March 12, 1966.

39. James L. Hicks, "The 'Uppity' Negro," *New York Amsterdam News*, March 26, 1966.

40. *Baltimore Afro-American*, April 1, 1967; A. S. "Doc" Young, "Black Day for Boxing," *Chicago Daily Defender*, May 2, 1967.

41. "Cassius Clay and the Draft," *Atlanta Daily World*, April 30, 1967.

42. William Worthy, "Draft Resistance Seen Increasing," *Afro-American*, May 6, 1967.

43. "Objectivity Called for in Clay Controversy," *Los Angeles Sentinel*, May 11, 1967. "Still Champion," *New York Amsterdam News*, May 13, 1967.

44. "Cassius Clay's Case," *Chicago Daily Defender*, May 15, 1967.

45. "Clay Deferment Rejected," *Chicago Daily Defender*, June 9, 1966.

46. "Clay's Sentence Termed 'Incredible,'" *Baltimore Afro-American*, July 1, 1967.

47. "The Case of Muhammad Ali," *Baltimore Afro-American*, July 1, 1967.

48. "Ali Wins One," *New York Amsterdam News*, September 19, 1970; "Ali Back after Paying Price," *Los Angeles Sentinel*, October 29, 1970. "Ali's Great Victory," *Chicago Daily Defender*, July 1, 1971.

49. "Amend This Unjust Law," *Baltimore Afro-American*, July 1, 1967. Herman Graham III, in a study of African Americans in Vietnam, reached a conclusion that laid substantial blame for the inequities of U.S. military manpower procurement during the war on Lyndon Johnson's management of the process. Graham concluded: "During the Vietnam War, most young African American males were marginal men in American society. President Johnson—concerned about a political backlash against the war among the middle class and about maintaining the viability of his Great Society programs—favored a draft system that would allow the sons of privileged whites to evade military service." According to Graham, this set of motivations prompted LBJ to avoid calling up reserves in favor of relying on draft calls and volunteers to fill U.S. combat manpower needs. Since only 5 percent of black men qualified for college deferments, and black poverty made enlistment an attractive employment option for African American males, the ranks of combat troops in Vietnam were populated by a disproportionate number of black draftees and recruits (Graham, *Brothers' Vietnam War*, 135).

50. "Clearing up the Draft Muddle," *Baltimore Afro-American*, March 18, 1967. While the figure for black induction is almost twice that of whites, a finding similar to that of the Kastenmeier study mentioned earlier in the chapter, the percentages themselves are quite different. The *Afro-American* editorial did not disclose the source of its data.

51. "Selective Service Abolishes Draft Deferments for Men in Critical Jobs, College Students," *Atlanta Daily World*, February 17, 1968.

52. President's Commission, *Report of the President's Commission*. For the timing of the end of the draft, see Joe P. Dunn, "Draft," in Tucker, *Encyclopedia of the Vietnam War*, 107.

53. *Pittsburgh Courier*, February 20, 1965. For statistics of African American deaths in Vietnam, see Lanning, *African-American Soldier*, 262, 263.

54. *Baltimore Afro-American*, February 20, 1965.

55. The full text of President Johnson's address is in *Public Papers of the Presidents of the United States: Lyndon B. Johnson*, 1:281–87.

56. "Two Wars," *New York Amsterdam News*, January 8, 1966.

57. The statistics of blacks in the infantry and their proportion of battle casualties are in Schomburg Center, *African American Desk Reference*, 287. Appy argues that it was not ethnicity but economic class that was the key determinant of the composition of American combat forces in Vietnam. Like poor nonwhites, poor whites were present in combat units in much higher percentages than middle-class whites; see Appy, *Working-Class War*, 17–38. Blacks bore two burdens: they were predominately poor, and they suffered systematic racial discrimination, particularly at the hands of overwhelmingly white southern draft boards.

58. "Negroes in Vietnam—the High Death Rate," *Los Angeles Sentinel*, March 17, 1966.

59. "Negro Deaths Exceed Whites' in Vietnam," *Pittsburgh Courier*, May 28, 1966.

60. "A Challenge to Democracy," *St. Louis Argus*, January 13, 1967.

61. For data on disproportionate black casualties and the efforts to reduce them, see "How Negro Americans Perform," and Johnson, "Negroes in 'The Nam,'" 33.

Also see Baskir and Strauss, *Chance and Circumstance*, 8, for a description of the Pentagon's efforts to reduce the exposure of blacks to combat and thereby reduce the black casualty rate.

62. U.S. Department of Defense, *Negro in the Armed Forces*, 231–43. The study presented annual data only for deaths "by hostile action." The summary data for all deaths, both "hostile" and "non-hostile" in the war, were included only through June 1971.

63. For the data on black casualties for the entire war, see "Why Quotas on Our Defense of Our Country," *Afro-American*, October 8, 1966; Appy, *Working-Class War*, 19. Guilmarten and Evans-Pfeifer put the black *enlisted* death rate for the period at 14.1 percent in "Casualties," in Kutler, *Encyclopedia of the Vietnam War*, 105.

64. Department of Defense, *Negro in the Armed Forces*, 4–7.

65. "The Black Soldier," *Chicago Daily Defender*, January 19, 1967.

66. "Cost of Freedom," *Milwaukee Star*, September 16, 1967.

67. Clifford Alexander, memo to President Johnson, February 14, 1967, Subject File, WHCF, box 4, LBJ Library.

68. Cyrus Vance, deputy secretary of defense, memo to the president, February 15, 1967, Subject File, WHCF, box 4, LBJ Library. At the bottom of the memo, Joe Califano stapled a note, also dated February 15, saying, "For the President's night reading."

69. President Johnson's "Special Message to the Congress on Equal Justice, February 15, 1967," *Public Papers of the Presidents of the United States: Lyndon B. Johnson*, 7:194.

70. Pentagon statement about black casualty rates in Vietnam, February 15, 1967, Subject File, WHCF, box 4, LBJ Library.

71. Johnson, "Negroes in 'The Nam," 33.

72. James L. Hicks, "Problem: Find the Real Enemy," *New York Amsterdam News*, March 19, 1966.

73. "Negro Casualties," *Chicago Daily Defender*, March 17, 1966.

74. "Congressmen Seek Investigation of Higher Vietnam Death Rate," *Baltimore Afro-American*, March 19, 1966.

75. David Llorens, "Why Negroes Re-Enlist," *Ebony*, August 1968, 87–93.

76. Ibid., 87.

77. Ibid., 87, 88.

78. Ibid., 88.

79. "No Disproportion Seen in Draft Call," *Baltimore Afro-American*, January 21, 1967.

80. McLean, "Black Man and the Draft," 62.

81. "LBJ Using Viet War to Kill Negroes: Nationalist Leader," *Chicago Daily Defender*, November 10, 1966.

82. Al Flowers, "Blacks Should Question Involvement in Vietnam," *Milwaukee Star*, December 13, 1969.

83. "Cannon Fodder in Vietnam," *Baltimore Afro-American*, March 4, 1967.

84. Ibid.

85. "No Room in the Cemetery," *Baltimore Afro-American*, June 4, 1966; also in

"Ala. Family Say Town Refuses to Bury Viet Hero," *Jet*, June 9, 1966, 9. The *Atlanta Daily World* covered the story on the front page of three issues of the newspaper: May 27, 29, and 31, 1966.

86. "Second-class Treatment," *Baltimore Afro-American*, June 11, 1966.

87. "With Honor and Distinction," *Baltimore Afro-American*, June 11, 1966.

88. The episode, which was widely reported in the black press, was also the subject of an essay by David L. Anderson in the collection of essays he edited, *Human Tradition in the Vietnam Era*, 135–51.

89. "GI Lost Life in Vietnam, Won Ala. Cemetery Battle," *Baltimore Afro-American*, January 3, 1970.

90. "Dead Soldier's Victory," *Baltimore Afro-American*, January 3, 1970; Glenn Stephens, UPI, "GI's Body in Cemetery He Selected," *Baltimore Afro-American*, January 10, 1970.

91. "White Fight—Black Burial," *New York Amsterdam News*, August 29, 1970.

92. "Negro Troops," *Chicago Daily Defender*, November 22, 1966.

4. African American Opposition to the War in Vietnam

1. Fairclough, "War in Vietnam," 113.

2. Weisbrot, *Freedom Bound*, 139.

3. "Words of the Week," *Jet*, April 1, 1965.

4. Whitney Young, "Use Troops in Selma," *Baltimore Afro-American*, March 20, 1965. A growing body of literature seeks to situate the domestic issues of race and civil rights in America within the larger context of America's standing in the world as the self-professed champion of personal liberty and civic freedom. The fountainhead for the core insights of this literature is the dissonance between U.S. preaching and practice in its racial life, as expressed with devastating effect by Gunnar Myrdal in his path-breaking 1944 book, *An American Dilemma: The Negro Problem and American Democracy*. Other works that explore aspects of this chronic U.S. struggle are Plummer, *Rising Wind*; Dudziak, *Cold War Civil Rights*; Borstelmann, *Cold War and the Color Line*; and Gilmore, *Defying Dixie*. The principal focus of Rosier's *Serving Their Country* is the Native American experience within a global perspective, but he also makes observations about the African American civil rights struggle as part of U.S. international relations.

5. The text of the speech can be found in *Public Papers of the Presidents of the United States: Lyndon Johnson*, 3:281–87. King's reaction is described in Weisbrot, *Freedom Bound*, 142.

6. Verney, *Black Civil Rights in America*, 65. The Moses quote appears in Branch, *Pillar of Fire*, 611.

7. Weisbrot, *Freedom Bound*, 152.

8. Ramsey Clark, interview by Harri Baker, March 21, 1969, Oral History Collection transcript, LBJ Library, 1, www.lbjlib.utexas.edu/johnson/archives.hom/oralhistory.hom/ClarkR/clark-r3.pdf.

9. Karnow, *Vietnam*, 682; D. Kaiser, "July 28, 1965," 390.

10. Boettcher, *Vietnam,*, 426.

11. Caro, *Means of Ascent*, xx, xxii.

12. Gallup, *Gallup Poll: Public Opinion, 1935–1971*, 3:1842–2338.

13. Boettcher, *Vietnam*, 426, 427.

14. Plummer, *Rising Wind*, 317.

15. "King Asks Peace Talks on Viet," *Atlanta Daily World*, March 3, 1965.

16. "King Calls for End of War, Poverty, Racism, Injustice," *Pittsburgh Courier*, July 17, 1965.

17. "Vietnam Negotiations a Must—M. L. King," *Baltimore Afro-American*, July 10, 1965.

18. Roberts and Olson, "Antiwar Movement," 35.

19. "Is Vietnam to Become a 'Civil Rights' Issue?" *U.S. News & World Report*, July 19, 1965, 12.

20. "Dr. King Out of His Depth in Vietnam," *Philadelphia Tribune*, July 13, 1965.

21. Beschloss, *Reaching for Glory*, 388.

22. Sparkman is quoted in "What They Say," *Baltimore Afro-American*, July 17, 1965. Weaver is quoted in "Raps King on Vietnam," *Baltimore Afro-American*, August 28, 1965.

23. Kotz, *Judgment Days*, 350.

24. Fairclough, "Martin Luther King, Jr.," 25.

25. "King, Not SCLC, to Seek Vietnam Peace Negotiation," *Baltimore Afro-American*, August 21, 1965.

26. "Dr. King and Vietnam," *Dallas Express*, August 21, 1965.

27. "Vietnam," *Dallas Express*, December 4, 1965.

28. "King Asks Viet Settlement, Seat in UN for Red China," *Baltimore Afro-American*, September 18, 1965.

29. Dan Day, "LBJ Fretting over Dr. King's Moves," *Baltimore Afro-American*, October 2, 1965.

30. Fairclough, "Martin Luther King, Jr.," 26.

31. West, "Religious Foundations," 117, 118.

32. See Huggins, "Commentary ," 86, 87.

33. Rowan, *Breaking Barriers*, 283, 286.

34. "Chides Sen. Dodd for His Attack on Dr. King," *Jet*, September 30, 1965.

35. *Jet*, October 7, 1965, 8.

36. "Have Right to Criticize U.S. Policy," *Baltimore Afro-American*, October 30, 1965.

37. "King and Vietnam," *Baltimore Afro-American*, October 2, 1965.

38. "The Right to Dissent," *Chicago Defender*, October 2–8, 1965.

39. Fairclough, "War in Vietnam," 114. According to Stewart Burns, King's words to his aides were part of a telephone conference call in mid-September 1965 recorded by the FBI (Burns, *To the Mountaintop*, 302, 303). The comment about *Profiles in Courage* appears in Fairclough, "Martin Luther King," 26.

40. Gardner, *Pay Any Price*, 263.

41. Ibid., 262, 263. For the 1969 data see Isaacs, *Vietnam Shadows*, 17.

42. Mueller, *War, Presidents and Public Opinion*, 143.

43. For the background of the SNCC statement and the full text of the declaration, see Forman, "Making of Black Revolutionaries," 753, 754.

44. According to David Halberstam in *The Children* (537, 538), Bevel became the SCLC's point man on the Vietnam War, doing the advance work for King's more activist antiwar appearances in New York in early 1967.

45. "King's Organization Critical of U.S. Role in Vietnam," *Baltimore Afro-American*, April 23, 1966.

46. "What They Say," *Baltimore Afro-American*, April 23, 1966.

47. King and Washington, *I Have a Dream*, 98.

48. An excellent discussion of the pros and cons of involving the civil rights movement with the antiwar drive is supplied by Robert S. Browne in his essay "Freedom Movement and the War in Vietnam."

49. Weisbrot, *Freedom Bound*, 193.

50. Andrew Young, interview by Thomas H. Baker, June 18, 1970, Oral History Collection transcript, LBJ Library, 11, www.lbjlib.utexas.edu/johnson/archives.hom/oralhistory.hom/YoungA/Young-a.pdf.

51. For a good summary account of the conference, including the behind-the-scenes lobbying by LBJ and his staff, see Weisbrot, *Freedom Bound*, 193. The conference drew its name, "To Fulfill These Rights," from the title of a commencement speech LBJ had delivered a year earlier at Howard University. During the speech, one of his most eloquent as president, Johnson announced his intention to hold a "conference of scholars, and experts, and outstanding Negro leaders—men of both races—and officials of the Government at every level." He even announced that "the theme and title will be 'To Fulfill These Rights'" and outlined what he intended to see accomplished at the ambitious meeting, boiled down nicely in the words "to shatter forever not only the barriers of law and public practice, but the walls which bound the condition of many by the color of his skin. To dissolve, as best we can, the antique enmities of the heart, which diminish the holder, divide the great democracy, and do wrong—great wrong—to the children of God." Near the end of the speech, he said: "So, it is the glorious opportunity of this generation to end the one huge wrong of the American Nation and, in so doing, to find America for ourselves, with the same immense thrill of discovery which gripped those who first began to realize that here, at last, was a home for freedom." See "Commencement Address at Howard University, 'To Fulfill These Rights,' June 4, 1965," in *Public Papers of the Presidents of the United States: Lyndon B. Johnson*, 4:635–40. Whitney Young's remark is quoted in Weisbrot, *Freedom Bound*, 193. For a mainstream newspaper report of Humphrey's address, see "A Fiery Humphrey Denounces Society," 27. Johnson's appearance is recounted in John Herbers's front-page story, "Rights Conference to Vote on Criticism of U.S. Policy," *New York Times*.

52. Harry C. McPherson Jr., summary of the president's remarks to the White House Conference "To Fulfill These Rights," June 2, 1966, President's Daily Diary, 6/1/66–8/31/66, LBJ Library.

53. The headline for a *New York Times* editorial called the affair, with considerable justification, "An Embattled Conference" (June 2, 1966, 42).

54. "The White House Conference," *Baltimore Afro-American*, June 4, 1966.

55. "Fulfillment Plan," *Chicago Daily Defender*, June 13, 1966.

56. Branch, *At Canaan's Edge*, 486; Weisbrot, *Freedom Bound*, 199, 200.

57. Roberts, "Story of Snick," 139, 140. Also see Joseph, *Waiting 'til the Midnight Hour*, 141, 142. Derision directed at King by young SNCC hotheads had a long history and reflected SNCC's impatience with King's early moderation and deliberation in making decisions. Shouts of "de Lawd" were directed at King on the Edmund Pettus Bridge at one stage in the second march out of Selma to Montgomery, Alabama, when he turned back, despite a clear path through the state troopers at the bridge. King was adhering to a secret compromise brokered by a federal mediator to allow some cooling off after troopers assaulted marchers two weeks earlier, on "Bloody Sunday," March 7, 1965. But some eager young activists at SNCC interpreted King's move as timidity. The raucous calls of "de Lawd" directed at King suggested he was holding himself above the fray like a remote deity (Weisbrot, *Freedom Bound*, 141). Even earlier, during the Freedom Rides, King's reticence to participate, for tactical reasons, was questioned by some of the youthful activists. When King justified his aloofness by saying, "I think I should choose the time and place of my Golgotha," the lofty association King chose with Jesus set the tone for the mocking references to deity in later snide attacks on him by fellow warriors in the civil rights movement (Branch, *Parting the Waters*, 467).

58. John Lewis, *Walking with the* Wind, 372–3; Good, "Odyssey of a Man,", 254.

59. John Goldman, "Stokely Carmichael, Black Activist, Dies," *Los Angeles Times*, November 16, 1998.

60. For the words of the unnamed radical, see Collier and Horowitz, *Destructive Generation*, 283.

61. Carmichael's original essay is "Power & Racism," 72. For Carmichael's UPI interview, see Stanley S. Scott, "We Must Be Black Led, Black Controlled, Black Dominated," *Baltimore Afro-American*, October 22, 1966.

62. Gary Gerstle, in his perceptive study of race and national identity in America, argues that, from the time of Theodore Roosevelt into the 1960s, a dominant white culture established a national identity into which minority groups were expected to assimilate, acquiescing in the dominant set of "Anglo-Saxon ideals." In Gerstle's view "the black nationalist challenge and Vietnam blew apart" this paradigm, as black nationalism and antiwar fervor began to strain and undermine the foundations of the core principles at the heart of a white culture that was losing its control over the definition of what constituted true Americanism. See Gerstle, *American Crucible*, 330.

63. "A *Time*-Louis Harris Poll: The Black Mood: More Militant, More Hopeful, More Determined," *Time*, April 6, 1970, 28, 29.

64. Robert Mullen, *Black Americans/African Americans*, 39.

65. Simeon Booker, "Negroes in Vietnam: 'We, Too, Are Americans,'" *Ebony*, November 1965, 89–99.

66. "Negro GIs Reject Viet Cong Propaganda Attempts," *Jet*, January 25, 1968.

67. Mueller, "Public Opinion and the President," 139; Lind, *Vietnam, the Necessary War*, 107, 108.

5. Martin Luther King Jr. and the Globalization of Black Protest

1. D. Lewis, "Martin Luther King, Jr.," 294.

2. Ohman interview, July 13, 2004.

3. Garrow, "Martin Luther King, Jr.," 26. See Lee's account of the episode in the collection of oral histories in Hampton, Fayer, and Flynn, *Voices of Freedom*, 342, 343. Adam Fairclough places the episode in the airport on the way to Jamaica for the vacation. In this version King himself bought the magazine and saw the article and the pictures as he was eating a meal at the airport. See Fairclough, "Martin Luther King, Jr.," 28, who cites as his source Lane and Gregory, *Code Name "Zorro,"* 54.

4. "The Casualties of The Vietnam War," *New York Amsterdam News*, two-part feature, June 17 and 24, 1967.

5. Fairclough, "Martin Luther King, Jr.," 29; Lyttle, *Chicago Anti-Vietnam War Movement*, 48–50.

6. "Dr. King Leads 5,000 Peace Marchers in Chicago Stroll," *Baltimore Afro-American*, April 1, 1967.

7. *Jet*, April 13, 1967.

8. Robinson, "Dr. King Proposes a Boycott," 1, 2.

9. D. Lewis, *King: A Biography*, 312.

10. For a full text of King's speech at the Riverside Church, see King, "A Time to Break Silence," in *A Testament of Hope*, 231–44.

11. In his study of Martin Luther King's preaching style, Richard Lischer refers to this shift in the mood and rhetorical strategy of King's preaching as moving from "identification to rage," a shift from conciliation and compromise to denunciation. See Lischer, *Preacher King*, 142–62.

12. Berman, *Lyndon Johnson's War*, 183. King's already weakened links to the White House were finally broken by the Riverside Church speech. According to Andrew Young, what was probably King's last conversation with the president occurred "about Thanksgiving time, 1966." Young was with King while he was speaking to the president, a conversation that lasted "about an hour," as Young recalled. King did most of the talking, emphasizing the "immorality of the situation more than tactics." Johnson conveyed a sense of being trapped between the Pentagon and the State Department, "under pressure from the generals on one side to . . . really escalate the war and try to win it in a hurry," while the State Department emphasized diplomatic strategy. "I think that was probably the last time they talked," said Young, to which the astonished interviewer said, "Oh really! That early." Young replied simply, "Yes" (Andrew Young interview).

13. For the SCLC resolution see "Dr. King Declares War on Viet War," *Baltimore Afro-American*, April 8, 1967. The SCLC document defending King's right to dissent is reported in Lentz, *Symbols*, 236n1.

14. Garfinkle, *Telltale Hearts*, 100. Also see Dougan and Lipsman, *A Nation Divided*, 108, which provides more details of Carmichael's role at the rally than does Garfinkle.

15. "Dr. King Sticks to Peace Guns," *Norfolk Journal and Guide*, April 22, 1967. Also see Small, *Covering Dissent*, 68.

16. Simeon Booker, "Dr. King's Viet Speech May Spur Army Boycott by Negroes," *Jet*, April 20, 1967.

17. Simeon Booker, "Ticker Tape U.S.A.," *Jet*, April 20, 1967, 15.

18. George Christian, White House press secretary, memo to President Johnson, April 8, 1967, Name File, WHCF, box 144, LBJ Library. The allegedly communist adviser to King to whom Rowan referred was the New York businessman and King insider Stanley Levison (Rowan, *Breaking Barriers*, 258). For Rowan's resignation from the administration and return to journalism, see pp. 277, 278.

19. Rowan, *Breaking Barriers*, 286.

20. Booker, "Dr. King's Viet Speech," 8.

21. "NAACP Board Raps Linking of Rights with Viet Strife," *Chicago Daily Defender*, April 11, 1967.

22. "King Raps NAACP 'Myth' on Views," *Chicago Daily Defender*, April 13, 1967.

23. King is quoted in Ansbro, *Martin Luther King, Jr.*, 264, 265. The omission of this portion of King's statement in the *Defender* likely simply reflected the paper's interest in brevity. Nothing in the substance of King's words would have caused the *Defender* to duck on ideological grounds, since the paper was fully engaged with coverage of the antiwar stance King had taken. It covered the views of both King and those who took issue with his opposition to administration policy in Vietnam.

24. "Wilkins in Bitter Attack on Dr. King's Peace Stand," *Chicago Daily Defender*, April 20, 1967.

25. Weiss, "Whitney M. Young, Jr.," 342, 343.

26. "Don't Link Viet, Rights: Dr. Jackson," *Chicago Daily Defender*, April 18, 1967.

27. "Brooke Raps Rights-Viet War Link," *Chicago Daily Defender*, April 20, 1967.

28. Frank W. Mitchell Sr., "King's Privilege to Speak," *St. Louis Argus*, April 21, 1967. Mitchell had been writing editorials about the war since 1965. See, for example, "Vietnam Demonstrations," November 5, 1965; "Vietnam Protests," November 12, 1965; "Why America Is at War in Vietnam," January 6, 1967; "Vietnam War," *St. Louis Argus*, March 10, 1967.

29. Mitchell, "Protesters and Vietnam," *St. Louis Argus*, April 28, 1967.

30. Mitchell, "Object Is to Win," *St. Louis Argus*, May 19, 1967.

31. Mitchell, "Test of U.S. Vietnam Policies," *St. Louis Argus*, May 26, 1967.

32. "Dr. King's Delayed Action Vietnam Bomb," *Norfolk Journal and Guide*, April 22, 1967.

33. Gordon B. Hancock, "King: Stepping Stone or Stumbling Block?" *Norfolk Journal and Guide*, April 15, 1967; "Shrinking Images of King and Carmichael," *Norfolk Journal and Guide*, May 6, 1967; "Dr. M. L. King: From Dissent to Dissension," *Norfolk Journal and Guide*, May 27, 1967.

34. "Where We Stand," *Dallas Post Tribune*, April 22, 1967.

35. "Dr. King's Tragic Doctrine," *New Pittsburgh Courier*, April 15, 1967. For the quotation from King's speech, see King, "A Time to Break Silence," 233.

36. "Why Blame the Viet War for Civil Rights Losses?" *Michigan Chronicle*, May 6, 1967.

37. Benjamin E. Mays, "Dr. King Is Sincere," *New Pittsburgh Courier*, May 20, 1967.

38. "Dr. King's Inherent Rights," *New Pittsburgh Courier*, May 27, 1967.

39. "War-Rights Link Brings about Break," *New York Amsterdam News*, April 22, 1967.

40. "American Tragedy," *New York Amsterdam News*, May 6, 1967.

41. "Fallacies in Dr. King's Stand on the Vietnam War," *Atlanta Daily World*, May 4, 1967.

42. "There Is No Disunity," *Baltimore Afro-American*, April 29, 1967.

43. "Dr. King Wins Approval," *Dallas Express*, May 6, 1967.

44. Wyatt Walker, "Reflections on Crime, Vietnam, and God," 13, 14.

45. "Two in One," *St. Louis Argus*, April 28, 1967.

46. Wolseley, *Black Press, U.S.A.*, 11, 12.

47. Fred Panzer, White House aide, memo to the president, May 19, 1967, "Advance Harris Survey, Monday, May 22, 1967," Name File, WHCF, box 144, LBJ Library.

48. Fred Panzer, memo to the president, "Harris Survey for May 22, 1967," Name File, WHCF, box 144, LBJ Library.

49. Fred Panzer, memo to President Johnson, "Advance Gallup for Sunday, June 11, 1967," June 9, 1967, Name File, WHCF, box 144, LBJ Library.

50. "Dr. King's Politics," *Chicago Daily Defender*, August 24, 1967.

51. "Dr. King's Triumph," *Chicago Daily Defender*, December 28, 1966.

52. Lyndon Johnson, letter to John Sengstacke, August 31, 1967, WHCF, EXEC FG, box 200, LBJ Library.

53. *Los Angeles Sentinel*, April 6, 1967. For descriptions of the event, see Evans, *Personal Politics*, 195–99; Fairclough, "Martin Luther King, Jr.," 35.

54. Jeffrey L. Hodes, "New Left in Disarray," *New Leader* 50, no. 18 (September 11, 1967): 6–8.

55. Garrow, *Bearing the Cross*, 573.

56. Garrow, "Martin Luther King, Jr.," 27.

57. *Pittsburgh Courier*, August 19,1967.

58. King, *Autobiography*, 342.

59. "Deliver Us from 'Friends,'" *Baltimore Afro-American*, May 6, 1967.

60. "Bedfellows," *Los Angeles Sentinel*, December 21, 1967.

61. Allan Morrison, "A. Philip Randolph Offers Civil Rights Plan: Wants a Social Revolution Involving Negroes and Whites," *Jet*, July 6, 1967.

62. A. Young, *An Easy Burden*, 432.

63. Garrow, *Bearing the Cross*, 576–77.

64. Rowan, "Martin Luther King's Tragic Decision"; Rowan, *Breaking Barriers*, 278.

65. "Rev. King's Vietnam Stand Harming Welfare of Negroes," *Dallas Express*, September 2, 1967. The *Express* did not include in its story any response from King to Rowan's attack.

66. Garrow, *Bearing the Cross*, 577.

67. King, "Drum Major Instinct," in *A Testament of Hope*, 264–67.

68. Burns, *To the Mountaintop*, 447–50.

69. King, "Drum Major Instinct," 267.

70. Among the black papers that had been critical of King's antiwar stance in the year before his death were the *Atlanta Daily World, Chicago Daily Defender, Dallas Express, Dallas Post Tribune, Los Angeles Sentinel, Michigan Chronicle, New York*

Amsterdam News, Norfolk Journal and Guide, Pittsburgh Courier, and the *St. Louis Argus. Jet* magazine also published negative stories about King's antiwar campaign during the same period. Notable for its generally supportive comments about the embattled King, despite the squalls being generated by his outspoken antiwar views during his last year, was the *Baltimore Afro-American.* The Baltimore paper had been an early opponent of the war, so its patience with the controversial pacifism of King was not surprising.

71. *Norfolk Journal and Guide,* April 20, 1968; *Michigan Chronicle,* April 13, 1968.

72. See chap. 2 for a thorough treatment of the issue of competition between the insatiable hunger of the Vietnam War for resources and the needs of black Americans, in particular, as discussed in the African American press.

73. Ray Zauber, "King's Peace Didn't Help Negro Cause," *Dallas Post Tribune,* April 13, 1968.

74. Alfred Duckett, "Killers of the Dream Were Not All White," *Dallas Express,* April 27, 1968.

75. For example, see editorial, "Rev. King's Vietnam Stand Harming Welfare of Negroes," *Dallas Express,* September 2, 1967. The editorial page of the *Dallas Express* carried a disclaimer of responsibility for opinions expressed in bylined items appearing on its op-ed page, so it cannot be stated categorically that the Duckett piece represented the opinion of the editor.

76. "Tribune Flooded with Letters: Senseless Viet War and Racism Caused Murder, Says Committee" and "King Called Inspiration to Men of All Colors," *Philadelphia Tribune,* April 9, 1968; "7 Peace Groups Picket," *Philadelphia Tribune,* April 23, 1968. Several months later the paper published an editorial strongly supporting Johnson for his management of the Vietnam War, headlined "Solution to War in Vietnam Not Easy." The editor wrote: "We believe that President Johnson is as dedicated to peace as any other American. However, he has the responsibility of solving the problem, while his harping critics offer no practical solution. They want peace but they give no feasible suggestions as to how it can be achieved" (*Philadelphia Tribune,* November 9, 1968).

In comparison with the spotty post-assassination coverage of King's antiwar views in much of the black press, the *New York Times* had a number of pieces on the subject. Examples include Herbert Mitgang, "The Race Crisis: A Non-Violent Man Is Martyred," April 7, 1968; Walter Rugaber, "Plea by Mrs. King: 'Fulfill His Dream,'" and "Statement by Mrs. King," April 7, 1968.

A survey of the *Chicago Tribune* and *Washington Post* found several examples of the same: "150,000 Pay Last Tribute to Dr. King," *Chicago Tribune,* April 10, 1968; "Pastor Blames King's Death on 'Sick Society' in America," *Chicago Tribune,* April 10, 1968; "Views of Dr. King's Funeral in Atlanta," *Washington Post,* April 10, 1968; "Homage Paid to Dr. King in Many Nations," *Washington Post,* April 10, 1968.

After the abrupt end to King's life, *Time* and *Newsweek* both found in the circumstances of King's death a perfect opportunity to resurrect King as "a reassuring symbol taken from simpler times and a simpler quest for justice." According to Lentz, this was done by stripping away the radicalism implicit in King's planned Poor People's

Campaign and his antiwar exertions, both aimed at the federal government, and by restoring the more reassuring symbolism of King in his strenuous confrontation with the dark forces of racism in the American South. Just as he rose to fame by facing down the racist city fathers in Montgomery and Selma, he died at the hands of a bigot wielding a rifle from the bathroom of a roominghouse in Memphis. It was a mythic end, which made it possible for the newsmagazines to create "a usable past for their readers" and signal the arrival of King as "once more a prophet from the South, from another country" (Lentz, *Symbols*, esp. 236–62 and 338–42).

77. Carl Wendell Hines, "King as Disturber of the Peace," in Griffith, *Major Problems in American History*, 378.

78. Examples of the reappearance of discussions of King's antiwar campaign in pieces in the black press, which had largely ignored this part of King's legacy in the immediate aftermath of the assassination, include "The Legacy of Dr. M. L. King Jr.," *Los Angeles Sentinel*, April 2, 1970, as well as two separate pieces in *Jet*: "King's Prophesy on Vietnam Now Haunts His Critics and Foes," *Jet*, May 22, 1975, 13; and a feature teased on the cover of the May 22, 1975, issue with the headline "Special Report: What the Vietnam War Did to Blacks," which included a "Words of the Week" section devoted entirely to a series of six brief antiwar pronouncements from King on p. 40.

6. "We're with You, Chief"

1. For the poll numbers see Harris, *Anguish of Change*, 56. As I detail in the introduction, the Gulf of Tonkin affair included two incidents, two days apart. The first, on August 2, 1964, saw a U.S. naval destroyer, the *Maddox*, attacked by three enemy patrol boats while on patrol along coastal waters just off the eastern shoreline of North Vietnam. The U.S. warship, aided by fighter-bombers from the carrier *Ticonderoga*, routed the enemy boats in a matter of minutes, with no casualties on the American side. Two days later the *Maddox* was joined by a second destroyer, the *Turner Joy*. In the darkness that night the U.S. skipper of the two-boat destroyer flotilla, Captain John J. Herrick, responding to radar blips and raw nerves, ordered his gunners to fire on unseen enemy boats in the blackness. After two hours of gunfire and swerving to avoid torpedoes, Herrick began doubting the existence of enemy boats or torpedoes. Maybe the blips were radar images caused by freak weather. He telegraphed his doubts up the chain of command to the Pentagon. Despite Herrick's doubts, within hours President Johnson launched air strikes against North Vietnam in retaliation. He also secured the Gulf of Tonkin Resolution from an eager Congress with few dissenting votes. A long escalation of the war followed. See Moise, *Tonkin Gulf,* xi. Moise's book is a detailed analysis of the incidents in the Gulf.

2. An example of coverage in the mainstream media is the treatment of the story in the *New York Times*. A check of daily issues of the newspaper from August 3 through 8, 1964, revealed extensive coverage of the Tonkin Gulf incident, retaliatory air strikes, and the Gulf of Tonkin Resolution, with headline stories each day through August 8, along with multiple stories, some of them lengthy features, in every issue, as

well as editorials on each of the six days. For the *Defender* editorial see "Vietnam and Rights," *Chicago Defender*, August 15–21, 1964.

3. The first front-page story in the paper was headlined "U.S. Air-Sea Force off Vietnam Waters" (*Atlanta Daily World*, August 4, 1964). The next day's more prominent war headline on the front page was "2 North Vietnam Gunboats Thought Sunk during 2nd Attack on U.S. Destroyers." (The banner headline that day was "FBI Digs Up Three Bodies in Philadelphia, Miss.," a story about the discovery of the grisly murders of the three civil rights workers.) The editorial in the *World* was "The Vietnam Crisis" (August 7, 1964).

4. A full text of the resolution appears in "The Tonkin Gulf Resolution, 1964," Paterson, *Major Problems in American Foreign Policy*, 2:571, 572.

5. Goldwater made this statement about the use of nuclear weapons in Vietnam when he was interviewed by Howard K. Smith on ABC-TV on May 24, 1964: "Defoliation of the forests by low-yield atomic weapons could well be done."

6. "Goldwater Retreats," *Chicago Defender*, October 17–23, 1964.

7. "LBJ Is Our Choice," *Baltimore Afro-American*, October 17, 1964.

8. "Our Position on the Presidential Election," *Atlanta Daily World*, October 22, 1964; "Time to Choose," *Pittsburgh Courier*, October 10, 1964.

9. *Jet*, December 13, 1963. For a transcript of the taped conversation of the president and Andrew Hatcher, see *Lyndon B. Johnson: The Kennedy Assassination and the Transfer of Power*, 2:772–75, 778, 779.

10. Caro, *Means of Ascent*, xvi–xviii. For Johnson's vivid characterization of Truman's civil rights proposal, see Dugger, *Politician*, 310.

11. Farmer interview by Baker, October 1969, 1, 2. Roy Wilkins, head of the NAACP, told an interviewer that the attitude of many civil rights leaders "was one of dismay" when Johnson was put on the ticket (Wilkins interview, 2, 3).

12. Martin interview by McComb, 5, 6.

13. Martin interview by Gillette, 12, 13.

14. Ellison, "Myth of the Flawed White Southerner," 212.

15. Even as Johnson won over black Americans with his wholehearted embrace of civil rights causes, he outraged white members of delegations from the Deep South and, according to one, white southerners generally. Representative F. Edward Hebert, a Louisiana Democrat, told an interviewer about the reaction to Lyndon Johnson's liberalism as president: "In Louisiana he was absolutely hated because they considered him a turncoat. They considered Lyndon Johnson the most horrible man that ever lived" (Hebert interview).

16. Wilkins interview, 7. In his autobiography, *Standing Fast*, Wilkins vividly recounts his first meeting with Johnson in the Oval Office on Friday, November 29, 1963 (295, 296). For the recollections of other black leaders about their contacts with Johnson in this period, see Whitney M. Young interview, 5; Farmer interview by Baker, 8, 9; Randolph interview. Transcripts from the taping system that was in operation from the earliest days of the Johnson presidency do not include early recordings of face-to-face conversations between LBJ and key African American leaders but do include contemporaneous, taped references by the president to these keys meet-

ings, including the first such meeting, which was with Roy Wilkins in late November 1963. Several phone conversations of the president and major black leaders were recorded in which they discussed civil rights matters or Johnson asked the various men to arrange for a later face-to-face meeting with him in the Oval Office. During his telephone conversation with Wilkins, the president asked for and received Farmer's phone number. Farmer recounts receiving Johnson's call in his interview with Harri Baker and in his autobiography, *Lay Bare the Heart*, 294–96. There is no published transcript of the telephone call; it may have been made from a phone not included in the taping system or the system may not have been activated at the time. For transcripts of the president's phone calls to other African American leaders early in his presidency, see *Lyndon B. Johnson: The Kennedy Assassination* 1:137–42 (Whitney Young); 1:161, 162 (King); 1:300, 301 (Randolph); 2:777–81 (Wilkins); 2:781–85, 3:181–84 (Whitney Young).

17. Garrow, *Bearing the Cross*, 308. For a summary of the meeting between the president and King, see *Lyndon B. Johnson*, 2:96, 97. The meeting itself was not tape-recorded.

18. Carl T. Rowan, memo to President Johnson, January 28, 1964, Name File, WHCF, box 117, LBJ Library.

19. Both the publisher's letter of September 2, 1964, and the president's reply on September 21 are in Name File, WHCF, box 117, LBJ Library. The editorial endorsing LBJ is "Why We Endorse Johnson and Humphrey," *Jet*, September 10, 1964.

20. President's Daily Diary, January 30, 1964, LBJ Library. The next meeting LBJ had with the board of the NNPA occurred on March 11, 1965. See Statement by Frank L. Stanley, president of the NNPA, made to LBJ, dated January 27, 1966, p. 3 of statement referring to meeting of March 11, 1965, Subject File, WHCF, box 4, LBJ Library. Three meetings led by Vice President Hubert H. Humphrey were held between LBJ's meeting with the NNPA in late January 1966 and October 16, 1967. These meetings were attended by members of the newly formed Governmental Affairs Committee of the NNPA; they met for daylong sessions each time with heads of various agencies responsible for implementing programs making up the Great Society. Additional sessions were held into late March 1968. For Humphrey's involvement see memos from Humphrey to LBJ dated October 16, 1967, and March 27, 1968, WHCF, EXEC PR, box 32, LBJ Library. Another meeting with the president and the full board of the NNPA was held on March 15, 1968. See White House memo from James R. Johns to W. Marvin Watson, March 15, 1968, Name File, WHCF, box 127, LBJ Library.

21. Goodlett to Watson, February 16, 1966, and Watson to Goodlett, February 24, 1966, Name File, WHCF, box 191, LBJ Library.

22. Watson to Goodlett, February 24, 1966, Name File, WHCF, box 191, LBJ Library.

23. One invitation to a White House dinner with the president called a purpose of the dinner "the exchange of views and ideas with other leaders of this country" (Draft of invitation dated September 16, 1965, Name File, WHCF, box 117, LBJ Library). An invitation to a stag luncheon for the president of Senegal, on September 28, 1965, is in the same file in box 117, as are the names of the members of the National Advisory Council, Office of Economic Opportunity. A letter from the president to John H.

Johnson thanked the publisher for serving on the National Advisory Commission on Selective Service, as his term of service on the body was ending (LBJ to John H. Johnson, March 24, 1967, Name File, WHCF, box 117, LBJ Library). For the president's appointment of the publisher to the Post Office Department Advisory Board, see the President's Daily Diary for December 11, 1967, LBJ Library.

24. According to the President's Daily Diary for 1966–68, the following events brought John H. Johnson, sometimes with his wife, to the White House to meet with LBJ on the dates indicated: meeting of the National Advisory Council of the Office of Economic Opportunity in the Oval Office, September 9, 1966; luncheon for President Leopold Senghor, Republic of Senegal, in the state dining room, September 28, 1966; luncheon to honor His Majesty Hassan II, King of Morocco, with receiving line followed by ballet, "The Moor's Pavane," February 9, 1967; meeting with International Executive Service Corps at the White House, May 25, 1967; state dinner in honor of William V. S. Tubman, president of the Republic of Liberia, and Mrs. Tubman, March 27, 1968, LBJ Library.

25. For an example of a social event to which the president invited Sengstacke, see draft of a list of guests to be invited to a dinner with the president, September 16, 1965, Name File, WHCF, box 117, LBJ Library. Sengstacke and his wife also appeared on the guest list for a small private dinner on the second floor of the White House on April 26, 1968. The guest list included Hubert and Muriel Humphrey, among other government and business luminaries, and, for good measure, the author John Steinbeck, who is listed as a houseguest at the White House. See President's Daily Diary, April 26, 1968, LBJ Library. For the USO appointment see President Johnson, letter to John Sengstacke, April 28, 1965, WHCF, EXEC FG, box 200, LBJ Library. The letter from LBJ to Sengstacke about his service on the Committee on Equal Opportunity in the Armed Forces is also in WHCF, EXEC FG, box 200, LBJ Library. The president's appointment of Sengstacke to the National Alliance of Businessmen is in WHCF, EXEC SP, box 200, LBJ Library. The appointment of Sengstacke to the USO committee and the reference to Sengstacke's service on the Committee on Equal Opportunity in the Armed Forces reflect Lyndon Johnson's recognition of Sengstacke's long history of involvement with U.S. military matters. The apex of Sengstacke's service came when he served on the presidential commission that deliberated the status of African Americans in the military during the Truman administration and recommended to the president the full desegregation of the armed forces. This led to Truman's Executive Order 9981 of July 26, 1948: "It is hereby declared to be the policy of the President that there shall be equality of treatment and opportunity for all persons in the armed services without regard to race, color, religion or national origin. This policy shall be put into effect as rapidly as possible, having due regard to the time required to effectuate any necessary changes without impairing efficiency or morale." Full compliance with the order took years, culminating in racial integration in the military under battlefield conditions during the Korean War, when casualties among white troops led to critical shortages of frontline combat units. The solution was integration of black troops into previously all-white units. Recalcitrant white commanders finally yielded to the stern realities of the manpower needs on the ground in Korea

and ushered in the era of racial integration in the U.S. military. The war in Vietnam was the first military conflict fought, from the beginning, by the U.S. military with fully integrated forces. For Truman's Executive Order 9981, as well as deliberations leading up to its issuance, see the online archives of the Truman Presidential Library. For the history from issuance of the desegregation decree to full implementation, see Astor, *Right to Fight*, 321–98.

26. T. C. Jervay, letter to Marvin Watson, White House staff, March 12, 1968, in the back-up material for the President's Daily Diary, March 12, 1968, LBJ Library.

27. President's Daily Diary, March 15, 1968, LBJ Library.

28. Martin interview by Gillette, 20, 21. Martin had intimate White House access as the Kennedy administration ended and the Johnson years began. Arthur M. Schlesinger Jr. describes how Martin was among a small group of family and presidential aides at the White House to receive the body of President Kennedy when it arrived from Bethesda Naval Hospital in the early morning hours of November 23, 1963, to lie in state in the East Room (Schlesinger, *Journals*, 204). During the Johnson administration, Martin was so effective as a contact between the White House and key African American leaders that Martin Luther King Jr. came to view him as his most reliable link with LBJ before the Vietnam War finally became a virtually insurmountable obstacle between King and the president (Kotz, *Judgment Days*, 289).

29. White House internal memo from Perry Barber to Jack Valenti, "Idea from Louis Martin," Name File, WHCF, box 127, LBJ Library.

30. Memo to the president, September 8, 1964, Name File, WHCF, box 127, LBJ Library.

31. The *Atlanta Daily World* was almost always supportive of U.S. policy, at times differing to advocate a more vigorous prosecution of the war effort and seldom voicing outright opposition. Among 122 editorials expressing support or opposition to America's role in the war in the *Daily World*, 116 supported U.S. policy and only six opposed it. The *Daily World* remained resolutely hawkish throughout the war. Despite its stout Republicanism, the paper generally supported Lyndon Johnson's policy in Vietnam throughout his administration. The *Atlanta Daily World* editorialized about the war in geopolitical, military terms without reference to issues of concern to African Americans. The paper was unabashedly aggressive: "We believe more of our military power should be used to stop the Communists in South Vietnam." And: "We hope that U.S. forces will not be withdrawn except under circumstances which will not lower our prestige" ("Vietnam, a Serious Problem," *Atlanta Daily World*, February 10, 1965).

32. The *Baltimore Afro-American* overwhelmingly opposed the war. Of its fifty-six editorials taking a position for or against the U.S. role in Vietnam, only three supported American policy in the region.

33. "LBJ All the Way," *Baltimore Afro-American*, March 5, 1966.

34. "We Stand with LBJ," *Baltimore Afro-American*, December 23, 1967.

35. "Few Know What the President Knows," *Philadelphia Tribune*, June 29, 1965.

36. "Doesn't Make Sense," *Pittsburgh Courier*, January 2, 1965.

37. "Send in the First Team," *Pittsburgh Courier*, February 13, 1965.

38. "No Immediate End to War in South Vietnam," *Pittsburgh Courier*, May 15, 1965.

39. "Bond Issue Puts in Focus Civil Rights vs. Vietnam," *Pittsburgh Courier*, February 5, 1966.

40. "Reason for Pause," *Pittsburgh Courier*, August 26, 1967.

41. "Young's Vietnam Tour," *Los Angeles Sentinel*, August 25, 1966.

42. "Puppets' Masters," *Los Angeles Sentinel*, November 9, 1966.

43. "Bedfellows," *Los Angeles Sentinel*, December 21, 1967.

44. "A Firm Hand," *New York Amsterdam News*, January 22, 1966.

45. "Weakened Argument," *New York Amsterdam News*, December 24, 1966.

46. "A Strong LBJ," *New York Amsterdam News*, November 25, 1967.

47. "*L'Affaire* Kitt," *New York Amsterdam News*, January 27, 1968; Lady Bird Johnson, *A White House Diary* (New York: Holt, Rinehart and Winston, 1970), 623.

48. "Love of Country," *New York Amsterdam News*, April 6, 1968.

49. "Tell Us the Facts," *Chicago Defender*, February 27–March 5, 1965.

50. For John Sengstacke's role in desegregation of the military, see Nalty, *Strength for the Fight*, 245, 246. For Sengstacke's influence in both the Roosevelt and Truman administrations see Nikolas Kozloff, "Vietnam, the African American Community, and the Pittsburgh Courier," *Historian* 63, no. 3 (2001): 8.

51. For Ethel Payne's ties to the Democratic National Committee, see Payne interview, September 24, 1987, 7, 8.

52. *Chicago Defender*, July 3–9, 1965.

53. *Chicago Daily Defender*, December 7, 1966.

54. Ibid., September 5, 1967.

55. Ibid.

56. Yet another draft cartoon drawing in Ohman's private collection exhibits her strong perspective on the consequences of Johnson's war policies. It depicts LBJ in the foreground broadcasting a plea for Americans to beautify their highways, while in the background U.S. helicopters drop bombs onto the pristine countryside of South Vietnam.

57. For the blitz of propaganda on the status of the war, see Herring, *America's Longest War*, 182, 183. For Wheeler's remarks see Address by General Earle G. Wheeler before the Economic Club of Detroit: Vietnam—a Year End Appraisal," December 18, 1967, box 9, folder 4, Larry Berman Collection (Presidential Archives Research), December 18, 1967, Vietnam Archive, Texas Tech University. For Westmoreland's remarks on NBC's *Meet the Press* on November 19, 1967, see Selected Statements on Vietnam by DOD and Other Administration Officials: July 1–December 31, 1967, January 11, box 1, folder 18, Glenn Helm Collection, Vietnam Archive, Texas Tech University. A full transcript of the interview is available at www.salon.com/news/primary_sources/2007/09/13/westmoreland_petraeus. For the quotation from Westmoreland's speech, see Address by General W. C. Westmoreland to National Press Club, Washington D.C., November 21, 1967, box 1, folder 5, Veteran Members of the 109th Quartermaster Company (Air Delivery) Collection, Vietnam Archive.

58. Dougan and Weiss, *American Experience in Vietnam*, 203, 204.

59. Cronkite is quoted in Spector, *After Tet*, ix. Whatever the influence of Cronkite's

pronouncement on succeeding events, it came at what turned out to be a turning point in the Vietnam struggle. That turning point was determined by events unfolding over several months in 1968. As Spector wrote: "In the long run the costly struggles of 1968, which began with Tet and continued through August and September, were a political success for the Communists. They convinced almost all influential Americans that the war could not be won at an acceptable price or in an acceptable time. Yet because they failed to break the political and military deadlock in Vietnam itself, the Communists doomed themselves to four more years of war" (312). Henry Kissinger characterized Cronkite's pronouncement as hyperbole but shrewdly noted that the news anchor's statement "contained a major element of truth: Hanoi's breaking point clearly exceeded America's" (Kissinger, *Diplomacy*, 671). That observation, as it turned out, would prove to be correct, as the diminishing U.S. political and popular support for the war would ultimately show.

60. "The Logic of the Battlefield," *Wall Street Journal*, February 23, 1968, 14, quoted in Kissinger, *Diplomacy*, 671, 672; "The War," *Time*, March 15, 1968, 14, also quoted by Kissinger (672).

61. Dallek, *Flawed Giant*, 506.

62. Carroll and Noble, *Free and the Unfree*, 405.

63. Dallek, *Flawed Giant*, 525, 526.

64. W. W. Rostow, Special Assistant to the President for National Security Affairs, memo to President Johnson, in back-up materials to the President's Daily Diary, March 15, 1968, LBJ Library.

65. President's Daily Diary, March 15, 1968.

66. White House memo from James R. Jones to W. Marvin Watson, March 15, 1968, Name File, WHCF, box 127, LBJ Library.

67. Elizabeth Murphy Moss, letter to President Lyndon B. Johnson, March 18, 1968, WHCF, EXEC PR, box 32, LBJ Library.

68. President Johnson, letter to John H. Murphy, III, President of the NNPA, on March 15, 1968, in back-up materials to the President's Daily Diary, March 15, 1968, LBJ Library.

69. Dallek, *Flawed*, 519; Maraniss, *They Marched into Sunlight*, 189–93.

70. Karl von Vorys, *American National Interest: Virtue and Power in Foreign Policy*, 215. For the text of Johnson's television address on March 31, 1968, see *Public Papers of the Presidents of the United States: Lyndon Johnson*, 9:469–76.

71. Johnson is quoted in Lawrence Wright, *In the New World*, 130.

72. Gordon Hancock, "The Shameful Attacks on President Johnson," *Norfolk Journal and Guide*, January 13, 1968.

73. *Chicago Daily Defender*, April 2, 1968.

74. "President Johnson," *Chicago Daily Defender*, April 3, 1968.

75. "War and Racism," *Norfolk Journal and Guide*, October 12, 1968.

76. For the tabulation of votes for the 1968 election, see Black, *Richard M. Nixon*, 558, 559.

77. "President Johnson," *Chicago Daily Defender*, April 3, 1968.

78. "The Peace Talks," *Chicago Daily Defender*, May 16, 1968.

79. "Negro Delegates," *Chicago Daily Defender*, August 13, 1968.

80. "What Humphrey Faces," *Chicago Daily Defender*, September 3, 1968; "The Humphrey Warning," *Chicago Daily Defender*, September 18, 1968.

81. "Johnson, Peace-Maker," *Chicago Daily Defender*, November 13, 1968.

82. "1968—The Year That Was," *San Francisco Post*, January 1, 1969.

83. "Lyndon Johnson and Vietnam," *San Francisco Sun Reporter*, January 27, 1973.

84. *Crisis*, April 1973, 113.

85. Dallek, *Flawed Giant*, 623.

7. The Black Press and Vietnam in the Nixon Years

1. "Nixon and the Black Press," *San Francisco Sun-Reporter*, January 18, 1969.

2. "The Election," *Baltimore Afro-American*, November 9, 1968.

3. Nixon Correspondence, 1968, box 29, folder 68, Abbott-Sengstacke Family Papers (hereafter Abbott-Sengstacke Papers).

4. "The New Congress," *Chicago Daily Defender*, January 8, 1969.

5. Ambrose, *Nixon: The Triumph of a Politician,*, 220.

6. Garthoff, *Détente and Confrontation*, 279.

7. Inglis, *Cruel Peace*, 240.

8. Szulc, *Illusion of Peace*, 3. In his diaries Nixon confidant H. R. Haldeman noted that the president, at a cabinet meeting on March 20, 1969, "stated flatly that war will be over by next year" (Haldeman, *Haldeman Diaries*, 42).

9. "Nixon and the Black Press," *San Francisco Sun-Reporter*, January 18, 1969.

10. "Let's Give Him a Chance," *Ebony*, April 1969, 52.

11. Nixon Correspondence, 1969–71, box 79, folder 46, Abbott-Sengstacke Papers.

12. Ibid. Nixon fired off a third telegram to Sengstacke on February 28, confirming the March 15 meeting of the National Alliance of Businessmen (NAB). Sengstacke was still serving on the NAB's executive board in the last year of the Ford administration; the publisher attended a reception for the NAB board hosted by Ford at the White House on April 6, 1976 (The Daily Diary of President Gerald R. Ford, April 6, 1976, Ford Library).

13. For the reference to publisher John H. Johnson's presence at the White House ceremony at which Nixon signed Executive Order 11458, see the President's Daily Diary, March 5, 1969, appendix C, Nixon Library.

14. President's Daily Diary, May 12, 1969, appendix B, Nixon Library. John Sengstacke's papers contain a copy of his letter to the social secretary at the White House, accepting "with pleasure the President's invitation to dinner on Monday, May 12, 1969, at eight o'clock" (in box 79, folder 46, Abbott-Sengstacke Papers).

15. President's Daily Diary, May 25, 1969, appendix B, Nixon Library.

16. President's Daily Diary, May 28, 1969, appendixes E and F, Nixon Library. This was not Nixon's first encounter with a group of African American publishers. In early 1957 then–vice president Nixon traveled to Africa to attend ceremonies celebrating Ghana's independence. The trip also included stops in Liberia, Ethiopia, Uganda, Sudan, Libya, Tunisia, and Morocco, as well as a side trip to Italy. Nixon traveled

with a group of thirty journalists, more than half of whom were from the "Negro press." For a reference to the Africa trip, see Black, *Richard M. Nixon*, 349. Black does not fix the date of the beginning of the Africa trip but says that Nixon returned to Washington on March 21, 1957.

Two weeks before Nixon met with the black publishers and editors, he had met with Ralph Abernathy, King's successor as head of the SCLC, in the Roosevelt Room of the White House. with The meeting had been coordinated by Daniel Patrick Moynihan, then an assistant to the president for urban affairs, in conjunction with a session of the Urban Affairs Council. After what seemed to Nixon to have been an affable meeting with Abernathy, the civil rights leader thanked the president profusely, as Nixon remembered the encounter. Abernathy then went straight to the press room, where he called the session with Nixon and his aides "the most disappointing, the most fruitless of all the meetings we had had up to this time." A horrified and seething Moynihan arrived in the Oval Office and said to Nixon, "After the way you and the rest of us listened and indicated our sincere desire to find solutions to the problems, he goes into the press room and pisses on the President of the United States. It was unconscionable and I promise it will never happen again." Abernathy's recollection of the episode was essentially the same. He attributed his comments to the press corps to the extreme anger he had felt during the meeting, presumably because of what he perceived to be Nixon's unresponsiveness to Abernathy's specific demands. The President's Daily Diary for May 13, 1969, available at the Nixon Library, lists those who attended the Urban Affairs Council meeting at the White House but sheds no light on the substance of discussions. For Nixon's recollection of the episode, see his book, *RN*, 436. Abernathy's version is in his autobiography, *And the Walls Came Tumbling Down*, 553, 554.

17. Joan Hoff cites studies showing that fifty-six of the top one hundred black firms, and forty-five of the top one hundred Latino businesses, were formed between 1969 and 1976, the first five years of which coincide with the Nixon presidency. For a good summary of the history and results of the Office of Minority Business Enterprise, see Hoff, *Nixon Reconsidered*, 95–97.

18. "The Same Old Stuff," *Chicago Daily Defender*, November 6, 1969.

19. "Black Leader's Chance," *New Courier*, August 31, 1968.

20. "The Fight on Poverty," *New Courier*, April 19, 1969.

21. "Veterans Day," *Los Angeles Sentinel*, November 7, 1968.

22. Ibid., November 13, 1969.

23. "A Noble Effort," *Los Angeles Sentinel*, November 20, 1969.

24. "Our Backyard," *New York Amsterdam News*, May 22, 1965.

25. "The Moon Race," *New York Amsterdam News*, July 12, 1969.

26. "Men on the Moon," *Oakland Post*, July 24, 1969.

27. "March on Washington," *San Francisco SunReporter*, January 11, 1969.

28. "Nixon's Tricky Dickering," *San Francisco Sun-Reporter*, July 12, 1969; "Nixon's Madness Continues," *San Francisco Sun Reporter*, November 8, 1969.

29. "An 'Honorable' Peace," *San Francisco Sun-Reporter*, May 17, 1969. For a sampling of *Sun-Reporter* editorials supporting the antiwar movement early in the Nixon

years, see: "Our Children—The Nation's Conscience," April 26, 1969; "Nov. 15 Peace Offensive," September 27, 1969; "Step Up the Peace Offensive," October 18, 1969; "The Things That Unite Us Are More Important," October 25, 1969; "Peace Struggle Must Continue," November 22, 1969; "The Tragedy of Vietnam," April 25, 1970.

30. "Nixon Must Listen on Vietnam," *San Francisco Sun-Reporter*, November 15, 1969.

31. John Lewis, "Black Voices," *Baltimore Afro American*, August 2, 1969.

32. Whitney M. Young Jr. interview, 8.

33. "Young Takes Stand against War in Vietnam," *Jet*, October 30, 1969, 9.

34. Nixon, *RN*, 409.

35. Sorley, "Vietnamization," 474–75.

36. Nixon, *RN*, 410.

37. Sorley, *A Better War*, 169. For the text of Nixon's speech, see *Public Papers of the Presidents of the United States: Richard Nixon,* 1:901–9.

38. Alonzo L. Hamby deftly explores the consequences of Nixon's strategic choices in *Liberalism and Its Challenger*, 302–8.

39. Kenneth Hunt, "America in the Far East: Political and Military Dimensions," in Rosecrance, *America as an Ordinary Country*, 136. Also see John G. Keilers, "Nixon Doctrine and Vietnamization," June 29, 2007, www.army.mil/article/3867/nixon-doctrine-and-vietnamization.

40. Sorley, "United States: Involvement in Vietnam, 1969–1973," in Tucker, *Encyclopedia of the Vietnam War*, 426, 427.

41. Melvin Small, "The Impact of the Antiwar Movement," in McMahon, *Major Problems in the History of the Vietnam War*, 491.

42. For the June 1969 poll see Pratt, *Vietnam Voices*, 406. For the July and September 1969 polls, see William M. Hammond, "Media and the War," in Kutler, *Encyclopedia of the Vietnam War*, 320.

43. Evans-Pfeifer, "American Public Opinion," 462, 463.

44. "A Castor Oil Prescription by Dr. Nixon and Intern Agnew," *St. Louis American*, March 5, 1970. The editorial was referring to the nominations of Clement F. Haynsworth Jr. and G. Harrold Carswell, both southerners and both ultimately rejected by the Senate, in November 1969 and April 1970, respectively, on the basis of allegations of racism and, in Carswell's case, of professional inadequacy. See Hoff, *Nixon Reconsidered*, 44–49.

45. Daniel Patrick Moynihan, "Memorandum for the President," January 16, 1969, 7, Nixon Library.

46. John H. Sengstacke, "Moynihan Memorandum," *Chicago Daily Defender*, March 9, 1970.

47. Nixon, *RN*, 440.

48. "A *Time*-Louis Harris Poll: The Black Mood: More Militant, More Hopeful, More Determined," *Time*, April 6, 1970, 28, 29.

49. Hoff, *Nixon Reconsidered*, 229.

50. See Caputo, *Thirteen Seconds*, for a reconstruction and analysis of the episode by a newspaper reporter who arrived at the Kent State campus shortly after the shootings occurred.

51. Tim Spofford wrote a scholarly and thoroughly readable book about the Jackson State shootings, *Lynch Street.*

52. "Record Is Not Good," *Michigan Chronicle,* May 30, 1970.

53. "Death in Black and White," *Dallas Post Tribune,* May 30, 1970.

54. MacPherson, *Long Time Passing,* 588.

55. Roy Wilkins, "Questions on College Deaths," *Baltimore Afro-American,* May 23, 1970.

56. "Has President Nixon Already Mounted a White Horse?" *St. Louis American,* May 7, 1970.

57. "We Are Concerned," *Chicago Daily Defender,* October 29, 1969.

58. "History on Their Side," *Chicago Daily Defender,* November 18, 1969.

59. In *Defender* editorials that distinguished opponents of the war by race, twelve editorials featured blacks who were against the war, whereas only six identified whites against the war. When we consider editorials that explicitly identified individuals from both races as opponents of the conflict, blacks opposing the war are involved in 70 percent of the pieces. An examination of editorial comments on the war in four other prominent black newspapers found the same tendency to identify black Americans with opposition to the war. (The comparable figures were *Pittsburgh Courier,* 78 percent; *Baltimore Afro-American,* 88 percent; *New York Amsterdam News,* 88 percent; *Los Angeles Sentinel,* 100 percent). This tendency was less prominent in the *Atlanta Daily World,* which spoke out against antiwar activity on the part of blacks. In editorials that identified opponents of the war by race, sixteen editorials in the paper featured white antiwar figures, and twenty, or just over 55 percent, featured opponents of the war who were black. When the paper's editorials discussed black opponents of the war, it was usually to pass judgment on their ideology or to reprimand them for encouraging the nation's foes by their irresponsible actions (for example, see "Anti-War Protests Deplored," October 22, 1966, and "God Bless America," November 13, 1969, both in the *Atlanta Daily World*).

60. "Black Poll on Vietnam," *Chicago Daily Defender,* March 18, 1970.

61. "The Black Man's Stake," *San Francisco Post,* May 28, 1970.

62. Abernathy, "Some International Dimensions," 237.

63. "The Agony of Vietnam," *New Pittsburgh Courier,* April 24, 1971. The massacre occurred in March 1968, and the *New York Times* published Seymour Hersh's stories about it in November 1969. For the date of the massacre see Karnow, *Vietnam,* 468.

64. "Calley's Peers Did Their Duty," *Baltimore Afro-American,* April 10, 1971. The other witness is quoted in FitzGerald, *Fire in the Lake,* 465.

65. Terry, "Bloods," 395.

66. "The War Keeps Killing," *Baltimore Afro-American,* May 6, 1972.

67. "Baptist Unit Tells U.S. to Quit Vietnam," *Baltimore Afro-American,* May 20, 1972.

68. "Vietnam Dishonor," *Baltimore Afro-American,* June 17, 1972.

69. "American Genocide Continues—Now the Dikes n' Dams," *San Francisco Sun-Reporter,* August 5, 1972.

70. "South Vietnam, Cambodia and Laos," *San Francisco Post,* February 25, 1971.

71. "Fact vs. Fiction: Who's Kidding Whom?" *San Francisco Post,* March 3, 1971.

72. "Viet War Must End," *Chicago Daily Defender*, April 25, 1972.

73. "Wanted Badly: A 'Scapegoat' for the Renewed Bombing in Vietnam," *St. Louis American*, April 27, 1972; "The One and Only Campaign Issue . . . Vietnam," *St. Louis American*, August 24, 1972.

74. "Vietnamization Folly," *San Francisco Sun-Reporter*, May 6, 1972..

75. "The Pentagon's 'Secret Papers,'" *Freedomways* 11, no. 3 (1971): 235, 236.

76. Rosecrance, *America as an Ordinary Country*, 16.

77. Schuman, "Two Sources of Antiwar Sentiment," 527.

78. The derivation of the phrase "peace is at hand" is noted in Ambrose, *Nixon: Ruin and Recovery*, 16. The phrase was picked up in the titles of several editorials in the *San Francisco Sun-Reporter*: "'Peace Is at Hand' Was a 'Nice Phrase,'" December 23, 1972, "'Peace Is at Hand' Was a Cruel Hoax," January 6, 1973, and "Peace Is at Hand or More Bombs?" January 20, 1973.

79. "Viet Peace, a Cruel Hoax," *Chicago Daily Defender*, December 26, 1972.

80. Tilford, "Operation Linebacker II," 233–35.

81. "'Peace Is at Hand' Was a 'Nice Phrase,'" *San Francisco Sun-Reporter*, December 23, 1972.

82. Eleanor Ohman, "A Christmas Plea," *San Francisco Sun-Reporter*, December 23, 1972.

83. Stanley O. Williford, "1972: In Review," *Los Angeles Sentinel*, December 28, 1972.

84. For the full text of the peace agreement see "Agreement on Ending the War."

85. For Nixon's words see Drew, *Washington Journal*, 208.

86. Joe P Dunn, "Draft," in Tucker, *Encyclopedia of the Vietnam War*, 107. The transition from the draft to an all-volunteer army began a long gestation after the Commission on an All-Volunteer Armed Force submitted its final report on on February 21, 1970. The commission included Roy Wilkins, head of the NAACP. The report recommended that the draft system be replaced by a system made up entirely of recruited volunteers. See the memo written by White House aide Martin Anderson, dated February 21, 1970, referencing the meeting of the commission and documented in President's Daily Diary for February 21, 1970, appendix A, Nixon Library.

An interesting omission from the membership of the commission was John Sengstacke, publisher of the *Chicago Defender* and dean of African American newspaper publishers. As someone who had served on presidential commissions dealing with military issues since the administrations of FDR and Truman, Sengstacke would have been a natural for Nixon's panel. Early in his first administration Nixon had cultivated Sengstacke, but perhaps the president had cooled on the publisher. Or perhaps the president simply preferred substantive policy input from Wilkins, who was the most moderate of the major civil rights leaders.

87. Laird, *Final Report*, 13, 14.

88. Drew, *Washington Journal*, 208. The "decent interval" and the final unraveling of South Vietnam are covered by Frost in "United States: Involvement in Vietnam, 1973–1975," 428–29.

89. "Lyndon Baines Johnson," *Los Angeles Sentinel*, January 25, 1973.

90. "Aftermath of Peace," *Los Angeles Sentinel*, February 22, 1973.

91. Nixon's promotion of the aid program for North Vietnam is described in Ambrose, *Nixon: Ruin and Recovery,* 57, 58.

92. "A Budget—More Than Money," *Ebony*, April 1973, 154.

93. "Nixon and Vietnam," *Atlanta Daily World*, March 27, 1968.

94. "A Commendable Move," *Atlanta Daily World*, June 12, 1969.

95. "We Are Honored," *Atlanta Daily World*, May 28, 1972.

96. "The Publishers' Visit," *Atlanta Daily World*, June 24, 1971.

97. "Not So," *Atlanta Daily World*, October 5, 1972.

8. Race Relations in an Integrated Military

1. Thomas A. Johnson, "Black Soldiers in 'The Nam,'" *Ebony*, August 1968, 38.

2. "War at Home, Abroad," *New York Amsterdam News*, May 13, 1967. Several cartoons in the black press made similar points about the contrast between brotherhood in combat in Vietnam and the failure back home in the United States to reconcile blacks and whites in a fully integrated community. For examples see the *Pittsburgh Courier*, February 26, 1966, and December 11, 1966. The *Los Angeles Sentinel* carried a cartoon with the same theme but displaying a tone of bitterness and disillusionment missing in earlier examples. The bitterness reflected changes in the quality of interracial relationships among U.S. military personnel in Vietnam that occasionally even spilled over into combat situations (which I address later in the chapter). These tensions had been commonplace in the United States for some time.

3. The number of African American Medal of Honor winners appears in Thad Martin, "The Black Vietnam Vet: Still Looking for Respect," *Ebony*, April 1986, 123.

4. "Dead Viet G.I. from Chicago to Be Awarded Medal of Honor," *Atlanta Daily World*, April 21, 1966; "President Says 'Men Like Milton Olive Die for Honor,'" *Atlanta Daily World*, April 22, 1966.

5. *Baltimore Afro-American*, April 30, 1966. The father's letter to the president was also highlighted in an editorial in *Ebony*, "Heroes and History," June 1966, 160; and Ragni Lantz, "Chicago Youth Joins 46 Other Negroes Who Won Top U.S. Medal," *Jet*, May 5, 1966, 6–10.

6. Marie S. Moore, "Integrate," *New York Amsterdam News*, January 21, 1967.

7. "No Time for Self-Pity but Renewed Dedication," *Pittsburgh Carrier*, April 30, 1966.

8. "Birdmen with Black Rifles," *Ebony*, October, 1966, 42.

9. Mike Davis, "They Couldn't Care Less What Color You Are," *Baltimore Afro-American*, July 22, 1967. Davis filed another front-page story, also emphasizing how distinctions of color disappeared in combat in Vietnam, for the *Baltimore Afro-American* of October 7, 1967.

10. "Negro Dies but Saves White Buddy," *Pittsburgh Courier*, January 27, 1968.

11. "GIs in Vietnam Ask *Jet* for Help against Bigotry," *Jet*, December 12, 1968, 54.

12. Terry, *Bloods*, xiii–xv. David Cortright summarizes stormy black-white relations in the Vietnam-era military, particularly as the U.S. armed forces began their transition toward an all-volunteer model. See Cortright, *Soldiers in Revolt*, 201–19.

13. "Unrest in Army," *New York Amsterdam News*, December 6, 1969.

14. Mike Davis, "GIs Shocked by U.S. riots," *Baltimore Afro-American*, August 12, 1967.

15. Davis, "They Couldn't Care Less."

16. Ethel Payne, "Crowded Saigon Is Lonely, Black GIs Find," *Chicago Daily Defender*, February 7, 1967.

17. Donald Mosby, "Filth, Bias, Prostitutes in Saigon's 'Soulville,'" *Chicago Daily Defender*, May 28, 1968.

18. "Racism in U.S. Army," *Norfolk Journal and Guide*, November 16, 1968.

19. The Seabee was scarcely alone in his observation of virulent prejudice directed at black soldiers by Vietnamese. Donald Mosby, writing for the *Defender*, reported conversations with black GIs that provide anecdotal evidence of the constant discrimination they faced from individual Vietnamese. Mosby also attributed Vietnamese antiblack prejudices to the influence of the rampant racism expressed by white American soldiers. See two feature stories by Mosby—"What's This? Jim Crow Found in Saigon Brothels," *Chicago Daily Defender*, May 13, 1968, and "Young and Old Vietnamese Wish Black GIs Would Leave Country," *Chicago Daily Defender*, May 21, 1968.

20. Thomas Picou, "Threaten Race Riots in Viet," *Chicago Daily Defender*, March 20, 1968.

21. Ethel L. Payne, "Navy Answers Complaint about Negro GIs' Mistreatment in Viet," *Chicago Daily Defender*, May 13, 1968. Payne's article appeared verbatim in the *New Pittsburgh Courier* on May 25, 1968, under the headline "Navy Plays Down Bias Complaints in Vietnam." Barry Wright's experience eventually led him to establish the Concerned Veterans From Vietnam (CVFV) to help black vets adjust to civilian life. It was a productive conclusion to his frustrating brush with the brass, when he complained through the media about the discrimination he faced in Vietnam. For the piece about Wright's group, see "Racism Led to New Group for Viet Vets," *Jet*, November 5, 1970, 25.

22. "No Dixie Flag in Armed Forces," *Baltimore Afro-American*, February 19, 1966.

23. "Complains of Viet Troop Bias, Confederate Flag before Death," *Jet,* April 4, 1968, 8, 9. Kitchen was not the first black soldier who died in Vietnam in early 1968 after writing home about the daunting challenges of life in the battle zone. On March 2, 1968, the *Baltimore Afro-American* published a poem written by a black marine lamenting his anguish at having to fight in Vietnam when his real battle was at home, combating injustice for black Americans. Before the young leatherneck got back "to the battle at home," he was killed in combat in Vietnam.

24. Terry, *Bloods*, 172.

25. James Russell, "Racism Rising in U.S. Army," *Chicago Daily Defender*, December 2, 1969. The story appeared in the *Baltimore Afro-American* on December 6, under a slightly different headline: "Racial Strife Up in Military."

26. "Racial Conflicts in Vietnam," *New Pittsburgh Courier*, December 27, 1969; reprinted by the *Courier* under the headline "Racial Bias in Vietnam," January 24, 1970.

27. "Race Riots Hit the GIs," *Baltimore Afro-American*, September 7, 1968.

28. "Marines Charge They Fight Two Wars: Racism, Viet Foe," *Baltimore Afro-American*, June 14, 1969.

29. "White v. Black Confrontations Are Increasing," *Pittsburgh Courier*, August 23, 1969, 14. A good summary of the clashes at Camp Lejeune appears in Westheider, *Fighting on Two Fronts*, 94–96.

30. "Marines Troubled by Racial Clashes at N.C. Camp," *Baltimore Afro-American*, August 23, 1969.

31. "Marine Admit Racial Problems," *Baltimore Afro-American*, August 23, 1969.

32. "GIs in Vietnam Ask *Jet* for Help against Bigotry," *Jet*, December 12, 1968, 54.

33. "People Are Talking About," *Jet*, May 1, 1969, 42.

34. "Black GIs Caught in Vise of Military Injustice," *Jet*, December 2, 1971, 12–17.

35. "Asks Probe of GI Bias," *Chicago Daily Defender*, June 16, 1970.

36. "Marines Approve 'Afro' Haircut, Black Power," *Baltimore Afro-American*; "Black Marines Get OK for Afros, 'New Salute,'" *Chicago Daily Defender*, September 4, 1969.

37. "An Army Beginning," *Baltimore Afro-American*, October 25, 1969.

38. "Racial Bias in Vietnam," *Chicago Daily Defender*, December 11, 1969.

39. A sample of stories about such studies includes these in the *Defender*: "Military Racism," August 21, 1969; James Russell, "Racism Rising in U.S. Army," December 2, 1969; "Racial Bias in Vietnam," December 11, 1969; "Racism in the Army," January 28, 1970; "Bar Black Caucus in Navy Riot Quiz," December 6, 1972. In the *New Pittsburgh Courier*: "Military Racism," September 6, 1969; "Racial Conflict in Vietnam," December 27, 1969; "Racism in the Army," February 7, 1970; "Armed Services Probe States: 'Racial Tensions on Increase,'" February 7, 1970. In the *Baltimore Afro-American*: James Russell, "Racial Strife Up in Military," December 6, 1969; "Military's Racial Crisis," February 7, 1970; "Study Sees More Bloodshed from GI Racial Troubles," January 31, 1970. In *Jet* magazine: "Render's Probe of Military Put Spotlight on Racial Injustices," December 2, 1971.

40. Johnny Bowles, "Gathering Storm: Clashes among GIs, Missing Guns," *Baltimore Afro-American*, May 16, 1970.

41. "Watch out! Vietnam 'Dope Outrages' May Be Charged to Black Veterans," *St. Louis American*, August 12, 1971.

42. "Black Viet Vets Not Returning Home to Riot Says UPI," *Jet*, August 15, 1968, 22; Ponchitta Pierce and Peter Bailey, "The Returning Vet," *Ebony*, August 1968, 150.

43. "Bad Discharges 'Brand' Veterans," *Jet*, May 22, 1975, 24; also see John Grady's article, "The 'Less Than Honorable' Solution," *Nation*, February 19, 1973, 233–36. For more on the issue of bad discharges, see Starr, James, and Bonner, *Discarded Army*, 167–81.

44. The final version of the speech said, "And after years of effort, we negotiated, under the most difficult of circumstances, a settlement which made it possible for us to remove our military forces and bring home with pride our American prisoners." The final ignominious moments of the long-deferred, but inevitable, end of the dismal conflict were a difficult time for a U.S. president and commander in chief, and a proud man. For the full text of the president's message, see *Public Papers*

of the Presidents of the United States: Gerald R. Ford, 2:459–72. For Ford's editing of the speech, see Berman, *No Peace, No Honor,* 3.

45. "A Tragedy in Vietnam," *Atlanta Daily World,* May 2, 1975.

46. Vernon Jordan, "Humiliating: End of the Line in Vietnam," *Los Angeles Sentinel,* May 15, 1975.

47. Shirley Lens, "A Land Torn by Tragedy," *Chicago Defender,* May 1, 1975.

48. "King's Prophesy on Vietnam Now Haunts His Critics and Foes," *Jet,* May 22, 1975.

Bibliography

African American Newspapers and Newsmagazines

I used microfilm of the newspapers in the following libraries: Auburn Avenue Research Library on African American Culture and History, Atlanta (*Atlanta Daily World*); State Historical Society of Wisconsin Archives (*Baltimore Afro-American, Dallas Express, Dallas Post Tribune, Los Angeles Sentinel, Milwaukee Star, New York Amsterdam News, Norfolk Journal and Guide, Oakland Post, Philadelphia Tribune, San Francisco Post, San Francisco Sun Reporter, St. Louis American, St. Louis Argus*); University of Illinois at Chicago (*Chicago Daily Defender, Pittsburgh Courier*); and Michigan State University (*Michigan Chronicle*).

Both *Ebony* and *Jet* are available on microfilm at the University of Illinois at Chicago. Articles from other African American periodicals and journals are cited individually in the bibliography under "Books, Articles, Essays, and Other Documents."

Atlanta Daily World
Baltimore Afro-American
Chicago Daily Defender
Dallas Express
Dallas Post Tribune
Ebony
Jet
Los Angeles Sentinel
Michigan Chronicle
Milwaukee Star
New York Amsterdam News
Norfolk Journal and Guide

Oakland Post
Philadelphia Tribune
Pittsburgh Courier
San Francisco Post
The San Francisco Sun Reporter
St. Louis American
St. Louis Argus

Interviews by Author and Oral Histories

Alsop, Stewart. Interview by Paige E. Mulhollan. July 15, 1969. Oral History Project, Online Archive, Lyndon Baines Johnson Library and Museum, www.lbjlib.utexas.edu/johnson/archives.hom/biopage.asp.

Ball, George. Interviews by Paige E. Mulhollan. July 8 and 9, 1971. Oral History Project, Johnson Library.

Chancellor, John William. Interview by Dorothy Pierce McSweeny. April 25, 1969. Oral History Project, Johnson Library.

Clark, Libby. Former reporter, *Los Angeles Sentinel*. Interview by author. August 11, 2004.

Davis, Belva. Interviews by Shirley Biagi. July 27 and November 21, 1992. Women in Journalism, Washington Press Club Foundation Oral History Project, Special Collections, Michigan State University, East Lansing.

Evers, Charles. Interview by Joe B. Frantz. April 3, 1974. Oral History Project, Johnson Library.

———. Interview by Robert Smith. December 3, 1971. Center for Oral Histories and Cultural Heritage, University of Southern Mississippi, Hattiesburg, www.usm.edu/oralhistory/alphandx.html#.

Farmer, James. Interview by Harri Baker. October 1969. Oral History Project, Johnson Library.

———. Interview by Paige E. Mullholan. July 20, 1971. Oral History Project, Johnson Library.

Fleming, Thomas C. Founder and editor, *San Francisco Sun Reporter*. Interview by author. July 14, 2004.

Fowlkes, William. Columnist, *Atlanta Daily World*. Interview by author. July 7, 1998.

Gilliam, Dorothy. Interviews by Donita Moorhus. December 14, 1992; February 8 and March 17, 1993. Women in Journalism, Michigan State University, East Lansing.

Hamer, Fannie Lou. Interview by Neil McMillen. April 14, 1972. Center for Oral History and Cultural Heritage, University of Southern Mississippi, Hattiesburg.

Hebert, F. Edward. Interview by Dorothy Pierce McSweeny, July 15, 1969. Oral History Project, Johnson Library.

Humphrey, Hubert H. Interview by Michael L. Gillette. June 21, 1977. Oral History Project, Johnson Library.

Lancaster, Johnson. Editor, *St. Louis Argus*. Interview by author. August 9, 2004.

Martin, Louis. Interview by Michael L. Gillette. June 12, 1986. Oral History Project, Johnson Library.

———. Interview by David G. McComb. May 14, 1969. Oral History Project, Johnson Library.

———. Interview by Robert Wright. March 25 and 27, 1970. The Civil Rights Documentation Project, Moorland-Spingarn Research Center, Howard University, Washington, DC.

McRae, Frank. Reporter, *Los Angeles Sentinel*. Interview by author. September 12, 2002.

Mitchell, Clarence. Interview by Thomas H. Baker. April 30, 1969. Oral History Project, Johnson Library.

Murphy, Frances L. Interviews by Fern Ingersoll. October 25, 1991; April 25, May 23, and August 1, 1992. Women in Journalism, Michigan State University, East Lansing.

Newson, Moses. Interview by Henry G. La Brie III. June 29, 1971. Black Journalists Oral History Project, Columbia University, New York.

Ohman, Eleanor. Former cartoonist and columnist, *San Francisco Sun-Reporter*. Interview by author. July 13 and 27, 2004.

Payne, Ethel. Interviews by Kathleen Currie. August–November 1987. Women in Journalism, Michigan State University, East Lansing.

Randolph, A. Philip. Interview by Thomas H. Baker. October 29, 1969. Oral History Project, Johnson Library.

Rusk, Dean. Interview by Paige E. Mulhollan. July 28, 1969. Oral History Project, Johnson Library.

Saunders, Warner. News anchor, at the NBC-TV affiliate WMAQ in Chicago, and former columnist, *Chicago Daily Defender*. Interview by author. August 6, 2004.

Scott, Alexis. Publisher, *Atlanta Daily World*. Interview by author. July 7, 1998.

Sengstacke, John. Interview by Henry G. La Brie III. June 22 and 24, 1972. Black Journalists Oral History Project, Columbia University, New York.

Smith, John B. Jr., Editor, *Atlanta Inquirer*. Interview by author. August 6, 2004.

Wilkins, Roy. Interview by Thomas H. Baker. April 1, 1969. Oral History Project, Johnson Library.

Young, Andrew Jr. Interview by Thomas H. Baker. June 18, 1970. Oral History Project, Johnson Library.

Young, Whitney Jr. Interview by Thomas H. Baker. June 18, 1969. Oral History Project, Johnson Library.

Manuscript Collections

Abbott-Sengstacke Family Papers. Vivian G. Harsh Research Collection of Afro-American History and Literature. Carter G. Woodson Regional Library, a branch of the Chicago Public Library.

Ford, Gerald R. Digitized Memoranda of Presidential Conversations. Gerald R. Ford Presidential Library and Museum, Ann Arbor, Michigan, www.fordlibrarymuseum.gov/library/dmemcons.asp.

Harry S. Truman Presidential Library and Museum. "Desegregaton of the Armed Forces: Chronology," n.d., www.trumanlibrary.org/whistlestop/study_collections/desegregation/large/index.php?action=.

Johnson, Lyndon Baines. Presidential Papers. Lyndon Baines Johnson Presidential Library and Museum, Austin, Texas.

Mosby, Sisi Donald, Papers. Vivian G. Harsh Research Collection of Afro-American History and Literature. Carter G. Woodson Regional Library, a branch of the Chicago Public Library.

Nixon, Richard M. Virtual Library. Richard Nixon Presidential Library and Museum, Yorba Linda, California, www.nixonlibrary.gov/virtuallibrary/index.php.

Payne, Ethel L., Papers. Library of Congress. Washington, DC.

———. Manuscript Department, Moorland-Spingarn Research Center, Howard University. Washington, DC.

Vietnam Center and Archive. Texas Tech University, Lubbock. www.vietnam.ttu.edu/.

Books, Articles, Essays, and Other Materials

"A Fiery Humphrey Denounces Society for Lag on Civil Rights." *New York Times*, June 2, 1966, 21.

"A Symptom of Anger." *Newsweek*, August 22, 1966, 59, 60.

Abernathy, Ralph. *And the Walls Came Tumbling Down: An Autobiography*. New York: HarperPerennial, 1990.

———. "Some International Dimensions of the Peace Movement." *Freedomways* 11, no. 3 (1971): 237–40.

"Agreement on Ending the War and Restoring Peace in Vietnam." In *United States Treaties and Other International Agreements, Vol. 24, Part 1: 1973*. Washington, DC: U.S. Government Printing Office, 1974.

Albert, Peter J., and Ronald Hoffman, eds. *We Shall Overcome: Martin Luther King, Jr., and the Black Freedom Struggle.* New York: Da Capo, 1993.

"Ali, Muhammad—The Measure of a Man." *Freedomways* 7 (Spring 1967): 101, 102.

Ali, Muhammad, with Richard Durham. *The Greatest: My Own Story.* New York: Random House, 1975.

Ambrose, Stephen E.. *Nixon: Ruin and Recovery, 1973–1990.* New York: Simon & Schuster, 1991.

———. *Nixon: The Triumph of a Politician, 1962–1972.* New York: Simon & Schuster, 1989.

Anderson, David L. "Bill Henry Terry, Jr., Killed in Action: An African American's Journey from Alabama to Vietnam and Back." In *The Human Tradition in the Vietnam Era*, edited by David L. Anderson, 135–51. Wilmington, DE: Scholarly Resources, I2000.

———. *The Columbia Guide to the Vietnam War.* New York: Columbia University Press, 2002.

"An Embattled Conference." *New York Times*, June 2, 1966, 42.

Ansbro, John J. *Martin Luther King, Jr.: Nonviolent Strategies and Tactics for Social Change.* New York: Columbia University Press, 2002.

Appy, Christian G. *Working-Class War: American Combat Soldiers and Vietnam.* Chapel Hill: University of North Carolina Press, 1993.

Aptheker, Herbert, ed. *A Documentary History of the Negro People in the United States.* New York: Citadel, 1992.

Arnold, James R. *The First Domino: Eisenhower, the Military, and America's Intervention in Vietnam.* New York: William Morrow, 1991.

Astor, Gerald. *The Right to Fight: A History of African Americans in the Military.* Novato, CA: Presidio, 1998.

"A *Time*-Louis Harris Poll: The Black Mood: More Militant, More Hopeful, More Determined." *Time*, April 6, 1970, 28, 29.

Barbeau, Arthur E., and Florette Henri. *The Unknown Soldiers: Black American Troops in World War I.* Philadelphia: Temple University Press, 1974.

Barber, James David. "Man, Mood, and the Presidency." In Tugwell and Cronin, *Presidency Reappraised*, 205–14.

Barbour, Floyd B., ed. *The Black Power Revolt: A Collection of Essays.* Boston: Collier, 1969.

Barnes, Peter. "Mr. Brooke of Massachusetts." *New Leader* 50, no. 3 (1967): 13, 14.

Barone, Michael. *Our Country: The Shaping of America from Roosevelt to Reagan.* New York: Free Press, 1990.

Barringer, Mark. "Antiwar Movement, United States." In Tucker, *Encyclopedia of the Vietnam War*, 18–19.

Baskir, Lawrence M., and William A. Strauss. *Chance and Circumstance: The Draft, the War, and the Vietnam Generation.* New York: Vintage, 1978.

Bates, Milton J., Lawrence Lichty, Paul Miles, and Ronald H. Spector, eds. *Reporting Vietnam: American Journalism, 1959–1975.* New York: Library of America, 2000.

Beckman, Aldo. "Civil Disobedience Hurts Rights Cause, Negro Leader Says." *New York Times,* June 1, 1966, sec. 1A, 12.

Bennett, Lerone Jr. *Before the Mayflower: A History of Black America.* 6th ed. New York: Penguin, 1987.

———. *Great Moments in Black History: Wade in the Water.* Chicago: Johnson, 1979.

———. *Pioneers in Protest.* Chicago: Johnson, 1968.

———. *The Shaping of Black America.* Chicago: Johnson, 1975.

———. *What Manner of Man: A Biography of Martin Luther King, Jr.* Chicago: Johnson, 1976.

Berg, Rick, and John Carlos Rowe. "The Vietnam War and American Memory." In *The Vietnam War and American Culture,* edited by Carlos Rowe and Rick Berg, 1–17. New York: Columbia University Press, 1991.

Berman, Larry. *Lyndon Johnson's War: The Road to Stalemate in Vietnam.* New York: W. W. Norton, 1989.

———. *No Peace, No Honor: Nixon, Kissinger, and Betrayal in Vietnam.* New York: Free Press, 2001.

———. "Waiting for Smoking Guns: Presidential Decision-making and the Vietnam War, 1965–67." In *Vietnam as History: Ten Years after the Paris Peace Accords,* edited by Peter Braestrup, 15–21. Washington, DC: University Press of America, 1984.

Beschloss, Michael, ed. *Reaching for Glory: Lyndon Johnson's Secret White House Tapes, 1964–1965.* New York: Simon & Schuster, 2001.

———. *Taking Charge: The Johnson White House Tapes, 1963–1964.* New York: Simon & Schuster, 1997.

Binkin, Martin, and Mark J. Eitelberg. *Blacks and the Military.* Washington, DC: Brookings Institution, 1982.

"Black America 1970: A *Time* Special Issue." *Time,* April 6, 1970, 1.

Black, Conrad. *Richard M. Nixon: A Life in Full.* New York: PublicAffairs, 2007.

"Black Power: Road to Disaster?" *Newsweek,* August 22, 1966, 32, 34, 36.

Boettcher, Thomas D. *Vietnam: The Valor and the Sorrow: From the Home Front to the Front Lines in Words and Pictures.* Boston: Little, Brown, 1985.

Booker, Simeon. *Black Man's America.* Englewood Cliffs, NJ: Prentice-Hall, 1964.

Borstelmann, Thomas. *The Cold War and the Color Line: American Race Relations in the Global Arena.* Cambridge, MA: Harvard University Press, 2001.

Braestrup, Peter. *Big Story: How the American Press and Television Reported and Interpreted the Crises of Tet 1968 in Vietnam and Washington*, Abridged ed. New Haven, CT: Yale University Press, 1983.

Branch, Taylor. *At Canaan's Edge: America in the King Years, 1965–68*. New York: Simon & Schuster, 2006.

———. *Pillar of Fire: America in the King Years, 1963–1965*. New York: Simon & Schuster, 1998.

Brinkley, Douglas. "The Man Who Kept King's Secrets." *Vanity Fair*, April 2006, 156–71.

Brodie, Fawn M. *Richard Nixon: The Shaping of His Character*. New York: W. W. Norton, 1981.

Brooke, Edward W. "Address to the 1967 National Convention of the NAACP." In Williams and Williams, *Negro Speaks*, 113–22.

———. "The United States and Vietnam." *World Affairs* 130, no. 1 (1967): 5–12.

Brooks, Maxwell R. *The Negro Press Re-Examined: Political Content of Leading Negro Newspapers*. Boston: Christopher, 1959.

Brown, H. Rap. "'How Many White Folks You Kill Today?'" In Kai Wright, *African-American Archive*, 639–41.

Brown, Joshua. "Cartooning." In *The Princeton Encyclopedia of American Political History*, edited by Michael Kazin, with Rebecca Edwards and Adam Rothman, 115–19. Princeton, NJ: Princeton University Press, 2010.

Brown, Warren Henry. *The Social Impact of the Black Press*. New York: Hearthstone, 1994.

Browne, Robert S. "The Freedom Movement and the War in Vietnam." In *Vietnam and Black America: An Anthology of Protest and Resistance*, edited by Clyde Taylor, 67–76. New York: Anchor, 1973.

Buchanan, A. Russell. *Black Americans in World War II*. Santa Barbara, CA: Clio, 1977.

Buni, Andrew. *Robert L. Vann of the* Pittsburgh Courier: *Politics and Black Journalism*. Pittsburgh: University of Pittsburgh Press, 1974.

Burns, James MacGregor. *Vietnam and the Transformation of American Life*. Malden, MA: Blackwell, 1999.

Burns, Stewart. *To the Mountaintop: Martin Luther King Jr.'s Sacred Mission to Save America: 1955–1968*. New York: HarperCollins, 2004.

Bush, Rod. "The Civil Rights Movement and the Continuing Struggle for the Redemption of America." *Social Justice* 30, no. 1 (2003): 1–17, www.the-freelibrary.com/The+Civil+Rights+Movement+and+the+continuing+struggle+for+the…-a0108197665.

Caputo, Philip. *Thirteen Seconds: A Look Back at the Kent State Shootings*. New York: Chamberlain Bros., 2005.

Carbado, Devon W., and Donald Weise. *Time on Two Crosses: The Collected Writings of Bayard Rustin.* San Francisco: Cleis, 2003.

Carmichael, Stokely. "Black Power." In Kai Wright, *African-American Archive,* 624–27.

———. "Power and Racism." In Barbour, *Black Power Revolt,* 63–76.

Carmichael, Stokely, with Ekwueme Michael Thelwel. *Ready for the Revolution: The Life and Struggles of Stokely Carmichael (Kwame Ture).* New York: Scribner's, 2003.

Caro, Robert. A. *Master of the Senate.* Vol. 3, *The Years of Lyndon Johnson.* New York: Alfred A. Knopf, 2002.

———. *Means of Ascent.* Vol. 2, *The Years of Lyndon Johnson.* New York: Alfred A. Knopf, 1990.

Carper, Jean. *Bitter Greetings: The Scandal of the Military Draft.* New York: Grossman, 1967.

Carroll, Peter N. *It Seemed Like Nothing Happened: America in the 1970s.* New Brunswick, NJ: Rutgers University Press, 1990.

Carroll, Peter N., and David W. Noble. *The Free and the Unfree: A New History of the United States.* 2d ed. New York: Penguin, 1988.

Carson, Clayborne, ed. *Civil Rights Chronicle: The African-American Struggle for Freedom.* Lincolnwood, IL: Legacy, 2003.

Carson, Clayborne et al., eds. *Eyes on the Prize: Civil Rights Reader, Documents, Speeches, and Firsthand Accounts from the Black Freedom Struggle.* New York: Penguin, 1991.

Chafe, William H. "The African-American Struggle as an Unfinished Revolution." In Griffith, *Major Problems in American History,* 384–98.

———. "The Social Politics of Race and Gender." In Griffith, *Major Problems in American History,* 31–48.

Cheng, Charles W. "The Cold War: Its Impact on the Black Liberation Struggle within the United States." *Freedomways* 13 (1973): 184–99.

"The Civil Rights Act of 1964." In *The New South,* edited by Paul D. Escott and David R. Goldfield. Vol. 2, *Major Problems in the History of the American South,* 561–63. Lexington, MA: D.C. Heath, 1990.

Colaiaco, James A. *Martin Luther King, Jr.: Apostle of Militant Nonviolence.* New York: St. Martin's, 1988.

Collier, Peter, and David Horowitz. *Destructive Generation: Second Thoughts about the Sixties.* New York: Summit, 1989.

Cone, James H. "Martin Luther King, Jr., and the Third World." In Albert and Hoffman, *We Shall Overcome,* 197–221.

"Congress and Vietnam." *New York Times,* August 8, 1964, 18.

Cortright, David. *Soldiers in Revolt: The American Military Today.* New York: Anchor Doubleday, 1975.

"Crisis of Color '66." *Newsweek*, August 22, 1966, 20–59.

Dalfiume, Richard M. *Desegregation of the U. S. Armed Forces: Fighting on Two Fronts, 1939–1953*. Columbia: University of Missouri Press, 1969.

Dallek, Robert. *An Unfinished Life: John F. Kennedy, 1917–1963*. Boston: Little, Brown, 2003.

———. *Flawed Giant: Lyndon Johnson and His Times, 1961–1973*. New York: Oxford University Press, 1998.

———. *Lyndon B. Johnson: Portrait of a President*. Oxford: Oxford University Press, 2004.

Danky, James P., ed. *African-American Newspapers and Periodicals: A National Bibliography*. Cambridge, MA: Harvard University Press, 1998.

Dann, Martin E., ed. *The Black Press, 1827–1890: The Quest for National Identity*. New York: Capricorn, 1972.

Davies, Philip. "U.S. Presidential Election Campaigns in the Vietnam Era." In Dumbrell, *Vietnam and the Antiwar Movement*, 124–36.

DeBenedetti, Charles. *An American Ordeal: The Antiwar Movement of the Vietnam Era*. Syracuse, NY: Syracuse University Press, 1990.

Dellums, Ronald V. "Institutional Racism in the Military." *Congressional Record*. 92d Cong., 2d sess., March 2, 1972, pt. 6:118.

"Democracy in the Foxhole." *Time*, May 26, 1967, 15–19.

"Desegregation Yes, Integration No." *Time*, April 6, 1970, 11, 12.

Domke, David. "The Black Press in the 'Nadir' of African Americans." *Journalism History* 20, no. 3–4 (1994): 131–38.

Dougan, Clark, and Samuel Lipsman. *A Nation Divided*. Boston: Boston Publishing, 1984.

Dougan, Clark, and Stephen Weiss. *The American Experience in Vietnam*. New York: W. W. Norton, 1988.

"The Draft: The Unjust vs. the Unwilling." *Newsweek*, April 11, 1966, 30–34.

Drew, Elizabeth. *Washington Journal: The Events of 1973–1974*. New York: Random House, 1975.

"Dr. King's Error." *New York Times*, April 7, 1967, 36.

"Dr. King to Weigh Civil Disobedience If War Intensifies." *New York Times*, April 2, 1967, 1, 76.

Dudziak, Mary L. *Cold War Civil Rights: Race and the Image of American Democracy*. Princeton, NJ: Princeton University Press, 2000.

Dugger, Ronnie. *The Politician: The Life and Times of Lyndon Johnson: The Drive for Power from the Frontier to Master of the Senate*. Old Saybrook, CT: Konecky & Konecky, 1982.

Dumbrell, John, ed. *Vietnam and the Antiwar Movement: An International Perspective*. Aldershot, UK: Avebury, 1989.

Dunn, Joe P. "Draft." In Tucker, *Encyclopedia of the Vietnam War*, 107–8.

Dunnigan, James F., and Albert A. Nofi. *Dirty Little Secrets of the Vietnam War.* New York: Thomas Dunne Books, 1999.

Dyson, Michael Eric. *I May Not Get There with You: The True Martin Luther King, Jr.* New York: Simon & Schuster, 2000.

Ellison, Ralph. "The Myth of the Flawed White Southerner." In *To Heal and to Build: The Programs of President Lyndon B. Johnson,* edited by James MacGregor Burns, 207–16. New York: McGraw-Hill, 1968.

Emery, Edwin, and Michael Emery. *The Press and America: An Interpretive History of the Mass Media.* 5th ed. Englewood Cliffs, NJ: Prentice-Hall, 1984.

Evans, Sara. *Personal Politics: The Roots of Women's Liberation in the Civil Rights Movement and the New Left.* New York: Vintage, 1980.

Evans-Pfeifer, Kelly. "American Public Opinion." In Kutler, *Encyclopedia of the Vietnam War,* 461–62.

Ewers, Justin. "Making History." *U.S. News & World Report,* March 22–29, 2004, 76–80.

Fairclough, Adam. "Martin Luther King, Jr., and the War in Vietnam." *Phylon* 45, no. 1 (1984): 19–39.

———. "The War in Vietnam and the Decline of the Civil Rights Movement." In Dumbrell, *Vietnam and the Antiwar Movement,* 113–23.

Farber, David. *Chicago '68.* Chicago: University of Chicago Press, 1988.

Farmer, James. "Annual Report to the National Core Convention." In Williams and Williams, *Negro Speaks,* 169–77.

———. *Lay Bare the Heart: An Autobiography of the Civil Rights Movement.* New York: Penguin, 1985.

Farrar, Hayward. *The Baltimore Afro-American, 1892–1950.* Westport, CT: Greenwood, 1998.

"F.B.I. Finds 3 Bodies Believed to Be Rights Workers." *New York Times,* August 5, 1964, 1.

Finkle, Lee. *Forum for Protest: The Black Press during World War II.* Rutherford, NJ: Fairleigh Dickinson University Press, 1975.

Fishel, Leslie H., and Benjamin Quarles. *The Black American: A Documented History.* Rev. ed. of *The Negro American.* New York: William Morrow. 1970.

FitzGerald, Frances. *Fire in the Lake: The Vietnamese and the Americans in Vietnam.* New York: Vintage, 1972.

Fleming, G. James. "The Afro-American—One of Many." In La Brie, *Perspectives of the Black Press,* 75–77.

Foner, Jack D. *Blacks and the Military in American History.* New York: Praeger, 1974.

Foner, Philip S. *The Civil War, 1851–1865.* Vol. 3, *The Life and Writings of Frederick Douglass.* New York: International, 1952.

Forman, James. "The Making of Black Revolutionaries." In *Brotherman: The Odyssey of Black Men in America,* edited by Herb Boyd and Robert L. Allen, 748–55. New York: One World, 1995.

———. "SNCC-SCLC Relations." In Carson et al., *Eyes on the Prize,* 217–20.

Frady, Marshall. *Martin Luther King, Jr.* New York: Penguin, 2002.

Franklin, John Hope. *From Slavery to Freedom: A History of Negro Americans.* 3d ed. New York: Alfred A. Knopf, 1967.

Franklin, John Hope, and August Meier, eds. *Black Leaders of the Twentieth Century.* Urbana: University of Illinois Press, 1982.

Franklin, John Hope, and Alfred A. Moss Jr. *From Slavery to Freedom: A History of African- Americans.* 8th ed. New York: Alfred A. Knopf, 2002.

Frey-Wouters, Ellen, and Robert S. Laufer. *Legacy of a War: The American Soldier inVietnam.* Armonk, NY: M. E. Sharpe, 1986.

Frost, Peter K. "United States: Involvement in Vietnam, 1973–1975," in Tucker, *Encyclopedia of the Vietnam War,* 428–29.

Gaines, Kevin K. *Uplifting the Race: Black Leadership, Politics, and Culture in the Twentieth Century.* Chapel Hill: University of North Carolina Press, 1996.

Gallup, George H. *The Gallup Poll: Public Opinion 1935–1971.* New York: Random House, 1972.

———. *The Gallup Poll: Public Opinion 1972–1977.* Wilmington, DE: Scholarly Resources, 1978.

Gardner, Lloyd C. *Pay Any Price: Lyndon Johnson and the Wars for Vietnam.* Chicago: Ivan R. Dee, 1997.

Garfinkle, Adam. *Telltale Hearts: The Origins and Impact of the Vietnam Antiwar Movement.* New York: St. Martin's, 1995.

Garland, Phyl. "The Black Press: Down but Not Out." *Columbia Journalism Review* 21 (September–October 1982): 43–50.

Garrow, David J. *Bearing the Cross: Martin Luther King, Jr., and the Southern Christian Leadership Conference.* New York: Perennial Classics, 2004.

———. "Martin Luther King, Jr., and the Spirit of Leadership." In Albert and Hoffman, *We Shall Overcome,* 11–34.

Garthoff, Raymond L. *Détente and Confrontation: American-Soviet Relations from Nixon to Reagon.* Rev. ed. Washington, DC: Brookings Institution, 1994.

Gerstle, Gary. *American Crucible: Race and Nation in the Twentieth Century.* Princeton, NJ: Princeton University Press, 2002.

Gilmore, Glenda Elizabeth. *Defying Dixie: The Radical Roots of Civil Rights, 1919–1950*. New York: W. W. Norton, 2008.

Goff, Stanley, and Robert Sanders, with Clark Smith. *Brothers: Black Soldiers in the Nam*. New York: Berkley, 1985.

Goldman, Eric F. *The Tragedy of Lyndon Johnson*. New York: Alfred A. Knopf, 1974.

Good, Paul. "Odyssey of a Man—and a Movement." In Meier and Rudwick, *Black Protest in the Sixties*, 252–66.

Goodman, Allan E. "What Went Wrong." In McMahon, *Major Problems in the History of the Vietnam War*, 582–94.

Goodwin, Richard N. *Remembering America: A Voice from the Sixties*. New York: Harper & Row, 1988.

Gottlieb, Sherry Gershon. *Hell No, We Won't Go: Resisting the Draft during the Vietnam War*. New York: Viking, 1991.

Grady, John. "The 'Less Than Honorable' Solution." *Nation*, February 19, 1973, 233–36.

Graham, Herman III. *The Brothers' Vietnam War: Black Power, Manhood, and the Military Experience*. Gainesville: University Press of Florida, 2003.

Graham, Lawrence Otis. *Our Kind of People: Inside America's Black Upper Class*. New York: HarperCollins, 1999.

Grant, Joanne, ed. *Black Protest: 350 Years of History, Documents, and Analyses*. New York: Fawcett Columbine, 1968.

"The Great Society—in Uniform." *Newsweek*, August 22, 1966, 46, 48, 57.

Greenberg, Stanley B. *Middle Class Dreams: The Politics and Power of the New American Majority*. New York: Times Books, 1995.

Griffith, Robert, ed. *Major Problems in American History since 1945*. Lexington, MA: D. C. Heath, 1992.

Guilmarten, John F. Jr., and Kelly Evans-Pfeifer. "Casualties." In Kutler, *Encyclopedia of the Vietnam War*, 103–5.

Halberstam, David. *The Best and the Brightest*. 25th anniv. ed. New York: Ballantine, 1992.

———. *The Children*. New York: Random House, 1998.

Haldeman, H. R. *The Haldeman Diaries: Inside the Nixon White House*. New York: G. P. Putnam's Sons, 1994.

Haldeman, H. R., with Joseph DiMona. *The Ends of Power*. New York: Times Books, 1978.

Hallin, Daniel C. *The "Uncensored War": The Media and Vietnam*. Berkeley: University of California Press, 1986.

Hamby, Alonzo. *Liberalism and Its Challengers: From F.D.R. to Bush*. 2d ed. New York: Oxford University Press, 1992.

Hammer, Richard. "One Morning in the War." In Marcus and Burner, *America since 1945*, 223–36.

Hammond, William M. *Reporting Vietnam: Media and Military at War.* Lawrence: University Press of Kansas, 1998.

Hampton, Henry, and Steve Fayer, with Sarah Flynn. *Voices of Freedom: An Oral History of the Civil Rights Movement from the 1950s through the 1980s.* New York: Bantam, 1991.

Harding, Vincent. "Black Power and the American Christ." In Barbour, *Black Power Revolt*, 94–105.

———. "Commentary." In Albert and Hoffman, *We Shall Overcome*, 159–66.

———. "King as Disturber of the Peace." In Griffith, *Major Problems in American History*, 266–71.

———. *The Other American Revolution.* Vol. 4, *Afro-American Culture and Society.* Los Angeles: Center for Afro-American Studies, University of California, 1980.

———. *There Is a River: The Black Struggle for Freedom in America.* New York: Vintage, 1983.

Harrington, Oliver W. *Why I Left America and Other Essays.* Jackson: University Press of Mississippi, 1993.

Harris, Louis. *The Anguish of Change.* New York: W. W. Norton, 1973.

Haskew, Michael, and Douglas Brinkley, eds. *The World War II Desk Reference.* New York: HarperCollins, 2004.

Hayden, Tom. *Reunion: A Memoir.* New York: Collier, 1988.

Herbers, John. "CORE Seeks New Agenda for Right Talks Today." *New York Times*, June 1, 1966, 1, 33.

———. "Rights Conference Averts Showdown on War Policy." *New York Times*, June 3, 1966, 1, 21.

———. "Rights Conference to Vote on Criticism of U.S. Policy." *New York Times*, June 2, 1966, 1, 21.

Herring, George C. *America's Longest War: The United States and Vietnam, 1950–1975.* New York: John Wiley, 1979.

Hodgson, Godfrey. *America in Our Time.* New York: Doubleday, 1976.

Hoff, Joan. *Nixon Reconsidered.* New York: Basic, 1994.

Hogan, Lawrence D. *A Black National News Service: The Associated Negro Press and Claude Barnett, 1919–1945.* Rutherford, NJ: Fairleigh Dickinson University Press, 1984.

Hoopes, Townsend. "Lyndon Johnson and Vietnam: 1968." In Marcus and Burner, *America since 1945*, 210–22.

Horne, Gerald. *Black and Red: W. E. B. Du Bois and the Afro-American Response to the Cold War, 1944–1963.* Albany: State University of New York Press, 1986.

Houser, George M. "Freedom's Struggle Crosses Oceans and Mountains: Martin Luther King, Jr., and the Liberation Struggles in Africa and America." In Albert and Hoffman, *We Shall Overcome*, 169–96.

"How Negro Americans Perform in Vietnam." *U.S. News & World Report*, April 15, 1966, 60–63.

Huggins, Nathan I. "Commentary." In Albert and Hoffman, *We Shall Overcome*, 84–92.

Hynds, Ernest C. *American Newspapers in the 1970s*. New York: Hastings House, 1975.

———. *American Newspapers in the 1980s*. New York: Hastings House, 1980.

Inge, M. Thomas, ed. *Dark Laughter: The Satiric Art of Oliver W. Harrington: from the Walter O. Evans Collection of African-American Art*. Jackson: University of Mississippi.

Inglis, Fred. *The Cruel Peace: Everyday Life and the Cold War*. New York: Basic, 1991.

Isaacs, Arnold R. *Vietnam Shadows: The War, Its Ghosts, and Its Legacy*. Baltimore: Johns Hopkins University Press, 1997.

"Is Vietnam to Become a 'Civil Rights' Issue?" *U.S. News & World Report*, July 19, 1965, 12.

Johnson, Lyndon Baines. *The Vantage Point: Perspectives of the Presidency, 1963–1969*. New York: Holt, Rinehart and Winston, 1971.

Johnson, Thomas A. "Negro Veteran Is Confused and Bitter." *New York Times*, July 29, 1968, 1, 14.

———. "The U.S. Negro in Vietnam." *New York Times*, April 29, 1968, 1, 16.

———. "The U.S. Negro in Vietnam: Black Servicemen and the War: 1968." In Bates et al., *Reporting Vietnam*, 615–27.

Jordan, William G. *Black Newspapers and America's War for Democracy, 1914–1920*. Chapel Hill: University of North Carolina Press, 2001.

Joseph, Peniel E. *Waiting 'til the Midnight Hour: A Narrative History of Black Power in America*. New York: Henry Holt, 2006.

Kaiser, Charles. *1968 in America: Music, Politics, Chaos, Counterculture, and the Shaping of a Generation*. New York: Weidenfeld & Nicolson, 1988.

Kaiser, David. *American Tragedy: Kennedy, Johnson, and the Origins of the Vietnam War*. Cambridge, MA: Belknap, 2000.

———. "July 28, 1965: End of an Era, Start of a War." In *Days of Destiny: Crossroads in American History*, edited by James M. McPherson, Alan Brinkley, and David Rubel, 387–401. New York: Dorliing Kindersley, 2001.

Karnow, Stanley. *Vietnam: A History*. New York: Viking, 1983.

Katz, William Loren. "The Afro-American's Response to U.S. Imperialism." *Freedomways* 11 (Summer 1971): 284–91.

Kearns, Doris. *Lyndon Johnson and the American Dream*. New York: Harper & Row, 1976.

Kerlin, Robert T. *The Voice of the Negro, 1919*. New York: Arno, 1968.

Killian, Lewis M. *The Impossible Revolution: Black Power and the American Dream*. New York: Random House, 1968.

Kimball, Jeffrey. *The Vietnam War Files: Uncovering the Secret History of Nixon-Era Strategy*. Lawrence: University of Kansas Press, 2004.

"King and Vietnam, 1965–1967: 'His Philosophy Made It Impossible Not to Take a Stand.'" In Hampton and Fayer, *Voices of Freedom*, 335–48.

King, Martin Luther Jr. *A Testament of Hope: The Essential Writings and Speeches of Martin Luther King, Jr.*, edited by James Melvin Washington. San Francisco: HarperSanFrancisco, 1986.

———. *The Autobiography of Martin Luther King, Jr.*, edited by Clayborne Carson. New York: Warner, 1998.

———. "Beyond Vietnam." In Boyd and Allen, *Brotherman*, 392–94.

———. "'I Have a Dream,' 1963." In Griffith, *Major Problems in American History*, 361–64.

———. "Martin Luther King, Jr., Declares His Opposition to the War, 1967." In McMahon, *Major Problems in the History of the Vietnam War*, 470–75.

———. "Where Do We Go from Here?" In *A Testament of Hope*, 245–52.

"King, Martin Luther, Jr." In *Africana: The Encyclopedia of the African and African American Experience: The Concise Desk Reference*, edited by Kwame Anthony Appiah and Henry Louis Gates Jr., 518–24. Philadelphia: Running Press, 2003.

King, Martin Luther Jr. et al. *Martin Luther King, Jr., John C. Bennett, Dr. Henry Steele Commager, Rabbi Abraham Heschel Speak on the War in Vietnam*. New York: Clergy and Laymen Concerned About Vietnam, 1967.

King, Martin Luther Jr., with James M. Washington, ed. *I Have a Dream: Writings and Speeches That Changed the World*. San Francisco: HarperSanFrancisco, 1986.

Kissinger, Henry. *Diplomacy*. New York: Simon & Schuster, 1994.

———. *White House Years*. Boston: Little, Brown, 1979.

———. *Years of Renewal*. Boston: Little, Brown, 1999.

———. *Years of Upheaval*. Boston: Little, Brown, 1982.

Kohn, George C. *Dictionary of Historic Documents*. New York: Facts on File, 1991.

Kolko, Gabriel. *Anatomy of a War: Vietnam, the United States, and the Modern Historical Experience*. New York: New Press, 1994.

Koontz, E. C. "Pittsburgh Courier Leads Fight for American Negro Equality." *Quill* 54, no. 10 (October 1966): 44.

Kotz, Nick. *Judgment Days: Lyndon Baines Johnson, Martin Luther King Jr., and the Laws That Changed America.* New York: Houghton Mifflin, 2005.

Kutler, Stanley I., ed. *Encyclopedia of the Vietnam War.* New York: Charles Scribner's Sons, 1996.

La Brie, Henry G. III. *A Survey of Black Newspapers in America.* Kennebunkport, ME: Mercer House, 1979.

———. *The Black Newspaper in America: A Guide.* Iowa City: Institute for Communication Studies, School of Journalism, University of Iowa, 1970.

———. *Perspectives of the Black Press: 1974.* Kennebunkport, ME: Mercer House, 1974.

———. "Text of Testimony—'The Mass Media and the Black Community,' Ad Hoc Congressional hearing." In La Brie, *Perspectives of the Black Press,* 87–101.

Laird, Melvin R. *Final Report to the Congress of Secretary of Defense Melvin R. Laird.* Washington, DC: U.S. Department of Defense, 1973.

Land, Adam. "African-Americans." In Kutler, *Encyclopedia of the Vietnam War,* 3–5.

Lane, Mark, and Dick Gregory. *Code Name "Zorro": The Murder of Martin Luther King, Jr.* East Rutherford, NJ: Prentice Hall, 1977.

Langguth, A. J. *Our Vietnam: The War, 1954–1975.* New York: Simon & Schuster, 2000.

Lanning, Michael Lee. *The African-American Soldier: From Crispus Attucks to Colin Powell.* Secaucus, NJ: Carol, 1997.

Laurence, John. *The Cat from Hue: A Vietnam War Story.* New York: PublicAffairs, 2002.

Lentz, Richard. *Symbols, the News Magazines, and Martin Luther King.* Baton Rouge: Louisiana State University Press, 1990.

Lewis, David Levering. *King: A Biography.* 2d ed. Urbana: University of Illinois Press, 1978.

———. "Martin Luther King, Jr., and the Promise of Nonviolent Populism." In Franklin and Meier, *Black Leaders of the Twentieth Century,* 277–303.

———. *W. E. B. Du Bois: The Fight for Equality and the American Century, 1919–1963.* New York: Henry Holt, 2000.

Lewis, John, with Michael D'Orso. *Walking with the Wind: A Memoir of the Movement.* New York: Simon & Schuster, 1998.

Lewy, Guenter. *America in Vietnam.* New York: Oxford University Press, 1978.

Lind, Michael. *Vietnam, the Necessary War: A Reinterpretation of America's Most Disastrous Military Conflict.* New York: Simon & Schuster, 1999.

Ling, Peter. "We Shall Overcome: Peter Ling Analyses Martin Luther King's Involvement with Nonviolent Protest in the USA." *History Review* (2003): 1–5.

Lischer, Richard. *The Preacher King: Martin Luther King, Jr. and the Word That Moved America.* New York: Oxford University Press, 1955.

Lyle, Jack. *The Black American and the Press.* Los Angeles: Ward Ritchie, 1968.

Lyndon B. Johnson: The Kennedy Assassination and the Transfer of Power, Vol. 1: November 1963–January 1964, edited by Max Holland. New York: W. W. Norton, 2005.

Lyndon B. Johnson: The Kennedy Assassination and the Transfer of Power, Vol. 2: November 1963–January 1964, edited by Robert David Johnson and David Shreve. New York: W. W. Norton, 2005.

Lyndon B. Johnson: The Kennedy Assassination and the Transfer of Power, Vol. 3: November 1963–January 1964, edited by Kent B. Germany and Robert David Johnson. New York: W. W. Norton, 2005.

Lyndon B. Johnson: Toward the Great Society, Vol. 4: February 1, 1964–March 8, 1964, edited by Robert David Johnson and Kent B. Germany. New York: W. W. Norton, 2007.

Lyndon B. Johnson: Toward the Great Society, Vol. 5: March 9, 1964–April 13, 1964, edited by David Shreve and Robert David Johnson. New York: W. W. Norton, 2007.

Lyndon B. Johnson: Toward the Great Society, Vol. 6: April 14, 1964–May 31, 1964, edited by Guian A. McKee. New York: W. W. Norton, 2007.

"Lyndon, the Liberator." *Crisis: A Record of the Darker Races,* April 1973, 113.

Lyttle, Bradford. *The Chicago Anti-Vietnam War Movement.* Chicago: Midwest Pacifist Center, 1988.

MacPherson, Myra. *Long Time Passing: Vietnam and the Haunted Generation.* New York: Doubleday, 1984.

Maguire, John David. "Martin Luther King and Vietnam." *Christianity and Crisis* 27, no. 7 (1967): 89, 90.

Mann, Robert. *A Grand Delusion: America's Descent into Vietnam.* New York: Basic, 2001.

———. *The Walls of Jericho: Lyndon Johnson, Hubert Humphrey, Richard Russell, and the Struggle for Civil Rights.* New York: Harcourt Brace, 1996.

Marable, Manning. *Race, Reform, and Rebellion: The Second Reconstruction in Black America, 1945–1990.* 2d ed. Jackson: University Press of Mississippi, 1991.

Maraniss, David. *They Marched into Sunlight: War and Peace, Vietnam and America, October 1967.* New York: Simon & Schuster, 2003.

Marcus, Robert D., and David Burner, eds. *America since 1945*. 4th ed. New York: St. Martin's, 1985.

McAdam, Doug. *Political Process and the Development of Black Insurgency, 1930–1970*. Chicago: University of Chicago Press, 1982.

McCutheon, John T. Jr. "Inflammatory Talk." *Chicago Tribune*, April 6, 1967, 20.

McMahon, Robert J., ed. *Major Problems in the History of the Vietnam War*. 2d ed. Lexington, MA: D.C. Heath, 1995.

McNertney, Edward M. "U.S. Economy and the War," in Tucker, *Encyclopedia of the Vietnam War*, 113–14.

Meier, August, and Elliott Rudwick. *Along the Color Line: Explorations in the Black Experience*. Urbana: University of Illinois Press, 1976.

———. *From Plantation to Ghetto*. Rev. ed. New York: Hill and Wang, 1970.

———, eds. *Black Protest in the Sixties*. Chicago: Quadrangle, 1970.

———, eds. *The Making of Black America: Essays in Negro Life & History*, vol. 2. New York: Atheneum, 1969.

Mershon, Sherie, and Steven Schlossman. *Foxholes and Color Lines: Desegregating the U.S. Armed Forces*. Baltimore: Johns Hopkins University Press, 1998.

Mohr, Charles. "President Makes Offer to Start Vietnam Talks Unconditionally; Proposes $1 Billion Aid for Asia." *New York Times*, April 8, 1965, 1.

———. "Racial Integration in the Armed Forces." *American Journal of Sociology* 72 (September 1966): 132–48.

Moise, Edwin E. *Tonkin Gulf and the Escalation of the Vietnam War*. Chapel Hill: University of North Carolina Press, 1996.

Moynihan, Daniel Patrick. *The Negro Family: The Case for National Action*. Washington, DC: U.S. Government Printing Office, 1965.

Mueller, John E. "Public Opinion and the President." In Tugwell and Cronin, *Presidency Reappraised*, 133–47.

———. *War, Presidents and Public Opinion*. New York: John Wiley & Sons, 1973.

Mullen, Robert W. *Black Americans/African Americans: Vietnam through the Gulf War*. Needham Heights, MA: Ginn, 1991.

———. *Blacks in America's Wars: The Shift in Attitudes from the Revolutionary War to Vietnam*. New York: Anchor Foundation, 1973.

Mullen, William F. *Presidential Power and Politics*. New York: St. Martin's, 1976.

Murray, Charles. *Losing Ground: American Social Policy, 1950–1980*. New York: Basic, 1984.

Myrdal, Gunnar. *An American Dilemma: The Negro Problem and American Democracy*. New York: Harper & Row, 1944.

Nalty, Bernard C. *Strength for the Fight: A History of Black Americans in the Military.* New York: Free Press, 1986.

———. *The Vietnam War.* New York: Barnes & Noble, 2000.

National Advisory Commission on Civil Disorders. *The Kerner Report: The 1968 Report of the National Advisory Commission on Civil Disorders.* New York: Pantheon, 1968.

Nelson, Stanley, dir. *The Black Press: Soldiers without Swords.* PBS, A Half Nelson Production, 1999.

Newkirk, Pamela. *Within the Veil: Black Journalists, White Media.* New York: New York University Press, 2000.

Newman, John M. *JFK and Vietnam: Deception, Intrigue and the Struggle of Power.* New York: Warner 1992.

Nicosia, Gerald. *Home to War: A History of the Vietnam Veterans' Movement.* New York: Crown, 2001.

Nixon, Richard. *RN: The Memoirs of Richard Nixon.* New York: Gossett and Dunlap, 1978.

———. *The Real War.* New York: Warner, 1980.

Oak, Vishna V. *The Negro Newspapers.* Yellow Springs, OH: Antioch, 1948.

Oates, Stephen B. *Let the Trumpet Sound: A Life of Martin Luther King, Jr.* New York: HarperPerennial, 1994.

O'Brien, Lawrence F. *No Final Victories: A Life in Politics from John F. Kennedy to Watergate.* New York: Doubleday, 1974.

Office of the Assistant Secretary of Defense for Manpower and Reserve Affairs. *Project One Hundred Thousand: Characteristics and Performance of "New Standards" Men.* Washington, DC: U.S. Government Printing Office, 1969.

O'Neill, William L. *Coming Apart: An Informal History of America in the 1960s.* New York: Time Books, 1971.

Pach, Chester J. "And That's the Way It Was: The Vietnam War on the Network Nightly News." In *Conflict and Consensus in American History*, edited by Allen F. Davis and Harold D. Woodman, 532–51. New York: Houghton Mifflin, 1997.

Palmer, L. F. Jr. "The Black Press in Transition." *Columbia Journalism Review* 9 (Spring 1970): 31–36.

Paterson, Thomas G., ed. *Since 1914.* Vol. 2, *Major Problems in American Foreign Policy.* Lexington, MA: D. C. Heath, 1989.

Payne, Ethel L. "Loneliness in the Capital: The Black National Correspondent." In La Brie, *Perspectives of the Black Press*, 153–61.

Penn, I. Garland. *The Afro-American Press and Its Editors.* 1891. Reprint, New York: Arno, 1969.

Peplow, Michael. *George S. Schuyler*. Boston: Twayne, 1980.

Peters, Charles. *Lyndon B. Johnson*. New York: Times Books, 2010.

Pfautz, Harold W. "The New 'New Negro': Emerging American." In *Black Revolt: Strategies of Protest*, edited by Doris Yvonne Wilkinson, 35–45. Berkeley, CA: McCutchan, 1969.

Plummer, Brenda Gayle. *Rising Wind: Black Americans and U.S. Foreign Affairs, 1935–1960*. Chapel Hill: University of North Carolina Press, 1996.

Pratt, John Clark, ed. *Vietnam Voices: Perspectives on the War Years, 1941–1982*. New York: Penguin, 1984.

Prattis, P. L. "Days of *Courier* Past." In La Brie, *Perspectives of the Black Press*, 67–74.

———. "The Role of the Negro Press in Race Relations." *Phylon* 7 (1946): 273–83.

"The President Acts." *New York Times*, August 5, 1964, 32.

Presidential Recordings Program. Miller Center of Public Affairs, University of Virginia. http://millercenter.org/academic/presidentialrecordings.

President's Commission on an All-Volunteer Armed Force. *The Report of the President's Commission on an All-Volunteer Armed Force*. New York: Collier, 1970.

"The Press: Beyond Ghetto Sniffing." *Time*, April 6, 1970, 88, 89.

Pride, Armistead S., and Clint C. Wilson II. *A History of the Black Press*. Washington, DC: Howard University Press, 1997.

Prochnau, William. *Once upon a Distant War: Young War Correspondents and the Early Vietnam Battles*. New York: Times Books, 1995.

Public Papers of the Presidents of the United States: Gerald R. Ford. 6 vols. Washington, DC: U.S. Government Printing Office, 1975–79.

Public Papers of the Presidents of the United States: John F. Kennedy. 3 vols. Washington, DC: U.S. Government Printing Office, 1962–64.

Public Papers of the Presidents of the United States: Lyndon B. Johnson. 10 vols. Washington, DC: U.S. Government Printing Office, 1965–70.

Public Papers of the Presidents of the United States: Richard Nixon. 6 vols. Washington, DC: U.S. Government Printing Office, 1971–75.

Purnell, Karl H. "The Negro in Vietnam." *Nation*, July 3, 1967, 8–10.

Radvanyi, Janos. *Delusion & Reality: Gambits, Hoaxes and Diplomatic One-Upmanship in Vietnam*. South Bend, IN: Gateway, 1978.

Rampersad, Arnold. *Jackie Robinson: A Biography*. New York: Alfred A. Knopf, 1997.

Reedy, George. *Lyndon B. Johnson: A Memoir*. New York: Andrews and McMeel, 1982.

"Report from Black America." *Newsweek*, June 30, 1969, 16–35.

Rivers, William. *The Adversaries: Politics and the Press.* Boston: Beacon, 1970.

Roberts, Gene. "The Story of Snick: From 'Freedom High' to Black Power." In Meier and Rudwick, *Black Protest in the Sixties,* 139–53.

Roberts, Randy, and James S. Olson. "Antiwar Movement." In Kutler, *Encyclopedia of the Vietnam War,* 29–47.

Robertson, James Oliver. *American Myth, American Reality.* New York: Hill & Wang, 1980.

Robinson, Douglas. "Dr. King Proposes a Boycott of War." *New York Times,* April 5, 1967, 1, 2.

———. "Jewish Veterans Attack Dr. King's Stand on War." *New York Times,* April 6, 1967, 10.

Rosecrance, Richard, ed. *America as an Ordinary Country: U.S. Foreign Policy and the Future.* Ithaca, NY: Cornell University Press, 1976.

Rosier, Paul C. *Serving Their Country: American Indian Politics and Patriotism in the Twentieth Century.* Cambridge, MA: Harvard University Press, 2009.

Rowan, Carl T. *Breaking Barriers: A Memoir.* New York: Harper Perennial, 1991.

———. "Martin Luther King's Tragic Decision." *Reader's Digest,* September 1967, 37–42.

Rulon, Philip Reed. *The Compassionate Samaritan: The Life of Lyndon Baines Johnson.* Chicago: Nelson-Hall, 1981.

Salisbury, Harrison E. *A Time of Change: A Reporter's Tale of Our Time.* New York: Harper & Row, 1989.

Schlesinger, Arthur M. Jr. *Journals, 1952–2000.* Ed. Andrew Schlesinger and Stephen Schlesinger. New York: Penguin, 2007.

Schomburg Center for Research in Black Culture. *The New York Public Library African American Desk Reference.* New York: John Wiley & Sons, 1999.

Schuman, Howard. "Two Sources of Antiwar Sentiment in America." *American Journal of Sociology* 78, no. 3 (November 1972): 513–36.

Schuyler, George S. *Black and Conservative: The Autobiography of George S. Schuyler.* New Rochelle, NY: Arlington House, 1966.

———. *Fifty Years of Progress in Negro Journalism.* Pittsburgh: Pittsburgh Courier, 1950.

———. "King: No Help to Peace." In *Rac(e)ing to the Right: Selected Essays of George S. Schuyler,* edited by Jeffrey B. Leak, 104–5. Knoxville: University of Tennessee Press, 2001.

Senna, Carl. *The Black Press and the Struggle for Civil Rights.* New York: Franklin Watts, 1993.

Shapley, Deborah. *Promise and Power: The Life and Times of Robert McNamara.* Boston: Little, Brown, 1993.

Sherwood, John Darrell. *Black Sailor, White Navy: Racial Unrest in the Fleet during the Vietnam War Era.* New York: New York University Press, 2007.

"Shortages in Defense." *New York Times*, August 7, 1964, 28.

Simmons, Charles A. *The African American Press: A History of News Coverage during National Crises, with Special Reference to Four Black Newspapers, 1827–1965.* Jefferson, NC: McFarland, 1998.

Simon, Dennis M., and Charles W. Ostrom Jr. "The President and Public Support: A Strategic Perspective." In *The President and Public Policy Making*, edited by George C. Edwards III, Steven A. Shull, and Norman C. Thomas, 50–70. Pittsburgh: University of Pittsburgh Press, 1985.

Small, Melvin. *Antiwarriors: The Vietnam War and the Battle for America's Hearts and Minds.* Vol. 1, *Vietnam: America in the War Years.* Wilmington, DE: SR Books, 2002.

———. *Covering Dissent: The Media and the Anti-Vietnam War Movement.* New Brunswick, NJ: Rutgers University Press, 1994.

———. "The Impact of the Antiwar Movement." In McMahon, *Major Problems in the History of the Vietnam War*, 487–94.

———. "Public Opinion." In *Explaining the History of American Foreign Relations*, edited by Michael J. Hogan and Thomas G. Paterson, 165–76. New York: Cambridge University Press, 1994.

SNCC Staff Working Paper. "The Basis of Black Power." In *The American Left: Radical Political Thought in the Twentieth Century*, edited by Loren Baritz, 364–70. New York: Basic, 1990.

Sorley, Lewis. *A Better War: The Unexamined Victories and Final Tragedy of America's Last Years in Vietnam* . New York: Harcourt Brace, 1999.

———. "Vietnamization." In Tucker, *Encyclopedia of the Vietnam* War, 474–75.

Spector, Ronald. *After Tet: The Bloodiest Year in Vietnam.* New York: Free Press, 1993.

Spencer, David R. "Visions of Violence: A Cartoon Study of America and War." *American Journalism* 21, no. 2 (2004): 47–78.

Spofford, Tim. *Lynch Street: The May 1970 Slayings at Jackson State College.* Kent, OH: Kent State University Press, 1988.

Stacewicz, Richard. *Winter Soldiers: An Oral History of the Vietnam Veterans Against the War.* New York: Twayne, 1997.

Starr, Paul, with James Henry and Raymond Bonner. *The Discarded Army: Veterans after Vietnam: The Nader Report on Vietnam Veterans and the Veterans Administration.* New York: Charterhouse, 1973.

Stokes, Louis. "Racism in the Military: A New System for Rewards and Punishment." Congressional Black Caucus Report. *Congressional Record.* 92d Cong., 2d sess., October 14, 1972.

Stone, Chuck. "The National Conference on Black Power." In Barbour, *Black Power Revolt*, 225–37.

Sundquist, James. "Building the Great Society: The Case of Equal Rights." In Marcus and Burner, *America since 1945*, 194–209.

Szulc, Tad. *The Illusion of Peace: Foreign Policy in the Nixon Years*. New York: Viking, 1978.

Takaki, Ronald. *A Different Mirror: A History of Multicultural America*. Boston: Back Bay, 1993.

Terry, Wallace. "Black Power in Vietnam: Racial Tensions in the Military, September 1969." In Bates et al., *Reporting Vietnam*, 396–400.

———. "Bloods." In Boyd and Allen, *Brotherman*, 395–99.

———. *Bloods: An Oral History of the Vietnam War by Black Veterans*. New York: Ballantine, 1991.

Thomas, Velma Maia. *We Shall Not Be Moved: The Passage from the Great Migration to the Million Man March*. New York: Crown, 2002.

Tilford, Earl H. Jr. "Operation Linebacker II." In Tucker, *Encyclopedia of the Vietnam War*, 231–33.

TRB. "LBJ Isn't JFK." In *The Face of Five Decades: Selections from Fifty Years of The New Republic, 1914–1964,* edited by Robert B. Luce, 470. New York: Simon & Schuster, 1964.

Truman, Harry. "Equality of Treatment and Opportunity for All Those Who Serve in Our Country's Defense." In Kai Wright, *African-American Archive*, 522–24.

Tucker, Spencer C. *Vietnam*. Lexington: University Press of Kentucky, 1999.

———, ed. *Encyclopedia of the Vietnam War: A Political, Social, and Military History*. New York: Oxford University Press, 2000.

Tugwell, Rexford G., and Thomas E. Cronin, eds. *The Presidency Reappraised*. New York: Praeger, 1974.

Turner, Morrie. "Reflections of a Black Cartoonist." In La Brie, *Perspectives of the Black Press*, 163–66.

U.S. Department of Defense. *The Negro in the Armed Forces: A Statistical Fact Book*. Washington, DC: Office of the Deputy Assistant Secretary of Defense for Equal Opportunity and Safety Policy, Department of Defense, 1971.

Unger, Irwin. *The Best of Intentions: The Triumphs and Failures of the Great Society under Kennedy, Johnson, and Nixon*. New York: Doubleday, 1996.

Unger, Irwin, and Debi Unger. *LBJ: A Life*. New York: John Wiley & Sons, 1999.

Van Deburg, William L. *New Day in Babylon: The Black Power Movement and American Culture, 1965–1975*. Chicago: University of Chicago Press, 1992.

Verba, Sidney et al. "Public Opinion and the War in Vietnam." *American Political Science Review* 61, no. 2 (1967): 317–33.

Verney, Kevern. *Black Civil Rights in America.* London: Routledge, 2000.

Von Vorys, Karl. *American National Interest: Virtue and Power in Foreign Policy.* New York: Praeger, 1990.

Walker, William O. "55 Years with the Black Press." In La Brie, *Perspectives of the Black Press,* 17–26.

Walker, Wyatt T. "Reflections on Crime, Vietnam, and God." *Negro Digest* 17, no. 2 (1967): 9–15.

"Warning to Hanoi." *New York Times,* August 4, 1964, 28.

Washburn, Patrick S. *A Question of Sedition: The Federal Government's Investigation of the Black Press during World War II.* New York: Oxford University Press, 1986.

Waters, Enoch P. *American Diary: A Personal History of the Black Press.* Chicago: Path Press, 1987.

Weisbrot, Robert. *Freedom Bound: A History of America's Civil Rights Movement.* New York: Penguin, 1991.

Weiss, Nancy J. "Whitney M. Young, Jr.: Committing the Power Structure to the Cause of Civil Rights." In Franklin and Meier, *Black Leaders of the Twentieth Century,* 331–58.

West, Cornel. "The Religious Foundations of the Thought of Martin Luther King, Jr." In Albert and Hoffman, *We Shall Overcome,* 113–29.

Westheider, James E. *Fighting on Two Fronts: African Americans and the Vietnam War.* New York: New York University Press, 1997.

Westmoreland, William C. *A Soldier Reports.* New York: Doubleday, 1976.

White, Theodore H. *America in Search of Itself: The Making of the President, 1956–1980.* New York: Warner, 1982.

———. *The Making of the President, 1972.* New York: Atheneum, 1973.

Whittemore, L. H. *Together: A Reporter's Journey into the New Black Politics.* New York: William Morrow, 1971.

"Wider War." *New York Times,* August 6, 1964, 28.

Wilkins, Roy, with Tom Mathews. *Standing Fast: The Autobiography of Roy Wilkins.* New York: Viking, 1982.

Williams, Jayme Coleman, and McDonald Williams, eds. *The Negro Speaks: The Rhetoric of Contemporary Black Leaders.* New York: Noble and Noble, 1970.

Williams, Oscar R. *George S. Schuyler: Portrait of a Black Conservative.* Knoxville: University of Tennessee Press, 2007.

Wilson, Clint C. II. *Black Journalists in Paradox: Historical Perspectives and Current Dilemmas.* New York: Greenwood, 1991.

Wilson, George C. "The Military." *Washington Post*, April 16, 1985, A1.

Wolseley, Roland E. *The Black Press, U.S.A.* Ames: Iowa State University Press, 1971.

Wright, Kai, ed. *The African-American Archive: The History of the Black Experience in Documents.* New York: Black Dog & Leventhal, 2001.

———. *Soldiers of Freedom: An Illustrated History of African Americans in the Armed Forces.* New York: Black Dog & Leventhal, 2002.

Wright, Lawrence. *In the New World: Growing Up with America from the Sixties to the Eighties.* New York: Vintage, 1989.

Wyatt, Clarence R. *Paper Soldiers: The American Press and the Vietnam War.* New York: W. W. Norton, 1993.

Yglesias, Jose. "Dr. King's March on Washington, II." In Meier and Rudwick, *Black Protest in the Sixties*, 267–83.

Young, Andrew. *An Easy Burden: The Civil Rights Movement and the Transformation of America.* New York: HarperCollins, 1996.

Young, Marilyn. *The Vietnam Wars, 1945–1990.* New York: HarperPerennial, 1991.

Young, Whitney M. "A 'Domestic Marshall Plan.'" In Kai Wright, *African-American Archive*, 618–20.

———. *To Be Equal.* New York: McGraw-Hill, 1964.

Zelikow, Philip, Ernest May, and Timothy Naftali, general editors. *The Presidential Recordings, Lyndon B. Johnson: The Kennedy Assassination and the Transfer of Power, November 1963–January 1964*, 3 vols. New York: W. W. Norton & Company. Vol. 1, Max Holland, ed.; vol. 2, Robert David Johnson and David Shreve, eds.; vol. 3, Kent B. Germany and Robert David Johnson.

Index